Heidegger's Conversations

SUNY series in Contemporary Continental Philosophy

Dennis J. Schmidt, editor

Heidegger's Conversations
Toward a Poetic Pedagogy

KATHERINE DAVIES

Published by State University of New York Press, Albany

© 2024 State University of New York

All rights reserved

Printed in the United States of America

No part of this book may be used or reproduced in any manner whatsoever without written permission. No part of this book may be stored in a retrieval system or transmitted in any form or by any means including electronic, electrostatic, magnetic tape, mechanical, photocopying, recording, or otherwise without the prior permission in writing of the publisher.

Links to third-party websites are provided as a convenience and for informational purposes only. They do not constitute an endorsement or an approval of any of the products, services, or opinions of the organization, companies, or individuals. SUNY Press bears no responsibility for the accuracy, legality, or content of a URL, the external website, or for that of subsequent websites.

For information, contact State University of New York Press, Albany, NY
www.sunypress.edu

Library of Congress Cataloging-in-Publication Data

Name: Davies, Katherine, author.
Title: Heidegger's conversations : toward a poetic pedagogy / Katherine Davies.
Description: Albany : State University of New York Press, [2024] | Series: SUNY series in Contemporary Continental Philosophy | Includes bibliographical references and index.
Identifiers: ISBN 9781438499116 (hardcover : alk. paper) | ISBN 9781438499130 (ebook) | ISBN 9781438499123 (pbk. : alk. paper)
Further information is available at the Library of Congress.

For my teachers,
for my students

Socrates (to Callicles): If we closely examine these matters often and in a better way, you'll be persuaded.

—*Gorgias* 513c–d

Contents

Acknowledgments	ix
Notes on Abbreviations and Conventions	xi
Introduction: Conversations, with Heidegger	1
Chapter 1 The "Triadic Conversation": Non-Oppositional Pedagogy	23
Chapter 2 The "Tower Conversation": Mistaking Pedagogy	69
Chapter 3 The "Evening Conversation": Communal Pedagogy	101
Chapter 4 The "Western Conversation": Poetizing Pedagogy	133
Chapter 5 "From a Conversation of Language": Endangering Pedagogy	169
Conclusion: Learning from/through/beyond Heidegger	211
Notes	223
Bibliography	269
Index	281

Acknowledgments

An enduring fascination with the performative dimension of Plato's writing first ignited my interest in Heidegger's conversational texts at the 2013 convening of the Collegium Phaenomenologicum in Città di Castello, Italy, directed by Drew Hyland and featuring lecture courses by Bret Davis, Dennis Schmidt, and Danela Vallega-Neu. I defended a dissertation at Emory University on the topic in 2017 under the direction of Andrew Mitchell with John Lysaker, Cynthia Willett, Sean Kirkland, and Drew Hyland as committee members. Though I remain a touch mournful about jettisoning ambitions for a larger comparative project on Heidegger's conversations *and* Plato's dialogues, I am nevertheless grateful for Andrew's encouragement to forgo writing what would have been, in his words, a fine "dissertation" to instead pursue a project that could one day become a "book." His prescient vision and unparalleled guidance led to the materialization of this very achievement.

Though I rewrote every word, this book presents the hermeneutical efforts to contend with Heidegger's reanimation of the Platonic spirit of dialogical philosophizing that I first began in my dissertation. I have since cultivated my readings with the immense benefit of intellectual engagement and support from many institutions, students, and colleagues. Invitations to speak at the philosophy department at Whitman College, the North Texas Philosophical Association, and several occasions at the North Texas Heidegger Symposium, as well as papers given at a number of meetings of the Heidegger Circle of North America, have helped me hone my ideas in response to generative questions and comments. I am grateful to the American Philosophical Association Diversity Institute Alumni Fund, Miami University of Ohio, and the University of Texas at Dallas for supporting my travel for some of these presentations. I came to refine my views in graduate seminars I offered on "Heidegger's Conversations" in 2020 and 2023 with dedicated students that greatly enriched this manuscript. Among those who have most shaped my thinking of Heidegger, I would be remiss not to name—first and foremost—my colleague and friend Charles Bambach, but also Julia Ireland, Krzysztof Ziarek, Ian Moore, Bret Davis, Will McNeill, Denny Schmidt, Richard Polt, Jen Gaffney, Shane Ewegen, Ted George, Jess Elkayam, Jill Drouillard, Jim Bahoh, Dana Belu, Gregory Fried, Iain Thomson, Becca Longtin, Joel Reynolds, Jen Gammage, Lily Levy, Simon Truwant, and the members of the DASEIN reading group since 2018. Thank you—all—for your generous conversation. I have learned more from you than you likely know.

I must thank Michael Rinella at SUNY Press for his expert shepherding of my manuscript through the review and publication process and, again, Dennis Schmidt, for his support as series editor. The suggestions and encouragement I received from three anonymous reviewers were deeply gratifying and constructive as I made final revisions.

I am grateful to the University of Texas at Dallas for providing me a pre-tenure research sabbatical during which I completed the bulk of the writing of the manuscript. The support of dean Nils Roemer and my colleagues in the History and Philosophy program have been integral to bringing this project to fruition.

Finally, I wrote this manuscript largely confined to my home by the global pandemic. As such, those with whom I share my domestic space played an outsized role in its materialization. These include hundreds of plants, four cats, and one dedicated partner, who routinely went above and beyond to support my writing efforts by preparing staggeringly delicious meals, proofreading pages, and offering companionship and respite amid the joys and struggles to realize this book. I couldn't have done it without you.

Notes on Abbreviations and Conventions

All references to primary works of Martin Heidegger are provided parenthetically throughout the text. I refer first to the pagination of the *Gesamtausgabe* volume (abbreviated GA), followed by a slash with a reference to the English pagination, when an appropriate translation is available. Some frequently cited English translations are abbreviated. These can be found in the bibliography. Any modifications to published translations are indicated by the abbreviation "tm" and the addition of emphasis by "em." Where no English translation is available, translations are my own. References to all other works are provided in endnotes.

Introduction

Conversations, with Heidegger

In five conversational texts written between 1944 and 1954, Martin Heidegger depicts characters discussing various themes that arise throughout his work. Heidegger auditioned a number of genres across his corpus. *Being and Time* is a treatise. In the 1930s, Heidegger experimented with a fragmentary, solitary, and esoteric form of writing Vallega-Neu has called "poietic."[1] Essays are replete, in both short- and long-form, and Heidegger delivered many public and semi-public speeches. Heidegger's teaching materials are also relevant. His collected lecture notes and student protocols from his seminars offer windows into the evolution of his thinking, which inform larger developments in the works he elected to publish. Privately, Heidegger composed poetry, kept journals, and exchanged copious epistolary correspondence.[2] A shared feature, however, runs through the various genres Heidegger employed; in one form or another, they all consist of a conversation—a conversation with himself, his readers, audience members, recipients of letters, students in the classroom, or the figures that constitute the Western tradition such as Plato, Aristotle, Descartes, Kant, Hegel, Nietzsche, but also Heraclitus, Trakl, Rilke, and, especially, Hölderlin.[3]

That Heidegger's thinking was sustained in conversational engagement with so many is a significant yet under-regarded dimension of his work.[4] This book explores the role conversation plays in Heidegger's thinking through a close study of his five explicitly conversational manuscripts. These texts are unique in Heidegger's corpus insofar as they enact *how* Heidegger imagines a group of people collaboratively learn to think beyond the metaphysics that shape the Western philosophical tradition. In other words, Heidegger's conversations stage the pedagogy implied by his efforts toward non-metaphysical thinking. They concretely demonstrate how Heidegger imagines a conversational engagement with his thinking might—or even should—unfold.

Conversations, between 1944 and 1954

Heidegger composed conversational texts during a crucial decade in his life and in European history. He experienced Germany's defeat in World War II, both of his sons went missing at the Eastern front and were held captive for several years, he faced denazification proceedings, suffered a mental breakdown, and was banned from teaching. Heidegger only returned to his position as an emeritus professor in the early fifties. Though Heidegger had faced challenges and setbacks throughout his life and academic career, the ending of the war and the beginning of the postwar period was a particularly difficult and revealing period.[5]

The winter semester of 1944/45 proved turbulent. Heidegger announces a lecture course titled *Introduction to Philosophy—Thinking and Poetizing*, which was to engage Nietzsche and Hölderlin. Heidegger will soon instead turn to the conversational genre of writing to illustrate the connection between thinking and poetizing. He does not, however, discover this possibility while delivering these lectures. After only two sessions, the course is canceled when Heidegger is briefly drafted into the *Volkssturm* in the middle of November. Freiburg is heavily bombed on the 27th of November, forcing the university's philosophy faculty to set in motion an earlier plan to fall back to Castle Wildenstein above Beuron in the Upper Danube Valley. Heidegger does not initially travel with the group of ten faculty members and thirty graduate students, who make the harrowing journey by foot through the Black Forest.

Heidegger is instead granted leave to spend several months cataloging and correcting his manuscripts. He initially deposits them for safekeeping in the vault of a Meßkirch bank where his brother Fritz worked.[6] While working on this project, Heidegger wrote to Elfride on February 2, 1945: "Now that I've looked through older writings, some of which go back two decades, & recognized their intrinsic connection with what has now been achieved; now that I've looked back over the path on which I've been led with many a detour & deviation, & I draw comparison with everything else that is there, I cannot leave it all to chance."[7] In the wake of holding this intensive editorial conversation with himself, Heidegger begins composing conversational texts, which wind their way through ostensive detours to arrive somewhere that could not be more different than the reality facing Germany at the time.

The composition of the *Country Path Conversations*—containing the first three of Heidegger's five conversational texts—is dated 1944/45 in volume 77 of the *Gesamtausgabe*. Many of the ideas Heidegger folds into these works likely began to germinate in 1944, as he surveyed the course of his thinking while cataloging his manuscripts. However, the texts were penned in March, April, and May 1945, after his editorial duties are completed. During these months, Heidegger joins the exiled philosophy faculty in the idyllic Upper Danube Valley—the scene of Hölderlin's *Der Ister*—rather than returning to Freiburg.[8] He spends his days traveling back and forth between Meßkirch and the forester's lodge at Hausen im Tal where his lover Princess Margot von Sachsen-Meinungen takes up residence, helping with the hay harvest and even holding informal class sessions with students.[9] These three conversational texts—of the ten interrelated conversations Heidegger planned to compose[10]—are written in the context of a rural, bucolic, erotic experience that facilitates his intensive study of Hölderlin, which could hardly contrast more strikingly with most Germans' experience of the end of the war. In his final days in the Upper Danube Valley in the end of June, Heidegger delivers the "Poverty" address, urging his fellow colleagues and students to prepare themselves to withstand impending hardship by reading Hölderlin.

His return to Freiburg is a jolt back to the realities of the immediate aftermath of Germany's surrender. His home and library are under threat of confiscation, and the future of his affiliation with the university is uncertain. The French begin denazification proceedings—known as *l'épuration*—and Heidegger's case is set to be tried. After the case is initially decided in January 1946, Heidegger suffers a nervous breakdown and is sent to the sanitorium in Badenweiler for treatment by Dr. Viktor von Gebsattel. Though Heidegger subsequently claimed his stay was only three weeks, he remains in residence for treatment for somewhere between three to six months of 1946.[11] In the midst of this episode, Heidegger undertakes an imaginative, poetic return to the Upper Danube Valley. Still uncertain of his sons' fates, facing the apparent ending of his own career, and caught between Elfride and Margot, Heidegger begins work on the "Western Conversation," which is set along the banks of the Danube near the sheep shed where his grandfather was born as Hölderlin wrote *Der Ister*. Between 1946 and 1948, Heidegger writes this apparently unfinished conversational text, in which he revisits and revises his earlier Hölderlin interpretations as he also prepares *Holzwege* and *Der Feldweg* for press.[12]

At the end of March 1954, the Japanese professor of German literature Tezuka Tomio meets with Heidegger in Freiburg. The historical conversation that resulted from their visit may have partly inspired Heidegger's final conversational text, "From a Conversation of Language between a Japanese and a Questioner." However, Tezuka Tomio's own published account of their meeting shows that Heidegger's text largely deviates from their discussion.[13] Further, Heidegger was already considering his thinking in relation to the East before this meeting, by way of his Hölderlin interpretations. The "Conversation of Language" is composed after Heidegger's teaching ban was lifted, his emeritus professorship is reinstated, and many of the hardships of Germany's defeat begin to ease. It is set indoors in a comfortable office space where the conversational partners are seated, rather than hiking through the forest, fields, or along the banks of a river. Though his final conversational text is an apparent outlier, it nevertheless demonstrates Heidegger's reconsiderations both of what he achieved and what he failed to achieve in his preceding conversational oeuvre, composed amid the chaos and threatened destruction of his personal, professional, and philosophical life.

Heidegger's turn to writing conversations may seem anomalous. However, it is notable that he composed them during a period of loss—of his audience, classroom, and many of his own preferred conversational partners—and ceased to write in this form once his belonging to the scholarly world is relatively restored. The conversational genre is also not without significant precedent in the history of Western philosophy, with which his thinking was intimately bound up. Yet Heidegger insists that his conversations are radically different from other philosophers' dialogues. In the first of the *Country Path Conversations*, Heidegger's character "the Guide" distinguishes between *Dialog* and *Gespräch*[14] for "the Scientist":

> GUIDE: But what is the conversation [*Gespräch*] itself, purely on its own? You evidently don't consider just any mere speaking with one another [*Miteinandersprechen*] to be a conversation. A speaking with one another can be found in every chat [*Unterhaltung*], discussion [*Unterredung*], debate [*Aussprache*], or negotiation [*Verhandlung*]; in a broader and vaguer sense these too are "conversations." Yet in the emphatic sense of this word we mean something else. Albeit what we mean is difficult to say. But it seems to me as though in a proper conversation an event takes place wherein something comes to language [*zur Sprache kommt*].

SCIENTIST: [. . .] could authentic conversation and what you understand by that be any different from what one customarily conceives of as "dialogue" [*Dialog*]? After all, it belongs to a conversation that it is a conversation about something and between speakers [*daß es Gespräch über etwas ist und dies zwischen Sprechenden*].

GUIDE: Yet a conversation first waits upon [*wartet erst darauf*] reaching that of which it speaks. And the speakers of a conversation can speak in its sense only if they are prepared for something to befall them in the conversation which transforms their own essence [*was ihr eigenes Wesen verwandelt*]. (GA 77: 56–57/CPC 36–37)

For the Guide, a dialogue presupposes the availability of the object about which subjects speak. Dialogue relies on what Heidegger calls metaphysical or representational thinking, which reduces things to objects and human beings to subjects. A conversation, on the other hand, endeavors to wait for non-metaphysical thinking—that releases any reliance on the subject/object metaphysical distinction—to unfold. It does not presume that the topic of which the conversationalists would speak is available in advance. Conversation instead calls for its speakers to remain open to the possibility that the event of conversation will fundamentally change them. Where dialogue depicts subjects carrying out a detached examination of a given object, conversation unfolds an unforeseeable and uncontrollable transformational event.

Heidegger starkly distinguishes *Gespräch* from *Dialog* because dialogue has been established as a staple of the Western philosophical tradition since its beginning. Heidegger's criticisms of Plato are well-known.[15] Since his early lecture courses in the 1920s and 1930s[16] culminating with his 1940 essay[17] "Plato's Doctrine of Truth," Heidegger has charged Plato with inaugurating Western metaphysics. As late as the 1964 essay "The End of Philosophy and the Task of Thinking," Heidegger still insists that "metaphysics is Platonism" (GA 14: 71/BW 433). Yet on March 11, 1945, in the midst of composing the *Country Path Conversations*, Heidegger writes a letter to his wife. He tells Elfride he is busy reading Hölderlin's theoretical works in search of a "simple saying"[18] to resolve his thinking efforts of the last seven years. Two weeks later, Heidegger writes again that he "suddenly found a form of saying . . . [in which] poetizing & thinking saying [*das dichtende und denkende Sagen*] have attained a primordial unity, & everything flows along easily & freely."[19] This form of saying was *Gespräch*. Though Heidegger

6 | Heidegger's Conversations

worries that his own writings might be compared to Plato's dialogues, he admits that "only from my own experience have I now understood Plato's mode of presentation."[20] His discovery of the primordial unity of "poetizing & thinking saying"[21] impelled Heidegger to write the *Gespräche*.[22] Over the course of his career, Heidegger becomes increasingly interested in what he called the neighborhood of poetizing and thinking. He mostly pursued this interest through essays and lectures. The five conversational texts figured as experiments in depicting this neighborhood are therefore unique in Heidegger's oeuvre. What does the conversational form of writing—as the unifying of "poetizing and thinking saying"—particularly enable for Heidegger? This book offers a response to this question.

Many scholars have already demonstrated the importance of contending with Heidegger's conversations. Bret Davis translated the *Gesamtausgabe*, volume 77: *Feldweg-Gespräche* as *Country Path Conversations*[23] and completed a careful study of Heidegger's thinking of the will,[24] which, he argues, underwent radical transformation when Heidegger introduced *Gelassenheit* in the conversations.[25] Drew Hyland has shown how the themes of the conversations essentially relate to the form of conversation itself[26] and how this form exhibits a debt to Plato's dialogues.[27] Andrew Mitchell demonstrates how many of the conversations contribute to Heidegger's later thinking of the Fourfold.[28] Silvia Benso,[29] Charles Bambach,[30] Robert Bernasconi,[31] Bret Davis,[32] Lin Ma,[33] Ian Moore,[34] Eric Nelson[35], Robert Savage,[36] Francisco Gonzalez,[37] Holger Zaborowski,[38] Tobias Keiling,[39] Shane Ewegen,[40] and I[41] have turned to particular conversations to shed light on the philosophical stakes of Heidegger's relation to figures including Plato, Hölderlin, and Eckhart and his elaboration of certain philosophical topics such as art, plurality, evil, love, technology, and the possibility of cross-cultural exchange. Heidegger's conversational texts have even more to offer. Across his corpus, Heidegger interrogates the meaning of representational metaphysics for thinking and launches a particularly poignant analysis in these texts.

(Non-)Representational, (Non-)Metaphysical Thinking

For Heidegger, the term "metaphysics" can and does take on a myriad of meanings.[42] In the introduction to *Being and Time*, Heidegger famously declares the question of the meaning of being has been forgotten, "although our time considers itself progressive in again affirming 'metaphysics' " (GA 2: 2/BT 1). Metaphysics does not study what it claims—being—because it converts being into an object of analysis that abstracts a universalized form from beings and assumes this abstraction holds in an atemporal sense. In short, metaphysics initiates the human ambition to study being scientifically—in the way we study all other beings—and this means to elevate its claims to an objective and ahistorical register. However, the aspiration that metaphysical claims would operate like laws of nature implies that we must assume being adheres to laws that apply to beings. For Heidegger, this assumption is misguided. Being *exceeds* that which we could scientifically know about it and therefore requires an entirely different way to know it. In *Being and Time*, this takes the form of the existential and phenomenological inquiry of Dasein into fundamental ontology.

After *Being and Time*, Heidegger continues to excoriate metaphysics for failing in its aspirations. In his inaugural lecture for the faculty at Freiburg titled "What Is Metaphysics?," Heidegger further develops his critique by showing how metaphysics forgets not only "being," but also the question of "nothing." Building on the phenomenological method introduced in *Being and Time*, in "What Is Metaphysics?," Heidegger shows how the questioner of this question must herself be placed into question, drawing a distinction between the transcendental totality to which metaphysics aspires and the immanent wholeness of being, which can only be approached by way of the nothing that renders being essentially finite.[43] In his subsequent lecture course *Introduction to Metaphysics*, Heidegger continues his thinking pursuit of being beyond the limitations of metaphysics as a philosophical science.[44] Here, he emphasizes that the metaphysical occlusion of being is grounded in a certain historical formation of grammar and language. The very distinction between subject and object is baked into syntax, so to speak, but is itself a product of metaphysical distortion. Thinking beyond metaphysics will require a different way of inhabiting language as well. Though metaphysics has attempted to also dominate the interpretation of art—as Heidegger shows in his later lecture course *Hölderlin's Hymn "Der Ister"*—it will be in unfolding poetizing language and letting it resonate that this challenge to metaphysics will be levied.

For Heidegger, metaphysics has guided the development of the history of Western philosophy. The philosophical discipline has configured itself as progressing toward a better, more correct determination of being. Heidegger rejects such claims—instead, he urges a turn back to the origin of metaphysical thinking to discover the possibilities its invention foreclosed—but recovers a valuable insight. Metaphysics claims that its aspirational objective determination of being is universal and atemporal but that our subjective understanding of it is progressive and therefore under historical development. For Heidegger, being itself is historical.[45] This means that being sends itself in temporal epochs in which the meaning of being is received differently. As he outlines in "The Age of the World Picture," there are at least three different major ages: antiquity, the Middle Ages, and modernity.[46] Only in the modern age is it possible to inquire into what Heidegger calls the modern "world picture" (GA 5: 89/HR 217–18). Within this epochal sending of being, science and technology develop rubrics to objectify the meaning of being. This is accomplished through the calculative representation of the subject. Since the philosophical investment in mathematics coupled with a newly autonomous and capacitated subject—founded in Descartes and honed by Kant—the subjective representation of objective being, using the rubric of science and technology and exemplified in the modern experiment, has dominated the meaning of being. For Heidegger, *representational* metaphysics is the form of thinking that must be confronted today.

In this book, I show that Heidegger launches his own version of an experiment with the conversational genre of writing as a way to learn to think beyond representational metaphysics. The conversations—especially the first three *Country Path Conversations*—serve as a pivot point between Heidegger's early and mature thinking of the relationship between science and technology. Put simply, Heidegger articulates a vision of this relation that upends the traditional notion of technology as applied science. Rather, Heidegger insists science is applied technology because, prior to simply studying nature, science itself is reliant on a representational "mathematical projection of nature" (GA 77: 5/CPC 3) that technologically constructs nature as calculable in advance. The metaphysics of such a scientific rendering of being is only possible because of the technological representation that the historically modern investment in rationality promotes.

Heidegger attempts to recover a more originary thinking of being, one that would think being non-metaphysically—without recourse to the representational thinking that modernity has honed. Plato inaugurated metaphysics with his analogy of the sun and metaphysical thinking may seem to shed light on its objects. But for Heidegger, this celebrated clarity instead functions to obscure and conceal its source. Instead, non-metaphysical thinking is native to the night and allows for thinking otherwise. Though day and night are different, they are not opposed—one emerges from out of the other. Representational metaphysics itself generates the terms needed to think first in and then beyond binary oppositions. The true challenge for following Heidegger's attempt to think non-representationally and non-metaphysically[47] is to learn how such an attempt can itself be engendered from out of representational metaphysics itself. This pedagogy requires terms that transform—that are on the move—as this attempt unfolds. This transformation is performed in Heidegger's conversational writings. Heidegger does not aim to reject, oppose, or even overcome representational metaphysics.[48] Rather, he seeks the grammar to demonstrate the limits of representational, metaphysical thinking—and how these very limits offer the gift of inaugurating thinking otherwise.

Heidegger's non-representational, non-metaphysical thinking cannot be reduced to a collection of discreet claims that constitute a systematic alternative to representational metaphysics. He does not aim to challenge Western representational, metaphysical thinking by replacing past systematic philosophies with his own version. Rather, his thinking calls for an elaboration—or performance—of its own unfolding. His philosophy cannot be reduced to a set of propositions because the *way* Heidegger thinks is as important as *what* he thinks, if not more so. His non-metaphysical thinking requires its own grammar—its own language, even—to emerge as such. This grammar would radically overturn an understanding of the ostensible given distinction and relation between subjects and objects. In these texts, Heidegger challenges the predominance of representational, metaphysical thinking. Such thinking presumes the subject/object distinction that may purport to grasp beings but forgets the being of these beings. Metaphysics professes to hold universally, but in truth it is a historically specific phenomenon that obscures our thinking of being. Representational, metaphysical thinking conceals its own provenance as a historically specific way of thinking—which takes the form of scientific and technological thinking in our epoch. Heidegger works to loosen up the universal claim and domination of such thinking and remind us that other ways of thinking are possible. At the very least, to think with Heidegger is to *unlearn* the traditional terms for thinking with the hope that practicing waiting for another way of thinking together will teach us how to think beyond our current limits.

In what follows, I argue that Heidegger's non-representational, non-metaphysical thinking is pedagogical in essence. I find the most poignant elaboration of this pedagogy in his conversational texts because the importance of teaching and learning is taken up in each of them. This book endeavors to provide a comprehensive overview of Heidegger's five conversations. It undertakes this task through elaborating the pedagogy[49] Heidegger articulates and performs in these texts. Each conversation raises the question of pedagogy uniquely and by emphasizing a different element of Heidegger's overall pedagogy. By reading the five texts in succession, I describe a development in Heidegger's pedagogy across the decade in which he composed these conversations. As Heidegger portrays teaching, he also learns. In his conversational texts, we witness Heidegger attempting to teach and learn the pedagogy of non-representational, non-metaphysical thinking.

Conversational, Poetizing Pedagogy

The interest Heidegger demonstrates in the philosophical status of the constellation of conversation, language, and pedagogy in his conversational texts finds precedent in his earlier work and is sustained in his later thought. Already in the 1936 essay "Hölderlin and the Essence of Poetry," Heidegger draws conversation and language together. A section of this essay is devoted to an excerpt of Hölderlin's poetry ". . . Since we have been a conversation / And able to hear from one another . . ." (GA 4: 38/EHP 56). To interpret these lines, Heidegger writes, "language is not merely a tool [*Werkzeug*] which man possesses alongside many others; rather, language first grants the possibility of standing in the midst of the openness of beings [*inmitten der Offenheit von Seindem zu stehen*]. Only where there is language, is there world" (GA 4: 37–38/EHP 55–56). Language constitutes the human being as a being who belongs to world. In further questioning the essence of language, Heidegger finds himself compelled to think with Hölderlin's poetizing. Of these lines, he writes,

> We—human beings—are a conversation [*Gespräch*]. Man's being is grounded in language [*Sprache*]; but this actually occurs only in *conversation*. Conversation, however, is not only a way in which language takes place, but rather language is essential only as conversation [*sondern als Gespräch nur ist Sprache wesentlich*]. What we usually mean by "language," namely, a stock [*Bestand*] of words and rules for combining them, is only an exterior aspect of language. But now what is meant by "conversation"? Obviously, the act of speaking with one another about something. Speaking, then, mediates [*vermittelt*] our coming to one another [*Zueinanderkommen*]. (GA 4: 38–39/EHP 56)

For Heidegger, conversation does not become possible because the human being first has language as a tool[50] and so equipped only then undertakes to exchange language with another in conversation. Rather, language itself is originally and essentially conversational. Though Heidegger will refine his notion of conversation in the wake of his thinking of the event,[51] already in 1936 Heidegger understands conversation as the essence of language, and this very insight is drawn from poetizing. The importance of poetry and poetizing for Heidegger cannot be overstated. In his later career, Heidegger will increasingly generate readings of the poetry of Hölderlin, principally, but also Trakl, Hebel, and Rilke.

In the 1935/36 lecture course,[52] while differentiating between modern natural science and ancient and medieval natural science, Heidegger reflects on what it means to learn. He notes that the word mathematics stems from the Greek τὰ μαθήματα. On his interpretation, this word means "the *learnable* and hence, simultaneously, the teachable; μανθάνειν means to learn and μάθησις means the doctrine of teaching, and indeed in a twofold sense: the process of learning [*in die Lehre gehen und lernen*], on the one hand, and the doctrine taught [and learned], on the other" (GA 41: 69–70/47). Learning is what Heidegger refers to subsequently as a taking, but not all taking is a learning. The mathematical, he suggests, sets out the possibility to know something in advance: "authentic learning [*eigentliche Lernen*] is therefore an extremely remarkable taking [*Nehmen*], a taking whereby the taker only takes what he or she at bottom already has [*im Grunde schon hat*]. Teaching [*Lehren*] also corresponds to *this* learning. Teaching is a giving [*Geben*], an offering; but what is offered in teaching is not the learnable, for the pupil is only given instruction [*Anweisung*] to take for himself or herself what he or she already has" (GA 41: 73/49). That true learning is a self-giving does not diminish the role of the teacher, but amplifies what it essentially is. Heidegger continues: "learning is more difficult than teaching; for only someone who can truly learn—and only as long as he or she can—he or she alone can truly teach. The true teacher differs from the pupil only in that he or she can learn better and more authentically wants to learn [*lernen will*]. In all teaching, the teacher learns most" (GA 41: 74/50). In the 1930s, for Heidegger, learning is the task of both teacher and student.

In the 1951/52 lecture course *What is Called Thinking?*, Heidegger reconsiders the question of pedagogy. Nearly two decades later, he initially rehearses much of his thinking from 1935/36. He still resists a model of teaching and learning whereby students simply amass information the teacher would present.[53] He insists that the teacher has more to learn than her students. Yet his later remarks differ in one crucial respect. In the 1930s, Heidegger argues that learning is more difficult than teaching. But in the

1950s, Heidegger reverses course and instead contends that "teaching is even more difficult than learning" (GA 8: 17/WCT 15).[54] He elaborates:

> Teaching is more difficult than learning because what teaching calls for is this: to let learn [*lernen lassen*]. The real teacher [*eigentliche Lehrer*], in fact, lets nothing else be learned than—learning. His conduct, therefore, often produces the impression that we properly learn nothing from him, if by "learning" we now suddenly understand merely the procurement of useful information [*nutzbarer Kenntnisse*]. The teacher is ahead of his apprentices in this alone, that he has still far more to learn than they—he has to learn to let them learn. (GA 8: 17–18/WCT 15)

Why is teaching now more difficult than learning? I argue that two interventions in Heidegger's thinking contribute to this reversal. First, as Davis has shown, Heidegger's thinking of the will undergoes substantial alteration in the 1940s. Whereas the teacher in the 1930s *wants* to learn, the teacher of the 1950s *lets* learning unfold. It seems that Heidegger has found that the letting or yielding of *Gelassenheit* is also relevant for pedagogy. In teaching and learning, *Gelassenheit* generates a more proper comportment for thinking of being than the assertion of the will he earlier valorized. Achieving the comportment of such released teaching is thereby decisively more difficult than learning. Second, Heidegger develops this notion of *Gelassenheit* in his conversational texts in which "the Teacher" is often a character and in which the topic and performance of teaching and learning play central roles. In these texts, the teacher must come to relate to the students concretely, engaging with them in their alterity and specificity.

Heidegger's depiction of pedagogy in the 1930s emphasizes the separate relations of the student to himself and teacher to herself, respectively, but the nuances of the relation *between* the student and teacher become more salient for the later Heidegger. In the "Triadic Conversation," Heidegger's character "the Guide"[55] tells the others, "participating in a conversation [*An einem Gespräch teilzunehmen*] is in fact difficult. It is even more difficult than leading [*führen*] a conversation. Since we met for the first time on this country path for a conversation, I have attempted to learn but one thing . . . The art [*Kunst*]—or the forbearance [*Langmut*], or whatever you would like to call it—of speaking together in conversation [*im Gespräch mitzusprechen*]" (GA 77: 46/CPC 29–30). The question of what it means to speak *together* has become compelling for Heidegger, and at a pivotal personal and political turning point. In the wake of losing his ability to engage in philosophical conversations at the university and while the meaning of community is being radically challenged by the imminent collapse of Germany, Heidegger reconsiders the importance of the role others play in the endeavor of thinking.

In rethinking pedagogy, it is no accident that Heidegger turned to the conversational genre of writing. Hyland has argued that it was a "necessity of thought"[56] that spurred Heidegger towards this style of composition. For Hyland, this turn suggests that Heidegger may have learned something about Platonic dialogues: "the possibilit[y] of exceeding the propositional content of sentences uttered, of allowing the unsaid and that which withdraws to emerge as such, which the Platonic dialogues exhibit, is just what Heidegger now comes to appreciate."[57] In four letters to his wife between 1945 and 1954, Heidegger directly expressed his desire to dedicate a book on Plato to Elfride. Though the book was never written, it was during these years that Heidegger was writing conversations. Hyland,[58] Davis,[59] and I[60] have suggested that the conversations may contain the germs of a more genuine reading of Plato. For his part, Heidegger claims the possibility of harboring the unspoken drew him to conversation. In the supplements to the "Triadic Conversation," Heidegger writes:

The Conversation

Where else could the unspoken [*Ungesprochene*] be purely kept, heeded, other than in true conversation [*wahrhaften Gespräch*].

Of all goods the most dangerous is language, because it cannot keep safe the unspoken—(not because it veils [*verhüllt*] too much, but rather because it divulges [*preisgibt*] too much). (GA 77: 159/CPC 104)

Conversation is capable of safeguarding what is not said, of harboring the alterity of this possibility. Zaborowski explains: "Whoever speaks is in danger of saying too much. Words, where they become truthful, indicate silence. In genuine conversation, therefore, it is necessary to be mindful of what is unsaid, of pauses, silence, the hiatus between words."[61] Zaborowski suggests that the significance of conversation for Heidegger extends far beyond his explicit conversational texts or his mentions of conversation in the (apparently) monological texts, raising the question of whether Heidegger's thinking as a whole may enact a conversation "between the thinking of the first beginning and an other beginning to thinking, one that is no longer metaphysical."[62] Though Heidegger never explicitly acknowledged Plato's sensitivity to the power of dialogue, perhaps he came to realize how Plato had also found a way to unsay what he was compelled to speak of in his writing.[63] Regardless, Heidegger himself came to appreciate how the unsaid remains guarded within and between the silences that punctuate what is said in conversation, unifying "poetizing & thinking saying" at last.

Toward Thinking, Otherwise

In each of the five conversations, one or more of Heidegger's characters interrogate the philosophical meaning of representational metaphysics. Though Heidegger does not announce a polemic against metaphysics or express the hope to overcome metaphysics, he is invested in demonstrating that its purported claim to universality is misplaced. For Heidegger, being is excessive; it surpasses our representations of it—other ways of thinking of being are possible. Demonstrating the limits of metaphysics requires attending to that which remains unsaid within the terms of representational thinking that metaphysics puts forth during any historical epoch. In these texts, Heidegger unfolds how learning to think non-metaphysically and non-representationally is a task for which collaborative conversation is needed.

In the conversations, Heidegger probes the limits of metaphysics through elucidating the historical guise it assumes in our age as scientific and technological thinking. In the first of the *Country Path Conversations*, the Guide describes the mathematical projection of nature as the technological, representational production that enables science to proceed. The Scientist claims that technology is applied science. The Guide instead insists that science is applied technology (GA 77: 5–15/CPC 3–10). Modern science follows Galileo[64] in claiming that nature is inherently mathematical. For Heidegger, such a presumption conceals that nature far exceeds this limited view of it. Even further, the mathematics we supposedly find in nature is in fact the result of a historically specific form of *techne*—a human way of knowing—that is projected onto nature. Where different forms of metaphysical thinking have dominated the ancient and medieval epochs,[65] in the conversations Heidegger understands modernity to be governed by a representational, mathematical projection of nature produced by an essentially technological form of scientific inquiry.

In the mid- to late 1940s, Heidegger is on the cusp of a philosophical breakthrough in his thinking of technology. As Mitchell notes, "it is in the

1949 Bremen lectures where Heidegger first introduces the fourfold that he likewise first introduces the thought of 'positionality' (*das Gestell*),[66] that is the ineluctable demand placed upon all that exists that it be available to the point of replaceability."[67] The account of scientific and technological thinking found in the *Country Path Conversations* apparently resembles his earlier thinking of machination in the mid- to late 1930s insofar as the characters seem concerned with articulating subjective representational[68] thinking and the metaphysics of objectification that follows from such an account. Heidegger goes so far as to introduce the notion of standing reserves—*Beständen*—in the "Tower Conversation" (GA 77: 196/CPC 128), but in an embryonic state. Heidegger here defines "standing reserves" as describing "things [that] were susceptible to being changed into objects" (GA 77: 196/CPC 128). In his mature thinking of technology, he will no longer be concerned with objects at all but rather with positionality as circulative replacement.[69] This circulation will reach such a pitch that nothing remains stable enough to function as a discrete object.

Though Heidegger will not come to understand how deeply circulative replacement will invite a reconsideration of his ontology as a whole[70] until 1949 and after, the conversations composed in the wake of World War II reveal a growing discord in his thinking, which Heidegger will turn to the fourfold and positionality to address more fully. Yet there are precursors to this revolution in Heidegger's thought, especially in the conversations.[71] In these texts Heidegger explores the significance of movement for thinking. He is not grappling with the vacuous circulative movement of technology's standing reserve, but rather what it means to think in/as motion.[72] The motto he crafted for his *Gesamtausgabe*—"ways, not works"—can hardly gain more purchase than on the texts Heidegger stages as unfolding in motion—on walks in the country. In the first of the *Country Path Conversations*, the characters describe the path on which they walk as the very releasement that moves them. The Guide clarifies that the path as "releasement [*Gelassenheit*] would not just be the way [*Weg*], but rather the movement (on a way) [*Bewegung*]" (GA 77: 118/CPC 77). In these texts, Heidegger is not yet depicting the endless circulation of that which essentially is what it is not, but rather the inherently conversational movement that allows the singular essence of being to unconceal itself as excessive.

This released movement along a way that can recover from the vacuous movement of technology is found in poetizing. For Heidegger, poetizing is eminently concerned with that which is singular and originary. Heidegger has not yet realized his mature thinking of technology, but in the years leading up to this development he is already exploring what it could mean to respond to it. As I will show, learning to let oneself into an involvement with poetizing as a fundamental event of being is the guiding thread that runs through each of Heidegger's five conversations. In finding the limits of representational, metaphysical thinking, the characters of Heidegger's conversations do not simply turn to poetry as a pedagogical tool or exercise that the teacher may deploy at will to replace one way of thinking with another. Rather, in these conversations, poetizing is revealed to be inherently pedagogical and pedagogy, in turn, to be inherently poetic.

Poetry appears—either explicitly or implicitly—in each of Heidegger's conversations. Of course, poetizing is not simply reducible to poetry.[73] As Ziarek writes, "Heidegger claims that poetry, understood in the narrow sense [namely, *Poesie*], only at certain moments—for example, ancient Greek literature, Hölderlin's late poetry—participates in *Dichtung*."[74] *Poesie*—poetry— and *Dichtung*—poetizing—are not necessarily always found together. In his first lecture course on Hölderlin, Heidegger emphasizes this: "Saying and saying [*Sagen und Sagen*] are not the same thing. To repeat [*nachsprechen*] a poem or even to be able to recite [*hersagen*] it by heart does not yet mean being able to follow poetically the telling [*mitsagen*] of the poetry" (GA 39: 42/41). Yet sometimes poetizing does occur in poetry. Lysaker notes, for Heidegger "some poems . . . unfold an originary language, which grounds being by figuring the event of unconcealment."[75] This is especially true for Heidegger of Hölderlin's poetry, which essentially poetizes.

Poetizing marks a comportment of language—a way in which being is unconcealed—not a linguistic form or genre. In 1951, Heidegger will describe poetizing as that which is, "not by seeking to wrest what is concealed [*das Verborgene*] out of its concealedness, but only by guarding the concealed in its self-concealment [*das Verborgene in seinem Sichverbergen hütet*]" (GA 7: 201/PLT 220–21). In the *Country Path Conversations*, scientific and technological thinking wrests what is concealed out of its concealedness through calculation based on the mathematical projection of nature. In 1951, Heidegger will think of poetizing as a sort of measuring as well, but of an entirely different kind than the mathematical measuring of science and technology: "we, in order to think of poetry,[76] must ever and again first give thought to the measure [*Maß*] that is taken in poetry [*im Dichten genommen wird*]; we must pay heed to the kind of taking [*Nehmens*] here, which does not consist in a clutching [*Zugriff*] or any other kind of grasping [*Greifen*], but rather in a letting come [*Kommen-lassen*] of what has been dealt out [*Zu-Gemessenen*]" (GA 7: 203/PLT 222). As in Heidegger's articulation pedagogy in 1935/36, poetry also unfolds as a form of taking, now in the comportment of releasement that corresponds with the reconsideration of teaching and learning in 1951/52. Poetizing as this letting come may occur in poetry. But it may also unfold in other artworks,[77] in a certain comportment of thinking, and, as I will show, in collaborative, conversational engagement with another.

As I've noted above, Heidegger claims he turned to conversation in 1944/45 for a particular reason: "Where else could the unspoken be purely kept, heeded, other than in true conversation" (GA 77: 159/CPC 104). Keeping and heeding the unspoken as such relies on guarding the concealed in its self-concealment of poetizing, because conversation enables those conversing to wait together for something to befall them in the conversation that transforms their own essence. Conversational partners rely on each other to extend, modify, and question their attempts to say what they are coming to think, necessarily disabusing one another of any exclusive claim to the final discovery of the meaning of what they think. The event of conversation unfolds in the midst of speakers in fits and spurts—never revealing itself as a metaphysical totality—and thereby guards the performance of their collaboration in its concealment as well.

On my reading, the collaborative sense of conversation Heidegger is choreographing in his conversational texts is poetic. Heidegger's characters learn how to become receptive to and levy the claim of poetizing together. That which is poetic emerges from itself alone, that is, it calls a renewed sense of world into being. This guarding of what is concealed in its concealment makes a claim of its own accord, without the need to appeal to evidence beyond its own poetic telling. Heidegger's characters who are caught up in the throes of metaphysical thinking find themselves instead reliant on the rubrics and frameworks of various (academic) disciplines in order to formulate their thoughts. Bypassing philosophical investment in a correspondence theory of truth,[78] poetizing illuminates another world, one that unfolds when and where language is thoroughly relational. Within the world of poetizing, no single word stands isolated or defined on its own—each word and phrase modifies and supports the others, helping each to come into its own by way of this mutual support, mirroring the non-metaphysical relationality of being and beings.

This is what conversation—and the conversational form of writing—accomplishes for Heidegger. Elaborating his experience of the unification of "poetizing & thinking saying," these texts depict thinkers—never the solitary thinker alone—collaboratively coming to think non-metaphysically together. The Guide tells his conversational partners that he only wants to learn one thing on their walk, "the art—or the forbearance, or whatever you would like to call it—of speaking together in conversation" (GA 77: 46/CPC 29–30). Speaking together means also to guard the unspoken that accompanies such an endeavor. They must learn to converse by first tolerating and then coming to celebrate the richness of their differences, alterity, and plurality. The silences, affects, and hiatuses that permeate their conversation preserve the conversation's essence as unsaid. Put simply, Heidegger's conversations enact a distinctly poetic pedagogy.

The Five Conversations

Each of Heidegger's five conversational texts choreographs this poetic pedagogy differently, under distinct conditions, and for various characters. This book argues that a distinct element of Heidegger's poetic pedagogy is elaborated in each conversational text. I draw out five such elements: non-oppositionality, making mistakes, thinking in community, poetic interpretation, and the danger of pedagogy. In elaborating these elements, I show how Heidegger's understanding of poetic pedagogy undergoes a development—and even revision—over the course of composing these five texts. Finally, I demonstrate that Heidegger enacts his poetic pedagogy through the deployment of five distinct pedagogical techniques that recur in each conversational text: openness to others, sensitivity to affect,[79] reversal, remembering, and silence. My examination of each conversational text elaborates both the distinct element of pedagogy Heidegger is emphasizing and demonstrates how Heidegger uses these five pedagogical techniques to stage a performance of that pedagogical element. His use of these pedagogical techniques changes relative to whether he is emphasizing the importance of poetic interpretation or making mistakes, for example. Nevertheless, these same five techniques enable us to discern both the architecture of Heidegger's poetic pedagogy and how it evolves between 1944 and 1954.

The first chapter unfolds the importance of non-oppositionality for Heidegger's pedagogy and provides an overview of Heidegger's first and longest of the *Country Path Conversations*—"Αγχιβασίη: A Triadic Conversation on a Country Path between a Scientist, a Scholar, and a Guide."[80] On my reading, the "Triadic Conversation" presents the most traditional view of teaching and learning Heidegger can muster. Though the Guide hardly provides step-by-step instructions for the Scientist or the Scholar, he does navigate the conversation to its apparently successful conclusion. The Scientist and Scholar inhabit the roles of students whom the Guide is provoking to learn to think non-representationally and non-metaphysically. The "Triadic Conversation" is chiastic in structure. While the light lingers, the Scientist and the Scholar cling to the metaphysical objectivity and subjectivity that support representational thinking. Yet after night falls, the Guide can invite first the Scholar to think beyond subjectivity and then the Scientist to contend with the limits of his investment in metaphysical objectivity. This pedagogical triumph is marked by their interpretative engagement with a poem and an episode of collaborative poetizing. In tracking their journey, I show how the Guide relies on five pedagogical techniques, which allow both him and his students to release themselves toward non-representational, non-metaphysical thinking. If Heidegger had only written the "Triadic Conversation," his pedagogy would be quite limited. Though the teaching modeled in the first conversation is one grounded in a released, poetic attunement toward the student, the Guide nevertheless is more experienced in non-representational, non-metaphysical thinking than his conversational partners. His agility and experience may inadvertently foster a sense of the teacher as authoritative despite his insistence otherwise.

In the second chapter, I show how Heidegger depicts making mistakes as critical for his pedagogy of non-representational, non-metaphysical thinking. The second of the *Country Path Conversations*—"The Teacher Meets the Tower Warden at the Door to the Tower Stairway"[81]—begins to counter the central misstep of the "Triadic Conversation," namely that the teacher is an authority figure. In this text, "the Teacher" is hardly cast in an authoritative role. The Teacher struggles the most to learn and makes repeated mistakes in his attempts to do so. The other characters—the Tower Warden and the Guest—facilitate the Teacher's approach to a picture he finds deeply unsettling. What the Guide had been urging his students to learn in the previous text—how to engage in a released waiting by sustaining moments of discomfort and distress rather than recoiling—now becomes the Teacher's own task. I show how Heidegger uses the same five pedagogical techniques in this conversational text to show that to be a teacher is not to have gained mastery, but instead to become ever more a student. Further, it is only *because* (not *despite* the fact that) the Tower Warden and the Teacher repeatedly make mistakes that they learn to practice releasement in the face of the strange, culminating in their encounter with the strange(r) Guest. For Heidegger's pedagogy, mistakes are positive invitations that grant the occasion to learn the limits of representational, metaphysical thinking.

In the third chapter, I elaborate the centrality of thinking in community for Heidegger's pedagogy. In the "Evening Conversation: In a Prisoner of War Camp in Russia, between a Younger and an Older Man,"[82] Heidegger elaborates a claim that non-metaphysical thinking must be shared and sharable. This means that his pedagogy is an essentially plural, collaborative endeavor. No teaching figure readily presents herself in the prisoner of war camp. The Younger Man and the Older Man find themselves abandoned, powerless, and suffering in their condition as prisoners. The situation of these conversational partners is determined by devastation and evil stemming from the scientific and technological thinking proffered by the Western metaphysical philosophical tradition. Yet even at the zenith of the poverty of representational metaphysics, the conversational partners share a healing experience. That ostensibly "individual" experiences are not confined to the individual is the most compelling claim of the "Evening Conversation." Though the Younger Man is ostensibly healed, something remains unsettled and outstanding in his experience. This leads him to seek out a conversation with the Older Man during which they realize that his companion is also suffering and in need of healing. In coming together—to converse and, in so doing, to challenge the concurrent confinement of experience itself to the individual—they become those who wait in the mode of *Gelassenheit*, relying on the five pedagogical techniques I have identified in the earlier conversations. Heidegger shows that these characters become able to teach themselves how to learn to heal *because* there is no authoritative teacher readily available. There would be no surer sign of any teacher's failure than for her students to remain students forever, dependent on another's instruction. In this chapter, I describe the healing these two characters find precisely because they are without the guidance of a teacher managing the five pedagogical techniques at play. Instead, they come together in community with one another as students-become-teachers of non-representational, non-metaphysical thinking.

In the fourth chapter, I unfold the importance of poetic language for Heidegger's pedagogy. Heidegger composed the first three *Country Path Conversations* in rapid succession during 1944 and 1945. Between 1946 and 1948, he wrote his fourth conversation, titled "*Das abendländische Gespräch.*"[83] This second-longest of Heidegger's conversations—the "Western Conversation"—revisits and revises Heidegger's earlier interpretations of the poet Hölderlin. It also returns to the "Evening Conversation," reimagining what may have been possible for the Older Man and the Younger Man if they had met under different circumstances. In a sense, it was Hölderlin's poetizing that the Older Man and the Younger Man in the "Evening Conversation" were waiting upon. The genuine, poetic liberation they needed (and remained without in the camp) is enabled through the circumstances envisioned in the "Western Conversation." The poet does not appear as an embodied character in this text, but I argue that Hölderlin's poetizing enables the characters to learn how to think in responding to poetizing. The students-become-teachers' task is one of teaching themselves how to harmonize with the "singing of the poet's poetizing," which they do by harnessing the five pedagogical techniques Heidegger repeatedly deploys. Their conversation delineates the need that everything—especially Hölderlin's poetry—has for interpretation. Meaning is not given as such. Rather, it emerges from an engagement and released involvement with that which is to be interpreted. The "Western Conversation" elaborates how Heidegger's pedagogy unfolds when students attend to how historical poetizing enables them to learn to teach themselves non-representational, non-metaphysical—which is to say poetic—thinking.

In the final chapter, I show how Heidegger warns of the danger of his pedagogy exceeding its proper limits. Though the "Western Conversation" marks the apogee of his poetic, conversational pedagogy, Heidegger composed a final conversational text in 1953/54, titled "From a Conversation of Language between a Japanese and a Questioner."[84] Though Hölderlin's poetizing opens the possibility for non-metaphysical thinking, this possibility remains tethered to Western metaphysics. For Heidegger, Hölderlin is the poet of the Germans. This means that the poetic pedagogy Heidegger shapes across his conversational texts has developed in response to the Western historical course of events. While depicting a discussion of the danger of conversation between the West and the East, Heidegger describes, but also—intentionally or not—*demonstrates*, how mistranslation and misappropriation remain omnipresent risks. A German "Questioner" and a "Japanese" guest—both of whom are depicted as professional teachers—discuss a slew of topics pertaining to the professors' distinct cultures and languages. They try to determine whether West and East—and indeed their distinctive origins and worlds—can enter into conversation with one another. Though the characters agree on several philosophical points, danger nevertheless haunts. Their apparent agreement may conceal deeper misunderstandings and foreclose the possibility for radical alterity to emerge. I show that the corrective Heidegger provides to the poetic pedagogy he developed in the first four conversational texts intensifies the imperative for such a pedagogy to address this danger by cultivating a sensitivity to and regard for alterity, even (and especially) when non-representational, non-metaphysical thinking *seems* already to have been learned and shared.

Conversational Ways

If the conversations accomplish all this for Heidegger, why did he stop composing them? It is vital to notice that he turned to the conversational genre during a chaotic and violent period, one full of hardship, uncertainty, and devastation for so many—to a far greater degree than for Heidegger. Nevertheless, at several points, Heidegger believed that the ending of the war may claim his life and prematurely end his work. Believing himself to be immanently facing such a possibility, Heidegger frantically composed conversations in which a teaching character makes a (potentially final) bid to explain and clarify the path of his originary thinking of being. Plato's dialogues follow upon his teacher Socrates's death; Heidegger's conversations may have been an attempt to preempt his own death, to perform the roles of both teacher and student in one fell swoop. Yet, once the urgency of the war and the hardships that followed faded, so too did his efforts to write conversations. He returned to the classrooms of the University of Freiburg as an emeritus professor, and invitations to share his work with audiences across the world proliferated anew. Heidegger had an active hand in shaping his legacy once again. Yet this does not mean that Heidegger's conversations were simply an unfinished or superfluous experiment. On the contrary, his conversational texts are themselves in conversation with one another—together they render a robust account of the grounding of his thinking of pedagogy in the indispensability of both collaboration and poetizing. There is a philosophical architecture and wholeness to this sub-corpus of Heidegger's writings. In what follows, I show that only in reading the conversations together and in sequence does Heidegger's poetic pedagogy emerge.

This book takes seriously Heidegger's assertion that conversation is a significant waystation in his thinking. I demonstrate that each of Heidegger's five conversations uniquely contributes to fleshing out the mechanisms, stakes, and limits of his poetic pedagogy. Only in reading the five texts together do its contours and range emerge. This poetic pedagogy does not and cannot hold itself out as a static set of rules or steps oriented toward a predetermined goal. It can only emerge in/as a collaborative performance. In exploring the conversational essence of language, I show that a thinking of and through pedagogy is also found at the heart of Heidegger's "ways, not works." In doing so, I argue that Heidegger presents a challenge to us to take up this task ourselves—to learn how to learn from, through, and beyond Heidegger.

1

The "Triadic Conversation"

Non-Oppositional Pedagogy

The first of Heidegger's *Country Path Conversations*—"Αγχιβασίη: A Triadic Conversation on a Country Path between a Scientist, a Scholar, and a Guide,"[1]—is his most ambitious conversational text.[2] It spans nearly 160 pages and surveys a vast number of themes seen in his later thinking, including the relationship between science and technology, *Gelassenheit* or releasement, and what constitutes a thing. Scholars have already demonstrated the richness of the thinking Heidegger initiates in this text.[3] I revisit many aspects of the philosophical content of the "Triadic Conversation" in this chapter, but I do so to draw out the form of the text and its import for the pedagogy that Heidegger performs. The performance of pedagogical thinking is compelling in the "Triadic Conversation"—*how* Heidegger accomplishes what he does. This dramatic unfolding uniquely comes to the fore in Heidegger's conversational texts and is the feature of the "Triadic Conversation" to which I most closely attend. I structure my reading by noting how the different characters do or do not initially understand one another and how—over the course of their conversation—they come into accord with what has been given them to think and they learn to speak together of this in conversation.

Put simply, the "Triadic Conversation" follows three characters as they transition from representational, metaphysical thinking to learn non-representational, non-metaphysical thinking. For Heidegger, representational thinking is supported by a history of metaphysics that endeavors to represent beings, but thereby forgets being. This history has culminated in an epoch dominated by science and technology. Non-representational thinking attests to another history of being, one that remains to be founded in poetizing as a saying and naming of that which is non-metaphysical. Heidegger dramatizes this transition for the characters of the "Triadic Conversation" through a pedagogy that is historically and geographically specific, offering a window into how Heidegger imagines three characters might—or even should[4]—learn to guide themselves out of an oppositional stance of resistance toward a non-oppositional, poetic pedagogy.

Conversational Context

The Scientist, the Scholar, and the Guide

The key to uncovering this text's pedagogy lies in attending to the roles of the conversational partners. As the title indicates, the three characters are *Der Forscher*, *Der Gelehrte*, and *Der Weise*[5]—the Scientist, the Scholar, and the Guide.[6] At first blush, these characters may seem lifeless, flat, or little more than mouthpieces for what readers of Heidegger may well find articulated in his essays, lectures, and addresses. Hyland notes that these Heideggerian characters are "largely without developed personalities [because] . . . they represent, and I think Heidegger's point is that he wants them *only* to represent, certain *types*, certain standpoints, certain disciplines: scientist, scholar, guide."[7] Gonzalez similarly claims, "while there are different interlocutors in these dialogues, they are never different individuals with names, but only general types."[8] The characters have no personal names and share only scant biographical information.[9] Though this apparent fault may be attributed to Heidegger's novice status as a writer of such texts, it is also possibly an intentional authorial choice. Plato was writing at a particular point in Western philosophy, at a moment where being may not have yet (or had only just) been forgotten, according to Heidegger's tracing of this history. Perhaps in the wake of the Western forgetting of being and predominance of metaphysics, Heidegger's characters can only represent certain types rather than emerge as refined and developed dramatis personae. Within the "Triadic Conversation," the philosophical need for this apparent lack is discussed by the Scholar and the Scientist:

> SCHOLAR: . . . those who might help us with saying and naming [*Sagen und Nennen*] could least of all concern themselves with names.

[. . .]

SCIENTIST: . . . In our conversations, it always seems to me as if [one's] standing and name—indeed, even one's own accustomed daily being [*tägliche Wesen*]—were to vanish.

SCHOLAR: Would this not be due to the fact that during the conversations another horizon opens up? (GA 77: 84–85/CPC: 53–54)

The daily horizon to which they are accustomed is what the characters will later call horizonal-transcendental thinking, delimited by the representational metaphysics the Guide will help the characters to leave behind, together. To let this other horizon open up during their conversation, the sayers and namers they learn to become must remain nameless. Though personality is not the driving force in the text, upon closer inspection it becomes evident that each character plays an utterly distinct role, challenging readers to attend to *who* they are and become as thinkers, not merely to *what* their personalities may indicate about them.[10]

The Scientist is named first in the title, for good reason. Though this conversation is not dramatic like a Platonic dialogue[11] or a theatrical script, the Scientist is largely responsible for animating Heidegger's text, and his demeanor alters radically as the conversation proceeds. Professionally, he is trained in the methodology of theoretical physics. He shares that he is researching and performing experiments concerning cosmic radiation.[12] At the outset, the Scientist is adversarial and quick to challenge what he deems to be the Guide's "strange" (GA 77: 10/CPC 5) contributions. Yet by the same token he is also the most open to pursuing new ways of thinking. The Scientist is typically the first of the three to articulate a breakthrough that propels their conversation to a new stage. He is unsettled often and thoroughly. The Guide tells him that philosophizing "appears to greatly unsettle [*beunruhigen*] you. That is good [*gut*]" (GA 77: 22/CPC 14), thereby articulating one of Heidegger's few attributions of positive valuation.

The Scientist is so unsettled and un-settleable because he is committed to competing—even contradicting—professional goals. On the one hand, he wants to listen to and be thoroughly guided by "nature and nature alone" (GA 77: 17/CPC 11). On the other, he admits that he is driven by a "feeling of domination [*Gefühl der Beherrschung*]" (GA 77: 31/CPC 19) to manipulate nature for the sake of progress and achievement (GA 77: 55/CPC 35). He finds himself caught in a dilemma whereby he wants to understand nature, but also manipulate it. Because the Scientist genuinely wants to listen to and understand what he has devoted his life to study, the Guide has an opening. He helps the Scientist see this methodology requires him first to project a metaphysics onto nature, which is at cross-purposes with his own desire to learn what nature is. In realizing that his aims frustrate one another, the Scientist adapts and gradually lets go of the project of domination and technological manipulation. The Scientist is open to learning and to undergoing his learning experience *with* the other characters. As such, he will be the character who first surmises what it means to think differently.

The Scholar often fades into the background of readings of the "Triadic Conversation." While the Scientist and the Guide obviously play counterpoint to one another,[13] the Scholar's role is subtler. Professionally, he is a historiographer of philosophy specializing in humanistic inquiry,[14] referring to his research in "intellectual history" (GA 77: 33/CPC 21). The Scholar is well suited to relate to both the Scientist and the Guide, holding something in common with each. Where the Scientist engages in scientific research, the Scholar pursues research in the humanities. The Scholar also shares an interest in philosophy with the Guide. He displays facility with concepts from Heraclitus, Plato, Aristotle, Leibniz, Kant, Hegel, and Nietzsche. The Scientist recognizes this affinity between the Scholar and the Guide, calling both "philosophers" (GA 77: 21/CPC 13). In general, the Scholar is adept at asking questions, but his experience with philosophy can be an impediment[15] to his learning process.

The Scholar is also caught in a dilemma. As a student of the history of philosophy, the Scholar wants to think along with the philosophers he admirers, but also wants to appear knowledgeable. When a new insight emerges, the Scholar often (perhaps unwittingly) arrests the unfolding of thinking, instead preferring to (re)cite doctrines of prior philosophers. Evincing a quasi-Kantian orientation, the Scholar is caught between wanting to think and wanting to know. This is clear when the Scholar repeatedly returns to perplexing statements from the Guide that do not obviously lead to any pre-given philosophical response, which leaves him at a loss. Because the Scholar aspires to thinking, the Guide can help him see that thinkers always remain silent about their greatest insight, perhaps because it is unknowable as such. The Scholar is more difficult to teach than the Scientist. He isn't as initially shaken by their conversation, precisely because the Scholar reductively renders its topics philosophically familiar. The pedagogy he requires is one of first unlearning the desire to *know* to then learn to *think*. The Scholar is initially more cautious, but then learns to move beyond simply knowing and (re)citing the doctrines of historical philosophers.

Despite their distinct pedagogical dilemmas, the Scientist and the Scholar have much in common. They are both practitioners of their disciplines as employees of a university. Given Heidegger's view that the organization of disciplines within academia is symptomatic of representational metaphysics,[16] the framework each relies upon to conduct his research will be questioned. The apparent distinction between the methodology of the Scientist and the historiology of the Scholar becomes a sustained conversational theme.[17] At first, it appears that modern natural science is "dedicated to the object" whereas the humanities are grounded in "the subjectivity of the researcher" (GA 77: 42/CPC 27). Methodology and historiology are, however, revealed to be mutually reliant and ultimately based in the metaphysics that constitutes both the subject and the object. At the outset, the Scholar remarks to the Scientist upon the "similarity of our occupations" (GA 77: 3/CPC 1), and by the conclusion, both disciplines are mentioned as obstacles to a releasement into non-representational thinking (GA 77: 153/CPC 100). In the thick of the conversation, more than once the Scientist and Scholar misremember who asks particular questions or introduces certain topics, further indicating that the apparent distinction between them is obviated to some extent by their shared metaphysical outlook.[18]

The Guide is the third and final character in the "Triadic Conversation." Unlike the Scientist and Scholar, the Guide has no professional identity. Apparently, the Guide spends his days engaged in philosophical work (GA 77: 4/CPC 2), but there are no indications that he carries this work out in a classroom or has students in any formal sense. About halfway through the conversation, the Guide explains what he takes *ein Weise*—a "guide"[19]—to be: "there are presumably no wise ones, no sages [*Weisen*]. However, this does not preclude that one may be a *Weiser* in the sense of a guide, where by this word I do not mean one who knows [*Wissenden*], but rather one who is capable of pointing [*weisen*] into that wherefrom hints come to humans. Such a guide [*Weiser*] is also able to show [*weisen*] the manner [*Weise*], the way, in which these hints are to be followed" (GA 77: 84–85/CPC 54). The Guide knows that he does not know but is less interested in Socratic perplexity than in pointing beyond representational, metaphysical thinking. This cannot be metaphysically represented but instead only hinted at, and this deeply informs the Guide's pedagogy.

Throughout the conversation, the Guide maintains a consistent demeanor. Whereas the other characters exhibit growth, the Guide attempts to practice non-representational thinking from the outset. Though he reaches out to the Scientist and the Scholar differently, he remains dedicated to the hope that he will learn "forbearance" or the "art of speaking together in conversation" (GA 77: 46/CPC 29–30). This art of conversation has nothing to do with willing, but rather is an "event . . . wherein something comes to language" (GA 77: 57/CPC 36). This notion of conversation-as-event is distinguished from a notion of "dialogue" that is "about something [*über etwas*] and between speakers [*zwischen Sprechenden*]" (GA 77: 57/CPC 37) and thereby reliant on metaphysical notions of objectivity and subjectivity. The forbearance needed to forgo participating in such an exchange relates to the Guide's early reply to the Scholar's question about what he wants from their conversation: "Since you so directly put me on the spot to say something, I must also directly, and therefore insufficiently, reply. What I really will [*will*] in our meditation on thinking is non-willing [*Nicht-Wollen*]" (GA 77: 51/CPC 33), that is *Gelassenheit* or releasement.[20] Though the Guide remains oriented toward non-metaphysical thinking, his conversational partners react to his comments and provocations differently, prompting the Guide to learn to teach differently in response.

The Guide also experiences an apparent dilemma in the "Triadic Conversation." He repeatedly insists he has nothing to teach, often falling silent when questioned. Yet he freely engages in surmising. The Guide is learning how to guard the unsaid in silence but also how to surmise what can be said of the unsaid in a way that properly guards it as such. This requires a certain sense of being through or "by way" of language; that is, not speech as correspondence between referent and reference, but rather as poetic. The Guide therefore walks a precarious path, still learning himself while also helping the Scientist and the Scholar learn. This may lead to the reading that the Guide functions as the teacher[21] in this (con)text, an interpretation that Heidegger later confirms. In 1959, Heidegger published an excerpt of nearly one-fourth of the "Triadic Conversation" in the collection *Gelassenheit*. Heidegger made several minor edits[22] to the text, the most significant of which is that Heidegger renames the Guide *der Lehrer*—the Teacher. Though Heidegger does not make this explicit until nearly fifteen years after composing the "Triadic Conversation," this text illustrates the challenges and dangers of assuming a pedagogical role with and for others, particularly when attempting to learn non-representational thinking. The Guide tells those he is attempting to teach, "I am far less sure of matters than you, because I perhaps experience its difficulty a little more clearly, from the sense I have that we are altogether still far away [*noch weit entfernt*] from the essence of thinking" (GA 77: 20/CPC 13). It is a sense of nearness and farness to that which can never be represented as an object—not any knowledge he might possess—that appoints the Guide as teacher in the "Triadic Conversation."

On a Country Path, as Night Falls

The country path that enables the characters' walk is introduced before the characters in Heidegger's title. This path is created and re-created by the preceding, collective efforts of others in founding and maintaining the path—events that are geographically and historically specific. Others have walked this path before, repeatedly,[23] including the three characters. They walked this path one year earlier—the preceding autumn—and discussed cognition (GA 77: 3–5/CPC 2). In returning, they rely on their earlier walk—consolidated with the walks of others—for the path's continued existence. That many have trodden the country path enables the possibility of their future walks. Their shared past thus enables futural possibilities, which they presently enact in the "Triadic Conversation." On Heidegger's account,[24] the temporality of the path is thus historical because what remains outstanding in the past constitutes that which is coming out of the future and shaping their current conversation. Further, this temporality is necessarily bound up with a historically and geographically specific community. Time and community constitute the country path as such.

The path incites movement. It is not the river of Hölderlin's poetizing, which first makes the earth arable and habitable for human beings.[25] But the country path does move human beings along its course. It prepares them to release themselves from representational, metaphysical thinking toward non-representational, non-metaphysical thinking. The motto Heidegger crafted for his *Gesamtausgabe*—"ways, not works"—suggests that he experienced his own thinking as attempts at charting a course through a philosophical landscape, leaving behind cartographies that others might follow. In the "Triadic Conversation," the Scholar suggests the way is "releasement." The Guide replies, "releasement would not just be the way [*Weg*], but rather the movement (on a way) [*Bewegung*]" (GA 77: 118/CPC 76–77). To practice non-representational thinking, they must come to understand that the way does not exist apart from the movement it engenders. It is tempting to represent movement as belonging to the activity of a subject walking along the path or to the objectified world passing by, but in thinking beyond metaphysics, the characters must let go of a worldview that depicts subjects advancing through a world of objects. On their country path walk together, they instead enact a "coming-into-nearness to the far" (GA 77: 116/CPC 75). Heraclitus's fragment 122—Αγχιβασίη[26]—serves as the proper title for this text and is translated variously by the characters. The Scholar says, "Αγχιβασίη names 'going' [*das Gehen*]. If it is thought with regard to the movement [*Bewegung*] that constitutes the essence of the human, then going means the mobile [*bewegliche*] relationship of the human to that which is" (GA 77: 154/CPC 101). The human's mobile relationship to being is further clarified by the Scientist as "letting-one-self-into-nearness" (GA 77: 155/CPC 102). In this, both the world and the travelers co-participate. For the first half of their conversation, the Scientist and Scholar repeatedly worry they are straying from the path of their conversation on the occasion of the Guide's apparently strange questions, as though the path's place were fixed. Over the course of their conversation, they come to understand that the path itself is on the move, harmonizing with the movement of their thinking. As they learn, non-metaphysical, non-representational thinking works with—never against—this doubled movement of being underway.

A "country" path evinces a particularly natural, pastoral setting.[27] The city—as a site of human habitation—appears briefly in the "Triadic Conversation," but the text largely moves outside the orbit of the *polis*. The only descriptions of the country path reside in the Guide's poetic musings. Their journey seems to lead them away from the city, through a forested area, and finally back to human habitation, indicating a circular route. The Guide suggests their task is not to arrive anywhere new but rather to learn to abide where they already are. In walking in a circle, they indeed return to where they began, but only at the cost of traveling the difficult ground they do.

At a pivotal moment, the three consider abandoning their conversation and retracing their steps home. Night is falling, so the Scientist proposes turning around. The Scholar also expresses concern their "steps will be doubly unsure on the forest path at night" (GA 77: 72/CPC 45). Their convention had been to discuss philosophical topics on their walk away from the city and to speak of "daily necessities and current affairs" (GA 77: 72/CPC 46) on the return to the *polis*.[28] On this occasion, the Scientist and Scholar convince themselves to press on into the night because "the manifold glimpses of light which, for all its opacity, the conversation granted us, are all too easily lost" (GA 77: 72/CPC 46). Though this decision, at the midpoint of the conversation, also eventually returns them to "human habitation [*menschlichen Behausung*]" (GA 77: 151/CPC 99), it does so not accompanied by a discussion of politics, but through an engagement in poetizing.

The country path covers substantial geographical ground and leads its travelers on a temporal journey. As their conversation touches upon the thoughts of historical figures and cultures, the light of day fades into evening and finally turns to night. Light and sunlight are significant in the history of philosophy. Light plays an outsized role in Plato's Allegory of the Cave, acting as a metaphor for the Idea of Ideas, that is the Idea of the Good.[29] In his 1940[30] essay "Plato's Doctrine of Truth," Heidegger presents an extended reading of this allegory. Though he finds it a rich text that elaborates the original and essential unity of education and truth (GA 9:124/167), Heidegger writes, "for Plato, [. . .] the expository power behind the images of the 'allegory' is concentrated on the role played by the fire, the fire's glow and the shadows it casts, the brightness of day, the sunlight and the sun. Everything depends on the shining forth of whatever appears and on making its visibility possible" (GA 9: 131/172). Because (un)hiddenness is only determined in its relation to this making visible, Heidegger finds "this 'allegory' contains Plato's 'doctrine' of truth, for 'allegory' is grounded in the unspoken event whereby ἰδέα gains dominance over ἀλήθεια. [. . .] The essence of truth gives up its fundamental trait of unhiddenness" (GA 9: 135–36/176). Thus, the possibility of our "most modern of modern times" (GA 9: 143/182) as determined by the dominance of representational, metaphysical thinking is born.

Light conceals its source. Paradoxically, that which enables visibility and seeing is itself invisible and unseeable. For Heidegger, this is what the metaphysics inaugurated by Plato's doctrine forgets. Where Plato's characters move in stages toward a proper relation to sunlight,[31] Heidegger stages his characters as gradually accustoming themselves to the falling night.[32] Heidegger charges Plato with preparing the metaphysical ground for a notion of education based on the correspondence theory of truth whereby a subject "correctly" apprehends an object. What Heidegger endeavors to teach and learn is rather a non-representational thinking that remains sensitive to the (hidden) conditions for emergence of that which becomes visible *otherwise* than metaphysically.

In traveling from day to night, Heidegger's characters are not on the hunt for knowledge. Rather, they are drawing near to the origin of thinking, shrouded as it is in "darkness" (GA 77: 103/CPC 66). It becomes apparent that darkness is needed to first allow light to shine forth as such; darkness may well be light's necessary and essential condition. As Hyland elaborates, "night obscures; it makes seeing more difficult. But strangely, in another register, it also can contain a remarkable brightness. It makes visible the stars, the very stars that, in the other brightness of day, remain hidden. The night that conceals also reveals . . . precisely what is usually hidden by the light of the everyday."[33] The sun is distinguished in proximity, but not in kind. It is simply one of many stars; likewise representational thinking grounded in metaphysics does not exhaust the possibilities for thinking as such.

As night falls and deepens, the conversation between the three characters flows more freely and easily. The Scholar and Scientist relax their exclusive investment in representational, metaphysical thinking. Their conversation becomes more collaborative and less adversarial, fulfilling the Guide's hope that they not "go forth 'against' [*gegen*] anything at all [because] whoever engages in opposition [*Gegnerschaft*] loses what is essential, regardless of whether he is victorious or defeated" (GA 77: 51/CPC 33).[34] Their various appeals to their environment and even the night itself evidence this gradual shift. By contrast, at the conversation's outset, the Guide's first utterance remarks upon the "coolness of the past autumn" (GA 77: 4/CPC 2) after the Scholar and Scientist already embarked upon an exploration of "cognition" by way of Kant. These two accuse the Guide of being unable "to follow [their] conversation" (GA 77: 4/CPC 2) because the natural environment seemed to distract him and impede their triadic exchange. Yet by the middle of the conversation, the Scholar and Scientist let go of the notion that a conversation requires a thematic object. The Scientist even begins to attribute his insights to the night, which, in his words, "compels concentration without using force [*ohne Gewalt anzuwenden*]" (GA 77: 107/CPC 69). When they return to human habitation at last, the night herself[35] is that which they have come to collaboratively poetize.

PEDAGOGICAL TECHNIQUES

The conversation that unfolds on the country path between the Scientist, the Scholar, and the Guide does not take the form of a lecture, debate, or even Heidegger's depiction of a dialogue. Rather, I contend that this conversation is structured pedagogically. As the conversational partners travel into the night, the Scientist and the Scholar become more receptive to pedagogical guidance. The Scientist and the Scholar initially rely on what could be called their disciplinary frameworks or technologies, terms I clarify below, to make sense of the world. Each conforms to the practices of research that accord with a discipline, in this case the disciplines of physics and history. The Guide instead relies on a pedagogy that is responsible only to itself—not to any external framework that would assess its correctness as metaphysical correspondence. Where the characters in Plato's Allegory of the Cave must be compelled—dragged even—to the next stage of their education in metaphysics, Heidegger's Guide has gentler pedagogical techniques. The transition these techniques engender does not consist in the three characters simply abandoning their metaphysical, disciplinary technologies to instead enact these non-metaphysical pedagogical techniques. Rather, both are mutually needful of one another and co-emergent.

It is evident that Heidegger understood the term "technology" in a variety of ways. In the 1930s, his thinking was focused on *Machenschaft* or machination. Mitchell explains, "machination names a systematic tendency toward objectification in all areas of life."[36] In his postwar writings, Heidegger refines his thinking of technology. Moving beyond objectification and representation as markers of the technological, he will later understand technology to operate according to an economy of circulative replacement. Heidegger's elaboration of the *Bestand* or standing reserve—defined by *Gestell*, which has been variously translated as enframing or positionality[37]—in no way indicates a collection of objects waiting to be used, but rather an ontological conversion into a commodity that is available, immediate, and orderable. This will first emerge in the 1949 Bremen Lectures.[38]

I distinguish between disciplinary technologies and pedagogical techniques by adhering to definitions Heidegger develops in the "Triadic Conversation." Circulative replacement is nowhere to be found. Technology is here defined as a metaphysical, representational, and calculative way of knowing that makes that which is known available for manipulation on the merits of the work and achievement its deployment requires. Heidegger in the mid-1940s still thinks technology as a metaphysics of objectification, but already he resists identifying technology with any apparatus. Technology is a way of knowing[39] that relies on the "mathematical projection of nature" whereby "thinking presents nature to itself as the spatiotemporally ordered manifold of moving points of mass" (GA 77: 11/CPC 7). This form of thinking's decisive fundamental trait is "work and achievement" (GA 77: 5/CPC 3). Metaphysical thinking is articulated methodologically as primarily spatial for the Scientist, whereas the Scholar enunciates metaphysics through a fundamentally temporal historiology. Both pursuits fall under the auspices of the work and achievement of research conducted as employees of a university. Heidegger stops short of linking his critique of a metaphysical exaltation of productivity to a critique of political economy, but he does show how the academic disciplines belonging to both the sciences and the humanities are organized as and by the philosophical version of "technology" he auditions in this text.

Resisting disciplinary technology, the Guide instead practices pedagogical techniques. In my usage, techniques are distinct from technologies because they are based in what the characters describe as τέχνη; *techne* characterizes a way of thinking that does not reduce that which is thought to mere knowledge. As the Guide describes it, *techne* is "the letting-see and bringing-into-view of that which a thing is according to its essence" (GA 77: 13/CPC 8). Below, I discuss the relation between *techne* and technology. For the moment, it is crucial to note that, with its newfound emphasis on the "thing" rather than the technological "object," the elaboration of *techne* here foreshadows the relationality of Heidegger's later thinking of the thing and the fourfold.[40] In the "Triadic Conversation," *techne* informs the practices the Guide engages in with the Scientist and Scholar, which I call techniques. Where the disciplinary technologies practiced by the Scientist and the Scholar presuppose the representational tradition of Western metaphysics to carry out their research, the Guide instead strives to think how that which is known is co-emergent with the unknown.

This describes the Guide's own thinking, but also the ways in which he relates his thinking to the Scientist and the Scholar. His pedagogical techniques proceed in two ways. First, the Guide's pedagogical techniques resist the representational thinking bolstered by metaphysics through a direct confrontation with metaphysics. Second, they engage a thinking that is otherwise than metaphysical, bypassing metaphysics by holding open the possibility for other forms of thinking. Though these techniques initially appear to his conversational partners as diversions, the Guide's techniques demonstrate the limits of metaphysical, representational thinking and ultimately how the possibility of non-metaphysical, non-representational thinking is spurned on by a more originary engagement with metaphysics.[41]

The Guide practices five pedagogical techniques throughout the "Triadic Conversation." First, the Guide practices openness to his conversational partners. He engages in their preferred modes of inquiry until their limitations become obvious, including structuring their conversation as an experiment by "testing th[e] case" (GA 77: 40/CPC 26) for the Scientist and contextualizing new ideas with historical precedents for the Scholar (GA 77: 53/CPC 34). Second, the Guide is particularly sensitive to affect, attending to feelings such as fear and anxiety (GA 77: 9/CPC 5). He shares his own feelings quite freely and recognizes that the feelings of his conversational partners are as significant as their thoughts. Third, the Guide often proposes reversals of ideas to enable a thinking past them. Though the Scientist and

Scholar at first complain that the Guide is "taking what sound common sense thinks and straightaway deliberately standing it on its head . . . one must attempt to stand on one's head and walk like that" (GA 77: 6–7/ CPC 4), soon enough they begin to anticipate these reversals and even to initiate them themselves. Fourth, the Guide reminds them what is at stake in their conversation. As the Scientist and Scholar are only beginners, they have difficulty recalling the course of their conversation as they try to orient themselves as non-metaphysical, non-representational thinkers. The Scholar and Scientist cope by repeatedly attempting to summarize their conversation in great detail at first,[42] later by only recapitulating the high points,[43] and finally by gathering the main currents of their conversation together in a commemorative mode[44] that the Guide models and promotes. Fifth, the Guide often falls—and remains—silent in the wake of the Scientist's and Scholar's struggles to (un)learn the limits of metaphysical, representational thinking. In sustaining silence, the Guide resists the temptation to metaphysically represent language as a tool of expression, which reveals and renders accessible that of which it would speak. In the final supplement appended to the "Triadic Conversation," implicitly citing Hölderlin, Heidegger writes, "of all the goods the most dangerous is language, because it cannot keep safe the unspoken—(not because it veils too much, but rather because it divulges too much)" (GA 77: 159/CPC 104). The Guide's many silences perform and teach this (poetic) thinking of language.

These pedagogical techniques permeate the "Triadic Conversation" and Heidegger's subsequent conversations. The dedicated readings I offer of each conversation in subsequent chapters also proceed according to the dual manner I rely on here. I first examine and elucidate the relevance of the differing dramatic structure of each of these texts. Second, I highlight the performance of these five pedagogical techniques as supporting the philosophical import of those structural shapes. Each conversation uniquely contributes to articulating a distinct element of Heidegger's poetic pedagogy of non-metaphysical thinking. Yet in each conversation, Heidegger relies on these same techniques to perform this pedagogy.

Pedagogical Transition(s)

CHIASMUS

The "Triadic Conversation" is a chiasmus.[45] After a brief opening, the first stage of the text introduces the Scientist's investment in metaphysical objectivity. The second stage unfolds the Scholar's commitment to metaphysical subjectivity. The crossing of the chiasmus marks the midpoint in the text, when the three together decide to continue along the path into the forest as night falls. The third stage of the text illustrates the Scholar letting go of his metaphysical understanding of subjectivity. The fourth stage provides the occasion for the Scientist to release his insistence on metaphysical objectivity. A conclusion celebrates this achievement through an episode of collaborative poetizing.[46]

While daylight shines, a polemical mood prevails whereby the Scientist and the Scholar extol how their disciplines proceed based on objectivity and subjectivity. In distinct moments, their worldviews are challenged, and each comes to terms with novel ways of thinking. Yet their responses show they may not yet understand how radical these challenges are. For example, they stop walking several times during their conversation—ostensibly to focus on pinning down a thought,—forgetting that the insight they are after is not an object to be examined, but an event that is itself on the move.

Once night falls, the conversation becomes increasingly collaborative. After their decision to turn into the forest at nightfall, the three return to the topics of subjectivity and objectivity, this time noting the *limits* of representational thinking. As they attempt to move beyond metaphysics to think non-representationally, they encounter two temptations—one that appeals to each disciplinary researcher—to return to that which is familiar. In resisting these temptations, they together learn how to come to non-representational accord with their topics of inquiry and with each other. These pedagogical achievements are illustrated and celebrated in their turn to poetry and collaborative poetizing at the closing of their conversation.

In what follows, I outline this chiastic structure of the "Triadic Conversation." I examine each stage I've just described and highlight its relevant thematic content. Following these expositions, I draw out the many performances of the five pedagogical techniques Heidegger embeds within these sections. Though not every pedagogical technique appears in each section, all five techniques nevertheless play an indispensable role supporting the pedagogical success the "Triadic Conversation" celebrates by its conclusion.

Science as Technology: Metaphysical Objectivity

The opening of the "Triadic Conversation" sets the tone, illustrating the characters' various philosophical commitments. For the first page and a half, the Guide does not speak. The Scholar and the Scientist engage one another, reminiscing how they had spoken together the year before. The Scholar voices that their prior conversation reminded him of an "old Greek word" (GA 77: 3/CPC 1) that seemed appropriate to their topic. However, he does not disclose the word and will not do so until the conversation's conclusion. The two determine to renew their prior interest in examining cognition along Kantian lines. When the Guide finally interjects to recall the "coolness of the autumn[47] day" (GA 77: 4/CPC 2) of their earlier walk, his companions accuse him of failing to pay attention to the "*thematic object* [Gegenstand] of discussion" (GA 77: 5/CPC 2). Reiterating cognition's combination of intuition and thinking, the Scientist boasts that in modern natural science, the role of intuition "vanished except for a small remainder" (GA 77: 5/CPC 3). This accords with his view that cognition's character is "work and achievement" (GA 77: 5/CPC 3)—an active, productive endeavor that exceeds the merely preparatory role of passive receptivity. The Scientist also depicts technology as applied science and claims that physics' reliance on technology to conduct experiments is immaterial to its disciplinary endeavor.

During their initial back-and-forth, it is readily apparent that the Guide and Scientist could hardly understand science—and its relation to technology—more differently. The Guide is not convinced by the Scientist's account of his discipline. In particular, he questions the Scientist's uncritical assumption of the alignment of his research efforts with science and his relegation of the application thereof to technology's domain. The Guide instead suggests, "what is technological does not consist in the use of machines" (GA 77: 8/CPC 4) and that they do not yet know what technology is, which baffles the Scientist. The Guide then provides a tentative explanation of how he understands the relation between the technological and the scientific. The Guide describes the "mathematical[48] projection of nature"—physics' crowning achievement in the Scientist's estimation—as the result of "thinking present[ing] nature to itself [*stellt sich die Natur . . . zu*] as the spatiotemporally ordered manifold of moving points of mass" (GA 77: 11/CPC 7). The scientific idea of nature is "pro-duced [*Her-gestellt*]" and ordered in advance as an "object [*Gegenstand*] of human representation" that renders nature, as a "re-presentat[ion] [*vor-gestellt*]" of a process of calculation become "deployable [*verwendbar*]" (GA 77: 11/CPC 7). This production of the object by way of calculation is the historical manifestation of metaphysical, representational thinking[49] with which the Scientist must learn to contend as merely one possible way of thinking. Because for the

Guide "objectification is the essence of technology" (GA 77: 12/CPC 7), he holds that science is applied technology, reversing the Scientist's initial claim that technology is applied science.

In countering the Scientist's characterization of his discipline, the Guide invokes a rendering of technology informed by τέχνη: "Τέχνη belongs to the stem τεκ—'to bring forth' . . . [which means] to bring something to presence and to let it appear" (GA 77: 13/CPC 8). For the Guide, *techne* is an event of appearance, whereas modern technology is merely one of many possible forms *techne* may take. Modern technology specifies in advance the form this event of appearance will take, namely as a mathematically represented object that is measurable, deployable, and manipulatable. This "setting-toward [*zu-stellen*]" (GA 77: 13/CPC 8–9) of technology, Davis notes, "may also imply 'ob-structing' [and] is later explained in terms of a representational setting-before that sets things toward us"[50] in a way that inappropriately overdetermines and distorts things rather than allowing them to appear from out of themselves.[51] In its originary sense, the Guide describes *techne* differently: "Τέχνη is the letting-see and bringing-into-view of that which a thing is according to its essence. 'Technology' in the modern sense is a kind of τέχνη. Modern technology is that letting-see and setting-toward in which nature comes to appear as a mathematical object" (GA 77: 13/CPC 8–9). As in all forms of appearance, modern technology also conceals what it apparently shows—nature. But it never acknowledges that it obstructs, even as it facilitates, an appearance of nature.

Throughout this exchange, the Scientist's and the Guide's positions are in conflict. The Scholar remains fairly neutral, at times coming to the aid of one or the other of his conversational partners. But clearly both the Scientist and the Scholar are skeptical of the Guide's contention that science is applied technology when characterized as *techne*. The Guide says he does not mean to "steer" the conversation away from "the question of the origin of technology" (GA 77: 16/CPC 10), but the three soon leave this topic behind. Instead, they discuss a wide array of other considerations,[52] which continues to put pressure on the purported universality that inheres in the claim to objectivity celebrated by the Scientist's view of science. The Guide shows that this claim to objectivity is supported by representational, metaphysical thinking, which is itself historically and geographically specific. The Scientist cannot yet contend with the limitations of metaphysical objectivity. At several points, the Scientist worries that his usually excellent memory for "long chains of inferences" is failing to retain the moves of their conversation, even as he repeatedly attempts to summarize the steps of their conversation

(GA 77: 25/CPC 16). He misses "having clear, graspable results" (GA 77: 26/CPC 17) to affix in his memory and grows exasperated that they cannot remain focused on the matter at hand—cognition—while the Guide doubts they have even found the matter of their conversation yet. Through what the Scientist understands as detours and false starts that elicit frustration and even fear, it is becoming evident that no topic of conversation can stand on its own—that is, objectively. Rather, their topic is already contextual and relational. Their route toward determining the matter of their conversation is neither direct nor progressive. The ways in which they discuss cognition demonstrate the limitations of the metaphysical objectivity that undergirds the Scientist's understanding of science and technology. The Guide gestures toward a significant difference between the cognition of the Scientist and a thinking that does not rely on producing its object as such or in advance. This phase of the conversation ends without the Scientist realizing the limitations of the metaphysical objectivity that support representational thinking. However, the Scientist's previously unquestioned faith in the capacity of science to objectively study nature via cognition is shaken.

In the overview of this first stage of the conversation, I mentioned that the Guide employs the five pedagogical techniques I identified above—silence, reversal, remembering, sensitivity to affect, and openness to others—to initiate a loosening up of the predominance of representing things as objects that pervades the Scientist's understanding of science and technology. I now turn to elaborating these techniques in greater detail.

First, the Guide initially remains silent. While the Scientist and the Scholar do the work of contextualizing and selecting the topic of their conversation, the Guide declines to speak. This allows the others to set their course and share what urges them to walk and talk together. The Guide then pedagogically responds to their concerns as an interested collaborator rather than an authoritative lecturer. Throughout their conversation, the Guide contributes what he calls "surmise[s]" (GA 77: 12/CPC 6–7): thoughts that are not quite statements and certainly not assertions. Surmising is how the Guide follows the hints or intimations of non-representational thinking. The Guide will often surmise, but then keep silent about the meaning or implications of his surmise,[53] allowing the Scientist and Scholar to elaborate the insight for themselves, thereby growing in confidence.

Next, the Guide reverses the Scientist's initial portrayal of the relationship between science and technology. The Scientist calls this a "tricky tactic" and the Guide responds, "what appears to be a reversal is at bottom something other than a mere rearrangement of words" (GA 77: 7/CPC

4). Where the Scientist reduces the work of philosophy to inverting "what sound common sense thinks and straightaway deliberately standing it on its head" (GA 77: 6/CPC 4), the Guide insists reversals are fertile moments for thinking beyond what initially appears as "nature" as instead an object produced in advance according to the representational, metaphysical rubric of the mathematical projection of nature. The Scientist and Scholar begin to discern this when considering the claim that science is applied technology, thereby acknowledging that the definitions of the terms of the reversal themselves undergo transformation. Technology no longer means applied science, but rather a way of seeing that which first makes science possible. Upon grasping this, the Scholar remarks, "there are clearly peculiar circumstances involved in this reversing" (GA 77: 15/CPC 10). In this early pedagogical phase, because the Scientist and Scholar can only notice these peculiar circumstances, it falls to the Guide to put words to their nascent sense that his reversal is not a *mere* reversal at all.

In contending with this reversal, the instability of objectivity also begins to challenge what it means for the Scientist and Scholar to think, know, and *remember*. Though the Guide does not (yet) actively assist the Scientist and the Scholar in remembering what is at stake in the course of their conversation, he lays the groundwork for the later distinction he will implicitly draw between merely *summarizing*—or, as the Scientist put it, memorizing long chains of (logical) inferences—and truly *commemorating* that which they are learning to think in a non-representational and non-metaphysical way. Allowing the Scientist to flounder in his sudden incapacity to memorize prepares the way for this yet-to-come pedagogy of remembrance.

Affect is also crucial at this stage. In confronting such a radical challenge to the reliability of objectivity and representational thinking, the Scientist shares that he feels exasperation, confusion, and—most notably—fear. His affective response provides an avenue for the Guide to build trust with the Scientist. The Scientist first expresses fear when the Guide insists that *theoretical* physics is essentially technological. The Guide suggests anxiety as the more proper affect.[54] But the Scientist repeats that he fears the Guide's speculations, in the face of which "every clear way and sure foothold breaks off," and the threat prevails of "the obvious uselessness of speculation, in the face of which we fear that we will fall into vacuity with it" (GA 77: 9/CPC 5). The Guide could have rejected the Scientist's characterization of speculation as useless. Though he does raise an argumentative question to the Scientist—"what is the useful useful for?" (GA 77: 11/CPC 5)—the Guide ultimately allows the Scientist to chart a course for their conversation that feels "safer" (GA 77: 11/CPC 6) to him. Yet fear erupts again when the Scientist realizes that he cannot study science itself using scientific methodology (GA 77: 36–38/CPC 23–24), saying he is afraid to find himself "a stranger[55] in my own house of physics" (GA 77: 37/CPC 24). The Guide praises the Scientist's excellent formulation of his predicament, which seems to encourage the Scientist. The Guide reassures him that strangeness need not arouse fear, but that this uncanny feeling could instead occasion astonishment, telling the Scientist "fear clouds sight. Astonishment clears it" (GA 77: 37/CPC 24).[56] Subsequently, the Scientist is able to see that the historiological view of the Scholar and his own methodological view are equally incapable of studying themselves on their own terms. Non-representational, non-metaphysical thinking is needed.

Finally, the Guide's pedagogy is not structured by authoritative debate. It is embedded within its context, which necessitates remaining radically open to his conversational partners. When the Scholar asks to bring their conversation back "onto the path," by summarizing their exchange, the Guide replies, "I am happy to entrust myself to your guidance," showing that the role of guide is commutable (GA 77: 10/CPC 6). The Guide requests "patience" from his conversational partners, both on his behalf and with themselves "in order to learn" (GA 77: 19/CPC 12). He is willing to revise his statements and "concede" points (GA 77: 29/CPC 18). The Guide engages in the preferred disciplinary modes of inquiry of his partners; he suggests that they might practice "testing th[e] case" (GA 77: 40/CPC 26), as the Scientist's methodology would construct an experiment or tracing the historiology of Aristotle's thinking of τέχνη with the Scholar (GA 77: 14–15/CPC 9). The Guide appreciates and learns from their preferred approaches. He even requests that the Scientist and Scholar "instruct" him regarding the "roaming away" from the conversation that they accuse him of (GA 77: 46/CPC 30). The Scientist especially relishes the opportunity to show the Guide how to resist taking bypaths, telling the Guide that it would bring him the "greatest pleasure" (GA 77: 46/CPC 30) to teach the Guide. This grants the Guide another opportunity to learn how to participate in conversation, which he claims as his own pedagogical task: "Participating in a conversation is in fact difficult. It is even more difficult than leading a conversation. Since we met for the first time on this country path for a conversation, I have attempted to learn but one thing . . . The art—or the forbearance, or whatever you would like to call it—of speaking together in conversation" (GA 77: 46/CPC 29–30). This shows that dispensing formal instruction could not be further from the Guide's intentions. The pedagogy the Guide enacts aspires to maintaining a genuine openness to his conversational partners.

This first stage of the "Triadic Conversation" is oriented by an initial loosening up of the predominance of scientific and technological thinking, grounded as it is in the purported objectivity of the Scientist's disciplinary methodology. In this way, the five pedagogical techniques employed in this stage are geared more toward the Scientist than the Scholar, though both of their disciplinary technologies are grounded in representational metaphysics.

The Soul and Its Faculties: Metaphysical Subjectivity

The Scientist and the Scholar have insisted the matter at issue in their conversation is cognition, which actively represents objects in their objectivity, that is, scientifically. The Scientist refuses to allow this theme to drop for long, though he tolerates the Guide's detours to a point. However, a moment arrives where the Scientist realizes it is possible to change course from interrogating the *object* of cognition—nature—to the *subject* of cognition—the human being. This ostensibly falls under the Scholar's purview as a humanist. According to the Scientist, where the "methodological analysis of physics . . . is entirely dedicated to the object . . . in the humanities . . . the subjectivity of the researcher is necessarily in play . . . [and can] never obtain to strictly objective, that is, to universally valid knowledge" (GA 77: 42/CPC 27). Though he believes the Scholar's knowledge cannot be objective, the Scientist comes to appreciate that the humanities may be able to account for the subject of cognition. The importance of the Scholar's research into metaphysical representations of the human comes to the fore as the two explore the ostensible structure of the soul.[57]

The turn to the soul follows on the heels of a philosophical high point in the "Triadic Conversation." Just after the Guide has agreed to be instructed by the Scientist to resist "roaming away" (GA 77: 46/CPC 30) from their path, he appears to abruptly jump away from science again. The Scientist becomes exasperated and worries that "soon there will be no more science" because he believes the Guide is "suspicious of science" (GA 77: 49–50/CPC 32). The Guide denies this, but his conversational partners are unconvinced. The Scholar presses him, and the Guide reiterates that he is not opposed to science: "I don't want to go forth 'against' anything at all. Whoever engages in opposition loses what is essential, regardless of whether he is victorious or defeated" (GA 77: 51/CPC 33). For the Guide, opposition essentially entails loss.

This implies that to learn how to speak together with others in conversation, the Guide must do so non-oppositionally. The Scientist has felt as though the Guide is opposing his and the Scholar's determination to examine cognition. The Scholar, responding to the Guide's remark on oppositionality, asks "[if] after all that has been said, you are not opposed to science, then it would be revealing and beneficial to the advancement of our conversation if you could say what it is that you really will to gain [*wollen*] from exerting yourself with us to illuminate the essence of cognition and especially thinking" (GA 77: 51/CPC 33). The Guide replies with one of the most cited passages from the "Triadic Conversation": "Since you so directly put me on the spot to say something, I must also directly, and therefore insufficiently, reply. What I really [*will*] in our meditation on thinking is non-willing [*Nicht-Wollen*]" (GA 77: 51/CPC 33). Though it will not be named as such for another fifty pages, this is the first appearance of releasement—*Gelassenheit*—in the "Triadic Conversation."

Gelassenheit is among the most significant developments in Heidegger's later thinking. Heidegger will later publish a selection from the "Triadic Conversation,"[58] preceded[59] by the "Memorial Address" in a 1959 collection titled *Gelassenheit*.[60] The fact that Heidegger prepared these texts for publication underscores his own sense of the importance of *Gelassenheit*. Davis argues that, in addition to the much-debated turn in Heidegger's thinking of being, another turn is discernable in Heidegger's work: away from his investment in willful assertion in the 1930s to the released non-willing of the 1940s and beyond.[61] Though the conversational partners refer to Meister Eckhart's coining of the word in the "Triadic Conversation," both within the text and in the supplements, Heidegger rejects the theological (and thereby metaphysical) determination Eckhart assigns.[62] The Guide describes how Eckhart failed to bring his own insight to fruition (GA 77: 109/CPC 70–71). As Davis explains, "*Gelassenheit* . . . names nothing less than the fundamental attunement (*Grundstimmung*) with which he says human beings are to authentically relate to other beings and to being itself. It contrasts with the fundamental attunement—or rather dis-attunement—of the will."[63] Yet this contrast is nothing simple to understand. Davis further elaborates, "this turn from will to *Gelassenheit* would *not* involve a mere reversal within what Heidegger calls 'the domain of the will,' a turnabout, for instance, from a will-ful assertion to passive submission. Rather, Heidegger's thought calls for a twisting free of this entire domain of the will and a leap into a region of non-willing letting-be that is otherwise than both will-ful activity and will-less passivity."[64] As Moore puts it, "rather than speaking of *Gelassenheit* as the state of having been released or as the state of having released oneself, it would be better to think of it as a middle-voiced event in which both the open-region and we are implicated."[65] As I will show, this endeavor to twist free into the middle-voice pertains not only to Heidegger's relation to the will, but also to the performative pedagogy of non-metaphysical thinking he is beginning to develop in the "Triadic Conversation." *Gelassenheit* cannot simply oppose the will just as non-metaphysical thinking cannot simply oppose metaphysics. As the Guide has already explained, going out against anything means that what is essential in it is already lost. The relation is otherwise than oppositional.

The conversational partners struggle to contend with the Guide's provocative reply that he wills non-willing. The Scientist notes that willing is related to thinking insofar as they are "often named together when one enumerates the main faculties of the soul: thinking, willing, and feeling" (GA 77: 52/CPC 33). In encountering a new framework—the soul—to direct their inquiry, for the first time the Scientist explicitly agrees to "let drop [*fallen zu lassen*][66] the thematic thread [*Leitfaden*] of our conversation" that he still insists had "been tightly maintained [*festgehaltenen*] up to this point" (GA 77: 52/CPC 34), at least by him. In letting the theme of scientific cognition and the representational framework of the mathematical projection of nature go, the Scientist expresses a hope—that with this new theoretical apparatus garnered from the Scholar's domain of humanistic inquiry, they will be able to pursue a discussion of "the unified domain of the soul's faculties" in a more "productive" (GA 77: 52/CPC 34) way so that he will, as he says, "become more at home in my own house" (GA 77: 52/CPC 34).

The homeliness the Scientist seeks is based in willful manipulation[67] as the essence of modern technology that drives the scientific, representational, and ultimately metaphysical thinking that undergirds the first phase of their conversation. Perhaps because of its implicit role throughout their exchange, the will becomes an appealing topic to the Scientist and he becomes willing to bring his interrogation of cognition to an end. The Scientist initially emphasized that science had minimized the role of intuition in cognition (GA 77: 5/CPC 3), and instead he works to underscore the maximal role of the object's objectivity. Once the primacy of activity and objectivity had been established, the Scientist could subsequently acknowledge that subjectivity plays a part in cognition. Since he felt that the Guide frustrated his efforts to think objectivity, the Scientist eagerly turns to the subject of cognition to recover his foothold in metaphysical thinking. The topic also appeals to the Scholar, who—as the disciplinary humanist—can draw from his extensive knowledge of the Western intellectual tradition to provide an overture of its historical account of the soul's faculties. While their discussion of scientific cognition remained mired in metaphysical *objectivity*, their discussion of the soul portrays the thinker, willer, and feeler as a metaphysical *subject*.

The Guide insists it is possible to "look out in various directions [*verschiedenen Richtungen*] from the same viewpoint [*Standort*]" (GA 77: 36/CPC 23) and that "the methodological view is a historiological view [*die methodologische Betrachtung sei eine historische*]" (GA 77: 40/CPC 26), a claim that baffles the Scientist further. Though the *object* emphasized in scientific cognition and the *subject* that unifies the faculties of the soul seem distinct, representational, metaphysical thinking produces them both. The Guide's provocation subtly implies how facile it may be to exchange the content of one academic discipline for another without disturbing the metaphysical presuppositions of research. Heidegger also performs this point dramatically. Though the Scholar had asked the Guide what he "will[s] to gain" from their conversation, the Scientist retroactively claims that *he* was the one to pose the question on five separate occasions.[68] That the attribution of ideas, intentions, and questions between the Scientist and the Scholar are so easily exchanged demonstrates the depth of the shared metaphysical foundation of their disciplines.

Though the Scholar's domain of research is highlighted in this phase, both the Scholar and the Scientist voice that they feel the conversation went astray when the Guide brought up willing non-willing (GA 77: 60–63/CPC 39–40). The Scientist further asserts that "willing non-willing" amounts to "willing willing" (GA 77: 61/CPC 39), and the Scholar insists that the Guide's claim reveals a "denial of the will to live" (GA 77: 62/CPC 39). The two demand a response to these charges. The Guide replies that he is not sure they have yet determined or experienced the essence of thinking[69] or of willing, despite their recourse to the framework of the faculties of the soul articulated by historical philosophers. The Guide revisits the metaphysical representation of negation—the question of how to think the "non" of "non-willing"—as they go on to discuss the relation between work and achievement versus rest and leisure. The Scientist and the Scholar understand rest as the cessation of work, though the Scholar attests that the ancients found in work "the interruption, and that means the negation, of leisure, the *neg-otium*" (GA 77: 69/CPC 44). The Guide questions "whether work and achievement [*Arbeit und Leistung*] are in general fitting measures [*gemäße Maße*] for the essence of the human. Assuming, however, that they are not, then one day the whole of modern humanity, together with its much extolled 'creative' achievements, will surely collapse in the emptiness of its rebellious self-oblivion [*in der Leere seiner aufständischen Selbstvergessenheit zusammenstürzen*]" (GA 77: 71/CPC 45). The Scholar and the Scientist to reassure themselves that "it cannot come to that" because the "new world order" is governed and secured by the essence of modern technological thinking (GA 77: 71/CPC 45). The conversational partners fail to resolve their disagreement as the conversation nevertheless moves on.

Although this stage of conversation—predicated on the metaphysical representation of the human as the unification of the three faculties of the soul—does not ultimately overcome the metaphysical framework of subjectivity it interrogates, the Guide persists in his pedagogy. He enacts the same five pedagogical techniques—silence, openness to others, remembering, sensitivity to affect, and finally reversal—that continue to loosen up representational thinking's claim to exclusive validity.

The Guide again relies on the pedagogical technique of silence. As the Scientist begins to see why the Guide is "averse to orienting our inquiry into the essence of thinking to scientific cognition" (GA 77: 54/CPC 35), the Guide prompts the Scientist to explain his own—that is the Guide's—aversion, rather than explaining it himself. In subsequently keeping silent for two pages and allowing the Scientist and the Scholar to offer their explanations of his response, the Guide discerns that a crucial representational and metaphysical presupposition is underlying their participation in the conversation, which prompts him to distinguish between dialogue and conversation.

The Guide doubts "whether a conversation is still a conversation at all if it wills something . . . [because] it seems to me as though in a proper conversation [*eigentlichen Gespräch*] an event takes place wherein something comes to language [*zur Sprache kommt*]" (GA 77: 56–57/CPC 36). The Scientist, confused, asks, "could authentic conversation and what you understand by that be any different from what one customarily conceives of as a 'dialogue' [*Dialog*]? After all, it belongs to a conversation that it is a conversation about something and between speakers" (GA 77: 57/CPC 37). For the Guide, an authentic conversation is not about something and between speakers. In activating both an object and subjects, dialogue is buttressed by metaphysical representation. The Guide distinguishes his understanding of *Gespräch* from the Scientist's rendering of *Dialog*: "Yet a conversation [*Gespräch*] first waits upon reaching that of which it speaks. And the speakers of a conversation can speak in its sense only if they are prepared for something to befall them in the conversation which transforms their own essence" (GA 77: 57/CPC 37). The Guide's reply upends the notion that the conversation is "about" an *object*, which is ostensibly already determined and available. Even more importantly, it also depicts who the speakers of a conversation are. They are not simply souls with faculties as *subjects*. They are those who are capable of and prepared for a radical transformation in their essence. The event of conversation cannot foresee *what* might be spoken of, and it does not know in advance *who* will participate in such a collaborative saying—the conversation itself is the event of this doubled emergence.[70] Metaphysics fails to depict what the Guide means by authentic conversation in its attempt to first represent the object and subjects of dialogue.[71]

In this, the Guide adheres to the pedagogical technique of remaining open to both of his conversational partners and whatever might emerge as the topic of conversation, resisting the impulse to trust any representation of either as inherently correct. Addressing the Scholar's preferred disciplinary technology—quoting the doctrines of historical philosophers he knows as a substitute for thinking himself—the Guide questions whether they've "caught sight of [thinking] originarily [*ursprünglich*]" and whether willing is necessarily the "striving" that the Scholar shows Leibniz insists it is (GA 77: 65/ CPC 41). Though his conversational partners suspect he has a "reason" for distinguishing thinking from willing that he is deliberately keeping secret, the Guide counters he does not (GA 77: 66/CPC 42). As he helps to stabilize their conversation by additionally practicing the pedagogical technique of remembering various themes they had discussed earlier, the Guide makes a point to affirm the contributions of the Scholar and the Scientist. He engages with the Scholar's historiological contributions and underscores that he "esteems" the Scientist's "readiness to get down to the facts of the matter that lives in every genuine scientist" (GA 77: 60/CPC 38). The couching of approval in affective terms particularly impacts the Scientist, also evoking the pedagogical technique of remaining sensitive to affect. Later, when the Guide uses the final pedagogical technique of reversing the traditional relation between work and rest—suggesting that it is not rest that is a failure in the face of the demands of work but rather that "work is a failure in the face of rest [*Versagen vor der Ruhe*]" (GA 77: 69/CPC 44)—it is the Scientist who replies, "having been previously instructed in this matter, I would not want to straightaway assert that you merely reverse [*umkehren*] the customary view" (GA 77: 70/CPC 44). These five pedagogical techniques are found again in this second stage of the conversation and continue to make headway in loosening up the dominance of representational, metaphysical thinking, especially as it has produced the notions of the soul and subjectivity that fall under the purview of the Scholar's research.

Night Falls at the Crossing: Learning (Non-)Metaphysical Thinking Together

At the midpoint, night falls. This marks a sea change in the "Triadic Conversation." The Scientist's and the Scholar's commitment to pursue clear and distinct representational thinking fades with the daylight. The arrival of night calls the conversational partners to a decision; they must choose whether to follow their path deeper into the forest or to turn around and walk home, an occasion during which they had previously habitually talked about personal or political—rather than philosophical—topics. In choosing to press on, they implicitly begin to challenge one of the most basic presuppositions of Western metaphysics—that clarity *clarifies*. Though the Scholar worries their steps will be "doubly unsure on the forest path [*Waldweg*] at night" (GA 77: 72/CPC 45), in the same breath he regrets suggesting "to break off our conversation so abruptly" (GA 77: 72/CPC 46). The Scientist and the Scholar decide to push on, with the Guide affirming that "clear evenings sometimes bring strangely bright nights" (GA 77: 74/CPC 47). What could it mean for obscurity to grant insight?

Though it may appear abrupt, the Guide has been preparing for this shift. Before nightfall, the Guide said he was attempting to learn how to speak together in conversation, that conversation is not a dialogue but an event wherein something comes to language, and that anyone who sets out to oppose anything has already lost what is essential. All of this informs the Guide's pedagogical role as teacher. Even though he is trying to enact a non-oppositional pedagogy of the event of the conversation they are collaboratively occasioning, before night falls the Guide is limited to challenging the established modes of scientific understanding and scholarly knowing. He did this by pushing these modes along their predetermined paths to their outer limits, using the five pedagogical techniques I've described. After night falls, however, they together begin to think non-representationally. Their exchanges become increasingly collaborative and less adversarial. Even their personal distinctions from one another fade with the sunset. The Scientist and the Scholar become amenable to the Guide's suggestions to free themselves from "ties to everything thematic" and instead allow what is said to "bring itself to language [*zu Sprache bringen*]" (GA 77: 75/CPC 47). The Scientist initiates the next phase of conversation, pursuing *Gelassenheit* and suggesting they should "let ourselves engage in non-willing" while the Scholar clarifies this means to "think about it unthematically" (GA 77: 76/CPC 48). There is now a palpable collaboration distinct from the antagonism that persisted while daylight yet lingered.

The second half of the "Triadic Conversation" is oriented by a task akin to a group pedagogical project. Together, they define the contours of what they come to call the "transcendental-horizonal" (GA 77: 102/CPC 65) representing that Western metaphysics—following Kant, in particular[72]—has promoted as *the* particularly human form of thinking, challenging its purported exclusive claim to securing validity. Along the way, they encounter two stumbling blocks, which tempt the Scholar and Scientist to revert to their preferred disciplinary ways of thinking and thereby invite a check on their learning up to that point. In articulating how philosophical anthropology cannot provide a sufficient account of the human being, the Scholar will manage to move beyond the representational projecting of the human as metaphysical subject. Later, the three turn to an example of a jug. The Scientist automatically sets out to represent the jug as a physical object, yet he also notices the limitations of this way of thinking. In so doing, he sets aside his reliance on the representational production of metaphysical objectivity that scientific and technological thinking presupposes.

I discuss both learning checks below after I delineate the conversational partners' depiction of transcendental-horizonal representing.[73] As night falls, the three return to discussing *Gelassenheit*. The Guide says he does not take the "will" to be a "faculty of the soul, but rather that wherein the essence of the soul, mind, reason, love,[74] and life is based" (GA 77: 78/CPC 49). Though the framework of the soul and its faculties may have been useful earlier, especially to allow the Scientist to move beyond his focus on the objectivity of scientific and technological thinking, the Guide now emphasizes its inapplicability. The Scholar replies that the will is based in the human and that "the human is . . . a horizonal being [*Der Mensch ist . . . ein horizontales Wesen*]" (GA 77: 83/CPC 52) where horizonality "essentially entails an open circle-of-vision [*Gesichtskreis*] or a receding depth of vision [*Gesichtsflught*] *(fuga)*" (GA 77: 83/CPC 53). This open circle-of-vision allows us to "know our way around," which the Scholar recalls "is what the Greeks named τέχνη" (GA 77: 86/CPC 55). For example, *techne* produces the outward look of trees. The Scholar says that in looking at a tree, we also look "out into treeness [*das Baumhafte*] and so look over and away from what we see, and yet in such a manner that it is only through this looking out beyond what is to be seen and what has been seen, that we see the individual tree" (GA 77: 86/CPC 55). Here, the Scholar obviously draws from Plato's metaphysical doctrine of Ideas to define horizonality.[75] He also calls attention to the way in which the horizon compels looking out into and beyond it. He names this "climbing over and going-out-beyond" the "transcendental" following Kant (GA 77: 98/CPC 63) in tracing this particular motif of Western metaphysics.[76] The transcending that "prevails in such horizon-forming representation" (GA 77: 98/CPC 63) willfully turns away and climbs over both the human being and any being she would think, reducing such a relation to the subject's representational production of an object.

This claim—that the human being is a horizonal being who relies on *techne* to contend with the horizon of intelligibility—makes some sense to the conversational partners. But they soon realize that the relation of the human to the horizon is necessarily figured from the human's point of view, not the horizon's (or of what lies beyond its) perspective. The Scholar particularly worries that this means their consideration of the horizon and the horizonal essence of the human "would with a single blow be rendered untenable" (GA 77: 88/CPC 56) because it would be incomplete, biased, and based on circular reasoning. And if their considerations were aimed at *representing* the relation between the human and the horizon, and thus at recovering metaphysical thinking, their project would be undercut. However, the Guide assures that interpretation is a provisional first step: "In the representation of the human's horizonal going out beyond himself and of the horizonal transcending or climbing over objects, there presumably lies a particularly formed, but at the same time an initially necessary, interpretation of a relationship which could, however, in its time manifest itself otherwise and indeed in its originary truth" (GA 77: 88/CPC 56). The Guide acknowledges that they are themselves engaged in representational thinking by positing the human as a horizonal being and that the Scholar is right to point out that they do not achieve a complete representation. Nevertheless, engaging the metaphysics of representational thinking may be a waystation—even perhaps a necessary waystation—and one in which we must not remain mired such that we forget that other ways of thinking are also possible. The Scientist shows that their provisionary interpretation aligns with the "traditional determination of the essence of *homo* as *animal rationale*" (GA 77: 88/CPC 56), which the Guide stresses must be annihilated in its traditional and accepted determination to retrieve the essential and originary sense of the human that it may yet harbor.

After the physical light has faded, the Guide's pedagogical techniques appear to the Scientist and the Scholar in renewed ways. Now that the practitioners of disciplinary technologies have begun to see the limits of representational, metaphysical thinking, the Guide's provocations become more meaningful. The Scientist and the Scholar begin to believe the Guide when he says he doesn't know something (GA 77: 78–80/CPC 49–50), rather than insisting he must be keeping the answer secret, as they had before. This allows the Guide's pedagogy of silence to gain in nuance. The Guide affirms when the Scholar surmises in an attempt to clarify what it means for the human to be horizonal, but also to refrain from guidance in other instances, offering only encouragement as the Scientist and the Scholar work to unpack this surmise together (GA 77: 83–84/CPC 52–53), where he had before. With this newfound trust of his conversational partners, the Guide ventures to speak of the enigma of *aletheia*: "The more [something] shows itself, . . . [it] veils itself [*sich verhüllt*]" (GA 77: 81/CPC 51) by "indicat[ing] [*hinweisen*] what is peculiar to our seeking in order to remain silent [*schweigen*] about finding from now on" (GA 77: 82/CPC 51). The Guide moves beyond merely keeping silent, but is now able to experiment with speaking itself as a certain form of keeping silent when his conversational partners learn to tolerate this enigma.

In the third and fourth stages of the conversation, the three together struggle at the limits of representational, metaphysical thinking. Their steps are nevertheless provisional. The Guide still must assuage the Scholar's fear that the introduction of the horizonal essence of the human stalls the progress of their conversation (GA 77: 90/CPC 57). When they try to think the horizon beyond the transcendental-horizonal thinking of the human, the Guide speaks of "a region" of openness, which the Scholar instead calls "the region of all regions" (GA 77: 112–13/CPC 73) or "*gegnet*" (GA 77: 114/CPC 73), a correction the Guide welcomes.[77] The Guide also initiates the pedagogical technique of reversal when he touches upon the alethic relation of unconcealment and concealment. This time, however, the Scientist anticipates the reversal and prepares himself to think it more deeply, in part, because he first raised the question the reversal provokes (GA 77: 81/CPC 51). In this way, the Guide increasingly steps back from the conversation, letting the Scientist and the Scholar notice that their steps are gaining in surety, despite—or even because of—the night. When their conversation moves on before the Scholar fully elaborates his surmises about the essence of the human, the Guide allows the conversation to wander. When the right moment arrives, he remembers what remained undone and invites the Scholar to return to his elaboration, recalling and reviving this apparently forgotten thread of conversation (GA 77: 85–86/CPC 54–55). Yet, in exercising this pedagogical technique, the Guide is not simply recollecting this or that topic. Rather, he is remembering themes in relation to the course of their conversation. Conceptualizing teaching as a unidirectional, progressive communication of information from the teacher to the student misses the essential role of what the Guide calls the transitional dimension of learning to think non-representationally—"perhaps it belongs to such a transition [*Übergang*] that it must at first pass over [*übergehen*] much, in order to retrieve it later" (GA 77: 124/CPC 81).

Philosophical Anthropology: Moving Beyond Metaphysical Subjectivity

The third stage of the chiasmus of the "Triadic Conversation" begins when, in wading into the waters of non-representational thinking, the Scholar is tempted to revert to his metaphysical conception of subjectivity. While they are struggling to determine how transcendental-horizonal thinking fails to touch on what is essential to the human, the Scholar offers a suggestion that seems compelling. Perhaps the historiological formulation of the human being as rational animal guarantees that the horizonal essence of the human is indeed representational and can thus be elaborated by philosophical anthropology (GA 77: 91/CPC 58). The Scientist enthuses at the suggestion while the Scholar remarks that it has suddenly become "quite bright" (GA 77: 92/CPC 58) over their path. This apparent solution to their quandary follows Kant, who himself followed the path of philosophical anthology,[78] and Plato, including his metaphysical analogy of light. This next phase of conversation consists in the three interrogating how and why the human being cannot be reduced to the philosophical anthropological representation of the rational animal. Together, they discharge the temptation toward thinking metaphysically while becoming even more familiar with what they have already begun to learn.

The relief that washes over the Scholar and the Scientist at this point is palpable. Maybe returning to the Scholar's metaphysical disciplinary framework will obviate the need to learn this difficult, new form of thinking after all! Because his conversational partners have suddenly been drawn back into representational and metaphysical thinking, the Guide presents an argument to challenge this framework. The Guide is not convinced that "the essence of thinking is an anthropological one" (GA 77: 92/CPC 58). He notes that if the human itself is the horizon of their conversation *and* the human has already been defined as horizonal, then they are confronting a *doubling* of the horizonality in question. This means that philosophical anthropology's promise to completely represent the subject cannot be fulfilled. Their discussion of horizonality is always already co-determined by horizonality, initiating an infinite regress[79] (GA 77: 93–94/CPC 59–60). Defining the human through philosophical anthropology, the Scientist realizes, is "a sheer impossibility" (GA 77: 94/CPC 60). This proclamation is all the more significant because the Scientist had insisted that he could not "discover anything confusing or unclear in our present inquiry" (GA 77: 92/CPC 59). The unfulfillable promise of clarity proffered by representational thinking had obscured how that very clarity hid the essence of what it ostensibly represented.

The conversational partners have realized that horizonality permeates both the supposed object of their conversation and themselves as ostensible subjects. Their belief in the very possibility of objective representation by a subject of the human is shattered. They are involved in—and experiencing—that of which they would converse. The Scientist says, "if, however, a meditation on the essence of the human cannot consist of a question about the human, then there is something amiss with the vociferous claims of philosophical anthropology in answering the question of what the human is" (GA 77: 102/CPC 65–66). The Scholar concurs: "For with regard to this question philosophical anthropology not only has nothing to answer, but also no longer anything to ask" (GA 77: 102/CPC 66). They have discovered that to ask *about* something is to pose no question at all, echoing the Guide's earlier resistance to describing their conversation as a dialogue.

Though fundamentally unrepresentable (GA 77: 123/CPC 80), they sense that their conversation is already supported by something other than metaphysical representation. This means that there is a way beyond metaphysical subjectivity; together they are discovering *who* (not *what*) they already are. The human is a being whose being is always already in relation to the world and things. In unfolding this relationality of the human being, the three move toward thinking altogether differently, with a thanking attentiveness, which waits upon the answers and even the questions such thinking may ask.

To elaborate this non-representational thinking of the human, the three return to *Gelassenheit*. The Scholar reminds the conversational partners that there are two possible meanings of "non-willing"—"on the one hand, a willing, in that a *No* prevails in it" but "non-willing also means: that which does not at all pertain to the will" (GA 77: 106/CPC 69). Though the Guide first suggests a transitional relation between the two, it is the Scientist—who had insisted that willing non-willing amounted to willing

willing (GA 77: 61/CPC 39)—who now shares a sudden insight into how releasement may occur:

> SCIENTIST: Am I right to assume the following determination of the relation between the one and the other non-willing: You will a non-willing in the sense of a renouncing of willing, so that through this renouncing we can let ourselves engage in—or at least prepare ourselves for an engagement in—the sought-for essence of that thinking which is not a willing. (GA 77: 107/ CPC 69)

Since representational thinking is driven by the will, the conversational partners must return to their brief initial consideration of releasement to learn non-representational thinking as non-willing. The alternative to a subject representing objects to herself via the transcendental horizon is a waiting upon things to come to rest in the open region of releasement, which enables thinking as "coming-into-nearness to the far" (GA 77: 116/CPC 75). Though the Guide still engages in his previous pedagogical techniques, especially by remembering relevant themes of their conversation, the three increasingly work together to overcome the metaphysical representation of the human being as subject, leaving behind any lingering hope that the Scholar's discipline could obviate the need to engage in non-metaphysical thinking.

THE JUG: MOVING BEYOND METAPHYSICAL OBJECTIVITY

In letting go of metaphysical subjectivity, the question of the thing that rests in the open region comes into view. For all their concern to rescue the essence of the human from metaphysical representation, the thing was neglected. Disambiguating the "thing" from the metaphysical representation of the "object" is the next challenge. This arises when the three turn to a jug to learn to draw this distinction between object and thing.[80]

The jug inaugurates the fourth pedagogical stage of the "Triadic Conversation." This episode provides an occasion for the Scientist to test his learning of the releasement needed for non-metaphysical thinking. In discerning its purpose, means, manufacture (by a potter), and clay substance,[81] the conversational partners figure the jug as metaphysical object. Upon this formulation, the Scientist suddenly reverts: "That of which the jug consists as manufactured and by means of which it also stands, is precisely also that in which it subsists as a jug-thing. And, as I now suddenly realize, something like the open-region is not also needed to characterize this standing-in-itself, that is, the thing-character of the thing" (GA 77: 127/CPC 82). Similarly to how the Scholar had been tempted to rehabilitate a tool of his discipline to think the human, the Scientist also launches his final attempt to turn back to science and technology to render the thing as metaphysical object.

The attempt is short-lived. The Guide reminds the Scientist of the distinction between *techne* and technology: "The objectiveness of objects cannot be grasped from τέχνη, but rather first from technology" (GA 77: 128/CPC 83). They recollect that scientific progress is the application of technological thinking governed by the metaphysics of production; the mathematical projection of nature has intervened to construct the jug as object in advance. This forecloses the possibility of experiencing the jug as a thing. The conversational partners determine that such foreclosure stems from what the Scholar calls the "firmly rooted habituation that we unawares end up looking at the intended thing in a horizon of outward looks and manufacturing" (GA 77: 129/CPC 83). The technology that prevails in our historical epoch informs our tendency to, as the Guide puts it, be "bewitched by what is actual" (GA 77: 129/CPC 84) without experiencing what is essential. Setting aside scientific and technological thinking that objectifies, they attempt anew to think the jug as thing instead.

They propose to restart their inquiry, paying careful attention to the point where the description of "the horizon of outward looks and manufacturing" (GA 77: 129/CPC 84) had put them off course. They note that even before the representation of the jug-as-manufactured arises, the jug as a completed thing first emerges for the potter, who has an outward look of a jug in his mind before he engages in manufacture. The three audition the idea that the jug is essentially a container, which contains by way of its sides and bottom. But they realize it is not the sides or bottom that truly contain, but rather the "emptiness" or "nothingness" (GA 77: 130/CPC 84–85) of the jug that the sides and bottom distinguish. The Scientist concludes, because "emptiness is the ungraspable . . . the potter does not and altogether cannot manufacture [it]" (GA 77: 130/CPC 85). Though the potter shapes the emptiness with the sides, bottom, and rim he manufactures, it is the *nothingness* of the jug that orginarily contains.

At this point, the Scientist reverts to his discipline of physics. He does not notice the (technological) manufacturing of the jug, but rather the (scientific) physical properties of the nothingness of the jug. The Scientist then brings up "something decisive"; he claims that "the jug, even when it seems to be empty, is not truly empty, and can never be empty. Even the allegedly empty jug is filled with air" (GA 77: 131/CPC 85). The Scholar tells the Scientist he has begun speaking again as a "physicist" and no longer as a "drinker of a drink" in insisting that filling the empty jug is really an "exchanging of the full" (GA 77: 131–32/CPC 85). The Guide acknowledges that the Scientist's statements are correct and pertain to the actual, but suggests considering "the question of whether or not what we are talking about has anything to do with what is actual" (GA 77: 132/CPC 85). The Scholar suggests that the Scientist (as physicist) has "forgotten the jug," to which the Guide adds, "and the relation between thing and open-region" (GA 77: 132/CPC 86).

This prompting enacts the pedagogical technique of helping the Scientist remember his own experience of releasement to the open-region just before. It was the Scientist who previously hit upon the depiction of non-representational thinking as a coming-into-nearness to the far. After several provocations to remember his previous insight, the following exchange unfolds:

> SCIENTIST: I am to say how I came to waiting and in what way a clarification of the essence of thinking came to me. Because waiting goes into the open, without representing anything, I attempted to release myself from all representing. And because what opens the open is the open-region, I, released [*losgelassen*] from representing, attempted to remain purely released over to [*überlassen*] the open-region.
>
> GUIDE: So you attempted, if I surmise correctly, to let yourself be involved in releasement [*sich auf die Gelassenheit einzulassen*].
>
> SCIENTIST: To be honest, I did not really think of this, even though we had previously talked about releasement. The occasion which led me to let myself into waiting in the manner mentioned was more the course of conversation, rather than the representation of any specific objects we considered. (GA 77: 117/CPC 76)

The Guide clarifies that the course of the conversation shows how releasement, rest, and movement are mutually related such that "releasement would not just be the way [*Weg*], but rather the movement (on a way) [*Bewegung*]" (GA 77: 118/CPC 77). Emphasizing movement—rather than the way itself (as object) or the one who would take the way (as subject)—invites thinking against the grain of representational, metaphysical thinking. However, movement also risks that in moving away from these moments of insight, they very well may be forgotten.

During this learning check, the Guide enacts pedagogy in reminding the Scientist of their earlier discussion of releasement and in further inviting him to reflect on the meaning of his insight when he tried to think of the jug as a physicist. With this prompting, the Scientist again loosens his grip on his disciplinary way of understanding. He confesses experiencing a "feeling of emptiness" when discussing the jug's emptiness. In yet again practicing letting go of the "workshop of science" where he feels at home, the Scientist claims that he both "know[s] and yet do[es] not know" how to have this conversation and think these thoughts (GA 77: 133/CPC 86). He finds the waiting hesitancy of their conversation sometimes insightful, but at other times he is overcome with impatience. The Scientist's radically honest portrayal of his feelings—as they inform his capacity to know—aids the Guide in further enacting the pedagogical technique of attending to affect. Noting these feelings of emptiness and impatience, the Guide can then invite him to consider ambiguity more deeply. Perhaps, as a learner, the Scientist needs to make mistakes, to grasp those mistakes as mistakes, and to derive a meaningful self-assessment therefrom. This work, far from indicating any pedagogical failure,[82] helps the Scientist reorient himself while also allowing his conversational partners to join in to help each other.

In this stage, the Scientist reaches out for assistance, rather than engaging in any polemics. He asks for guidance to see how he rushed his thinking of the jug-thing, indicating he is "grateful" (GA 77: 134/CPC 86) for such help. The Guide notes that in speaking of the air in the hollow space, the Scientist was no longer "speaking of the jug" itself (GA 77: 134/CPC 87). As the Guide and Scholar together show him, emptiness of the jug as thing is the emptiness of *drink*. The container that contains abides in the drink, which gathers the "event of drinking of what is offered and received as drinkable" (GA 77: 134/CPC 87). Heidegger has not yet established his thinking of the fourfold, but the Guide offers an account of the jug-thing as belonging to the event of the festival[83] that accords with his later ontology. In gathering the sunshine of the sky and the grapevine of the earth, the jug offers the wine it contains to the human to drink beyond the mere need to drink compelled by thirst (GA 77: 134–36/CPC 87–88). The Scientist replies, "I cannot bear for long this reveling in inklings of the wonderful. I need exact determinations" (GA 77: 137/CPC 89). This request helps them all to calibrate their conversation to better elaborate where the danger of exact determinations lies. The Guide says, "we tend to represent these relations objectively in a system, instead of waitfully letting ourselves be involved in what is named as open-region and releasement, open-region and thing" (GA 77: 138/CPC 89). A contrast is thereby developed between representational thinking and non-representational thinking, which is itself pedagogically significant. Even further, the contrast contextualized by the conversation illustrates how representational thinking itself may be of assistance in making the leap to non-representational thinking. Learning such non-metaphysical thinking requires metaphysical thinking in much the same way "willing willing" is needed to learn the "willing non-willing" named in *Gelassenheit*.

In the wake of this pedagogically laden exchange, the three conversational partners speak of various themes of non-representational thinking such as the open-region, enregioning, the thing, bethinging, *Gelassenheit*, and the historical sending of the essence of the human. The increasing fluidity they discover between representational and non-representational thinking enables a dynamic of radical openness to emerge, not only in the pedagogical technique that practices an openness to one another, but also an openness to non-representational, non-metaphysical thinking itself. For instance, at one point the Scholar asks to use familiar, scholarly terminology, but forms his request by acknowledging that non-metaphysical thinking may emerge from metaphysics: "I know that terminology not only rigidifies thoughts, but at the same time it also makes thoughts once again ambiguous," to which the Guide replies, "after that scholarly reservation you may freely speak in a scholarly manner" (GA 77: 139/CPC 90). Despite—or because of—the metaphysical, representational dimension of disciplinary terminology, the conversational partners have learned to engage with it, freely.

Collaborative Poetizing

Through engaging the limitations of representational metaphysics predicated on objectivity and subjectivity, the Scientist, the Scholar, and the Guide manage a pedagogical achievement. Davis writes, "at issue in the ["Triadic Conversation"] is a transformation from the modern essence of thinking as a kind of willing, specifically as a transcendental projection of world or positing of a transcendental horizon of meaning, to a more proper and more originary essence of thinking as an indwelling releasement to the worlding of the world as the regioning of the open-region."[84] This indwelling releasement that I have called non-representational, non-metaphysical thinking certainly requires a moving away from such transcendental thinking. But this moving away does not entail anything like a straightforward abandonment of metaphysics. To abandon something is to oppose it; for the Guide, opposing anything entails already losing what is essential. To practice a non-oppositional stance toward representational, metaphysical thinking is instead to learn to step back so as to see better what such thinking is in its essence. Despite its tendency to obscure its origins, such thinking sustains possibilities for thinking otherwise. The three have discussed the so-called enigma of nearness and farness at several points throughout the "Triadic Conversation," suggesting that nearness and farness are not objective opposites but instead stand in integral and dynamic relation. They even call upon this enigma to describe the essence of thinking as a coming-into-nearness to the far (GA 77: 28–34/CPC 18–21). The enigma is illustrated in their conversation; they must move away from representational, metaphysical thinking so as to first draw near to it, and, further, in nevertheless drawing nearer to non-representational, non-metaphysical thinking, they yet remain far from it. Simply moving from one system to another amounts to accomplishing no meaningful transition at all. Teaching and learning a different way of moving, moving on a way—*Bewegung*—is needed.

The pedagogical techniques the Guide enacts respond to this need. In remaining open to his conversational partners, attending to their affect, suggesting provocative reversals, remembering relevant themes of their conversation, and remaining silent when appropriate, the Guide illustrates the pedagogical role of the thinker. His role teaching those who would learn is not one of presenting information as an authoritative figure for students to absorb and regurgitate. He does not tell them what to think. He provokes them to practice thinking differently. As their conversation unfolds, the Scientist and the Scholar increasingly take up this task, even beginning to enact these pedagogical techniques themselves.

Yet, insofar as the language of their conversation remains mired in representational aspirations, their attempts to learn to teach themselves non-metaphysical thinking can only remain preparatory. The Guide addresses this: "The thinker even says more than he himself can know, such that he is surprised and above all surpassed by the inexhaustibility of his own word" (GA 77: 100/CPC 64). What is it that is inexhaustible about the thinker's speaking? It calls forth more than can be said and remains silent even as it speaks. The way of moving that these three learn is a way of speaking. They endeavor not simply to exchange one vocabulary for another, but to reimagine grammatical and syntactical dynamics. The notion that dialogue is an exchange of language about something and between speakers is contested. The Guide suggests that conversation instead consists in waiting upon an event that "first brings the word to language [*das Wort zur Sprache bringt*]" (GA 77: 57/CPC 37). Presumably this event also involves letting oneself and one's conversational partners together into the open-region where "the word . . . alone answers [*verantwortet*] for itself" (GA 77: 120/CPC 78). Earlier, a discussion of the relation of questions to answers arose. The Scientist and the Scholar found it a rather straightforward proposition that all answers respond to questions, but the Guide was not so confident. He doubted that "every answer is the answer to a question" because, on his view, "the answer [*Antwort*] is the counter-word [*Gegenwort*] . . . to the word" (GA 77: 23/CPC 14–15). Not every question allows a word to come to language such that a counter-word could respond. But there is a way of speaking together—released into the open-region—where the word becomes its own counter-word, where the word can "answer for itself."

This way of inhabiting language is poetic saying.[85] The modes of harnessing language that prevail in the Scientist's and Scholar's disciplinary frameworks proceed by anchoring every claim metaphysically, in the mathematical projection of nature or in the doctrines of past philosophers. By contrast, poetic saying supports itself by allowing what it shows to show itself of itself, without reference to any pre-given rubric. It requires no metaphysics. If a mode of speaking understands itself to be symbolic or metaphorical in function, it is not poetizing, but rather a metaphysical exercise.[86] If it were to happen that our historical age—dominated as it is by metaphysical and representational thinking—were able to raise a question of itself, poetic saying would provide the counter-word. For Heidegger, poetic saying may yet be able to save the "thing-essence [*Dingwesen*]" from its representation as "objects [*Gegenständen*]" and the "human-essence [*Menschenwesens*]" from a metaphysics of "egoity [*Ichheit*]" (GA 77: 140–41/CPC 91).

Once the metaphysical interpretations of the object and subject have been left behind, according the chiastic form I've shown informs the "Triadic Conversation," the conversation between the Scientist, Scholar, and Guide concludes in three parts. These increasingly turn toward poetizing saying as a way of moving between[87] representational, metaphysical thinking, and non-representational, non-metaphysical thinking.

First, the three interpret a poem together. In attempting to name what it means to endure the belonging of the human to the open-region, the Scholar suggests the word "indwelling [*Inständigkeit*]" (GA 77: 144/

CPC 94) because he once memorized a poem that concerns it. He recites it for the others:

> Indwelling
> Never one truth alone
> to receive intact
> the essential occurring of truth
> for far-extending constancy,
> place the thinking heart
> in the simple forbearance
> of the single magnanimity
> of noble recollecting. (GA 77: 144–45/CPC 94)

This poem[88] enables the three to speak of indwelling as the relation of the human to the open-region without metaphysically representing it as such. Once they experience non-representational thinking as poetic saying, the Guide explains it was impossible to accomplish this "so long as we will [*wollen*] to represent it to ourselves, and that means to violently [*gewaltsam*] bring it before ourselves as an objectively present-at-hand relation [*gegenständlich vorhandene Beziehung*] between an object called 'human [*Mensch*]' and an object called 'open-region [*Gegnet*]'" (GA 77: 146/CPC 95).

With the turn away from a violent metaphysics toward releasement, the three interpret the poem through a series of thematic rephrasings of insights that emerge across their conversation. The counter-word to the word of the poem is nothing other than their conversation as a whole. The Guide initiates this way of responding to the poem, saying, "I would like to attempt to rephrase [*umschreiben*] the statement about the relation of truth to the human in order to clarify what we have to meditate on if we are to consider this relation as such" (GA 77: 147/CPC 96). Through this rephrasing, he clarifies that though it is the open-region that occasions truth (not the human), independence from the human being is still *a* relation to the human. This clarity is a far cry from the systematic determination demanded by metaphysics. The Scholar responds, taking up this sort of clarificatory practice of rephrasing, "if this were so, then the human, as the indweller in releasement to the open-region [*Inständige in der Gelassenheit zur Gegnet*], would abide in the provenance of his essence, which we may rephrase [*umschreiben*] as: The human is he who is required in the essential occurrence of truth" (GA 77: 147–48/CPC 96). This proliferation of rephrasings functions pedagogically to illuminate the historical relation of the human to the essential occurrence of truth[89]—truth is no longer thought metaphysically as correspondence but instead as alethic event.[90]

In the second part of the conclusion, the conversational partners move from interpreting the poem to a particular word the Scholar remembers. At several points during their conversation, the Scholar shared that he was thinking of a word that had first occurred to him in their conversation the previous year. The very first lines of the "Triadic Conversation" introduce the Scholar expressing his desire to share "an old Greek word" (GA 77: 3/CPC 1). He never finds the requisite receptivity to properly disclose it until the conversation is in its final moments. In exploring all the depictions of thinking the poem engenders—as noble-mindedness, thanking, thanking for being allowed to thank, commemorating, and a relation and comportment to nearness (GA 77: 148–50/CPC 97–98),—the Scholar recalls the word again. He hopes it is capable of gathering the various definitions of thinking the poem had prompted even though he acknowledges "this probably no longer allows itself to be said in a single word" (GA 77: 150/CPC 98).

The word is Heraclitus's fragment 122: Ἀγχιβασίη—the title of the "Triadic Conversation" that is only disclosed as it concludes. The Scientist asks what it means. The Scholar replies, "the Greek word is translated into German as *Herangehen*, 'going-up-to" (GA 77: 152/CPC 100). The Scientist and Scholar agree that this word is a good name for the essence of cognition they began their conversation with: "the character of actively going-forward [*Vorgehens*] and going-to [*Zugehens*] objects is strikingly expressed in it" (GA 77: 152/CPC 100). Yet they also emphasize that this metaphysical model of representational thinking "does not at all suit that essence of thinking which we surmised [*vermuteten*] along the way today" (GA 77: 153/CPC 100). The Guide remains mostly silent, but interjects at this point to ask if there isn't another possible translation of the term. The Scholar admits there is another, more literal translation: "going-near [*nahengehen*]" (GA 77: 153/CPC 100). The Greek term is separated into two parts; "ἀγχί, 'near,' and βασίη, βαῖνειν, 'to stride,' 'to go' " (GA 77: 153/CPC 100), which can also mean "to walk."[91] This word names not only *what* they would like to think in drawing near to it, but the very *way* they have accomplished this—a walk.

The "Triadic Conversation" is a conversation that does what it thinks, performing and amplifying the infinite remainder that representational metaphysics can never capture. Their conversation has been a pedagogy of the limits of representational thinking and a movement toward a saying that can non-metaphysically disclose their insight. The Scholar says, "Ἀγχιβασίη names 'going' [*das Gehen*]. If it is thought with regard to the movement

[*Bewegung*] that constitutes the essence of the human, then going means the mobile [*bewegliche*] relationship of the human to that which is" (GA 77: 154/CPC 101). This mobility is what the characters have performed. This is demonstrated when the three go even further in their interpretation of the Heraclitus fragment, rephrasing "going" as "going-into-nearness [*In-die-Nähe-gehen*]" and as a "letting-one-self-into-nearness [*In-die-Nähe-hinein-sich-einlassen*]" (GA 77: 155/CPC 102). They refrain from granting finality to any particular interpretation. If they were to determine one interpretative translation of the term as definitive, it would cease to partake in its "mobile relationship" to being and instead solidify into something representational and metaphysical. They must strive to continue rephrasing their insight, which attests to its essential character. It must keep moving—as a *Bewegung*—to unfold non-representationally and non-metaphysically.

Because this word is capable of allowing such an event, the Scholar and Scientist remark in turn that in it, "something like a claim [*Anspruch*] could also be heard resounding [*erklingen*]," which is "why this word stands entirely by itself" (GA 77: 155/CPC 102). The fragment does not stand by itself because it has unambiguously determined what it means. Rather, because the word calls forth its counter-word(s), it can answer for itself by uncovering an originary conversational dynamic[92] that animates the word. Heraclitus's word—and the "words" of many other thinkers,[93] as the Guide acknowledged earlier (GA 77: 98–99/CPC 63–66)—bears many meanings. What was required in the interpretation of the poem they just engaged in is also required to interpret the meaning of such a word. Their conversation reveals how the word is already in conversation with itself by offering a multiplicity of interpretive translations of it.

In the third and final part of the conclusion, Heidegger will not yet make explicit that the counter-word to such a word takes the form of a poetizing saying. This will be found in Heidegger's subsequent conversational texts, especially the "Western Conversation." But he draws the "Triadic Conversation" to a close in a distinctive way[94]—they engage in collaborative poetizing. They are no longer interpreting another's poet's or another thinker's word. In their closing lines, they spontaneously create a collaborative poem:

SCHOLAR: Ἀγχιβασίη—going-into-nearness—the word of course in no way means the essence of modern research, be it that of the natural sciences or be it historiological research. But the word can, entirely from afar, stand as name over our walking course today—

GUIDE: a course which escorted us deep into the night—

SCIENTIST: a night which gleams forth ever more magnificently—

SCHOLAR: and over-astonishes the stars—

GUIDE: because it brings near the distances of the stars to one another.

SCIENTIST: At least in the mind of the naïve observer, but not so for the exact scientist.

GUIDE: For the child in the human, the night remains the seamstress [*Näherin*] who brings near [*nähert*], so that one star next to the other gleams in silent light.

SCHOLAR: She joins the lights together without seam or hem or yarn.

SCIENTIST: The night is the seamstress who in sewing brings near [*nähernd näht*]. She works only with nearness, which furthers farness.

SCHOLAR: if she ever works, and does not rather rest—

GUIDE: while she astonishes the depths of the height—

SCHOLAR: and in astonishment opens up what is closed shut—

SCIENTIST: and so like waiting harbors the arrival—

GUIDE: if it is a released waiting—

SCHOLAR: and the human remains a-propriated [*vereignet bleibt*] into there—

GUIDE: from where we are called. (GA 77: 156–57/CPC 102–3)

Though Heidegger continues to provide speaker designations in the manuscript, he need not have. The three together build phrases and sentences, rephrasing each other's contributions continuously, exemplifying the best of what conversation can be and what every teacher hopes her students may learn to become capable of. Commenting on this collaborative poetizing, Hyland writes, "if someone were to ask, 'who said this sentence?' the only answer could be either all three or more accurately 'no *one*.' For the thought of the sentence is not uttered *by* any one of them so much as it emerges from the convergence of them all."[95] Since nightfall at the midpoint of the conversation, at which the chiastic undoing of metaphysics is dramatically initiated, the characters increasingly leave behind their distinct personalities. As Hyland continues, "in an inspired self-referential closing, the three characters themselves sew together seamlessly—and as one—the thoughts which conclude the dialogue,"[96] appropriately taking night herself as that of which they would speak.

This collaborative poetizing exemplifies not only non-metaphysical thinking, but also the traces of the pedagogical techniques—openness to others, sensitivity to affect, reversals, remembering, and silence—that were first needed to allow non-representational, non-metaphysical thinking to unfold. In these lines, it becomes impossible to meaningfully distinguish which character is saying what. No one is really concluding their thoughts or articulating them as finalized assertions. There is instead a sense of a radical open-endedness to who they are and what they say. They seem to feel—as much as think—what the others say. They note and enact reversals. This poetizing commemorates themes from their conversation. And finally, for all their poetizing saying of the night, they practice remaining intentionally silent about the night's "there." In this way, their collaborative poetizing demonstrates that each has learned to practice the pedagogical techniques the Guide introduced and enacted to resist grasping the cognition of a subject as an object, instead learning to collaboratively poetize non-representational, non-metaphysical thinking precisely as they performatively engage in it.

The Question Concerning (Non-)Authoritarian Politics

Occupying the role of teacher, the Guide guides his students to take note of and learn to think beyond the limitations of representational, metaphysical thinking with apparent success. The Scientist and Scholar contended with the metaphysical presuppositions of their disciplines. Together, they have further learned to freely engage with the representational thinking that the history of metaphysics has encouraged. They can discern that whatever may appear as defined, measured, and available may yet harbor what remains undefined, unmeasured, and concealed. Responding to metaphysics freely takes the shape of poetic saying. In what constitutes a unique instance of collaborative poetizing in Heidegger's corpus, the three conversational partners come together to demonstrate how they have learned, suggesting that each character is indispensable to this pedagogy, though not as a distinct, subjective personality. The Guide speaking in monologue form could not have accomplished this on his own. The art of speaking *together* in conversation is the only way a non-oppositional pedagogy of non-representational, non-metaphysical thinking can be founded. In many respects, the "Triadic Conversation" is a pedagogical triumph.

And yet the destination of their conversation invariably aligns far more with the Guide's initial inclinations than with the Scientist's or Scholar's.[97] Though he claims not to will anything at all, the Guide often seems to function as a mouthpiece for Heidegger's own way of thinking. The Guide practices silence, yet the absence of his voice has all the more philosophical volume. Further, Heidegger chooses to note a place and date at the end of the text—"Messkirch, 7 April 1945" (GA 77: 157/CPC 103),—which is entirely out of step with the scene he has composed within the "Triadic Conversation." As Hyland notes, the text depicts

> a quiet, almost idyllic walk, uninterrupted by anything that might disrupt the course of their conversation. The three can pause from time to time, contemplate the stars in the bright sky above. But . . . in the spring of 1945, in the countryside outside of Freiburg? Any actual conversation along a country path in southern Germany during those days would surely have been interrupted by bombs and anti-aircraft fire as the Allies bombed Freiburg and the surrounding area into devastation and as the war ground toward its inexorable conclusion. Yet the conversation occurs as if in an idyllic world where the war and its destructive effects were non-existent![98]

Although Heidegger has laid the groundwork to found a non-oppositional pedagogy within the text, a provocative and troubling contrast persists between the political reality of Germany at that actual time and place and the alternate philosophical fantasy Heidegger composed. In loosening the grip of representational, metaphysical thinking and reconfiguring this non-oppositional relation between metaphysics and thinking, has Heidegger thereby reinforced another classical opposition, namely, the opposition between philosophy and politics?

Though the "Triadic Conversation" accomplishes much, it is clear that the non-oppositional pedagogy Heidegger has founded remains nascent. By default, the Guide has led the conversation, despite his aspiration toward a non-authoritarian pedagogy. Heidegger's silence about the larger political stage of this conversation is deafening.[99] In the wake of the composition of this text, Heidegger continues to write conversations. In the next "Tower Conversation," we meet the teacher again, this time without his students. The teacher will there be free to make (many and repeated) mistakes. We have already seen the important learning opportunities that errors have invited for both the Scientist and the Scholar. The question remains as to how a teacher might navigate committing and tarrying with her own mistakes.

2

The "Tower Conversation"

Mistaking Pedagogy

Despite its accomplishments, the tour de force of the "Triadic Conversation" left much undone. Heidegger himself indicated as much, highlighting a philosophical weakness in his postscript concerning how nature defends itself against technology by allowing the objectification of its domain. Concerns also loom about just how open the Guide was to the viewpoints of his conversational partners. The second of Heidegger's *Country Path Conversations*—"The Teacher Meets the Tower Warden at the Door to the Tower Stairway"[1]—begins to address the nuances of the pedagogical transition from representational, metaphysical thinking to non-representational, non-metaphysical thinking. The non-oppositional pedagogy founded in the "Triadic Conversation" may not complete this transition. The "Tower Conversation" further explores this possibility through a fresh meeting with the Teacher, who now finds himself without any students to teach.

The "Tower Conversation" emphasizes making mistakes.[2] If the transition from representational, non-metaphysical thinking to non-representational, non-representational thinking can never be fully completed, the locale of the *between* of these ways of thinking becomes paramount. This "in-between thinking," as Holger Zaborowski describes it,[3] tarries with the strangeness of finding oneself between the metaphysics that representational thinking relies on and an inkling of some other possibility. In this text, the Teacher finds himself stranded in this strange locale and repeatedly makes mistakes navigating himself. These mistakes are not mere errors that require correction. They themselves open up the possibility for a released, poetic pedagogy.

These mistakes bear the strangeness of non-representational, non-metaphysical thinking and invite the conversational partners' collaboration in exploring the "between-field" (GA 77: 202/CPC 131) that depicts "where we truly already are" (GA 77: 172/CPC 111). The "we" that comes into sharper relief is not understood as *who* they are as individuals,[4] but as constituted through a grappling with *where* this "we" finds itself. In the "Tower Conversation," the Teacher is dramatically suspended between a disconcerting picture and an unknown guest. The tower and the Tower Warden accompany him as he contends with the strangeness of where he finds himself, inviting the Teacher to form meaningful connections both with things and with others as he learns to make mistakes.

Conversational Context

Things and Characters

The "Tower Conversation" depicts several characters—the Teacher, the Tower Warden, and the Guest—speaking of themes drawn from Heidegger's larger philosophy. Yet this text distinguishes itself in granting roles to several important *things* that motivate the conversation that unfolds between these characters. These things—the picture, the tower, and their relation—are newly important because this conversation is faster paced and more philosophically agile. While the characters in the "Triadic Conversation" managed to arrive at a non-technological and non-scientific sense of the jug as a festive thing that gathers relations between the earth and sky, they could only do so after more than a hundred pages of the Scientist and the Scholar advocating for their respective disciplinary ways of thinking. In the "Tower Conversation," no one advocates for representational, metaphysical thinking. The characters are instead eager to approach the things that permeate their conversation as things,[5] not objects. But as they strive to remain sensitive to the gathering relationality of these things, the tendency toward representation, fathoming, and substantiating nevertheless intrudes.

Two things permeate the conversation. First, the picture—*das Bild*—is the occasion for the conversation. The Teacher arrives at the tower stairway hoping to continue a discussion from the night before about the picture hanging in the Tower Warden's tower room that shocked and distressed him. Though the conversation that ensues is more far ranging, the picture never entirely fades in importance, even as the Teacher confesses that he wishes it would. The picture is distinguished in never appearing in the text. Heidegger never reveals if it is a painting, a drawing, or a photograph; or what it depicts. It may present a raging storm over cliffs that drop into the sea or the periodic table of elements. For readers, the silence of the picture is deafening.

Yet the picture invites the recollection of several of Heidegger's preceding essays from the mid- to late 1930s, in particular "The Origin of the Work of Art" and "The Age of the World Picture." If the picture is a work of art, Silvia Benso suggests it is through the picture-as-art that the importance of the poetic is underscored in the "Tower Conversation." Benso writes, "the reader of Heidegger cannot avoid being reminded, at this juncture, of another artistic image that appears in one of Heidegger's texts and lets something otherwise concealed become manifest—it is, of course, the image of the pair of shoes in Van Gogh's painting."[6] What Van Gogh's painting reveals is the happening of truth, which, as Benso points to, means that "*all art*, as the letting happen of the advent of the truth of what is, is, as such, *essentially poetry*."[7] The picture calls and recalls the poetic into the "Tower Conversation" where no obvert invocation of poetry occurs. The poetic essence of the picture disturbed the Teacher and thereby occasions the dramatic engine of the conversation.

But the "Tower Conversation" is also propelled by the temptation to render the picture according to a different essay, namely "The Age of the World Picture." The characters discuss the threatening dominance of what they call the "ruling world-picture [*Weltbild*] of the natural sciences and technology" (GA 77: 193/CPC 126). Despite their best efforts, the Teacher and the Tower Warden mistakenly think of the picture representationally and metaphysically—as a world-picture, which "does not mean 'picture of the world,' [*Bild von der Welt*] but rather the world grasped as picture [*Welt als Bild begriffen*]" (GA 5: 89/218). The picture has the capacity to reveal itself poetically or as the modern world-picture dominated by science and technology. How the characters learn to attend to the picture *between* these possibilities organizes the course of their conversation.

The picture leads to the second thing that orients the text. The tower—*der Turm*—is both the site of the Teacher and Tower Warden's initial meeting and the place where the picture belongs. Readers learn that the picture was a gift from the Guest, who discerned that the picture belonged in the Tower Warden's tower room. Beyond serving as the dwelling place for the picture, the tower is designated as a "thing" (GA 77: 198/ CPC 128), not an object. The tower invites the characters to consider the relationality of things. Here, the tower assumes the place of the jug in the "Triadic Conversation"—it is the thing that "towers up into the sky and is engaged in the earth" (GA 77: 178/CPC 116). For the Tower Warden, dwelling in the tower fosters becoming more sensitive to "the trembling of the world . . . in further-reaching oscillations [*Schwingungen*]" (GA 77: 163/CPC 105). To contend with the sensitivity this relationality of the tower grants, the characters must walk away from the tower to come nearer to its essence. At several points, the characters turn back to see the tower during several "halting stays [*Aufenthalten*]" (GA 77: 184/CPC 120). They seem to effortlessly experience the same enigma of nearness and farness that the Scientist and Scholar from the "Triadic Conversation" struggled to understand. For Benso, the tower also invokes the poetic, nodding directly to Hölderlin: "It is in fact Hölderlin who, due to his declared incurable madness, was kept in care in an apartment within a tower in Tübingen, overlooking the river Neckar, for over 35 years."[8] Thus the tower is essentially related to the poetic.[9] Things—never objects—open the possibility of poetizing.

Three[10] characters speak of these things and more: the Teacher—*der Lehrer*,—the Tower Warden—*der Türmer*,—and the Guest—*der Gast*. The Teacher and the Tower Warden converse as a pair for most of the text. We know that the characters in the first "Triadic Conversation" had spoken together one year prior. The characters in the "Tower Conversation" have spoken the preceding evening and seem to converse regularly and often. They might be friends. Their pace of conversation is quicker, and, though the Teacher bemoans his limitations relative to the Tower Warden, they are both more adept non-metaphysical thinkers than the characters from the preceding text. Rather than engaging in something akin to philosophical combat, Heidegger's characters are already working in a collaborative, mutually supportive way. They are tarrying with difficult thoughts, which emerge through the questioners' working together to support one another with mutual vulnerability, confidence, and trust.

The Teacher illustrates how strange teaching is. Presumably the Teacher teaches professionally, though he does not mention any specific teaching experiences, yet he is grappling with more than a few unanswered questions. Unlike the Guide in the "Triadic Conversation," the Teacher in the "Tower Conversation" plays the role of *learner*, depicting teaching in an entirely different light. Reversing expectations, the Tower Warden is responsible for guiding the Teacher through their philosophical journey. It initially seems that Heidegger introduces a new cast of characters engaged in their own dynamics. However, in the 1959 publication of a selection from the "Triadic

Conversation," Heidegger renamed "the Guide" "the Teacher." It seems Heidegger only later realized the Guide was the Teacher, perhaps *because* he had more to learn. On closer inspection, the Teacher seems to recall specific formulations drawn from scientific and technological thinking and historiological thinking as they were expressed by the Scientist and the Scholar. I suggest that the Teacher we meet in the "Tower Conversation" fulfills the role of the Guide from the previous text;[11] being a teacher means to learn from and with one's students. This does not necessarily mean to advocate for the viewpoints they articulate, but rather to grapple with challenges their questions pose for the Teacher's own attempt to learn non-representational, non-metaphysical thinking. Perhaps Heidegger is further underscoring that teachers (most of all) need guides so as to learn to become pedagogues. As a teacher in search of a teacher, Heidegger's character arrives as an unexpected guest, both at the door to the Tower Warden's stairway and in the Tower Warden's meeting of his Guest. The Teacher is uninvited yet welcomed in his paradoxical pedagogical role.

The Teacher appears in distress. His affect responds to both the picture and the Guest. His distress is amplified when the Teacher repeatedly finds himself still trying to *grasp* non-metaphysical thinking representationally, rather than opening himself to surmising that which is inapparent. In short, the Teacher repeatedly tries and fails to represent non-metaphysical thinking, which cannot be represented as such. The Teacher is not straightforwardly fearful of the picture or Guest (as the Scientist had been of losing his theoretical framework), but he is not yet adept at letting object-oriented fear transform into an object-less anxiety that would properly prepare him for such thinking. Part of what the Teacher learns is that courage and trust are critical affects to cultivate for one who finds oneself in the "between-field [*Zwischenfeld*]" (GA 77: 202/CPC 131). The Tower Warden says the Teacher practices a "loosened up metaphysical manner [*eine aufgelockerte metaphysische . . . Denkweise*]" (GA 77: 175/CPC 114) of thinking. The pressing question becomes whether this is sufficient or whether there is anything more the Teacher can do to move beyond a metaphysical thinking grounded in representation. The Teacher learns to tolerate his restlessness in the face of this question and to allow its crescendos to pass through *Gelassenheit*. He first makes the apparent mistake of trying to solve his restlessness—as though it were a problem with a technical solution—and simply obliterate his tendencies toward metaphysical thinking. With the Tower Warden's guidance, he instead comes to interrogate those very mistakes as the locale of the possibility of non-metaphysical thinking. On my reading, for Heidegger to teach is to learn to make mistakes, properly. The Tower Warden notes he "cannot force this insight through mere instruction and decree" (GA 77: 179/CPC 117), but through repetition the Teacher becomes ever more sensitive to the concealed provenance of all forms of thinking.

The Tower Warden lives in the tower and presumably keeps and maintains it, experiencing the relationality of the world through this thing that is also his home. He does not remark upon the views[12] the tower's height grants, but instead highlights its sensitivity to the movement of the ground below. As he reminds the Teacher that representational, metaphysical thinking is limited, the Tower Warden suggests that "perhaps we overestimate the role to be played by such an examination of the world, and what we ourselves contribute to it, by holding it to be the work of our representing [*das Werk unseres Vorstellens halten*], and by remaining insensitive to that which touches us inconspicuously. He who lives in the height of a tower feels the trembling of the world sooner and in further-reaching oscillations [*Schwingungen*]" (GA 77: 163/CPC 105). The tower dweller *feels* what others do not. In his forward to the *Country Path Conversations*, Davis suggests that Heidegger's Tower Warden may resemble Heidegger himself, Hölderlin, or a character from Goethe's *Faust*,[13] all of whom aspired to or took up residence in towers. Benso insists the Tower Warden is the poet Hölderin.[14] These intriguing suggestions undoubtedly contain germs of truth. But the function Heidegger assigns to this figure is also significant—the Tower Warden is he who, because he sets himself farther from something, is more sensitive to and thus nearer to its essence. He is more practiced at feeling that which attends to the enigma of nearness and farness.

The Tower Warden is more experienced in practicing non-metaphysical thinking than the Teacher. This raises an intriguing pedagogical point. Perhaps the Teacher's *lack* of experience is part and parcel of what teaching *is* for Heidegger.[15] Yet the Tower Warden's experience does not immunize him against also making mistakes. What sets them apart is that the Tower Warden admits and draws attention to his own mistakes, even when the Teacher has not noticed. The Tower Warden's proactive vulnerability engenders the Teacher's confidence in himself and trust in his conversational partner to remain open to learning though interrogating these mistakes. Above all, the Tower Warden welcomes both his expected and unexpected guests, doing his utmost to guide them on their journey. They trust him because both the Teacher and the Guest have established relationships with the Tower Warden, if not (yet) with one another. The Tower Warden enables the Teacher to come more fully into his pedagogical role as a perpetual learner because he guides their conversation and models how to make a mistake properly. In exemplifying the courage and trust needed to contend with his mistakes, the Tower Warden preserves the vulnerability required to constitute a "we" capable of thinking non-metaphysically together.

The Guest is enigmatic. His presence in the text is largely defined by his absence. Despite the silence his physical absence compels, the Guest nevertheless exerts a great deal of influence on the Teacher and Tower Warden's conversation. His profession is never described, but it is mentioned that he gives gifts (GA 77: 169/CPC 109–10), perhaps may occasion the festive (GA 77: 198–99/CPC 129), and is in no way a source of information (GA 77: 169–70/CPC 110). Benso suggests the Guest may be Heidegger writing nature as *physis* into the text: "A plausible possibility in spirit with the overarching poetic and Hölderlinian aura of the entire conversation, a conversation that in any event is in itself an act of philosophical imagination, is that the guest be not a real (living or deceased) figure but an imaginary one—namely, I surmise, Mother Earth or, better, Nature."[16] Zaborowski rejects understanding the Guest as a "nihilist," a "god," or even "Zarathustra."[17] Rather, he turns to the philosophical description of a guest that Heidegger developed several years earlier in the *Ister* lecture course: "A guest is that foreigner who for a time becomes homely in a homely place foreign to them, and thus themselves bring what is homely for them into the homely of the foreign and are received by the homely of the foreign."[18] The Guest may thereby be distinguished as one who dwells in transit, who remains in the in-between of the homely and the foreign and illustrates their mutually needful relation to one another.

On my reading, the Guest troubles any easy distinction between presence and absence, thereby contesting metaphysical renderings of being. For all the silence he keeps during the majority of the text, his impending arrival is still very much in conversation with the others. As Heidegger later writes in "Language," "we are always speaking, even when we do not utter a single word aloud" (GA 12: 9/PLT 187). The Tower Warden describes the Guest as the "guest *par excellence*" because "he can listen" (GA 77: 180/CPC 117), which is thereby still a form of speaking. As Heidegger emphasized in "Hölderlin and the Essence of Poetry," language itself is conversational in essence. This means that not only is language already speaking with itself and with us, but that listening and hearing are also integral to language itself.[19] The Guest's silence is a way in which he participates in the conversational essence of language even before he partakes in the conversation between the Teacher and Tower Warden. The Guest is also the source of the picture that caused him such unrest. Even as the Teacher tries to distance himself from the picture, he finds himself unwittingly walking toward the Guest, who is likewise approaching him. This also illustrates Heidegger's thinking of history and of the origin. The historically originary is never something merely past. The origin remains outstanding yet ahead, coming out of the future. The Guest echoes this fundamental thinking of the origin in its connection to language and thus to conversation itself. It is this practice of originary thinking that engenders the Teacher's mistakes. The Guest is thus exceedingly generous in silently allowing himself—as origin—to become the site of an other's mistaken representation of him so that they can learn to think otherwise.

Across Days and Fields

This conversation is already underway, in several senses. It covers an enormous philosophical terrain rapidly and ends just as a new phase commences. Readers are privy to a mere snippet of a larger event sustained across meetings and relationships. The Teacher and the Tower Warden had been together the night before, discussing the picture that distressed the Teacher. He returns to the tower stairway uninvited in the hopes of finding relief by talking with the Tower Warden further about the picture. It also seems the Tower Warden and the Guest conversed the previous evening. Though these conversations were had separately, the Guest says these prior discussions have rendered the three "in the same condition [*im selben Fall*]" (GA 77: 202/ CPC 131) and prepared them to converse all together. Though the written text abruptly ends upon meeting the Guest, their conversation seems to continue. As Zaborowski suggests, "it is as though what is now discussed (or could be discussed) can no longer be written down."[20]

Though the preambles began in the darkness of the preceding evening, this conversation takes place during daylight hours. The conversational partners report seeing the tower at a distance several times, and they spot the Guest before they meet him. In the "Triadic Conversation," light was an impediment. The darkness after nightfall was the proper setting for that conversation. But the Teacher and the Tower Warden do not find the daylight problematic, though they speak disparagingly of the "artificial light" (GA 77: 172/CPC 111) of the scientific-technological world-picture and approvingly of the "darkness" (GA 77: 172 and 192/CPC 111 and 125) in which the origin of non-metaphysical thinking remains concealed. In the "Triadic Conversation," the moments where the conversational partners stopped walking along the path coincided with instances where representational thinking was activated, trying to arrest the movement of being, which such thinking attempts to measure metaphysically. In the "Tower Conversation," the "halting stays [*Aufenthalten*]" (GA 77: 184/CPC 120) that quietly punctuate their walk have no such effect. The moments in which the Teacher and the Tower Warden stop walking to turn back and take in the view of the tower as they draw farther away from it only enhance their conversation. The conversational partners in the "Tower Conversation" seem more capable than those in the "Triadic Conversation," easily managing what had been obstacles for those less practiced in thinking beyond representational metaphysics.

The second half of the "Tower Conversation" takes place on the country path. The first half unfolds *before* they arrive at the path. Upon reaching it, an important change can be discerned. The conversational partners begin to directly engage with metaphysical thinking. Before the Teacher and the Tower Warden reach the country path, they largely avoid explicitly metaphysical topics. The advanced level of their conversation is apparent as they move with a dizzying speed of philosophical virtuosity, touching on themes they clearly discussed before (and therefore find no reason to slow down or fill in gaps, least of all for the readers' sake). After reaching the country path, their pace does not necessarily slow, but their well-worn tracks seem to invite a relation to the metaphysical terms that have been discussed on this path many times before, including during the "Triadic Conversation."

Their conversation—or rather the written text of the "Tower Conversation"—begins at the base of the tower. The Tower Warden has just climbed down the tower stairs to set off for some unknown destination. The Teacher arrives unexpectedly, hoping to continue their conversation from the night before about the picture in the tower room at the top of the stairs. The two remain at the base of the tower, discussing how to proceed thinking of the distressing experience. Yet, as their conversation continues, the tower itself—and the upward and downward of it that the stairs take part in enabling—becomes an explicit theme. The Teacher struggles to follow the non-metaphysical sense of the tower the Tower Warden invokes. This struggle, coupled with the Tower Warden's need to meet the Guest, leads them to walk away from the tower. From a greater distance, the Tower Warden hopes the Teacher will more easily draw near to the essence of the tower as thing. At first, the Teacher is also glad to be walking away from the tower and the picture in the room, but he soon learns they are walking toward the source of picture—the Guest. As they approach the country path, Heidegger provides no explicit description of their surroundings. It seems appropriate to surmise that they are off-roading, walking through fields adjacent to the country path. As they navigate terrain not purposefully cultivated for human habitation, their conversation continues in a similarly untamed register. They remark repeatedly on the idiosyncratic style of their conversation, admitting the likelihood that hardly anyone else would understand them (GA 77: 173/CPC 112).

Once they reach the country path, the tenor and vocabulary of their conversation alters. The Teacher did not intend to accompany the Tower Warden beyond this point, but the conversation pulls him along. The Tower Warden continues welcoming his unexpected company, modeling the comportment the Teacher himself is struggling to embody toward the approaching Guest. From the country path, they are better able to turn back to see the tower. This non-metaphysical sense of the tower as thing is enabled by the conversational partners' newfound willingness to include overtly metaphysical topics in their discussion. Prior to walking on the country path, the conversational partners moved quickly and freely through a number of themes, many of which were metaphysically grounded though never explicitly acknowledged as such. Once they are walking along the familiar country path, the Teacher seems more equipped to name the metaphysical tendencies of his own representational thinking, despite his efforts at resistance. Identifying these latent tendencies prepares him to continue to learn.

Though the text culminates in the Teacher still struggling to properly welcome the Guest on the country path, Heidegger seems to intimate that the conversation continues after the text ends. There is no grand finale (like the collaborative poetizing of the "Triadic Conversation") or not one readers are invited to witness. Perhaps the conversational partners are only able to turn back, retracing their steps toward the tower once more after they have come to grips with the claim representational, metaphysical thinking continues to make even (and perhaps precisely) when they attempt to resist it.

The Mistake as Pedagogical

One of the most striking differences between the "Triadic Conversation" and the "Tower Conversation" is in their affective tenors. Though the "Triadic Conversation" resolves into a collaborative poetizing, initially it was a combative debate between the characters advocating for a form of representational, metaphysical thinking and the character who drew attention to the limits of such an approach. The "Tower Conversation," on the other hand, strikes a friendly and collaborative tone from the outset, but no resolution is found, at least none to which readers are privy. Despite this difference, the same pedagogical techniques employed in the "Triadic Conversation" can be discerned in the "Tower Conversation": openness to others, attention to affect, employing reversals, recollection, and silence. Here, these techniques do not simply reveal the limits of representational, metaphysical thinking; they further demonstrate the needfulness of those very limits as the site of the possibility of non-representational, non-metaphysical thinking.

In the "Tower Conversation," no character actively advocates representational, metaphysical thinking. Yet such thinking nevertheless irritates. Both the Teacher and the Tower Warden make mistakes in attempting to think otherwise. The Teacher struggles more, but as I will show, the Tower Warden is neither immune from committing his own mistakes nor from the reverberations of the Teacher's mistakes. At various points, there is a kind of pronoun trouble. Despite various efforts to clearly distinguish between the singular first- and second grammatical persons, over the course of their conversation it becomes clear that the first-person plural is most philosophically relevant. Because they are participating in the constitution of a "we"—and not just a "you" or an "I,"—the way either conversational partner thinks affects the other. These can occasion impediments or opportunities for growth. The characters grapple with how to teach and learn from one another under these conditions.

In the "Triadic Conversation," the Guide relied on pedagogical techniques to unveil the limits of representational, metaphysical thinking. The Tower Warden's use of these techniques in the "Tower Conversation" is put to a different purpose. The Tower Warden does not need to first draw attention to the limits of representational thinking, as the Guide did. The Teacher is acquainted with these limits and has already devoted time to attempt this. At stake is not a pedagogy of transition, but a pedagogy of sustaining a sensitivity to the *between* of this transition. If, as the Tower Warden suggests, it is not possible to simply progress from representational, metaphysical to non-representational, non-metaphysical thinking, then what is needed is a pedagogy not of accomplishment, but of what it means to be underway.

This pedagogy of the between is articulated in the "Tower Conversation" through a series of (compounding) mistakes. Though the term "mistake" appears only twice (GA 77: 201–2/CPC 131), the Teacher and Tower Warden make mistakes throughout the conversation. The Teacher especially learns how generative and necessary these mistakes are for learning to inhabit the between of representational, metaphysical and non-representational, non-metaphysical thinking. What he needs to learn, and then learn to teach, is not that representational metaphysics must be abandoned. Rather, he comes to experience—precisely through making mistakes—that such thinking cannot be abandoned. But this experience is not one of powerlessness and resignation. In coming together to recognize their condition, I argue that the conversational partners are engaged in a constitution of themselves as a "we" thanks to the gifts that these mistakes turn out to be. These mistakes provide the opportunity to exercise vulnerability with one another and strengthen the trust needed to recognize the "same condition" (GA 77: 202/ CPC 131) in which they all find themselves. As Heidegger emphasizes in the Hölderlin lecture courses, the task of the poet is the founding of a people (GA 39: 78–151/71–132). Though poetry does not appear explicitly in the "Tower Conversation," the conversational partners are learning to found a "we" out of their encounter in the most unlikely locale of all: the mistake of representational, metaphysical thinking.

Mistaking Pedagogy

Bidirectionality

The "Tower Conversation" delves into the nuances of how and why the Teacher must assume the role of a (non-authoritative) learner. Heidegger stages this pedagogical evolution by stranding the Teacher between the strangeness of the picture in the tower room and the strange(r) Guest. The physical and metaphysical trajectory of this walk shows their conversation begins in proximity to the picture, continues as they walk farther and farther away from the picture, and ends as they come into proximity to the Guest. Yet there is another non-metaphysical directionality at play. The Tower Warden reveals that the Guest himself is the origin of the picture, which he gifted to the Tower Warden because of its fittingness in the tower room. Heidegger's thinking of the sending of the history of being[21] is prominent at this time. His lecture courses on Hölderlin attempted to think the relationality of the river to its origin in a fundamentally historical sense (GA 53: 1–62/1–50). But the enigma Heidegger developed in the "Triadic Conversation" also describes the structure of the "Tower Conversation"—the enigma of nearness and farness. The continuing importance of this enigma is shown in the conversational partners' endeavor to walk away from the tower to better see what it is. The Teacher also tries to leave behind the distressing picture only to unwittingly draw nearer to its source. In a non-metaphysical sense, the Teacher is walking *toward* the picture insofar as he is drawing nearer to its origin through moving *farther* from the picture itself. His walk seems to be at cross-purposes with itself.

The "Triadic Conversation" was structured as a chiasm. The "Tower Conversation" now illustrates the relation between a metaphysical trajectory and a non-metaphysical trajectory, which appear opposed but in fact are revealed as selfsame. The Tower Warden helps the Teacher recognize that opposing representational metaphysics in order to "cross-over [*Übergang*]" (GA 77: 171/CPC 111) into non-representational, non-metaphysical thinking is mistaken. Yet *this* mistake serves as the occasion for the Teacher to learn that metaphysical thinking is the locale from which he can "turn-back [*Rückkehr*]" (GA 77: 171/CPC 111) toward the selfsame origin of both ways of thinking. There is also a distinct and philosophically significant midpoint to the "Tower Conversation"—reaching the country path. Before this midpoint, as they walk across the country fields, they resist explicitly naming how representational metaphysics informs their conversation. This resistance relates to the Teacher's desire to think in a more advanced way and his hope that he has (already) abandoned representational metaphysics. Once they reach the country path, however, they do name this. The Teacher articulates the shape of this thinking along the lines that the Scientist and the Scholar from the "Triadic Conversation" would have,[22] further suggesting that a teacher is only truly a teacher if and when she can listen to and learn from her students as well. The Teacher and the Tower Warden's willingness to name science and technology as well as historical references allows them to articulate the "critical point [*kritische Punkt*]" (GA 77: 186/CPC 121) that would allow the possibility of non-representational, non-metaphysical thinking to emerge.

In the sections that follow, I show how the characters make mistakes in hastily falling back into representational, metaphysical thinking rather than letting what they think be in all its strangeness. They use the five pedagogical techniques I've described above to learn from these mistakes. After providing an overview of the thematic context of the opening scene, the characters walk up to the country path, walking on the path, and finally meeting the guest, I offer an analysis of how these pedagogical techniques are at play in the various stages of this bidirectional movement that opens up the field *between* representational, metaphysical and non-representational, non-metaphysical thinking.

Meeting at the Tower

Unbidden and unexpected, the Teacher bursts onto the scene to find the Tower Warden who just climbed down from his tower room. Instead of first greeting the Tower Warden, the Teacher dejectedly remarks, "so I have come then too late" (GA 77: 163/CPC 105). His first line is neither a statement nor a question. It is an appeal that does not formally demand an answer, yet it calls for the welcoming response from the Tower Warden that he receives. This opening scene already indicates the thematic metaphysical mistake with which the Teacher is struggling. The Tower Warden suggests a non-metaphysical sense of time could never render an assessment that someone has arrived "too late"[23] because such temporality unfolds "singularly and then suddenly" (GA 77: 165/CPC 106) and can be neither comparative nor superlative. Though the Teacher is already somewhat aware of this distinction, metaphysical presuppositions slip into his contributions[24] across the "Tower Conversation."

The apparent origination of their conversation is deceiving. The "Tower Conversation" is only the latest in a series of conversations between these conversational partners. Their implied friendship accounts for the lack of formalities between them, which would be expected at the outset of an encounter between strangers, colleagues, or mere acquaintances. These two were together in the tower room the night before. This prior meeting was oriented by the Teacher's acute perplexity and distress aroused by the picture on the wall. The Teacher tells the Tower Warden that their previous conversation had caused him "deep unrest throughout the day" (GA 77: 163/CPC 105) and prompted his arrival as an unexpected guest.

Though the picture prompts the conversation, readers do not learn this is the occasion of the Teacher's unrest until the opening volley of conversation subsides. The Teacher clarifies that he believes he has arrived too late "to solve the wondrous [*Wundersame*], which has held me in unrest [*in der Unruh hält*] throughout the day" (GA 77: 163/CPC 105). The Tower Warden responds, "I scarcely still think of paying attention to something wondrous in order to solve it" (GA 77: 163/CPC 105), instead suggesting, "prior to that, the strange [*Seltsame*] is there for us to find" (GA 77: 164/CPC 106). It is the strange that first grants the possibility of unfolding a non-representational, non-metaphysical thinking. The wondrous is associated with representational, metaphysical thinking, motivated by a "willing-to-know [*Wissenwollen*]" that seeks to undertake an "examination of the world" (GA 77: 163/CPC 105). Heidegger hereby alludes to the famous Platonic association of philosophy and wonder, warning of the metaphysical destiny initiated with Plato.[25]

The Teacher attempts to understand the Tower Warden's depiction of the strange by opposing it to the wondrous. The Tower Warden builds on this: "The latter arouses our questioning; the former hints back into itself [*winkt in sich selbst zurück*]" (GA 77: 164/CPC 106). They come to agree that wondering seeks to assess that which is according to a predetermined framework. This seems to contrast with cultivating sensitivity to the strangeness of that which inconspicuously reveals itself, unsurmised. But the singular and sudden appearance of the strange contains its own paradox. The Tower Warden remarks, "the unsurmised [*Unvermutete*] always reaches only those who surmise [*vermuten*]" (GA 77: 165/CPC 106), which risks that surmising could become "the will-to-a-ground [*den Willen zum Grund*]" (GA 77: 165/CPC 107) that would overwrite the possibility of the strange with the wondrous. Though the Teacher is unsure how to guard against this, the Tower Warden maintains his confidence that surmising can nevertheless forego "seeking after supports and foundations" (GA 77: 166/CPC 107).

In their initial back-and-forth, the conversational partners draw a whirlwind of distinctions—primarily between the wonderous and the strange, but also between questioning and hinting, willing and passing by, and the surmised and the unsurmised. However, the Tower Warden expresses a concern that "hastiness remains a danger [*Gefahr*]" (GA 77: 166/CPC 107). The Teacher seems to rush to discern "what supports the confidence of such surmising" (GA 77: 166/CPC 107), which the Tower Warden notes is driven by wondering. Questioning the foundations of this provenance attempts to represent it metaphysically. Yet the Tower Warden's concern is also meant as a warning to himself. They *both* need to practice patience in surmising the unsurmised and, as the Teacher says, "to let the wondrous, and the craving to fathom it, pass by [*vorbeigehen lassen*]" (GA 77: 166/CPC 107). The Tower Warden responds: "This word is fitting. To let pass by, but not to will to go beyond and overcome [*nicht übergehen und überwinden wollen*]" (GA 77: 166/CPC 108).

Haste is grounded in the "will that is the danger" (GA 77: 166/CPC 108), threatening to lead surmising toward the representational, metaphysical thinking the Tower Warden is trying to help release the Teacher from. Here the Tower Warden offers a surprising self-critique:

TOWER WARDEN: I myself fell prey to it [the danger of the will] when we met a moment ago. You came to solve the wondrous that had unsettled you all day long.

TEACHER: And you pulled me away from that.

> TOWER WARDEN: Because of a haste that is difficult to recover from, a haste which never once wishes to abide with, to behold, what this wondrous might be. (GA 77: 167/CPC 108)

The Tower Warden not only outlines the danger of hastiness, but he also admits *he* fell prey to this very mistake with the Teacher. Though the speed of their conversation was partly born out of an advanced practice of thinking and conversing together, this speed also led the Tower Warden to make a mistake at the Teacher's expense. The Tower Warden admits he was not patient in drawing a severe distinction between the wondrous and the strange. He thereby discounted the Teacher's interest in the wondrous as perhaps *itself* strange. The Tower Warden proactively and humbly points out his own mistake and acknowledges this possibility. He acknowledges it is "difficult to recover from" this haste, but it is this very mistake that allows them to surmise the unsurmised, namely that metaphysics itself may be thought non-metaphysically.

Three pedagogical techniques undergird the first phase of the "Tower Conversation." First, the characters employ reversal. Despite his initial inclination to draw sharp distinctions, the Tower Warden initiates a reversal because he realizes it led the Teacher to make the mistake of positing an opposition between the wondrous and the strange. In challenging the distinction he initiated, the Tower Warden acknowledges this relation is non-oppositional and more nuanced than he initially suggested. Whereas the Guide in the "Triadic Conversation" reversed the terms the Scientist and Scholar used,[26] the Tower Warden engages in a pedagogically advanced maneuver—reversing his own depiction without being prompted to do so. The failure to practice the pedagogical technique of proper openness to the other is also ameliorated. The Tower Warden ensures to point out his mistake to his conversational partner, indicating he had not been properly open to the Teacher. He commits to remediating this failure by openly acknowledging his mistake now, hoping the Teacher's learning will be further enabled through such openness. Finally, the two together practice recollection, summarizing what had gone wrong and revisiting where their conversation had just veered off course. Employing these pedagogical techniques—reversal, openness to others, reversals of ideas, and recollecting—has a salutary and stimulating impact on the Teacher. Immediately after, the Teacher freely offers a fuller account of the unrest that brought him to the tower doorway.

Now the Tower Warden is prepared to listen to—and perhaps even teach—the Teacher. The Teacher shares that the picture in the tower room provoked him to "come here to climb up to you," to which the Tower Warden replies, "in the meantime I have climbed down" (GA 77: 167/CPC 108). The Teacher recalls a fragment from Heraclitus, which they translate: " 'The way upwards downwards one, and that means: the selfsame [*derselbe*]' " (GA 77: 167/CPC 108). Where the conversational partners in the "Triadic Conversation" complained of unnecessary detours and received significant pedagogical intervention before they could properly hear the fragment from Heraclitus that oriented their conversation, the Teacher and the Tower Warden can embrace these bypaths. The Teacher first senses the belonging together of the upward and downward Heraclitus speaks of by representing the stairs in the interior of the tower to himself. This runs a metaphysical risk. The Tower Warden insists the gathering of the upward and the downward in their belonging together is not limited to the inside of the tower. He admits perhaps this "does not allow itself to be easily said from the foot of the tower. It would be better for us to catch sight of the tower from a distance [*aus der Ferne*]" (GA 77: 168/CPC 109). The two agree to walk away from the tower to enable this experience.

The Tower Warden invites the Teacher to accompany him "just up to the country path" (GA 77: 169/CPC 109). He extends this invitation only after the Teacher questions the pronouns in the Tower Warden's suggestion: " 'We,' you say—and yet at the same time you must admit that in this view of the tower from a distance belongs an experience of the Tower Warden" (GA 77: 168/CPC 109). In raising the issue of the "we," and marking that he does not yet feel a part of this "we," the Teacher is touching upon one of the most philosophically central questions of the "Tower Conversation"—how it is that any community, especially a non-metaphysical community, comes to be. The Teacher intended to climb up to ask the Tower Warden about the picture. The Tower Warden meanwhile climbed down to go out to meet the Guest. As the next phase of their conversation will reveal, it is in coming to recognize the selfsameness of these apparently opposed movements that the meaning of their belonging together as a "we" is illuminated.

WALKING UP TO THE COUNTRY PATH

The two set off toward the country path with a caveat. The Tower Warden invites the Teacher to accompany him "just up to the country path" so as to leave the path itself "free for another conversation" (GA 77: 169/CPC 109). This suggests that the country path may not be the appropriate setting for their current discussion, for reasons that emerge in due course. The details of the scene are left undescribed, but the conversational partners seem to be walking in and between country fields, picking their way through an only semi-domesticated landscape that tolerates but does not actively support human sojourn.[27] Before reaching the country path, they also seem to be moving in the between-field of thinking, abstaining from representational metaphysics but not yet achieving non-representational, non-metaphysical thinking either. Despite their awareness of haste's danger, the two continue to speed along, committing different versions of their earlier mistakes. In part, this is enabled by their resistance to explicitly recognize the metaphysical presuppositions that intrude regardless. Once they reach the country path, they will name these as such. But as they make their way through the wild landscape, they mistakenly attempt to willfully remain free of representational, metaphysical thinking.

As they walk, the Teacher mentions his relief to be leaving the picture in the tower room behind them. The Tower Warden rejoins, "let us *not* leave the picture" (GA 77: 169/CPC 109), disclosing that the Guest recently gifted it to him. As the Teacher attempts to leave the picture behind, he finds himself walking toward its origin. The Teacher then makes his next mistake. He confesses a hope that the Guest "will be able to give me some direct information [*unmittelbare Auskunft*] about the picture" (GA 77: 169/CPC 110). The Tower Warden tries to dissuade the Teacher of this, urging him not to expect the Guest to either solve the wondrous of the picture or reveal what may be strange about it.

Contending with this new obstacle, the Teacher retorts, "yet, if he gave you the picture, he must have certainly had an acquaintanceship [*Kundschaft*] with it" (GA 77: 170/CPC 110). The Tower Warden is struck by the word *Kundschaft* and asks the Teacher where he learned the word. The Teacher replies, "I found it used in your speech" (GA 77: 170/CPC 110). The Tower Warden admits that the Guest "must have an acquaintanceship in relation to the picture" (GA 77: 170/CPC 110), though he is unsure of its precise shape. Together, they leave open whether the Guest's acquaintanceship takes the form of "expertise [*Kennerschaft*]" or the "gift [*Geschenk*] of a message [*Kunde*] . . . that comes to us inceptually [*die uns anfänglich zukommt*]" (GA 77: 170/CPC 110). Yet even before the notion of a gift is explicitly raised, it seems the three characters are already implicated in relations of giving and receiving gifts. The Guest gifted the picture to the Tower Warden. The Tower Warden had given the gift of this word *Kundschaft* to the Teacher. The Teacher then gave the Tower Warden's word back to him in their conversation. Now the Teacher and Tower Warden hold open the possibility that the Guest may, "when the moment is favorable [*günstig*]"

(GA 77: 171/CPC 111), share the gift of the inceptual message of the picture. Though the Teacher has not met the Guest, gifts already mediate the relations between the three, enlarging the meaning of the "we" they are coming to constitute.

The conversational partners catch sight of the tower and realize they are near the country path without yet having "entered into the interplay between Heraclitus's saying and the essence of the tower" (GA 77: 171/CPC 111). Though the Teacher has not yet freed himself from representing the upward and the downward of the tower, he tells the Tower Warden that he has "let the feeling of unrest that the picture brings me run its course," to which the Tower Warden responds, "this letting is good" (GA 77: 171/ CPC 111). Despite—or perhaps because of—their ostensible detour, the Teacher engaged in a practice of *Gelassenheit*[28] toward his distress. Clearing the way for the strange of the picture also opens the strange of the tower the Heraclitus fragment depicts. The Tower Warden says, "the picture belongs in the tower room . . . so we should not separate the strange of the picture and strange of the tower" (GA 77: 171/CPC 111).

The same pedagogical techniques used in the first stage of their conversation—reversal, openness to one another, and remembering—are discernible, with the addition of the pedagogical practice of releasing affect. The Teacher again tried to represent something—the Guest himself—metaphysically, as a source of information. The Tower Warden again chastised the Teacher for this impulse. In recognizing the returning of his unwitting gift of the word *Kundschaft*, the Tower Warden notes his own hasty decision to dissuade the Teacher, reversing course to remain open to him. In subsequently recollecting together how this ostensible detour postponed understanding the Heraclitus fragment, the Teacher mentions how he released his distress. The Tower Warden affirms that this practice—informed by *Gelassenheit* toward such an affect—is "good," a rare designation for Heidegger. As before, this response to a series of mistakes contributes to an increasing trust the conversational partners experience in relation to themselves and to one another.

Immediately before reaching the country path, they come to focus on the ontological issue underlying the Teacher's tendency to try to will himself to think non-metaphysically, that is to make the mistake of trying to metaphysically represent the possibility of non-metaphysical thinking to himself. This is the issue of provenance, which will become even more apparent once they reach the country path. The Teacher expresses a desire to cross over to the Tower Warden's way of thinking, which the Tower Warden tells him is impossible,

TOWER WARDEN: . . . so long as you struggle at a crossing-over rather than allowing a turning-back.

TEACHER: To where?

TOWER WARDEN: To that place where we truly already are. (GA 77: 171–72/CPC 111)

Directionality gives rise to the Teacher's confusion. He attempts to seek out non-metaphysical thinking in some other locale, but the Tower Warden insists that this possibility is not granted from somewhere else but is found where the two of them—as a "we"—already truly are. Though he strives to understand, the Teacher admits this remains in "darkness" (GA 77: 172/CPC 111).

The Tower Warden tries to guide him through his confusion, reminding him that they are not trying to know or understand but to properly "receive" what he calls "the look" that "brings us before the unapparent" (GA 77: 172/CPC 112). This non-representational look is hardly the view of the subject or "ego" (GA 77: 172/CPC 112) that takes itself as its own object. Their task is to understand not *what* or *who*[29] they are, but rather first *where* they find themselves. The Teacher says that they must "rather look away from ourselves in order to find ourselves where we truly are" (GA 77: 172/CPC 112).[30] The non-representational, non-metaphysical look of the tower as thing is the selfsame look they must have toward themselves. They must learn to practice sensitivity to the relationality of the locale rather than isolating and representing metaphysical objects as metaphysical subjects. This look of the unapparent is something that only shows itself of its own accord and on its own terms. It can never be signified or represented as a dictionary might purport to signify or represent something (GA 77: 173–74/CPC 113). Instead, they strive to "remain with the uniqueness of the matter" (GA 77: 174/CPC 113) rather than relying on a pre-given rubric to determine meaning in advance.[31]

The Teacher and the Tower Warden emphasize that their task is essentially collaborative. The Tower Warden insists he is only able to remain with the uniqueness of this "state of affairs" if the Teacher also takes part: "I not only catch sight of it and do catch sight of it only insofar as we—you as well as I—stay within it" (GA 77: 175/CPC 114). This is not an individual or individualized endeavor. It involves the "we" as *who* must turn back to where they already are. This raises the provocative suggestion that non-representational, non-metaphysical thinking may only be possible in collaborative conversation with others. The Teacher seems to accept this and offers a suggestion for how he might also come to catch sight of this uniqueness. He says he needs a "fitting word" (GA 77: 175/CPC 114) to follow the Tower Warden's thinking. The Tower Warden calls this an "ambivalent intention" that shows the Teacher's "loosened up metaphysical manner" of thinking, which displays a "prediction to follow" the Tower Warden's way of thinking, but continues to make the mistake of searching for a "passageway" between the two ways of thinking, rather than instead "turning back" (GA 77: 175/CPC 114) to more deeply interrogate how he is already engaged in such thinking. The Teacher still voices his desire to "abandon this manner of thinking" (GA 77: 176/CPC 114) that remains related to representational metaphysics. The Tower Warden asks how a thinking that is metaphysical, even in a loosened-up way, could come to call for its own abandonment. With this question ringing in the air, the two suddenly find themselves on the country path.

Walking on the Country Path

The Tower Warden signals they have reached the country path by putting a question to the Teacher: "Do you not notice that we are already walking on the ever reliable country path?" (GA 77: 177/CPC 115). Though Heidegger does not mark the precise moment the conversational partners return to the familiar path, the word "metaphysics" is first uttered one page before the Tower Warden poses his question. The explicit appearance of metaphysics and their acknowledgement that they are still caught within representational metaphysics seems to correspond with this return to the country path. Though they avoided inviting this way of thinking into their conversation, metaphysical thinking had accompanied them as another sort of uninvited guest all along.

Though the Teacher was only supposed to proceed up to—but not onto—the country path, the acknowledgement of metaphysics seems to activate its own sort of gravity. From this point on, the two do not shy away from directly speaking about the scientific, technological, and historiological manifestations of representational metaphysics while they nevertheless continue learning non-metaphysical thinking. Posed more definitively between such possibilities, their mistakes become increasingly legible as such. On the country path, the Teacher realizes that his mistakes *are* his opportunity to begin thinking non-metaphysically. This begins the most philosophically dense section of the "Tower Conversation." The conversation slows in pace as the conversational partners delve into representational, metaphysical terminology and explore both metaphysical and non-metaphysical questions. Mistakes abound. I focus here on elaborating the significance of one particular mistake that pertains to what the conversational partners call the "critical point" (GA 77: 188/CPC 121) of their conversation.

Before arriving at this "critical point," the Teacher and the Tower Warden revisit the tower, Heraclitus, scientific and technological thinking, and the question of history. Upon noticing they have reached the path, the two turn back to catch sight of the tower again. The Teacher says he had forgotten why they were reflecting on the essence of towerness. The Tower Warden recalls for him the saying from Heraclitus and the question of "how we would arrive at where we truly already are" (GA 77: 177/CPC 115). The Teacher can then finally see how "the tower towers up into the sky and is engaged in the earth" (GA 77: 178/CPC 116), which evinces a non-representational, non-metaphysical reflection on the thinghood of the tower. Though this may be an "everyday idea" (GA 77: 178/CPC 116), the Teacher suggests it "can no longer stand up to the forward march of modern natural science's manner of representing" (GA 77: 179/CPC 116), which is enabled by its essence as technology. Though they agree that understanding how a technological scientific metaphysics has come to dominate things and transposed them into objects is crucial, they also acknowledge they could never "force this insight through mere instruction and decree" and instead "leave the tower to its restful standing" (GA 77: 179–80/CPC 117).

Though they let the tower be, the Teacher is not quite prepared to practice releasement toward scientific and technological thinking itself. He revives a point the Scientist made in the "Triadic Conversation," namely that it seems so easy to "transpose the relation between science and technology back onto that between theory and praxis" (GA 77: 180/CPC 117) and thus to deny that science is an application of technological thinking. Though this view mistakenly figures "acts of human consciousness" (GA 77: 180/CPC 117) as grounded in a subject, the Tower Warden is also careful to point out that "representing, producing, and ordering are ways through which what presences reveals itself to us in its presence" (GA 77: 181/CPC 117). Scientific and technological thinking also allows being to unconceal itself; it cannot simply be opposed as inimical to non-metaphysical thinking. As the Tower Warden himself had needed to learn about wondering, even that which appears as the apex of representational metaphysics may yet garner a strange sensitivity to the non-representational and non-metaphysical.

The conversational partners then embark on an interlude on the question of what constitutes the human. The human is not a metaphysical subject who represents, produces, and orders objects, but rather one who sojourns—the one for whom these manners of comportment constitute a sojourn or *Aufenthalt*. As Davis points out, "*Aufenthalt* most often means 'sojourn' in the sense of staying (*Sichaufhalten*) somewhere temporarily. However, similar to our word 'residence,' *Aufenthalt* can refer not only to the act of staying, but also to the place where one stays (*Aufenthaltsort*) and the time-period that one stays there (*Aufenthaltzeit*)" (CPC 118). The human as sojourner finds herself staying somewhere in a temporally finite way.[32] Inhabiting space and time in this way does not align with the methodological or historiological renderings the Scientist and the Scholar advocated in the "Triadic Conversation." The place and temporality of the sojourn are not the exclusive result of the *human*'s view of being. They also must be thought of as originating in *being*'s first granting of the human's being. Upending representational metaphysics' presupposition that the subject produces reality, the conversational partners depict a relationality of the human and being whereby each needs and is "in view" (GA 77: 182/CPC 118) of the other. The Teacher says, "sojourn is both a matter of that which presences to—while viewing—the human, because it contains; and also a matter of the human, who stays [*sichaufhält*] in such a view and containing with-hold," which figures the human as "the self-restraining comporter [*der Sichverhaltende*]" (GA 77: 182/CPC 118–19).

To further unfold how this is distinct, the Teacher asks whether he can elaborate a "glimpse" of this possibility using what he calls "language that is familiar to me" (GA 77: 183/CPC 119). The Tower Warden graciously consents, with one condition. The Teacher shares that he wants to draw from the "history of thinking" (GA 77: 183/CPC 119) to articulate his insight, recalling the Scholar's references to the historiology of philosophy in the "Triadic Conversation." The Tower Warden introduces a distinction between "any mere modernization of the historically past" and how "what has historically been becomes a preview of what is yet to come, of what long approaches us" (GA 77: 184/CPC 119). The Teacher accepts this sense of history as futural[33] and inherently connected with the human essence as sojourn and is thereby able to proceed without making the Scholar's historiological mistake. His mistake will be different. The Teacher says he thought of this fragment when he first glimpsed the relationality of the human and being as speaking to the "still unresolved question of the relation between science and technology" (GA 77: 185/CPC 120). He is "disturbed" by the "stubbornness of the dominant representation" that "technology is the actualization of the knowledge and theories of the natural sciences" (GA 77: 185–86/CPC 121). The Teacher wants to "strive to break" (GA 77: 186/CPC 121) the dominance of this way of thinking, but the Tower Warden cautions that this is not possible for "mortals alone" who are only able to "think" (GA 77: 186/CPC 121) in response. This shows that the oppositional stance the Teacher is preparing to take only serves to mire him further in representational metaphysics.

With this encouragement, the Teacher finds the "courage" (GA 77: 186/CPC 121) to share a second fragment from Heraclitus—fragment 112—that the conversational partners now leave untranslated and uninterpreted, perhaps inviting the reader to concurrently practice non-metaphysical historical inquiry. As Davis points out, McKirahan translates this fragment: "Right thinking is the greatest excellence, and wisdom is to speak the truth and act in accordance with nature, while paying attention to it" (CPC 121). The Tower Warden seems to intuit what the Teacher is thinking of with the Heraclitus fragment: "Representing, producing, and ordering are not only each related to what presences, but also, prior to this, they are held into all relations to what presences by the presencing of what presences" (GA 77: 186/CPC 121). Not only is scientific and technological thinking grounded in metaphysics, but metaphysics in turn may be "held" by being itself, as one possible way of unconcealing itself as such.

Here the "critical point" is articulated. It concerns the way in which they are to understand how being holds metaphysics out as its own historical possibility:

> TEACHER: . . . with this reference there remains for me one reservation: I would like to consider whether going back to ancient thinkers can provide us with a clear explanation of how we are to think that which you have in view when you say that representing, producing, and ordering are held by the presencing of what presences. The critical point lies in this "held" [*gehalten*]. I know that speaking of a point [*Punkt*] is not fitting—I mean the focal-place [*Ort*] of the crisis of thinking.
>
> TOWER WARDEN: Whether it follows the track of metaphysics, or—
>
> TEACHER: I have a dim presentiment of this other possibility, but also know that we are not yet decisively and exclusively engaging in a meditative pursuit of it.

TOWER WARDEN: For we still lack the trust, or even the proper aptitude for this trust in what carries and what calls on non-metaphysical thinking.

TEACHER: Thus you are unable to get by without keeping one eye trained on metaphysics.

TOWER WARDEN: Certainly not, and especially not when it is a matter of a first indication of the other thinking, if you will allow me this naming, which implies no sense of superiority over against metaphysics. (GA 77: 186–87/CPC 121–22)

The Teacher and the Tower Warden describe this "critical point" and emphasize how difficult achieving a description of it is. In attempting to conceive of the relation between that which presences—being—and the representing, ordering, and producing indicative of scientific and technological thinking—the historical manifestation of representational metaphysics—a significant question arises. The Teacher considers whether the terms of this relation are metaphysical (which seems plausible because the result is metaphysical thinking) or whether the terms *themselves* can be thought otherwise. The Teacher acknowledges that even calling it a critical "point" is mistaken, but he does not seem to have any reservations in further depicting this point as a "crisis," rather than as an invitation to this other thinking.

The Tower Warden approaches the Teacher's mistake using all five pedagogical techniques: silence, openness to the other, affect, reversal, and remembering. In this case, he leads with silence. The Tower Warden prompts the Teacher to consider the possibilities for describing the relationality of the critical point by naming one option, but remaining silent about the other, entrusting it to the "—" that opens as an appeal to the Teacher to think further. In his initial response, the Tower Warden employs the pedagogical techniques of silence and openness to others. In his reply, the Teacher seems assured that whatever this "other possibility" may be, they are not yet engaging in it. The Tower Warden diagnoses one of the barriers they are facing in affective terms, noting they "lack the trust" to think non-metaphysically, grounding that which is to be learned by way of this third pedagogical technique. The Tower Warden also challenges the Teacher's assumptions about the Tower Warden's relation to metaphysics, reversing his expectations by affirming that he does keep "one eye trained on metaphysics." Finally, in articulating how the "other" thinking relates in a non-oppositional way to metaphysics, the Tower Warden remembers the

Teacher's earlier request. The Teacher had asked to use language that was familiar, though strictly "not fitting," to name it. The Tower Warden is also naming this possibility of thinking otherwise by describing its relation to metaphysics; the terms "non-metaphysical," "other," and even "inceptual" recall a relation to metaphysics. In recalling the Teacher's own acknowledged mistake, the Tower Warden intimates that thinking otherwise must take place by way of its relation to metaphysics for human beings as historical sojourners. In other words, this mistake may be entirely necessary.

The Tower Warden and the Teacher are in the process of learning the needfulness of this mistake. The Tower Warden insists, "any countermovement against metaphysics, and any mere turn away from it, always remain still caught in metaphysical representation" (GA 77: 187/CPC 122). The Teacher responds by sharing a fear. In pursuing the suggestion that being may allow itself to be objectified by scientific and technological thinking, the Teacher worries that their inquiry may amount to a justification of representational metaphysics. He asks "whether we are reflecting on the belonging-together of representing and producing precisely in order to metaphysically justify the scientific-technological world-picture, or—here I don't know what more to say" (GA 77: 193/CPC 126). The Tower Warden asks whether the Teacher wants to learn to think non-metaphysically in a way that "shakes science and technology's claim to truth" (GA 77: 193/CPC 126). The Teacher assents, admitting that a will to shake metaphysics motivates him, which risks ensnaring him in metaphysics even more. At the same time, he also realizes that such shaking would not accomplish much to unseat its dominance. Though they may recognize the artificiality of scientific-technological thinking, it has undeniably produced the "effectively actual world" (GA 77: 194/CPC 126), which contests the very distinction between the artificial and the natural. The Tower Warden commiserates, telling the Teacher that "mere shaking [*Erschütterung*] brings about nothing, unless it soon swings [*schwinge*]³⁴ within an older, sturdy bringing-to-rest" (GA 77: 195/CPC 127), which has no will toward a predetermined end because its "provenance [*Herkunft*] . . . kept itself concealed" (GA 77: 196/CPC 127).

Though the Teacher struggles to let the provenance of the critical point of the relationality of the human and being "remain in the dark" (GA 77: 192/CPC 125), as he puts it, the Tower Warden impels him toward instead speaking together of the "sturdy relation of things to us" (GA 77: 196/CPC 127) where the provenance of this relation is properly concealed. Though this may be the first explicit call to consider the relationality of human beings and things, the "Tower Conversation" has been permeated—from beginning to end—by a thinking of two things in particular: the tower and the picture. The two just mentioned that their view of the tower illustrates how they could take distance from determining it according to the "ruling world-picture of the natural sciences and technology" (GA 77: 193/CPC 126) by walking away from it, though what they are drawing near to in so doing remains obscure. They are also walking away from the picture, the origin of which they are on the cusp of encountering. In speaking of these things, they have glimpsed the possibility of an other, non-representational, non-metaphysical thinking. Even where conversion from things into objects seems complete, a remainder of their being-as-thing yet lingers. The very objectification of things seems to conceal the thing somehow safely behind its veneer. The momentary unconcealment of these things has occasioned their mistakes and invited them to further interrogate their relation to metaphysics in a non-metaphysical way. In short, these encounters with things prepare the conversational partners for their most challenging encounter yet.

MEETING (THE STRANGER) ON THE COUNTRY PATH

Perhaps upon reaching the apex of a gentle swell of the country path, the Tower Warden remarks that he can already see the Guest approaching. The Teacher worries the Guest is coming "too early, since we have not succeeded in getting very far in our attempt to catch sight of the tower as thing" (GA 77: 198/CPC 129). This response recalls the Teacher's opening line, which also mistakenly relied on a metaphysical representation of time, marking his own arrival as "too late" (GA 77: 163/CPC 105). From this repetition, it may seem that the Teacher has not pedagogically grown during the conversation. But such an interpretation would rely on the tacit assumption that mistakes are merely privative and that an adept thinker is practiced precisely in avoiding them. The "Tower Conversation" has upended this presupposition. A non-metaphysical thinker lets her mistakes be.

Unlike the last section of the "Triadic Conversation," the concluding pages of the "Tower Conversation" depict no obvious pedagogical triumph. Rather than constructing a scene where the three characters' meeting shows the Teacher has learned how to engage in a welcoming, released comportment toward the strange, Heidegger shows the Teacher continuing to make a series of mistakes. During this final phase of the (written) conversation, the Teacher repeatedly expresses anxiety in the face of their impending meeting with the Guest. Since they have not achieved the stated objective of their walk together—catching sight of the tower as thing and meditating on the unsettling picture—the Teacher cannot fathom how they could incorporate the Guest into their ongoing conversation. In a panic, he demands that he and the Tower Warden cut their conversation short to properly welcome the Guest. As both the Tower Warden and Guest will attest, this is a mistake.

In response to the Teacher's worry about meeting the Guest "too early," the Tower Warden reminds the Teacher that their objective is not to achieve "a purportedly better concept of tower and of thing" (GA 77: 198/CPC 129), but rather to turn back to where they already are. They are still underway and will ultimately return to the tower room to find themselves once more before the picture the Teacher still describes in its "wondrousness," a designation the Tower Warden now allows alongside his recollection that "we called it the strange" (GA 77: 198/CPC 129), demonstrating that these ways of thinking are not opposed, but can emerge from one another. This releasement—even toward metaphysical representation—awakens a sense of thinking as a "festival" (GA 77: 198/CPC 128), which the Tower Warden is first to note.[35] Though they are unsure whether the Guest or the country path itself will awaken this festival of thinking, the Tower Warden urges the Teacher to notice "how we ask everywhere about the selfsame" (GA 77: 199/CPC 130). That each and every thing celebrates a relationality to every other thing hails the limitations of a metaphysics that seeks to fix and manipulate objects through subjective representation. Even further, this festivity illustrates that "our thinking is nevertheless already initiated" (GA 77: 199/CPC 130) into this selfsame relationality.

The Teacher takes this to be a "question of provenance" (GA 77: 199/CPC 130) concerning the origin of our thinking and not only, as the Tower Warden puts it, "what we ask about, but also how" (GA 77: 199/CPC 130). This apparently "innate" (GA 77: 199/CPC 130) desire to know "wherefrom" beings spring cannot be accounted for in an appeal to human nature. Rather, the conversational partners find that they must allow themselves to get involved in "the question of the provenance of provenance, and thereby into the well-known infinite regress" (GA 77: 200/CPC 130). Drawing from Greek thought, the Teacher navigates this metaphysical conception of the problem so as to raise the question of the relation between provenance and ground: "Every kind of ground provides a provenance; but not every provenance is a kind of ground. And so provenance would have to be in play where no ground is given . . .—an audacious demand, to be sure, on the customary manner of representing" (GA 77: 200–1/CPC 130). To think provenance without reference to a representation of ground (or its mere negation, abyss) is the audacious demand of non-metaphysical thinking:

TOWER WARDEN: We cannot force something to acquiesce to an audacious demand, but rather can only free something for it.

TEACHER: So that we let it come to us. (GA 77: 201/CPC 130–31)

It is *Gelassenheit* that enables a response to this call, which takes place in the context of a "we." The use of the first-person plural is hardly incidental, particularly given the imminently expanding meaning of this pronoun about to take place when the Guest finally appears.

The Teacher commits his final mistake when the Tower Warden announces, "but there is the guest coming around the bend in the path" (GA 77: 201/CPC 131). The Teacher responds that they "should save the conversation we have begun about the essential occurring and prevailing of the provenance for another occasion" because the Guest could not possibly be interested in "such a general and wide-ranging question as that of the provenance of provenance" (GA 77: 201/CPC 131). The Tower Warden reassures the Teacher that the Guest "would like to listen" more than anything, though he allows the Teacher to "leave the question, as it were, lying under way" (GA 77: 201/CPC 131). However, when the Teacher announces that "the guest shall speak to us of his own accord about what concerns him," the Tower Warden becomes more forceful, telling him that he "may be mistaken" (GA 77: 201/CPC 131) about this prediction. This pronouncement from the Teacher resonates with the metaphysical description of dialogue the Scientist had articulated in the "Triadic Conversation": "It belongs to a conversation that it is a conversation about something and between speakers" (GA 77: 57/CPC 37). The Guest is not a subject who will speak about matters he formulates as objects. The Teacher must forgo wondering about the Guest to instead let the strange of this Guest—as a *stranger*—be on its own.

Though the Teacher tries to suggest they begin an entirely new conversation, their time to decide has run out. The Guest arrives. The Tower Warden tells the Teacher, "let me at once introduce you to him. In a certain sense he in fact knows you already, since yesterday evening in the tower room I first told him something about what has moved us for years" (GA 77: 201/CPC 131). Only at the conclusion of the text do we learn that the Guest was also with the Tower Warden the evening before in the tower room. Apparently both the Teacher and the Guest had been with the Tower Warden in his room at separate—yet non-metaphysically related—times. It seems they had not been prepared to come together—to expand the meaning of their "we"—until now. The Guest confirms his prior acquaintance with the selfsame topics that concern the Teacher, speaking for the first time in the conversation: "I am pleased to encounter both of you in conversation after having already heard a lot about what it is that you speak of," agreeing with the Tower Warden that any move to "break off" the conversation they had already begun would be a "mistake" (GA 77: 201–2/CPC 131). The term mistake[36] only explicitly appears at the end of the "Tower Conversation." However, the importance of mistakes—of interrogating and learning from mistakes and recognizing how mistakes can only be understood as such in relation to a metaphysical rubric—undergirds the entire textual exchange.

The final moments of the written text of the "Tower Conversation" offer no solution to these mistakes, but rather illustrate a communal released response to them. Responding to the Teacher's concern that the Guest does not "know what we are speaking about," the Guest affirms this, and the Tower Warden retorts that the Guest may be able to "guess what it is from what I told you" (GA 77: 202/CPC 131). This prompts the Teacher to recollect and summarize the essence of their conversation: "That we have long been moving ourselves on a between-field," which the country path enables them to "celebrate" such that the path itself "moves us" (GA 77: 202/CPC 131). The between of this between-field is strange indeed, illuminated only by the movement it facilitates. The country path—which I have argued is an invitation to engage with the historical manifestation of metaphysical thinking in our age, namely scientific and technological thinking grounded in representation—is not here an object that facilitates travel by subjects. The possibility of movement associated with the country path is not entirely appropriated by the conversational partners, as they say, "moving ourselves" along it, or by only understanding the path as something that "moves us" (GA 77: 202/CPC 131). Rather, the festival of mobility unfolds the relationality between these possibilities. In the non-metaphysical place and time opened up, the Tower Warden, the Guest, and the Teacher are also free to encounter one another. As the Guest puts it, "the three of us are in the same condition, and there is no reason to break off the conversation you have begun" (GA 77: 202/CPC 131). In responding to the Teacher's mistaken impulse to halt their conversation, the three come together as a "we" established by the sameness—and even the selfsameness—of their condition as those involved in a pedagogy of non-representational, non-metaphysical thinking. Though the text ends, readers have a sense that they take up their festive we-ness, conversing as they walk back to the tower room to encounter the picture together.

Poetizing Mistakes

In the "Tower Conversation," Heidegger shows that pedagogy is not corroded but instead enhanced by making—and collaboratively recovering from—mistakes. Even a teacher is not immune from mistakes. In authoring the characters as he has, Heidegger suggests it is pivotal for a teacher to inhabit the role of one who is yet learning her ostensible area of expertise. Mistakes are crucial way stations along the path toward learning non-representational, non-metaphysical (poetic) thinking. To conceive of pedagogy as a practice of learning to avoid mistakes entirely is, itself, mistaken. As the Tower Warden demonstrates for the Teacher, mistakes are not failures. They are invitations to respond non-metaphysically to both metaphysical and anti-metaphysical (which is to say, still metaphysical[37]) thinking. A pedagogy of mistakes is fundamental for learning to think otherwise.

The poetic appears only obliquely in this text, associated with the distressing picture that impelled the Teacher to return uninvited at the Tower Warden's door. However, the presence of this absent picture is felt at nearly every turn in the "Tower Conversation." In many ways, it seems, they may even take the detour out away from the tower and toward the Guest so that they can practice the courage and trust needed to turn back to where they already were (GA 77: 171–72/CPC 111)—namely, before the picture in the tower room. This text would then suggest that the move from scientific, technological, and historiological thinking to collaborative poetizing in the "Triadic Conversation" may have itself suffered from the danger of hastiness. Perhaps to prepare to poetize, we must first learn to swing within the between-field of representational, metaphysical and non-representational, non-metaphysical thinking, to learn to attend to the relationality of selfsameness even here, and to experience the constitution of a communal "we" that springs from such a shared pedagogical condition.

It is telling that the importance of mistakes emerges at this particular moment in political history and in Heidegger's personal experience of the ending of World War II and the impending fall of Nazi Germany. But telling of what is a question that remains both unquestioned and unanswered within the "Tower Conversation." Is Heidegger alluding to the political circumstances of the war as a mistake? If so, which side is mistaken? Or is Heidegger alluding to his own involvement with National Socialism as a mistake? If so, why would he not make this explicit? Though it offers no definitive answers to these lurking questions, the third and final of the *Country Path Conversations* will most directly address Heidegger's immediate political history and personal entanglements. Heidegger's character "the Teacher" may very well have found himself in need of guidance in the wake of committing his own mistakes in thinking. But if this is true of a fictional character, it is even more true for the German people as a whole. The "Evening Conversation" picks up where the "Tower Conversation" leaves off, elaborating how and why a "we" can be formed, even in the wake of the most egregious mistakes a community of people can commit.

3

The "Evening Conversation"
Communal Pedagogy

Heidegger's third and final *Country Path Conversation* is titled "Evening Conversation: In a Prisoner of War Camp in Russia, between a Younger and an Older Man."[1] Despite being the shortest of Heidegger's conversations, it covers a broad array of themes including evil, healing, silence, morality, death, politics, waiting, and poetizing. Heidegger may come the closest he ever will to accounting for his postwar silence about the Nazi genocide perpetuated against millions of Jews, though this raises more questions than it definitively answers about Heidegger's politics. This text was also deeply personal for Heidegger. He composed it while his own sons were missing at the eastern front.[2] In grappling with his fear as a father in such a position, Heidegger's inner turmoil about the political consequences of National Socialism are evident in this text, which he dates the "8th of May 1945" (GA 77: 240/CPC 157). The "Evening Conversation" is thus particularly salient for those interested in how Heidegger contends with questions of political accountability at the end of the war.

When read as the third installment of Heidegger's five conversations, this text plays a significant role in developing the pedagogy I argue undergirds these texts, continuing many of the dynamics introduced in the "Triadic Conversation" and the "Tower Conversation." These characters explore the formation of the collaborative sense of the "we" already at play in the preceding conversations. Here, Heidegger makes the rather stunning claim that it is not only *possible* to collaborate with others in non-representational, non-metaphysical thinking, but that collaborative sharing is *essential* to the task. The Younger Man tells the Older Man, "the more essential an insight is, the greater must also be the tact with which it awakens in fellow humans the knowledge that grows from it" (GA 77: 215/CPC 139). Because metaphysical thinking relies on the representations it produces to order and manipulate beings, it issues its own calculative rubrics according to which it can be assessed as correct. Non-metaphysical thinking, because it is non-representational, has no such access to ascertain whether it has been successful. On my reading of this text, Heidegger shows that the capacity to be shared with others is a non-accidental feature of non-representational, non-metaphysical thinking. Perhaps the only way we can experience such thinking is as a "we."

This communal and collaborative thinking is attested to by pedagogical dynamics. There is no distinguishable teacher. The two characters who converse should rather be understood as a pair of students bereft of their teacher in the context of their imprisonment in the camp. Without anyone to guide them, each sets the tone at times, but neither occupies the teaching role exclusively. Because there is no discernable teacher, Heidegger's pedagogy is at its most dynamic. The text concludes with an explicit discussion of pedagogy that depicts teaching as a form of learning, which avoids becoming merely another outlet for ideology. The teacher's absence means these students must learn to educate themselves—a hope any teacher would hold for her students. In the wake of the most grievous mistake a people could make, these students are still able to pedagogically collaborate to learn as a "we."

The "Evening Conversation" is about the possibility for healing in the context in which the conversational partners collectively find themselves. Only in learning together to wait and to poetize in the face of the evil brought to light by the domination of representational metaphysics can healing unfold. The conversational partners must invite others to share in the insights garnered from their turn away from metaphysical thinking so that the "we" needed for such healing can be founded. The question has shifted from "where" this thinking takes place in the "Tower Conversation" to the "who" that engages in such thinking. Plurality is paramount. But in thinking of what it means to come together as a community, the problem of Heidegger's personal and political accountability remains, even as he obliquely elaborates his reasons for remaining silent about the Holocaust. His silence cannot be justified. In a text that advances a thinking of evil and death, Heidegger's refusal to acknowledge the particular evil and the particular deaths perpetrated by Nazi Germany is even more reprehensible.

Just who does or does not belong in the community he is coming to think remains an important question to raise, particularly as Heidegger's ambiguity about the answer remains unresolved within the text.

Conversational Context

The Younger Man and the Older Man

Only two characters speak in the "Evening Conversation." These conversational partners share much in common and disagree very little. The Scientist, the Scholar, and the Guide in the "Triadic Conversation" needed nearly 150 pages before they could think together with (rather than against) one another. The Teacher, the Tower Warden, and the Guest in the "Tower Conversation" also required preparation to welcome engagement with one another properly. The Younger Man and the Older Man in the "Evening Conversation" relate differently. They have evidently spoken together often and frequently. They know one another well on personal and emotional registers. Each typically refines and extends the other's contributions. In the rare instance they diverge, there is nothing combative or competitive about how they proceed to explore their points of view. In moments, each asserts their distinction from the other in terms of their particular histories, comportments, and preoccupations. But these conversational partners largely share an interest in working out the meaning of the healing experience that initiates their conversation. In part, this may be due to their shared conditions as Germans, fellow soldiers, and prisoners of war in a foreign land. The bond these experiences forged between them is palpable in their evident care for one another. Yet in collaborating to unpack the Younger Man's healing experience, it gradually becomes apparent that further exploring their relationship along non-representational, non-metaphysical lines is a necessary precondition.

Unlike the preceding *Country Path Conversations*, the characters in the "Evening Conversation" are not distinguished by their professions. We learn both are prisoners and soldiers and that before they took on these identities, they both spent time at university as students. Heidegger names them simply "The Younger Man"—*Der Jüngere*—and "The Older Man"—*Der Ältere*. There is no sense of their proximity in age, but we can presume the Younger Man has lived fewer years and the Older Man has experienced more years. The "who" of these characters is explicitly configured temporally. In addition to the temporality denoted by the title itself, this signals the question of time is at play. When time is represented metaphysically, it is straightforward to measure time as a quantity of years. But as the conversational partners discuss, it is possible to think of "a still-concealed dimension of time [*eine noch verborgene Dimension der Zeit*]" (GA 77: 218/CPC 141). Even where tidy distinctions between past, present, and future are contested, the importance of the temporally differentiated relation between the two characters remains. The comparative force of their names—which retain their meaning only in relation to one another—marks who they are as emerging from the context of their relationship. The Younger Man is only younger relative to the Older Man and vice versa. In this way, the "Evening Conversation" suggests how community can be founded non-metaphysically.

The Younger Man initiates their conversation. He invites the Older Man into his experience, describing how he was overcome by "something healing [*etwas Heilsames*]" (GA 77: 205/CPC 132) as they marched that morning. Throughout the ensuing conversation, the Younger Man is relatively more brazen in his thinking. He is not as beholden to convention and engages in playful surmising. Representational metaphysics seem to have not (yet) shaped him as significantly as his conversational partner. Despite his youthfulness, the Younger Man has also suffered a deep wounding. The Older Man describes the Younger Man's decision to "bury in your silence [*Schweigen*] all the adversities that have befallen us" (GA 77: 206/CPC 133). The Younger Man's sustained youthfulness in the wake of such pain is hard won.

The Older Man is more cautious. Though he apparently enjoys the Younger Man's brash surmises, he does not allow himself to be swept up by them entirely. The Older Man often situates his questions in relation to other thinkers and poets, including Nietzsche, the significance of pre-Socratic "most ancient Greek" (GA 77: 222/CPC 144) thinking, Hölderlin, and even an excerpt from a "historiological account of Chinese philosophy" (GA 77: 239/CPC 156). His reserve contributes to his skepticism about the possibility of sharing in the Younger Man's healing experience, though he acknowledges that they are *both* wounded by their recent experiences and from being "barred from being young [*Es war uns verwehrt, jung zu sein*]" (GA 77: 219/CPC 142) by their political circumstances. Illustrating how these characters learn how to learn together without a teacher to guide them, Heidegger emphasizes that learning itself is the proper comportment for teaching. Pedagogy is not accidentally, but *essentially* collaborative.

Imprisoned, in the Evening

This conversation takes place in a prisoner of war camp for German soldiers in Russia.[3] Their imprisonment is occasioned by what the Older Man calls "a blinded leading-astray of our own people [*eine verblendete Irreführung des eigenen Volkes*]" (GA 77: 206/CPC 133). They have been led to a condition of confinement that delimits both a spacial constraint, "between the walls of these barracks, behind barbed wire" (GA 77: 206/CPC 132), and a temporal confinement whereby the two bemoan they "were barred from being young" (GA 77: 219/CPC 142). This dual sense of confinement determines both the physical and temporal condition in which the conversational partners find themselves. In several senses, they are at a standstill. Unlike the previous texts, this conversation takes place while the two are unable to move freely through the countryside. They are only able to walk in nature when they are marching between their workplace and the camp.

Yet even when "representing, producing, and ordering" (GA 77: 190/CPC 124) them as prisoners through confinement holds sway, this purported mastery fails to take absolute hold of them. As Mitchell puts it, "nothing can ever ultimately capture us or close us off from the world around us. However trapped we might be, there is always a beyond."[4] The Older Man and the Younger Man are trapped, but nevertheless, "something healing" overcomes the Younger Man "out of the rustling of the expanse of the forest" (GA 77: 205/CPC 132) as they walked to their workplace earlier that morning. This healing experience touches him as a human being who exceeds the subjectivity that attempts to constrain him. Despite all efforts to fix beings as objects to be represented, produced, and ordered by the scientific and technological thinking of the subject, being can never be brought to such a standstill by the human will. Being *itself* is on the move. The Younger Man describes the movement that occasioned his healing experience: "The capaciousness [*Geräumige*] of the forests swings out [*schwingt*][5] into a concealed distance [*in eine verborgene Ferne*], but at the same time swings back to us again, without ending in us" (GA 77: 205/CPC 132). This swinging invites the human being to take part in its swinging but would never grant her control over its motion. In the context of the "Evening Conversation," this swinging movement also opens a space for conversation to unfold *between* them, where that of which their conversation speaks nevertheless invites them to participate in the swinging of non-representational, non-metaphysical thinking.

The "Evening Conversation" takes place (as the title indicates) as evening careens toward night. The "Triadic Conversation" also took place as

106 | Heidegger's Conversations

the sun set and the stars came out. However, the darkness of the Russian prisoner of war camp seems darker. There is no discussion of starlight or any sense of a leisurely atmosphere that allows the conversational partners in the "Triadic Conversation" to continue walking together as late as they like. The Younger Man and the Older Man in the "Evening Conversation" are aware they are pressed for time. They express concern that they must sleep soon, presumably because they need their strength for physical labor the next day. Their politically produced condition impedes their capacity to fully engage with their locale. But even in the depth of this darkness, the conversational partners find in one another reassurance that together they can wait for a non-representational, non-metaphysical relationality to emerge. They may even need to fully confront the radical impoverishment that politics (as an expression of representational metaphysics) has activated to truly find healing—not just for themselves, but also for their larger community. They draw from their past experiences in the hopes that they can bring about a different kind of future, as a historical people that need not be confined by such politics.

LEARNING WITHOUT A TEACHER

Because of the lack of any clear teaching figure, there is hardly any distinction between who is teaching and who is learning in this text. Nevertheless, the Younger Man and the Older Man practice the same five pedagogical techniques found in the previous conversations: openness to others, attention to affect, reversals, remembrance, and silence. Neither is primarily interested in convincing the other of the limitations of their way of thinking or of illustrating the potential fruitfulness of interrogating those limitations. Rather, each engages in mutually recognizing their woundedness produced by representational metaphysics.

There is no teacher available in the camp. This means that those who find themselves impelled by their pain to learn must play both pedagogical roles. On the one hand, this underscores their impoverished condition, bereft of guidance. But on the other hand, this can mark a pedagogical accomplishment. Any teacher hopes that her work ultimately brings about her own obsolesce. That is, if a student were to remain a student forever, the teacher has clearly failed. In the "Evening Conversation," students learn how to teach themselves and thereby prepare to teach others.

The pedagogy of self-teaching the Younger Man and the Older Man practice is oriented by healing, but not from any intentional or unintentional mistakes in activating representational, metaphysical thinking. In fact, these characters fall into such thinking much less than the preceding characters. Their wounding has already been accomplished. On the other side of this pain, they find the experience of non-representational, non-metaphysical thinking serves as a healing salve. These characters do not make the same mistake as the Teacher in the "Tower Conversation." Instead, the impulse to such thinking seems almost instinctive for these characters. Because they have no choice, they learn that to heal does not mean to close themselves off, but rather to open themselves out toward the world of others. Mitchell summarizes the meaning of the healing Heidegger has in mind: "Healing is not a restoration to a lost integrity, but an acceptance that healing never comes, or is only ever coming, is an infinite task at the heart of finitude (to call it asymptotic is to privilege completion too much). Instead of trying to restore oneself to go it alone, to heal is to let oneself be borne by the world. To heal is to open."[6]

These characters are bereft of any assistance a teacher might provide, confined in a camp with a recollection of something that happened on an earlier (forced) walk through the forest. Though they are physically confined, thinking and poetizing nevertheless initiates the movement of their conversation. Far away from the country path, perhaps they are finally able to draw nearest to it.[7] Or perhaps only from such a distance are they in a position to recognize that the path of the German people has gone off course, led astray by the evils of politics. The task may now no longer be to simply return to the country path post-haste, but to delve deeper into the forest and, ever farther from the encroaching *polis*, to renew the historical destiny of what the characters will call "the people of poets and thinkers [*das Volk der Dichter und Denker*]" (GA 77: 233/CPC 152). This possibility emerges from the "we" (that the "Tower Conversation" could only indicate roughly) capable of a "conversational surmis[ing] [*gesprächlichsweise vermuten*]" that exceeds "propositional statements [*aussagenden Sätzen*]" (GA 77: 231/CPC 150).

In a sense, the "Evening Conversation" is still unfolding in the between-field of the "Tower Conversation." But the conversational partners move from interrogating the "where" of this between-field to the "who" that inhabits this locale. Extending the depiction of the human being as the one who sojourns in the between-field, here two senses of the human being are developed. These two descriptions—the human being as the rational animal and the human being as the mortal—are ultimately shown to be selfsame insofar as they both rely on an experience of waiting as the characters come to describe it. Understood in this way, the human being comports herself in the between-field as the one who waits, out-waiting even a politics grounded in representational metaphysics that insists on producing a worldview rather than supporting the "we" that waits toward the poetizing conversation that first allows such a community to emerge.

The ostensible goal of this pedagogy is not to accomplish such thinking in opposition to representational, metaphysical thinking. Its impetus lies in recognizing and accepting the consequences of such thinking together, in conversation. Yet an unresolved question arises already here about the claim Heidegger seems to levy at National Socialist politics. In advocating for a comportment of *Gelassenheit* toward this political manifestation of metaphysics, Heidegger also seems to attempt to justify his own silence about the horrors perpetrated by the Nazis, which took place not in the Russian prisoners of war camps Heidegger writes about, but in the Jewish death camps he does not mention. In insisting on the importance of the communal "we" in healing from this politics, Heidegger seems to be implicitly re-inscribing a criterion for inclusion and exclusion within such a community. In privileging the healing of *German* survivors of Nazism, Heidegger expresses care and concern for those least affected by the evil and devastation he philosophizes, raising the question of whether he has come to grips with the incomparable effect on those who died in the Holocaust or whether he is only interested in supporting healing for the surviving Germans.

Healing Pedagogy

Standstill

The "Evening Conversation" is at a standstill. The imprisoned characters cannot walk along a country path, leisurely discussing philosophy. But even within this experience of spatial and temporal confinement, the possibility of a mobility of conversation essential to healing remains. Heidegger here works out the terms of this mobilization. He elaborates how this experience needs to be *shared* to emerge at all. The healing in question belongs to a community, never only to an individual. The movement the "Evening Conversation" initiates, despite the characters' standstill, is one of singular pronouns becoming meaningful only as plural, and of revealing themselves to have always already been constituted as a plurality. The meaning of pronouns was troubled already in the "Tower Conversation," but this importance is developed in the "Evening Conversation."

These characters learn how to teach themselves to engage in non-representational, non-metaphysical thinking as a way of being and speaking with one another. Contributing to the efforts of characters from the preceding conversations, they also endeavor to think past the individualism of subjectivity to instead reveal a shared sense of what it means to be human. As I will show, this involves what the Older Man calls "a still-concealed dimension of time" (GA 77: 218/CPC 141). This dramatic dual releasement, opening the individual to the collective, on the one hand, and temporality to a sense of the historical destiny of a people, on the other, unfolds in the "Evening Conversation" in three parts. In the first part, the five pedagogical techniques already emerge as relevant dynamics. But because there is no teacher to guide those dynamics, they initially remain under-regarded. Not until the second conversational phase—once the characters begin to learn *who* they are in the plural—are the conversational partners further able to enact these pedagogical techniques as such, and to learn to teach themselves. As the conversation concludes, they contend with poetizing as a way of building community and as they move toward non-representational, non-metaphysical thinking.

Evil and Healing

The "Evening Conversation" begins most abruptly. There are no introductions, pleasantries, or even solicitations of consent to engage in conversation. Any time these two find to speak is likely so limited that there is not a moment to waste. In the opening line of the text, the Younger Man reports an experience from earlier in the day: "As we were marching to our workplace this morning, out of the rustling of the expansive forest [*aus dem Rauschen des weiten Waldes*] I was suddenly overcome by something healing" (GA 77: 205/CPC 132). As soon becomes apparent, the Younger Man's experience of something healing is not yet complete. It has raised a question as to the origin and possibility of such an experience. He feels impelled to bring this to the Older Man because this experience has left something unsettled in him. Such a response hardly evinces a sense of calm or relief that might arise from healing.

The two consider "wherein this something that heals could rest [*beruhen*]" (GA 77: 205/CPC 132). In clarifying the experience the forest occasioned, the conversational partners struggle to identify *how* the forest's expanse is healing and *why* they need healing in the first place. Both tasks prove difficult. The Older Man suggests, "perhaps it is what is inexhaustible [*Unerschöpfliche*] of the self-veiling expanse [*sich verhüllenden Weite*] that abides in these forests of Russia" (GA 77: 205/CPC 132). In attempting to make sense of this suggestion, the Younger Man mistakenly identifies the "capaciousness [*Geräumige*]" of the forest as the source of healing. The Older Man rejoins that it is not simply a metaphysical representation of space that is at stake, but rather a self-veiling movement, which space takes part in, that enables healing. The Younger Man describes that which "swings out [*schwingt*] into a concealed distance, but at the same time swings back to us again, without ending with us" (GA 77: 205/CPC 132). Mitchell writes, "there is an activity to the expanse . . . We extend through a space that is itself on the move . . . It swings out, but not without bearing a relation to us, one that simultaneously pulls it back to us."[8] It is not that the forest reveals open (but still metaphysically objective) space to a confined subject such that the "contrast" (GA 77: 206/CPC 133) provides some measure of relief to the prisoners "while we here—between the walls of these barracks, behind barbed wire—incessantly run up against and wound ourselves on what is objective [*gegen das Gegenständliche*]" (GA 77: 206/CPC 132). It rather calls for non-representational, non-metaphysical thinking. The Younger Man insists, "the expanse carries us to what is objectless [*Die Weite trägt uns dem Gegenstandlosen zu*]" (GA 77: 205/CPC 132).

The Older Man then asks why healing is needed in the first place. He wants to know "what is wounded [*wund*]" in the Younger Man (GA 77: 206/CPC 133). This flows from the domination of representational metaphysics, attested to by what the conversational partners call devastation and, ultimately, evil. In introducing this, the Older Man offers what may be an attempt to justify Heidegger's own silence about the Holocaust:

> I don't want to press you any further, however, since I know how strictly you bury in your silence [*Schweigen*] all the adversities that have befallen us here these past months. Nevertheless, in order to comprehend what has become healing for you, I would have to know what is wounded in you. And what is not all wounded and torn apart in us?—us, for whom a blinded leading-astray of our own people is too deplorable to permit wasting a complaint on, despite the devastation [*Verwüstung*]

that covers our native soil and its helplessly perplexed [*ratlose*] humans. (GA 77: 206/CPC 133)

There are at least two crucial elements of this passage: the pronoun usage and the philosophical investment in silence.

The pronouns in this passage undergo a significant evolution. The Older Man's prompting of the Younger Man to articulate his woundedness demonstrates a slippage between the use of the singular pronouns "you" and "I" into the plural pronoun "us." An implicit claim facilitates this. In inquiring into the Younger Man's healing experience, the Older Man requests to "know what is wounded" in him. Next, he uses the pronoun "us" to describe the location of that wound, which suggests that gaining such knowledge of an other would thereafter entail the constitution of a "we"—and no longer a "you" and an "I." This early passage indicates that what is at stake in this text is not a causal effect on a single individual, but rather the meaning of shared experience. This gains in philosophical importance as the conversation unfolds.

Silence also figures prominently in this passage. It seems the Younger Man is suffering from a trauma about which he prefers—or even needs— not to speak. But the Older Man attributes these traumas to a "blinded leading-astray" of the Germans, about which he justifies silence as the appropriate response. There is much to say about this silence, particularly its political dimension.[9] In considering Heidegger's own description of human beings as those who "are always speaking, even when we do not utter a single word aloud" (GA 12: 9/PLT 187), it is clear that this silence does not evade bearing significance. It is drenched in meaning. In a certain light, this passage rehearses Heidegger's critique of polemics, outlined in the "Tower Conversation"[10] and in the "Triadic Conversation."[11] This would allow the possibility to think non-representationally and non-metaphysically, rather than ensnaring one further in the logic of that which threatens ideological domination—in this instance, perhaps National Socialism itself. Yet, in this case, Heidegger would be presuming that politics is just another manifestation of certain configurations of metaphysics. This presumption itself attests to a certain social, political, and professional privilege Heidegger experiences, but does not acknowledge as significant for guiding his philosophical work.[12]

These characters' decision to keep silent about the atrocities of the Holocaust is inadequate and abhorrent. This silence does not allow Heidegger to escape implication. Though the characters criticize the standpoint of "moral superiority [*moralische Überlegenheit*]" as unable "to grasp, much less abolish or even mitigate, evil" (GA 77: 209/CPC 134), they nevertheless determine that they should only speak of their political situation in a "collected manner, according to the highest standards, and without false passion" (GA 77: 207/CPC 133). To speak of the aftermath of National Socialism in this manner requires, first, that one has survived the Shoah and, second, that one must be able to remain calm and composed, which implies an exclusion of those too severely impacted to be capable of speaking of the effects on them and their communities. Of course, both conditions apply to Heidegger himself, but do not apply to millions of others, including many of Heidegger's teachers, colleagues, and students. The dissonance between rejecting moral superiority and the delegitimizing and excluding voices and accounts that decline to speak of this devastation "according to the highest standards" is undeniable. Heidegger's meager attempt to reconcile them fails from the outset.

Heidegger's silence about the Holocaust speaks volumes, and not only in the ontological register he intends. Though he has developed a framework for acknowledging and addressing mistakes in the "Tower Conversation," Heidegger declines to employ it to interrogate his own set of personal and philosophical failings regarding politics (if he indeed recognizes them as such, a question that has and continues to garner crucial study and debate[13]). Heidegger instead devotes his efforts to the ontological conditions that wounded "our own people." The question inevitably arises: whom does "our" people include? And whom does it exclude? If it is only those who are in such a privileged position as to be able to decide how and when to speak about the Shoah, then Heidegger remains fundamentally and willfully ignorant of the true extent of Germany's devastation.

Though the Younger Man and the Older Man acknowledge this devastation's collective impact at the political level, it is the *ontology* of devastation they proceed to discuss. According to these characters, this devastation "has not, after all, existed just since yesterday" (GA 77: 207/CPC 133), but "is deeper and comes from farther away" than what is reflected in "an enumeration of instances of destruction [*Zerstörungen*] and the obliteration [*Auslöschung*] of human lives [*Menschenleben*]" (GA 77: 207/CPC 133). For these characters, "the devastation [*Verwüstung*] of the earth and the annihilation [*Vernichtung*] of the human essence [*Menschenwesens*] that goes with it are somehow evil itself [*das Böse*]" (GA 77: 207/CPC 133). The essential evil of this devastation cannot be understood through traditional accounts of morality, because they worry morality itself may be a "monstrous offspring of evil [*Ausgeburt des Bösen*] . . . [which seeks] to envision a world order [*Weltordnung*] and make certain of a world-security [*Weltsicherheit*] for the national peoples [*Völkern*] by means of morality" (GA 77: 209/CPC 135). Morality offers a metaphysical representation of evil that fails to attend to the relation between evil [*Bösen*] and that which is malicious [*bösartig*].[14] According to the Younger Man, "malice is insurgency [*Bösartige ist das Aufrührerische*], which rests in furiousness [*Grimmigen*] . . . [and] conceals its rage [*Ingrimm*], but at the same time always threatens with it" (GA 77: 207–8/CPC 134).

The "essence of evil," the Younger Man continues, is such that it "never entirely breaks out, and which, when it does break out, still disguises itself, and in its hidden threatening is often as if it were not [*als sei er nicht*]" (GA 77: 208/CPC 134). The healing swinging expanse of the forest is self-veiling such that the concealment in which it participates is, in a certain sense, transparent in its concealment. It is unconcealed as something that nevertheless remains concealed. In this way, it maintains a relation to itself—to its origin—and is therefore selfsame as self-veiling, in the sense developed in the "Triadic Conversation" as a belonging-togetherness by way of difference. Evil, by contrast, "disguises itself . . . [and] is often as if it were not." Evil also conceals itself. But it does so by denying its own origin, cutting off the possibility of relating to itself, and instead presenting itself as identical in the way the Guide in the "Triadic Conversation" understood it, namely as that which is self-separate and therefore cannot belong to anything, even to itself.[15] In this way, the characters determine that the essence of evil consists in the lack of the ontological possibility of relationality, not in a failure to adhere to any given imperative or set of moral standards.

As the characters come to understand the importance of difference in the ontological register, a significant difference between the two simultaneously emerges. In contending with how "evil rests in malice," the Older Man says, "I could almost think that malice is something pertaining to the will [*etwas Willensmäßiges*]" (GA 77: 208/CPC 134). The Younger Man replies, "perhaps in general the will itself is what is evil," to which the Older Man responds, "I shy from even surmising [*vermuten*] something so audacious [*Gewagtes*]" (GA 77: 208/CPC 134). Aside from the association suggested between evil and the will,[16] we learn that the Younger Man is comfortable making audacious leaps while the Older Man is more reserved, shying away from surmises he cannot necessarily prove. Though the Younger Man responds, "I too only said 'perhaps,' and what I said is also not my thought, even though it has not let go of me ever since I once heard it"

(GA 77: 208/CPC 134), he nevertheless introduced the suggestion. Perhaps this brashness speaks of the Younger Man's youth or his healing experience. The distinction between what is young and what is old will soon become philosophically relevant. The Older Man responds to this surmise by sharing that he feels "a contrary will of an aversion [*Widerwille*]" welling up in him that would "rather stop me from [speaking of this devastation], pressuring me to seek out a standpoint of superiority [*überlegeneren Standort*] in an attitude that no longer pays heed to the devastation" (GA 77: 210/CPC 135–36). This impulse to combat the evil of the will with a "contrary will," however, would only lead them to make the mistake of oppositionality.[17] This is, in part, why the Older Man claims that any standpoint of "moral superiority" will fail to "grasp, much less abolish or even mitigate, evil" (GA 77: 209/CPC 134).

Instead, they must will non-willing, engaging in *Gelassenheit* so as to "first be granted the privilege" of a thinking that is "free" (GA 77: 210/CPC 136). The Younger Man thinks that if they were to receive such a privilege "here in this camp," they may be able to see how "devastation is probably a far-reaching event [*Ereignis*] through which any and all possibilities for something essential to arise and bloom in its dominion are suffocated at the root" (GA 77: 210–11/CPC 136). The Older Man thinks this suffocation "announces itself in the form of the purportedly highest ideals of humanity: progress, unrestrained escalation of achievement in all areas of creating, equal employment opportunities for everyone, and above all the allegedly highest rationale—the uniform welfare of all workers" (GA 77: 211/CPC 136). This is one of the ways that the devastation conceals itself, unfolding itself "as if it were not" by disguising itself where it may be least expected—contaminating humanist principles. The conversational partners do not claim these ideals are inherently evil, but that they may contribute to devastation through leading "the various realms of humanity to become obsessed with devoting everything to their realization" (GA 77: 211/CPC 136) at the expense of all else. Yet even when the realization of these ideals becomes obsessive to the point of imposing a dominant ideology, it must still be understood as an effect—not the cause—of the deeper event of devastation. In this way, the conversational partners agree that "the World War is for its part only a consequence of the devastation that has been eating away at the earth for centuries" (GA 77: 211/CPC 136). For Heidegger, representational metaphysics is ultimately at fault.

In contrast to that which is healing being occasioned by the self-veiling expanse of the forest, the conversational partners conclude that the meaning of the devastation is "that everything—the world, the human, and the earth—will be transformed into a desert [*Wüste*]" (GA 77: 211/ CPC 136). They liken the desert to the ocean and a wasteland, both of which embody the "deserted expanse of the abandonment of all life [*die verlassene Weite der Verlassenheit von allem Leben*]" (GA 77: 212/CPC 137), which forecloses in advance the possibility for anything to emerge, or even to perish. Opposed though they may seem, the forest and the desert are, as Bernasconi notes, "intimately connected."[18] The Younger Man and the Older Man come to this description of the desert only after the swinging occasioned by the forest is intimated. For Bernasconi, this shows that "the desert and the forest are not simply opposed to each other . . . it is in and out of the experience of the forest that the desert is experienced as such."[19] Such an insight may be also uncovered through considering the between-field and the pedagogy of mistakes Heidegger developed in the "Tower Conversation." To be let into the possibility of non-representational, non-metaphysical thinking does not mean that representational metaphysics is absolutely abandoned. The transition itself is a lingering in the between-field of these possibilities. Representational metaphysics—as a desert—can also occasion non-representational, non-metaphysical insight to unfold when its limits are recognized as such.

Not only will any attempt to abandon representational, metaphysical thinking be unsuccessful, but metaphysics' own attempt to abandon being will also fail. The abandonment of being by representational metaphysics is nevertheless still a relation to being, albeit an ambiguous one. The Younger Man emphasizes that the concurrent abandonment of beings by being is "an abandonment which nonetheless still lets beings be [*noch sein läßt*]" (GA 77: 214/CPC 138). This leads the Older Man to conclude that "the being of all that is, remains ambiguous [*zweideutig*] to the core" (GA 77: 213/CPC 138). Though they cannot describe[20] the provenance of being in its ambiguity, they acknowledge that being mysteriously enables both the being of beings and "nothing" (GA 77: 213/CPC 138) without contradiction.[21] Being is capacious enough for the possibilities of healing and of evil, suggesting a mutual necessity and even intimacy[22] that swings between and even beyond these possibilities, drawing us further into relation with this oscillation[23] of being. That being may itself be evil—or at least allow for evil to arise—is encapsulated for the conversational partners by "this thought, that evil would dwell in the essence of being" (GA 77: 215/CPC 139). They cannot simply oppose evil on moral grounds. This would indicate a failure to think the truth of being, which may include evil. They must rather learn to let being be, despite the challenge of managing this during "an age of devastation" (GA 77: 213/CPC 138).

Much is at stake in this releasement toward the evil of being. Navigating this ambiguity may exploit a vulnerability to the "malice of devastation" the conversational partners worry "reaches its extreme when it settles into the appearance of a secure state of the world, in order to hold out to the human a satisfactory standard of living as the highest goal of existence and to guarantee its realization" (GA 77: 214/CPC 138). Because evil "is often as if it were not"—by denying its origin and disguising itself behind that which is ostensibly good—it may be lurking behind even the most seemingly benign universal humanist principles for organizing society.[24]

Though being enables distraction, disguise, and errancy, it also supports the possibility of thinking what is essential. But how would we ascertain the difference since "the 'measures' [»*Maßnahmen*«] that humans take . . . are capable of nothing [*nichts vermögen*]"? (GA 77: 215/CPC 139). The answer is given by the Younger Man: "The more essential [*wesentlicher*] an insight [*Einsicht*] is, the greater must also be the tact with which it awakens [*weckt*] in fellow humans [*in den Mitmenschen*] the knowledge that grows from it" (GA 77: 215/CPC 139). This striking statement provides the interpretive key to understanding the pedagogy Heidegger develops in the "Evening Conversation." Because it is based on the logic of the identical, that which is evil isolates and divides subjects and objects by way of representational metaphysics. Healing from this would be attested to by a *plural* community of human beings who find themselves similarly awakened by this selfsame relationality that allows being to swing ambiguously rather than to represent, order, and produce the world as manipulatable. In the next phase of conversation, this insight becomes increasingly potent. The Younger Man and the Older Man are wounded; both fundamentally need to learn what this wound is and how it may be healed. But first they must come to share in an essential insight that founds their community. This unfolds through an exploration of their who-ness as those who wait.

Already in this first phase, the five pedagogical techniques Heidegger stages in his conversations have appeared. In the "Evening Conversation" there is no distinct teaching figure who might embody these techniques. Instead, the language itself—by which they explore the Younger Man's healing experience—gives rise to these pedagogical techniques and later enables them to come into their own as students-become-teachers. In this section, a reversal is enacted such that morality is no longer that which combats evil but is rather revealed as its source. The characters learn that they must attend to the importance of affects such as pain and feeling healed, but also the rage and malice of evil. The conversation itself was occasioned by the Younger Man approaching his friend for help, which signals he expected to be (and was) met with an openness from him. Together, they contend with what it means to remember what happened that morning, along with what led to their confinement. The characters determine such remembrance requires a certain way of keeping silent, especially about politics.

Who is the Human Being?

In the next phase, the Younger Man and the Older Man perform the pedagogy under discussion as they teach themselves how to ask "who is human being?" In exploring the meaning of the claim that an insight is "essential" only if it is sharable—that is, if it "awakens in fellow human beings the knowledge that grows from it,"—the conversational partners encounter a problem. The insight in question describes an age of devastation that is metaphysical, not moral. It is one thing to discuss this with those who are experiencing pain and confinement resulting from the malice of insurgency. It is an entirely different challenge to show to those whose "world shines with the gleam of advancement, advantages, and fortune" (GA 77: 216/CPC 139) that this too is symptomatic of devastation. On the one hand, the conversational partners face an explicitly pedagogical dilemma. They are tasked to "show, without haughtiness, the devastation to those who are affected and, without the slightest trace of paternalism, to give them advice for the long meditation which is required to become familiar with the devastation" (GA 77: 216/CPC 140). On the other hand, they must question whom the human being is such that she needs the "unnecessary" (GA 77: 216/CPC 140), which such a meditation undoubtedly appears to be, at least initially. These tasks lead the conversational partners to surmise that they must "learn to simply wait" (GA 77: 216/CPC 140).

Waiting is a temporal comportment. Without time, one cannot wait. Waiting is represented metaphysically as a span of linear time. How long, then, must the conversational partners wait until this insight into the age of devastation is widely shared? The response they come to is perplexing—until they are first prepared to wait upon the waiting. They must wait not as representing subjects of metaphysical objects. Rather, they must learn that being is on the move—swinging—and is also capable of waiting upon our waiting. The Younger Man notes that they would need "to wait for so long, as though waiting would have to outlast death" (GA 77: 217/CPC

140), which is, as the Older Man remarks, "like something that waits in us" (GA 77: 217/CPC 140). Unlike the Teacher in the "Tower Conversation," these conversational partners do not wonder why this is the case or insist on raising the question of provenance. Instead, they agree that this is a "strange" (GA 77: 217/CPC 140) waiting that waits neither upon something nor upon nothing, but nevertheless waits. This waiting is not long in the sense of stretching across the past, present, and future. Rather, this waiting is non-metaphysical, reaching "a still-concealed dimension of time" (GA 77: 218/CPC 141), which can never be represented but only experienced. The Younger Man performs this in his own silent pause as he notes that this waiting "we can only experience . . . by waiting. To will to take hold of pure waiting in haste would be like trying to scoop water with a sieve" (GA 77: 221/CPC 143). This waiting cannot be measured in a temporal span. The conversational partners can only surmise whether this experience is occurring by checking in with each other, to find out if the one waiting can share this experience with others. This means their being toward one another in collaborative conversation is not accidental, but *essential* to Heidegger's pedagogy.

Heidegger indicates this centrality of the "we" of conversation in several ways. As noted, the Younger Man's and the Older Man's names are comparative. This means they are inherently related to one another as characters since their names bear no meaning in isolation. The very names that identify them harbor this difference. Further being asked how he came to understand waiting in relation to this still-concealed dimension of time, the Younger Man refers to his healing experience from the morning, claiming that in it "what is healing draws near and is granted to us" (GA 77: 219/CPC 142). Though it happened in the morning, the Younger Man uses the present tense. The Older Man also initially balks at this pronoun usage: "You say 'to us,' and yet this healing *was* granted only to you" (GA 77: 219/CPC 142, em). The Younger Man counters that he would "like to share it now with you, because . . . you are pained by the same wound" (GA 77: 219/CPC 142). Though the Older Man is not yet able to partake in this healing, he is preparing to share in this essential insight.

Names and pronouns are not the only gestures of the relationality Heidegger refines in the "Evening Conversation." In considering the essence of the human as "one who waits" (GA 77: 230/CPC 150), the conversational partners explore two definitions of the human being: one that stems from a historiological account of Western philosophy—the younger definition of the human being—and another that arises from the poets—the older definition of the human being. Though these definitions seem initially opposed, they discover two distinct ways the definitions relate to one another. Though it is not explicitly named as such, the work they engage in together is interpretative.[25] In working out these interpretations, this section offers an extended example of the shape Heidegger's pedagogy can take in the wake of a healing event.

The conversational partners return to their "shared wound," describing it as arising from the devastation that "barred [them] from being young" (GA 77: 219/CPC 142). Being young is not measured as a quantification of years. Rather, the conversational partners suggest youth means to be "permitted to be there for the unnecessary" (GA 77: 219/CPC 142) and no longer "barred from thinking" (GA 77: 221/CPC 143). The two wonder what "thinking" means in what they remember as philosophy's definition of the human "as the thinking being" (GA 77: 221/CPC 143). In response, the Older Man suggests something critical is missing in this depiction of the human being. He worries that in its haste, the West reductively renders thinking as "rationality" (GA 77: 221/CPC 143). This "hastiness" has long "unsettled" him (GA 77: 221/CPC 143). For the first time in his conversations,[26] Heidegger indicates a break within a single character's line, rather than between different characters' lines. Presumably, the Older Man takes a moment of silence as he is speaking, illustrating the weightiness of the impending revelation (GA 77: 221/CPC 143).

After his silence, the Older Man confesses a "fear" (GA 77: 222/CPC 144). He recalls an even older definition of the human as "the mortal . . . [which is] incomparably deeper" (GA 77: 222/CPC 144). He articulates the human as mortal using a singular noun. However, the Older Man prefers this definition because it challenges the view that the human is "by himself, isolated and detached from the great relationships in which he properly stands" (GA 77: 222/CPC 144), including his relationships to other mortals.[27] In addition to drawing out this alternative rendering of the human, the Older Man here enacts two of Heidegger's pedagogical techniques: attending to affects of fear and being unsettled and keeping silent so as to learn how to engage these affects.

The characters posit that the younger definition of the human being is grounded in the historiological account of philosophy whereas the older definition is preferred by the poets. Yet this does not simply settle the matter through a decision to reject a metaphysical representation in favor of a poetic rendering. Again, Heidegger declines any polemical resolution. The task—prepared by the "Tower Conversation" and developed in the "Evening

Conversation"—is to learn to interpret these definitions as neither inherently metaphysically constructed (as with the younger definition) nor poetically informed (as with the older definition). They work to articulate how both definitions may be interpreted either metaphysically or non-metaphysically. Interpretation—not content alone—crucially participates in the enactment of non-representational, non-metaphysical thinking.

The Younger Man first sees that neither metaphysical isolation nor non-metaphysical opening out toward others is inherent to either definition. Either definition can be interpreted non-metaphysically through collaborative, non-representational interpretation.[28] The first way the conversational partners relate the definitions is through the original Greek of the younger definition. On this basis, the Younger Man contends, "the older definition can only be explained if the younger one is thought through" (GA 77: 223/ CPC 145). Once the Younger Man interprets the "logos" in the ζῷον λόγον ἔχον as "gathering toward the originally all-unifying One" (GA 77: 223/ CPC 145), the Older Man already sees the "inner relation of this [younger] definition to the older one" (GA 77: 223/CPC 145), namely the human as ὁ θνητός or the mortal. In further elaborating the all-unifying one as the divinity of the immortals from which the mortal distinguishes herself, the Older Man can now say "the two essential definitions—which initially appear as almost incompatible, or at least foreign to one another—basically think the selfsame" (GA 77: 224/CPC 145). Though the two seem to agree and thereby appease the Older Man's fear that rationality had overwritten mortality as the most significant feature of being human, their task is not yet complete. Heidegger senses a further danger that this interpretation invites a metaphysical, theological representing of the divinity that supports the selfsameness of these two definitions.

At this moment, Heidegger's pedagogical techniques unfold in their full amplitude. It is the Younger Man's turn to express affective concern. In responding to the Older Man's account of the selfsameness of these definitions, the Younger Man engages in a reversal by remembering the Older Man's original worry of hastiness. In so doing, the Younger Man illustrates his sustained openness toward his conversational partner through listening closely to him, including to his recent silence. He is open to revising the interpretation he touched off because of his friend's initial concern. The Younger Man shares that he worries the Older Man's interpretation of the selfsameness of the two definitions may inadvertently "hasten by the allegedly older [definition]" (GA 77: 224/CPC 145). The Younger Man points out that mortality relates the mortal not only to the immortals, but also to death.[29] The Older Man responds by voicing a metaphysical representation of death as "not at all . . . a distinguishing trait of the essence of the human . . . [because] the animal can also do that" (GA 77: 224/CPC 145). In the language of *Being and Time*, the Older Man here describes "perishing" not "death" (GA 2: 247/BT 238). The Younger Man clarifies that what he means by death is not something shared with animals "if to die means: to go toward death, to *have* death" (GA 77: 224/CPC 145). To be mortal is to be capable of appropriating one's ownmost expropriation, the possibility of impossibility or, as the Younger Man puts it, to wait upon death as "what waits in us" (GA 77: 225/CPC 146).

What the Older Man's response shows is that not everything that seems poetic or derived from the poets necessarily poetizes. The Older Man seemed to prefer the older definition of the human as the mortal (at least in part) because it is articulated by the pre-Socratic poets. Yet when pressed, it became clear that the representation of death supporting this preference was itself metaphysical in that it depicted death as objectively assessable. This underscores that the relationality marked by *interpretation* is what is essential, not anything that would inhere in an ostensibly poetic object. In a renewed return to the younger, historiological definition of the human being, the Younger Man sees that in logos "gathering toward the originally all-unifying One, something like attentiveness prevails, and if you begin to ask yourself whether attentiveness is not in fact the same as constant waiting . . . then perhaps one day you will sense that, also in the allegedly younger definition, the essence of the human as the being that waits is experienced [*erfahren wird*]" (GA 77: 225/CPC 146).

Interpretation holds the possibility for non-representational, non-metaphysical thinking. But historiological accounts also enable such interpretation, just as poetic accounts may. In both collaborative interpretations, the essence of the human as one who waits—which enables both accounts of the selfsameness of the relations between the definitions—remains "unspoken" (GA 77: 225/CPC 146). This *unspoken* sense of the waitfulness of the human being provides an added safeguard against the hastiness of metaphysical representation. Their first attempt to interpret the selfsameness of the definitions failed. But this failure set their interpretation into motion, opening the opportunity to wait for even another interpretation to swing their way. Their mistakes granted the gift of occasioning non-representational, non-metaphysical thinking.

Because each definition of the human being needed the other in order to arrive at a sense of its essence, the conversational partners conclude that each definition is "equally old, because equally originary and in their origin equally concealed" (GA 77: 225/CPC 146). What it means to measure time has itself changed. Age cannot be represented in objective years in interpreting these definitions as equally old. Such non-metaphysical thinking is only possible because each needed and learned from the other. Though the Older Man initially supplied the older definition of the human being, he did not understand its essential meaning. It was the Younger Man who interpreted how the initially "foreign" definitions nevertheless shared in an unspoken sense of the human being as one who waits. He pointed out the hidden metaphysical presupposition of the Older Man's interpretation of the older definition and called his own initial interpretation back into question. Without youth's brazen surmising, that which is truly old could not have been found. These characters needed one another. Neither could have arrived at this insight without the other. This illustrates the meaning of the formation of community underway in the "Evening Conversation." As the Younger Man already surmised, the healing experience is not meant for a "you" or "me" in isolation, but rather for the "we."

In this section, all five of Heidegger's pedagogical techniques are enacted: sensitivity to affect, openness to others, silence, reversal, and remembrance. Their sharing with each other matures through the pedagogical exchange concerning the two definitions of the human being and how they both relate to the unspoken essence of waiting. Both the Younger Man and the Older Man demarcate their affect in relation to the learning that takes place. At the conclusion of this phase of conversation, neither any longer expresses the fear that had motivated each in his initial objections. They are "glad" and "thankful" (GA 77: 225–26/CPC 146) that their exchange has provided the opportunity to learn to wait for the interpretation of selfsameness. By remaining open to one another and accepting the Older Man's silence and the Younger Man's reversal as they are further enabled to remember how the poets and philosophers have defined the human being, the characters ultimately experience the waiting of the "one who waits." Heidegger's pedagogical techniques unfold even without a teacher to guide those who would learn.

This pedagogical success allows the conversational partners to return to the question of healing with a renewed sense of their task to "guard themselves against straight away inquiring into what that which heals is in itself" (GA 77: 226/CPC 146). Because that which is essential to the human remains safeguarded as "unspoken" in the two definitions drawn from the Western tradition, the characters recognize that which is healing in the Younger Man's earlier experience may need to remain concealed to be healing. The sense of community they are cultivating contests whether non-representational, non-metaphysical thinking could be contained by and in one subjective experience. What if non-representational, non-metaphysical thinking exceeds itself, as that which essentially "awakens in fellow human beings the knowledge that grows from it"? The Older Man tells the Younger Man he somehow finds himself sharing in the Younger Man's experience of "that which is beginning to heal you and—as I now experience—me as well" (GA 77: 226/CPC 146). Once they have let this representational, metaphysical partitioning of humans as subjects and other beings as objects pass by, the meaning of sharing and collaboration begins to take shape.

The pedagogical upshot of the philosophical and poetic traditions' renderings of the human being is encapsulated in the following exchange:

OLDER MAN: It seems to me that those who wait first learn the right kind of humble contentment.

YOUNGER MAN: So that they can be the teachers of great poverty. (GA 77: 226/CPC 147)

To teach, one must first learn to endure the waiting of learning and find—even within this poverty of the devastation effectuated by representational metaphysics—the resources to generously invite others to learn to think otherwise. In his short lecture "Poverty," Heidegger draws on his recent work in the "Evening Conversation."[30] There, he engages with Hölderlin's poetizing of what it means to be poor and questioning whom the first-person plural includes. Heidegger understands "the genuinely being poor is in itself be-ing rich"[31] insofar as even in circumstances of the direst neediness, we can yet think how "man abides in a relation to that which surrounds him—a relation that is exalted above the relation of a subject to an object"[32] but rather is sustained in how the human being abides in relation to being itself, which can be found in "the alternating conversation of a people with one another."[33] This is the conversation Heidegger is laying the possibility for in the "Evening Conversation."

An interlude on the meaning of waiting follows the discussion of the human being. Once they have had an experience of waiting together, they are better prepared to describe waiting by protecting the essence of this experience from representational, metaphysical thinking through conversation and, increasingly, poetizing. The conversational partners return to many of the ways they had described waiting prior to their ostensible detour through these depictions of the human. Yet they do so having garnered a confidence that a different way of speaking of the waiting is appropriate to their task of describing what is healing. Some examples include "pure waiting would be like the echo of pure coming" (GA 77: 227/CPC 147), "As those who wait, we are the inlet for the coming" (GA 77: 227/CPC 147), "waiting is in essence otherwise than all awaiting and expecting, which are basically unable to wait" (GA 77: 227/CPC 148), and "we are like a string instrument of the most ancient provenance, in whose sound the primordial play of the world resounds" (GA 77: 227/CPC 148). In putting forth these increasingly poetic descriptions of human's waiting, the two learners let the question of provenance remain unspoken, indicating pedagogical growth beyond the point where the Teacher in the "Tower Conversation" had stalled. They call this the "freedom" (GA 77: 230/CPC 149) to sidestep the metaphysical representations of "objects for subjects" (GA 77: 228/CPC 149) to instead explore the possibilities poetic language might afford for further sharing in their communal healing.

To depict what they are attempting to think as poetic only partially elucidates what these characters are enacting. The Younger Man says, "what heals can also never be set forth in propositional statements," and the Older Man continues, "but rather can only be conversationally surmised, as happened just now with us" (GA 77: 231/CPC 150). Propositional statements are forms of language grounded in representational, metaphysical thinking, which would seek to objectively ascertain healing. This is not how what heals has been discussed in this text. Only in conversation—an event of language that necessarily involves more than a single person—can healing become meaningful. What enables healing from metaphysics is itself non-metaphysical. Following Heidegger's earlier claim that insights into what is essential can only be known as such through their sharability with others, it is clear that non-representational, non-metaphysical thinking belongs to humans in their *plurality*, never as individualized subjects atomized and isolated. Nevertheless, the devastation also plays a role in this healing. In first impoverishing the possibility of community by bringing about circumstances in which experiencing plurality seems impossible, representational metaphysics prepares the way for a pedagogy that generates community out of a collaborative interpretation related to poetizing, not politics.

BUILDING COMMUNITY: THE PEDAGOGY OF POETIZING

After the conversational partners conclude that what is healing can be conversationally surmised, the Younger Man voices an additional possibility—that they could also surmise what heals through poetizing. He shares a poem[34] he wrote with the Older Man:

> First in waiting
> do we come into our own,
> Granting to everything
> the return into resting.
> Like the tender
> sound of old master violins,
> which passed away unheard
> from instruments in hidden cases. (GA 77: 232/CPC 151)

The Younger Man also describes his compositional experience: "without their being willed, the following words spoke themselves to me" (GA 77: 231/CPC 150). This suggests that *Gelassenheit* pervaded the poetizing of this poem. The conversational partners do not find the poetizing of the poem competes with or displaces their earlier conversational surmising. Rather, it seems to complement conversation[35] by similarly enacting waiting. The Older Man responds to the Younger Man's poem by saying, "I have often pondered whether your thinking is not in fact a concealed poetizing," which he clarifies does not mean that the Younger Man expresses "what we are attempting to say with the help of verses and rhymes" but rather that "the poetizing of your thinking lies rather in that it is a waiting" (GA 77: 232/CPC 151). The poetizing of this poem is not reducible to its rhetorical form, but is found in its essence as waiting, which it shares with non-representational, non-metaphysical thinking.[36]

The broaching of poetizing in the "Evening Conversation" coincides with a turn toward discussing how the "people"—among whose ranks "poets and thinkers" (GA 77: 233/CPC 152) are found—are to be regarded. A discussion about politics ensues. Heidegger suggests that just as metaphysics reduces the human being to a subject that represents, produces, and orders objects, politics carries out a metaphysical project through solidifying aggregates of isolated, detached individuals who nominally belong to a nation-state or international union. Such detachment forecloses the possibility of waiting and healing from the devastation through sharing experiences in conversation or in poetizing. Relative to others, the conversational partners agree that a people guided instead by poets and thinkers would be "endangered like no other," not by anything external, but rather by "ignorant impatience . . . [that would] spur itself on to continual mistakes" (GA 77: 233/CPC 152). Poets and thinkers are not protected against mistakes by their poetizing and thinking. Echoing the pedagogy of mistakes depicted in the "Tower Conversation," Heidegger instead claims that those who wait are *more* vulnerable to making mistakes. Is Heidegger here tacitly admitting that he, as a thinker, made "continual mistakes" in his previous political thought and action? Perhaps. But he is neither explicit about this, nor does he specify what shape these mistakes might take. Where Heidegger's Tower Warden was able to proactively call attention to and admit his mistake, Heidegger himself is not.

The waiting of such a people is complex. The conversational partners agree that important aspects of learning to wait include that the people "would have to remain indifferent to whether others listen to it or not," could never "insist on its waiting essence as on a special calling or distinction," and would be "entirely unusable to others" because it is entirely unconcerned with "progress and raising the achievement curve, and for the brisk pace of business" because it is "the most elderly people" (GA 77: 233–34/CPC 152). Yet as this most elderly people, it is also the most youthful because it is devoted to what metaphysics deems "the unnecessary" (GA 77: 234/CPC 152), which belongs to the young. The selfsame relationality of the young and the old intimates that, for Heidegger, conventional, metaphysical ways of representing time gain no traction. Those who wait experience the still concealed dimension of time that the conversational partners are also experiencing through their mutual healing. What this healing enables the conversational partner to realize is the wider implication: "by becoming those who wait, we first become German" (GA 77: 235/CPC 153). What is meant by "German" is nothing based in nationalism, but rather in an ontological plurality.

The mistakes such a people make as they struggle to become this people who wait are to conceive of themselves representationally and metaphysically. The Younger Man describes this by noting a definition of Germanness he means to ignore: "We will not become German so long as we plan to find 'the German' by means of analyzing our supposed 'nature' " (GA 77: 235/CPC 153). The nature of a people is often depicted politically through nationalism. Though the Younger Man argues that in the wake of the devastation, "it has become unnecessary to still inveigh against the national"

(GA 77: 235/CPC 153), he nevertheless describes its metaphysical character: "The idea of a nation is that representation in whose circle-of-vision a people bases itself on itself as a foundation given from somewhere, and makes itself into a subject. And to this subject everything then appears as what is objective" (GA 77: 235/CPC 153). This metaphysical political grounding of "nationality" is further described as a "rebellious uprising into subjectivity . . . [in which] the devastation of the earth is everywhere prepared for and ultimately established as unconditional" (GA 77: 235–36/CPC 154). This version of politics is inexorably metaphysical in kind.

This holds for Heidegger's characters, regardless of whether the national or the international produces such a politics. The conversational partners conclude, "we cannot become German—which means those who poetize and think, that is, those who wait—so long as we chase after the German in the sense of something national," which the Younger Man elaborates, saying "if we are German, we also do not lose ourselves in a vague internationalism" (GA 77: 236/CPC 154). Yet to let go of both national and international renderings of what is German does not also mean to surrender the term. If what Heidegger means by "German" is nothing national or metaphysical but is instead born of a shared experience of waiting, why does he insist on retaining the name? The "Evening Conversation" provides no direct answer.[37] Clearly national affiliation played a role in the characters' imprisonment in Russia, and the need for the formation of a community of thinkers and poetizers remains palpable throughout the text. But why such a community need remain designated as "German" is left unexplained.

Once the conversational partners have come to terms with who the human being is, and the possibility that a "we" (not just an "I") may wait, the philosophical status of the experience of healing that prompted their conversation is transformed. The Older Man muses to the Younger Man: "You know, it seems to me as though I too am now beginning to feel that which heals" (GA 77: 237/CPC 154). Though it was not initially his, the Older Man shares in the healing that previously belonged only to the Younger Man. The experience of that which heals is neither subjective nor relegated to the past. It comes out of the future in such a way that it founds the possibility of a (non-political) community of people. For Heidegger, this event of healing is essentially historical and, in its historicality, can only be known as an insight that must be shared by a community.

The "something healing" that motivates the "Evening Conversation" has two elements. First, this healing event can only be unfolded non-representationally, through conversational or poetizing surmising. Propositional statements and other metaphysical attempts to assess this healing will fail to register what it is. Second, in engaging healing by way of conversational or poetizing surmising, this experience necessarily affects others. It enables a communal "we" that is founded otherwise than metaphysically out of the still-concealed dimension of time that makes possible a Heideggerian sense of history.

The sharing of this healing insight communally also implicates pedagogy. Though the Younger Man first began to experience that which heals earlier that morning, something was left radically outstanding in this experience. The Younger Man was compelled to seek out his friend to discuss what happened, which suggests that he is still undergoing this event *during* their conversation. To make sense of his own healing, the Younger Man concurrently *teaches* it to the Older Man, thereby opening it up for them both. In this way, he *learns* his own experience by and through his conversational partner coming to share in that selfsame experience. Yet the swinging of the healing experience between the two does not end with either of them, but rather, as they conclude, swings out beyond them and must be shared even more widely, with the others in the camp and then with their entire homeland (GA 77: 240/CPC 157). The conversational partners describe this sharing in explicitly pedagogical terms:

> OLDER MAN: Thus we must learn to know the necessity of the unnecessary and, as learners, teach it to the peoples.
>
> YOUNGER MAN: And for a long time this may perhaps be the sole content of our teaching: the need and the necessity of the unnecessary.
>
> Now I can also say to you more clearly what gave itself to be known in the healing that was granted to us today. It is the dark and the difficult that such a learning and teaching must bear on its shoulders, insofar as learning and teaching may only ever have their element in waiting. (GA 77: 237–38/CPC 155)

Learning is prioritized as a necessary precondition for teaching.[38] Within the Younger Man's elaboration on the Older Man's suggestion, note one of several instances in Heidegger's conversational corpus where one of his characters takes a moment of silence while speaking, indicated by the paragraph break. This break also performs the philosophical point in that it is not strictly "necessary" for expressing his idea. The depiction of a "dark and difficult" pedagogy suggests that learning and teaching must bear the metaphysical devastation and contend with the ambiguity of being that allows for evil—as the malice of insurgency—to arise. It must continue to wait upon the necessity of the unnecessary rather than allow itself to be drawn into the metaphysical economy of usefulness. As those who wait, they must guard themselves against any such haste because this pedagogy is not one that will be enacted immediately. As a historical endeavor to found a people, it is necessarily futural. The Older Man concludes, "on many evenings to come in this camp, we will ponder over how to advise those among us and among others, who only know the necessary, on the necessity of the unnecessary—and we will ponder over how to do this in such a way that those being advised do not fall into rashly making this teaching into a belief and a worldview and extolling it as such" (GA 77: 238/CPC 155). A teaching of non-representational, non-metaphysical thinking always risks becoming what it is not, echoing the very ambiguity of being that it would learn.

Underlying this call for non-representational, non-metaphysical pedagogy, another reason Heidegger refuses to speak directly about the horrors of the Holocaust may be discerned. Though the war has ended (on the very date he notes in the postscript), Heidegger writes in the supplements to the text that the world is celebrating "its victory" without realizing how with "the War at an end, nothing changed, nothing new" (GA 77: 240–41/CPC 157). Perhaps Heidegger is unconvinced that the evils stemming from the representational, metaphysical nationalism of National Socialism have fully emerged. Perhaps the devastation is still unfolding, unabated. Poets and thinkers are those who, for Heidegger, are most in danger of hastily capitulating to errancy. In choosing instead to wait, Heidegger may see himself as declining to participate in the construction of a "worldview" that necessarily belongs "to the age of, and in the dominion of, the devastation" (GA 77: 238/CPC 155–56) that might too quickly admit (and therefore too quickly absolve) guilt rather than "bear this burden together" (GA 77: 238/CPC 155). Heidegger instead relegates the truth of the devastation in which National Socialism participated to a long meditation on that which is still in need of healing, even after victory has been declared. Yet even in depicting this conclusion from a Heideggerian view, clearly his silence fails miserably, *especially* if it indeed is intended to mark his resistance to ideology. As was already evident in the "Tower Conversation," the mistakes of representational metaphysics provide a fecund site for learning to think otherwise, but only in the between-field. If his silence is a rejection of Nazism, Heidegger is assuming the polemical and ultimately self-righteous moral stance he condemned earlier in the "Evening Conversation." His failure continues.

Not only are Heidegger's views on the Holocaust in this text obscure, but the scope of the "we" and the "us" of this healing pedagogy of waiting is also troubling. The conversational partners identify two takeaways from their conversation. They must "learn to wait" and "attempt to tell friends" of the possibility of non-representational, non-metaphysical thinking (GA 77: 239/CPC 156). Who are these pedagogically capable friends? And on what terms does their friendship proceed? The Older Man offers what he calls "a good night parting . . . thanks" (GA 77: 239/CPC 156) to the Younger Man by relaying a short conversation he had memorized during his "student days . . . from a historiological account of Chinese philosophy" (GA 77: 239/CPC 156).[39] The conversation relates a parable concerning the "necessity of the unnecessary" (GA 77: 239/CPC 156) and is in this way a suitable coda to their own conversation. The Younger Man thanks the Older Man for sharing the conversation and the Older Man thanks the Younger Man for sharing his poem, again underscoring how the possibility of learning how to teach a collaborative thinking that waits may unfold *either* through conversational surmising or poetizing, underscoring a philosophical affinity between these ways of saying.[40] They end by wishing a good night to each other, to "all in the camp," and "to the homeland" (GA 77: 240/CPC 157). The addressee of this farewell is not limited to the conversational partners or even to those who are in a similar condition nearby, but to a much larger sense of "we."

The question of the status of the conversation excerpted from the *Zhuangzi* becomes even more urgent in the wake of this conclusion. Does Heidegger include it to show that the Chinese partners—in this conversation within a conversation—are somehow essentially really German because they are learning to wait upon the unnecessary? Or is Heidegger suggesting that even non-metaphysical representations of (national) identities lose their coherence, if only we wait long enough? Or is this a straightforward case of cultural appropriation that takes for itself what it finds "useful" about something foreign, despite Heidegger's own preceding case against following such an impulse? Is Heidegger making the mistake of hastily falling victim to his own "ignorant impatience"? These questions remain unanswered within the "Evening Conversation." Though it is the first, this is not the last time in his conversations that Heidegger engages with non-Western philosophy. In the "Conversation of Language,"[41] Heidegger wrestles with whether such an engagement is possible in great detail. But already in the "Evening

Conversation," the fact that Heidegger engages with Eastern philosophy signals that the "we" Heidegger is developing in relation to his pedagogy is ambiguous. But in considering the possibility of a community of thinkers that bridges the East and West, Heidegger neglects to disclose whether he considers Jews to be members of this non-metaphysical German community. His silence speaks volumes.

Healing as a "We"

In the "Evening Conversation," Heidegger shows how in the wake of devastation, non-representational, non-metaphysical thinking enables healing. This healing is not individualized or subjective. It does not close us off from the world. It rather opens us out toward it, despite the ambiguity of being, which may give rise to evil. The text explores how the founding of a non-metaphysical community is not accidental but *essential* to healing. And because there is no teacher in this conversation, the two characters learn to teach themselves. They learn how to enact pedagogical techniques for learning non-representational, non-metaphysical thinking, or rather they allow these techniques to reveal themselves as already enacted by conversational or poetizing language. In engaging in this pedagogy, these prisoners become those who wait as they prepare to teach others how to wait as well. Even in the wake of the rage and malice of insurgency, the possibility of collaboratively coming together as a "we" remains. The characters learn that only *together* can they sense whether they have achieved insight into that which is essential.

Yet for the triumph depicted within the conversation, the text is all the more noteworthy for its silences. Heidegger here seems to offer something like an oblique rationale for his own silence about the extermination of millions of Jews. There is no acknowledgment of his political privilege relative to his Jewish colleagues and students or his personal accountability for his vigorous participation in Nazi political organizing. The non-political sense of what it is to be "German" that Heidegger is trying to elaborate in this text, as the war is ending, is not an acceptable response to the genocide that had unfolded, nor is his silence about these millions of deaths justified. The pedagogy Heidegger develops in these texts does rely on silence as one of its techniques. But such silences pertain to non-metaphysical insights that can only be conversationally or poetically surmised because we do not yet know how to let language speak non-metaphysically. About metaphysics,

Heidegger has much to say. If we are to accept his claim that nationalistic politics stem from representational metaphysics, then Heidegger has more than enough resources to inveigh against this instantiation of scientific and technological thinking. Heidegger's thinking may have the resources to acknowledge genocide, but Heidegger the thinker does not. He chooses silence.

In his next conversation—the "Western Conversation,"—Heidegger writes not about the "German" but about the "West." In so doing, he will recast his same characters in a very different setting. The new versions of the Younger Man and the Older Man will not turn their attention to the Jews—as those most in need of healing and reformation of their community—but rather to a renewed effort to read and interpret Hölderlin's poetizing. As had already been suggested in the "Evening Conversation," conversation or poetizing are proper avenues toward enabling a collaborative sense of a "we," unconstrained by metaphysical politics. In the "Western Conversation," Heidegger returns to the swinging of being, poetizing, and Hölderlin to reimagine how the thinking of these characters may have been shaped if they had had Hölderlin's poetry to guide them.

4

The "Western Conversation"
Poetizing Pedagogy

After the *Country Path Conversations* were written in rapid succession at the conclusion of the war, Heidegger considerably slows his pace composing conversations. The fourth conversation—"*Das abendländische Gespräch*"[1] or "The Western Conversation"—was written between 1946 and 1948. As the immediate threat and radical uncertainty of the end of the war subsided, so too did Heidegger's frenzied attempt to recapitulate his philosophical efforts in conversational form.[2] This second longest of Heidegger's conversations is unfinished, in several senses. Replete notes left in the manuscript—both in-line notes and footnotes—indicate bypaths Heidegger planned to take, but never made legible for his readers. Not only does Heidegger append a note—"not completed" (GA 75: 196)—to the end of the manuscript, but the characters also remark upon the philosophical significance of the difference between something merely "unfinished" and that which "breaks off" and is thereby "completed in this breaking off" (GA 75: 194), like Hölderlin's poem "*Der Ister*."

It is Hölderlin's poetizing that Heidegger's efforts are devoted to unfolding in this conversation. This text undertakes this task in its historical and philosophical context. Robert Savage calls the "Western Conversation" a "ramble"[3] on Hölderlin's poetizing, touching upon nearly every corner of Hölderlin's poetic corpus. For Charles Bambach, this conversation makes good on one of Heidegger's earliest descriptions of "his relationship to the poet as a form of *Gespräch*."[4] Bambach argues Heidegger presents a distinctively postwar reading of Hölderlin. Previously, I have found in the

"Western Conversation" a subterranean corrective to his earlier readings of Plato, noting similarities in setting and themes with the *Phaedrus*.[5]

The "Western Conversation" grounds Heidegger's endeavor to learn to think non-representationally and non-metaphysically in interpreting Hölderlin's poetizing. In this text, Heidegger's pedagogical thinking culminates in learning poetic interpretation. Such interpretation does not rely on a pre-given rubric to uncover objective meaning of Hölderlin's verses and stanzas. Rather, it embraces the ambiguity of poetizing, which further reveals the ambiguity of being itself.[6] The characters in Heidegger's conversation do not seek explications of Hölderlin's poems on the basis of a range of already metaphysically authorized corresponding representational possibilities, but rather hope to teach themselves to learn how to resonate, or "sing with" (GA 75: 111) the singing of Hölderlin's poetic saying. This means, first and foremost, that they must shelter it in its essential ambiguity and remain, as they put it, in "twofold conversation [*Zwiegespräch*]" (GA 75: 158), with the singing of the singer.

Scholars of Heidegger's Hölderlin have probed the "Western Conversation."[7] In extant studies of Heidegger's conversational oeuvre, however, this text tends to be overlooked.[8] This is regrettable because, as I argue, the "Western Conversation" occasions the epitome of Heidegger's poetic pedagogy. The "Western Conversation" advances explorations begun in the *Country Path Conversations*. While the "Tower Conversation" was concerned with the "where" of non-metaphysical thinking and the "Evening Conversation" probed the question of "who" may undertake such thinking, the "Western Conversation" emphasizes that the locale constitutes the community capable of non-metaphysical thinking and vice versa, revealing an inherent and mutually necessary relationality. It further shows that the richness of such an encounter can unfold for conversational partners properly supported in non-representational, non-metaphysical thinking. They are engaged in something entirely different from the nascent pedagogy of such thinking in the "Triadic Conversation"[9]; they are prepared to learn to think *poetically*.

Reading the "Western Conversation" as an episode following the "Evening Conversation" is especially illuminating. As Savage argues, the "Western Conversation" can be read as "a kind of dream script that picks up the "Abendgespräch" where it left off, as the two friends fall asleep under a Siberian sky, evocations of *Dichtung* and *Heimat* still ringing in their ears."[10] Characters with the same impersonal names come together to converse. In the "Evening Conversation," the homophonous characters were confined in a prisoner of war camp. In the "Western Conversation," they are free to roam the banks of the Danube river and discuss lines of poetry from across Hölderlin's corpus. In the "Evening Conversation," the students-become-teachers were bereft of guidance. Now these two have an expansive collection of Hölderlin's poems at hand, never as a standing reserve of poetry, but as a wellspring of the possibility of non-representational, non-metaphysical thinking as *poetic*.

Significant developments in historical, political, and personal circumstances between the composition of the *Country Path Conversations* and the "Western Conversation" are also legible in this text. Between the years of 1946 and 1948, Heidegger underwent de-Nazification proceedings and was banned from teaching,[11] he had a mental breakdown and spent some months in a sanatorium,[12] and his sons were still missing at the eastern front.[13] He composed this conversation in a bombed-out Freiburg and at the sanatorium, yet within the text he makes a fantastical, postwar return to the Upper Danube Valley—where he wrote the *Country Path Conversations*. Additionally, Heidegger reveals his own genealogical connection to that place. In the first pages of the "Western Conversation," a footnote indicates Heidegger's grandfather was born in a sheep-stall in the Upper Danube Valley while Hölderlin was composing the Ister hymn. Rather than worrying about the plight of his sons, Heidegger remembers his ancestral origins, initiating a historical voyage backward that resounds across the "Western Conversation." In the course of this temporal reversal, Heidegger brings the pedagogical project begun in the *Country Path Conversations* to its (poetic) apogee.

Conversational Context

The (Explicit) Characters

Two characters are named as conversational partners in the "Western Conversation." They bear the same names as those in the "Evening Conversation": "the Younger Man"—*Der Jüngere*—and "the Older Man"—*Der Ältere*. They have similar temperaments and conversational styles too. The Younger Man tends toward daring surmises and the Older Man worries those surmises are too bold. But where the characters confined in the prisoner of war camp were severely limited—by time, physical constraint, and extreme metaphysical devastation—these characters have the opportunity to learn and grow more freely in their interpretive engagement with Hölderlin's poetizing, especially "*Der Ister*."

The Younger Man remains more willing to take philosophical risks. As they set out on their trek, the Younger Man's contributions are perceived by his conversational partner as bolder, brasher, and more opaque. In response to his initial esoteric foray, the Older Man remarks on this opacity, telling him, "your talk [*Rede*] is deeply veiled [*verhüllend*]" (GA 75: 59). This difficulty stems from the Younger Man's penchant for introducing new topics. For example, in describing how the river protects itself from those who aim at "interpreting the river song immediately [*unmittelbar*]," that is according to representational metaphysics, the Younger Man speaks of the "erstwhile love [*einstige Liebe*]" of a "mysterious allowing" that precedes all interpretive efforts and enables an "intimacy [*Innigkeit*]" of interpretation with the river song (GA 75: 64). His conversational partner generally is able to follow these new contributions rather adeptly. Nevertheless, the dynamic of their conversation typically consists in the Younger Man setting the pace and the Older Man working to keep up.

There are also ways in which the Younger Man of the "Western Conversation" seems different—and perhaps more mature—than Heidegger's earlier iteration of this character. For all his boldness, the Younger Man is more willing to interrupt the conversation when they stray too far from Hölderlin's poetizing. At times, the Younger Man even issues (grammatical) imperatives to slow down interpretive efforts and to simply listen ever more closely to the self-veiling of the poetizing (GA 75: 112–14). This challenges the more traditional dynamic one might expect between those of different ages. At other points, however, the Younger Man seems even more audacious, going so far as to rewrite one of Hölderlin's lines as he strives to listen ever more closely to its resonating (GA 75: 171).

The Older Man also exhibits characteristics akin to the character by the same name in the "Evening Conversation." He repeatedly worries that the Younger Man's surmises leap too far ahead without sufficient grounding and are "too daring" (GA 75: 160). He says that he isn't capable of following the Younger Man's "youthful exuberance" because he is "more deliberate" (GA 75: 89). This depiction is undercut when the Younger Man calls it a "half-organic representation [*halbbiologische Vorstellungen*], of youth and age" (GA 75: 89) that recalls metaphysical stereotypes rather than a thoughtful consideration of the meaning of youth and old age. The Younger Man muses instead, "perhaps youth is never old enough to be young" (GA 75: 89). The inherent relationality of youth and age that the conversational partners strove to unpack across many pages of the "Evening Conversation" is condensed into one sentence of the "Western Conversation." Despite the mutual needfulness of their experiences of the meaning of time, the Older Man also responds to the Younger Man's issuance of imperatives with his own, perhaps reactivating traditional meanings of their age difference. Even late in their conversation, the Older Man finds himself confused because the Younger Man is moving too fast. He asks for clarification, admitting that he isn't able to follow at the Younger Man's pace, but does so without shame or embarrassment (GA 75: 177).

There is growth in the Older Man's range as well. For instance, when they reminisce about their experience swimming together in the river "the other day" (GA 75: 64) and sensing the river spirit then, the Older Man subsequently takes the conversational lead. While the Younger Man may be more daring in his interpretive attempts, the Older Man is also committed to engaging with Hölderlin's poetizing and contributing to this effort. But he does so by first dwelling even more deeply with certain experiences and only then introducing new ideas into their conversation from his memory of those erstwhile experiences, not out of the boldness seemingly reserved for youth.

The most common pronoun these characters invoke to describe their relations to their thinking and interpreting is the grammatical first-person plural—"we." The force of this pronoun is supported by an enduring friendship. Many of the characters in the *Country Path Conversations* were also friends, but there is a palpable vivacity to the relation between these men, perhaps grounded in the sense of friendship[14] articulated at the end of the "Evening Conversation" that together "we must learn to wait" (GA 77: 239/CPC 156). In the "Western Conversation," this waiting happens in proximity. The characters are "neighbors" who not only dwell in the same place, but who know the same members of their community.[15] In the "Tower Conversation," both the Teacher and the Tower Warden recall earlier conversations with an unnamed "neighbor" (GA 77: 171 and 176/CPC 111 and 115). Perhaps Heidegger is finally illustrating the possibilities that lie in engaging in sustained and repeated conversations with those with whom one shares the same place and time, dwelling, as the Older Man and Younger Man apparently do, in communal proximity. They seem well-versed in conversing with one another, specifically regarding non-representational, non-metaphysical thinking.[16] These conversational partners begin completing one another's sentences only three pages into the "Western Conversation" (GA 75: 61), and this dynamic is sustained across the text (GA 75: 88, 142–43, and 191). Such conversational chemistry was only achievable after greater duration and expenditure of effort in the *Country Path Conversations*.

The pedagogical dynamic between these two characters is implicitly demonstrated rather than directly expressed. Though there is no explicit teacher or extended mediation on the meaning of teaching, the characters make passing references to the importance of learning (GA 75: 177 and 184). The absence of explicit invocation suggests these characters are enacting—rather than still learning—Heidegger's pedagogy, but they are doing so in a way that remains open to learning, specifically learning to sing with Hölderlin's poetizing. While these characters generally succeed in collaborating rather equally, they do so while following the lead of Hölderlin's poetizing. Heidegger perhaps inadvertently demonstrates how little the distinct identities of the characters matter relative to Hölderlin. Accidentally repeating the Younger Man's name, Heidegger writes two separate entries following one another attributed to the same speaker (GA 75: 75). This shows that Heidegger is not as earnestly differentiating his characters at this point in his conversational oeuvre. Perhaps in poetic interpretation, differentiation between interpreters is not as important as remaining sensitive to hearing the otherness[17] that thrives within poetizing itself.

Hölderlin himself is not an explicit character in the "Western Conversation," but his poems and poetizing resound across this text. It may be tempting to attribute a teaching role to Hölderlin since his poetry allows the conversational partners to engage in non-representational, non-metaphysical interpretation. But, just as no teaching figure appeared in the "Evening Conversation," there is no apparent teacher in the "Western Conversation" either.[18] This allows the characters to take responsibility for their own pedagogy. A significant difference between these texts shows, however, that the characters in the "Western Conversation" are students-become-teachers both because Hölderlin is absent and because his absence is marked by the traces of his poetizing,[19] which function as cairns, guiding their journey along the riverbank. Hölderlin's poetizing cannot be reduced to his poems—better described as poetizing's afterimage. As Krzysztof Ziarek explains, "*Dichtung* names that which, concealing itself in art, makes 'place' for art: it 'projects' and 'outlines' (*entwerfen*) in such a way that it keeps itself from emerging and, in this peculiar withdrawal, opens art. In other words, *Dichtung* marks the *Ur-sprung*, the 'origin' that remains unnamed . . . [and that] retreats from speech and writing."[20] Hölderlin himself also remains unnamed as a character in this text, withdrawing from their conversation, yet making a place for it as its origin. Perhaps this is because his poetizing is already essentially conversational, obviating the need for secondary illustration. In the 1936 essay "Hölderlin and the Essence of Poetry," Heidegger writes, in response to Hölderlin, "conversation, however, is not only a way in which language takes place, but rather language is essential only as conversation [*sondern als Gespräch nur ist Sprache wesentlich*]" (GA 4: 38–39/EHP 56). This depiction of language as inherently conversational relates to Heidegger's contention that Hölderlin is a historical figure, one who stands out yet ahead and who grants that which is outstanding in what has-been as a properly futural possibility.[21] Hölderlin's poetizing allows the realization that "we have been *one* conversation since the time when there 'is time.' Ever since time arose and was brought to stand, since then we *are* historical" (GA 4: 39/EHP 57). Conversation and the historical are thus selfsame. Hölderlin's poetizing *is* the occasion to come to terms with this relationality.

Conversation is also explicitly thematized, but only as the "Western Conversation" nears its end, after navigating a deluge of Hölderlin's verses. Attempting to articulate what they mean by the "Western world . . . [that] is no object" (GA 75: 158) in contradistinction to its corresponding metaphysical representation in the "occident" (GA 75: 157), the conversational partners note that theirs is a "uniquely Western conversation . . . that only speaks in the language of the Western world" (GA 75: 158). I raise the question of what Heidegger means by the non-metaphysical "West" below. But at this early point, it is important to consider how conversations could be construed as essentially "Western." Is this due to the founding of the Western metaphysical tradition in the Platonic dialogues? The next lines offer a hint. The Younger Man stipulates that the Western world can only speak conversationally "provided that our thinking conversation remains in twofold conversation [*Zweigespräch*] with the singing of the singer" (GA 75: 158). This twofold conversation certainly refers to Hölderlin's poetizing. Yet another conversational partner may be ambiguously indicated here.

I suggest Plato may be another non-explicit character in the "Western Conversation." The Older Man remarks, "conversation is only hearing [*Gespräch is nur Gehör*]" (GA 75: 190). On my reading, the conversational partners are not only practicing a poetic pedagogy in non-representationally and non-metaphysically interpreting Hölderlin's poetizing, but they are also illustrating the possibility of listening even more closely for such possibilities that may remain outstanding in the historical origins of the West. In constructing a pedagogy of learning to attend to representational metaphysics for the opportunities for making mistakes[22] that then would enable non-representational, non-metaphysical thinking, it is plausible that Heidegger returned to this origin(ator) of metaphysical thinking. In all of his conversations, Heidegger is engaging with the Western metaphysical tradition, which he variously attributes to beginning with Plato. But he does not want to oppose representational, metaphysical thinking.[23] Rather, Heidegger's characters are learning to appreciate the opportunities it affords for learning how to think otherwise. These opportunities are not accidental, but are part and parcel of representational metaphysics. In these texts, Heidegger's conversational partners are learning that metaphysics is not even *itself* essentially metaphysical but is instead fundamentally ambiguous. In his earlier work, Heidegger exhibits animus toward Plato, to the point of apparent willful misreading, which reaches a pinnacle in the 1942 essay "Plato's Doctrine of Truth."[24] However, in his later work in the 1950s and beyond, Heidegger seems to have reassessed his earlier confrontational stance.[25] Between these assessments stands the "Western Conversation," recalling themes from Plato's dialogue *Phaedrus,* which also takes place outside the city walls next to a stream between a younger and older man who discuss love, beauty, and the power of language.

On the Banks of the (Western) River

In the "Western Conversation," Heidegger returns to the Upper Danube Valley. On the first page, Heidegger notes that his grandfather[26] was born here as Hölderlin was composing *"Der Ister."* This is not the first instance in which Heidegger links his genealogical ties to the concern for thinking in his conversations. In the "Evening Conversation," his sons were implicitly significant. Where the third of the *Country Path Conversations* involved Heidegger's descendants, the "Western Conversation" recalls his ancestors.[27] On Bambach's reading, Heidegger's biographical-familial origin is a central focus of the text.[28] Bambach writes that Heidegger develops a "self-mythologizing account . . . [in] coupling Hölderlin's composition of the Ister hymn in 1803 with the birth of his grandfather in a sheep stall near the source of the Donau at 'the same time as the Ister hymn was written,'"[29] which links "the poet and the thinker in a destinal bond that confirms Heidegger's own place within the history of beyng."[30] For Heidegger, the Upper Danube Valley is the untransmutable locale of this destiny, to which he and Hölderlin must return.

This is also the location where Heidegger composed the *Country Path Conversations.* Though the grim ending of the war brought anxiety and foreboding in the spring of 1945, Heidegger makes an imaginative return to this place where he spent a series of idyllic days writing, which may have contrasted even more starkly in his memory with the postwar realities he experienced after he traveled home.[31] However, this return launches a recognizably *postwar*[32] reading of Hölderlin. At the conclusion of the "Evening Conversation" and in the attendant "Poverty" lecture, Heidegger envisions a gathering of the German essence in the course of Germany's defeat. His personal experience following the war's end did not bear this out. Instead, Heidegger physically and mentally breaks down.[33]

His return to the place where he composed the *Country Path Conversations* suggests several interpretations. Nostalgia may have drawn him. Or perhaps the ubiquity of Hölderlin's poetizing in the conversation suggests an association between Hölderlin's poetizing and the Upper Danube Valley, which is also found in the *Country Path Conversations*. As Bambach writes, "there is much about Hölderlin's work that appeals to Heidegger: his paratactic style that undermines the rationalistic metaphysics of modernity, his ethical attunement to dwelling in the age of the world's night, his grasp of the poetic character of art, his hymnal songs that call for a new language and a renewed relation to the natural world."[34] These themes are readily found in the *Country Path Conversations*[35] and may suggest that Heidegger composed all of his conversations thus far with Hölderlin in mind.

Regardless of any additional motivations, it is clear that in the "Western Conversation" Heidegger is making an imaginative visit to the Upper Danube Valley to reconsider the historical possibilities of Hölderlin's poetizing in the war's wake. The way he fashions the setting of his return continues his theme of ignoring the actual political circumstances of the day. Savage notes this text "shows not the slightest trace of the conditions under which it was written."[36] In the "Western Conversation," however, we may find a philosophical reason for this obviation. As commentators have noted,[37] Heidegger invokes several themes from Plato's *Phaedrus*. This Platonic dialogue does not take place in the *polis*, but rather ventures out into nature to discuss "love, mania, wings, the soul, beauty, music, and the limitations of written texts"[38] all of which explicitly appear in the "Western Conversation" as well. Perhaps Heidegger's conversational turn toward *Phaedrus* suggests he finds something significant in the non-political orientation of this dialogue, which resonates with a history of an entirely different sort in Hölderlin's poetizing. Hölderlin also turns eastward, toward the Greeks and, as Bambach writes, "offers a poetic geography and a poetic history for thinking through the turning at the limit, border, and boundary between East and West, Orient and Occident."[39]

In this conversation, I argue that Heidegger achieves the apogee of his pedagogy in staging his characters in conversation with Hölderlin's poetizing. A significant element of this pedagogy is learning how Hölderlin's senses of geography and history are drawn together and intertwined in their poetic essence. In his 1942 lecture course, Heidegger already declared that his interest in Hölderlin's work consists in redeeming representations of metaphysical "space" for a non-metaphysical "locality" and metaphysical "time" for non-metaphysical "journeying" (GA 53: 52–60/42–48). The journeying of the river is the locale of human dwelling *and* cannot be analytically distinguished like the concepts of space and time. In the "Western Conversation," the conversational partners define the *Abendland*—simultaneously the Western land and the land of evening—as that which no longer permits space and time to be pried apart, but occasions the intertwined "here" and "now" of poetic building such that they accomplish "the time-place [*Zeit-Ort*] of self-completing destiny" (GA 75: 157). In this locale, time is allowed to become an "abiding-while [*Weile*]" and space is released as "expanse [*Weite*]" (GA 75: 74). Despite the essential mutual needfulness of place and history in this text, I next attempt to hold them apart for a short while, to explore the philosophical significance of how Heidegger constructs the setting of the "Western Conversation."

By the "*Ister*"

The "Western Conversation" doubly unfolds along the banks of the Ister. In one sense, the two conversational partners are walking along the banks of the Danube river. In distinction from the earlier *Country Path Conversations*, there is no physical path—no *Feldweg*. Instead, the river itself cuts a way—a *Stromweg*—through the forested landscape. The river has made this land arable and promoted its natural flourishing. While a forest briefly appeared in the "Evening Conversation," as the site where the feeling of something healing was engendered before they spoke, here the forest is the sustained backdrop, drawing its sustenance from the river. The characters cannot rely on a pathway maintained by the historical community of fellow travelers because they are no longer amidst the fields where the natural and the agricultural meet. In the thick of the forest, they can only make their way by following the river, which has created its own route through the landscape. The newfound emphasis on and access to nature—as opposed to the *polis* as enabling forms of organization and extraction of value from the natural world—need not lead to the conclusion that Heidegger is no longer concerned with the consequences of representational, metaphysical scientific and technological thinking. Perhaps stepping even farther away from such thinking in this setting may allow him to draw even nearer[40] to that which makes it possible. Such clarity may show how instead poetizing—not scientific and technological thinking—offers a renewed sense of community.

The conversational partners are also discussing Hölderlin's poem "*Der Ister*." In the first lines of the conversation, the Younger Man announces that his hope is to remain with the resonating of Hölderlin's hymn. For Heidegger, this poem is neither separate nor separable from the Ister river. In his 1942 lecture course, Heidegger insists Hölderlin's "poetry must stand entirely outside of metaphysics . . . [such that] the rivers in Hölderlin's poetry are in truth not 'symbolic images'" (GA 53: 22/19). Hölderlin's poetizing of the river, then, does not represent the metaphysically actual river, but rather offers a "poetic telling" (GA 53: 24/21) of the river's essence. Hölderlin's hymn "*Der Ister*" poetizes the essence of the Ister—they are the selfsame,[41] as the characters emphasize (GA 75: 63). The setting of their conversation is its content. In following the river, they follow the poem, which provides the structure of their conversation. Hölderlin's poetizing is announced in the opening (GA 75: 59), and an interpretation of the poem is begun in earnest relatively early[42] in the conversation (GA 75: 73). Though substantial sections seem to depart from a close reading of the poem, the conversational partners eventually return to an intensive elaboration of the first stanza (GA 75: 131), a discussion of the second stanza (GA 75: 168), and even launch a brief elaboration of the last lines (GA 75: 194) as their conversation breaks off.[43]

This locale of the poetized essence of the river can only unfold when its journeying is accounted for. The poetized river's *where* slips ineluctably into a consideration of its *when*. As the conversational partners are walking toward the river's origin in the evening light, the Older Man remarks suddenly that he doesn't know how they have reached the valley of the river (GA 75: 63). This means the two have likely already been walking together for a while, perhaps even before[44] the text of the "Western Conversation" begins. There are replete suggestions they have conversed before and assume they will do so again. At one point, the Younger Man says he would like to show the Older Man how the resounding course of the river turns toward them (GA 75: 60), which he says, "you will only purely know when you behold the turn from the narrow peak of the highest cliff [*vom schmalen*

Gipfel des hohen Felsens]. Next time I would like to show you this view [*Anblick*]; but it is admittedly not any mere view. It is the open of the river's way [*das Offene eines Stromweges*], which you only enter if you have recognized *the* way in [*wenn du darin* den *Weg erkannt hast*] and know it from indwelling [*Innestehen*]" (GA 75: 60). Their conversation enacts this indwelling so that "next time" they speak, they might be prepared to hike up into the heights[45] to explore the meaning of the river's terrain from a new perspective.

Not only are the characters found at a particular moment during the day and within their ongoing relationship, but the riversong is itself in motion, journeying across the locale it has hewn into the landscape. This journeying gives rise to Heidegger's sense of Hölderlin's alternative cartography. Here, rivers and mountain ranges—not metaphysically informed representations of political borders—demarcate different lands, including the West and the East. The river's journeying across the landscape is what gives rise to this poetic geo-history linking the East and West, Greeks and Germans.[46] The river also fulfills the philosophical significance of the country path initiated in the "Triadic Conversation." There the path was human made, but nevertheless resulted from a historical and collective endeavor, though this remained concealed from some of its travelers. In the "Western Conversation," the river is naturally occurring, but it also carves a pathway through the forested landscape. It is essentially historical—in Hölderlin's and Heidegger's sense—such that it creates the possibility of the arability of the land and thus of human dwelling in proximity to the gods.[47] And finally, on Heidegger's reading, the river flows backward, toward its source. Where the river geographically runs eastward, in a historical sense it must be understood as flowing to the West. As Bambach puts it, "the Ister's journey eastward from Donaueschingen in the Black Forest to the shores of the Black Sea constitutes the poetic-philosophical journey of spirit as it moves *geographically* from west to east, even as its *historical* journey transpires from East to West."[48] In this way, the river travels in tandem with the historical migration of the fiery philosophical spirit of the Greeks to the most foreign land of German sobriety,[49] with the rising of the sun in the East and setting in the West, and echoes a temporality of healing first elaborated in the "Evening Conversation." Perhaps it is not until the evening [*Abend*] in the West [*Abendland*] that a healing event of the morning can be contended with, experienced as such, and ultimately shared with others in a poetic founding of community. Healing also flows backward, returning to the source of its own needfulness.

ON A SPRING EVENING

The "Western Conversation" takes place as spring is about to become summer. This seasonal turning is significant. The first "Triadic Conversation" took place as summer had just turned to autumn (GA 77: 4/CPC 2). Though the time of year is not remarked upon in either the "Tower Conversation" or the "Evening Conversation," the anguish of the prisoners of war turning into a waitful healing evokes the sense of a harsh winter hinting to resolve into a spring. This leads to the imaginative suggestion that the "Tower Conversation" may take place as autumn is turning to winter, when nighttime conversations are best held indoors, perhaps in a tower room. Heidegger's characters may have come full circle. In the "Western Conversation" they anticipate a renewed summer, when the weather allows them to freely roam even after the sun has set.

The conversational partners are also walking and talking as evening becomes night. In the first of the *Country Path Conversations*, the moment in which evening turned to night informed both crisis and chiasm.[50] In the "Western Conversation," the transition to darkness presents no predicament. The event of nightfall is unremarkable since the river's element is the nighttime, when the river is freed in "the magnanimity of its restraining brightness [*ihrer verhaltenen Helle*]" (GA 75: 62). Night is the river's native element, and this provides a guard against metaphysical representations of time (GA 75: 62). Further, a significant poetic event the conversational partners elucidate in "*Der Ister*" and Hölderlin's Night Songs (GA 75: 96) concerns the "festival in which the day with the night is reconciled" (GA 75: 148). The ostensible clarity of daylight (GA 75: 191), which the "Triadic Conversation" showed metaphysical methodology and historiology craved, is here shown to need the ambiguity of the night's darkness (GA 75: 185) such that learning to think beyond Western metaphysics can find its (conversational) partner in poetizing saying.

Such reconciliation becomes possible in the turning of the evening indicated in the title of the conversation. "*Das abendländische Gespräch*" translates literally to "The Evening-land Conversation." That Heidegger demarcates the West as the "land of evening" shows that its essence lies in its temporal status relative to the history of representational metaphysics, not in a strictly geographical location. The Younger Man tells the Older Man, "the evening land [*Abendland*] is properly the time-place [*Zeitort*] of destiny" (GA 75: 157), which means what is *abendländisch* is "still coming" (GA 75: 157) and is "no object" (GA 75: 158). Only because their conversations are *of*—never *about*—the Western world, the Older Man concludes, "our conversations are let into the Western conversation . . . which only means that we remain waiting in all thinking and are not allowed to presume anything" (GA 75: 158). The West is nothing metaphysically representable. It is a possibility for which they must wait, but never await[51] as a not-yet-present state of affairs.[52] The characters in the "Evening Conversation" also emphasized the importance of waiting, becoming a people whose essence it is to wait, and even to wait in the manner of poetizing (GA 77: 232–33/CPC 151–52), but they were confined to a prisoner of war camp in a foreign land. In the "Western Conversation," these characters are walking and talking not only at the right time—evening—but also in the right place, returning to the homeland after a sojourn in the foreign—along the banks of the river sung into being by the poet of the West.

The *Abend* of the *Abendland* is not the evening of a single day, but rather the twilight of an epoch of a particularly Western form of thinking: the age of representational metaphysics expressed by scientific and technological thinking. The conversational partners are thus concerned by a sense of time Hölderlin helps unfold, which could never be represented by a subject. Evening is a time of defeat and decline, both for metaphysics and for Germany. Yet, as Bambach notes, such an *Untergang* in no way obviates the special role Heidegger, through Hölderlin, ascribes to this destiny: "His inspiration for the shape of this destiny arc of Western thinking closely follows Hölderlin's own scheme of Hesperian destiny as tracing the path of the sun's ascent, reign, decline as a pattern of a day-night-day."[53] Savage also underscores Heidegger's faith in renewal following decline: "Accordingly, and all appearances to the contrary, the Fatherland has not been abandoned in "Das abendländische Gesprach," to be replaced by a Swabian parochialism and/or good Europeanism, but hibernates within the Occident whose fate it has come to share, and whose rejuvenation (or Orientalization) it is entrusted with precipitating."[54] As evening is essentially related to the morning that follows night, the West is—for Heidegger and Hölderlin—essentially related to the East. In the "Western Conversation," Heidegger thinks the East from a distinctly Hölderlinian vantage point,[55] but in his next and final conversation, he contends with the Eastern world[56] more expansively, engaging with a Japanese conversational partner (of his own devising). In some ways, Heidegger attempts to think beyond the Western philosophical tradition. But he is still engaged in a search informed by Hölderlin[57] for the other beginning of the *Western* tradition, refusing to abandon its promise for a "foreign" way of thinking. For all its errancy, Heidegger holds that the *essence* of Western representational metaphysics can be recovered through a pedagogically engaged, poetic thinking.

PEDAGOGICAL TECHNIQUES

The five pedagogical techniques I've traced in the preceding conversations are also found here: reversal, sensitivity to affect, remembering, openness to others, and silence. In what follows, I show that each of these techniques is at work in the "Western Conversation." What is distinct about the appearance of these techniques in the "Western Conversation," however, is that these techniques emerge without any apparent initiation by either character. At last, Heideggerian pedagogy unfolds from out of the event of non-representational, non-metaphysical interpretation of Hölderlin's poetizing that happens firmly *between* the characters and the poetry. In the "Western Conversation," Heidegger sculpts the apogee of his poetic pedagogy because these techniques are finally revealed *as techniques of poetic language itself*, not technologies a particular subject would enact for the purposes of realizing a given objective.

The preceding conversations were devoted to unfolding these techniques as supports for a praxis of non-representational, non-metaphysical thinking. The "Western Conversation" elaborates how this praxis unfolds without recourse to subjectivity or objectivity through poetizing—through the event of language itself. Teaching and learning are ways of letting this event unfold, not analytical practices that transmute this event into measurable outcomes from which knowledge can be derived and disseminated. These pedagogical techniques emerge topographically as dynamics of poetic language while the conversational partners sing with Hölderlin's poetizing through interpretation. This need for interpretation first emerged in the "Evening Conversation," but there the students-become-teachers were not accompanied by Hölderlin's poetry.[58] Strictly speaking, Hölderlin does not play the role of the earlier absent teacher in this alternative iteration of these characters' conversation. Hölderlin remains just as absent in the "Western Conversation" as he was in the "Evening Conversation." Yet because his poetizing resonates across the valley where the river cuts its path, his absence here is even richer.[59] His withdrawal from the conversational partners' company leaves behind traces of his poetizing in his poems for them to learn to interpret.

Poetic Pedagogy

The "Western Conversation" follows the river in the twofold sense already remarked upon. Though this text is the most meandering and unhindered of all of Heidegger's conversations, it is guided by the river as Hölderlin poetizes it. The discussion is nonlinear, dexterous, topographical, and self-referential. As in earlier conversations, these characters seem to anticipate insights they later elaborate, often through referring to quotations of Hölderlin's poetry. Though Heidegger's writing generally declines linear or progressive rhetorical models, this text illustrates this concretely[60] in the characters' interpretive engagement with Hölderlin's poetizing. Though the text is organized by Hölderlin's hymn "*Der Ister*," whenever the characters launch a close reading of a stanza, their efforts lead to a proliferation of engagements with many of Hölderlin's other poems. The conversational partners only manage a close reading of the first stanza, selections of the second stanza, a few points rehearsed in the third stanza, and the closing pair of lines in the fourth stanza. Much of "*Der Ister*" is passed over without direct engagement. But the spirit of the river may not be confined to this single poem.[61] The conversational partners note the resonances between this hymn and Hölderlin's many other poems.[62] For instance, the conversational partners note that "Germania" is a song that "speaks into [*hereinspricht*]" the Ister-song, and the Germania-hymn is "let into [*eingelassen*]" the Ister-song (GA 75: 85) such that their meaning is enigmatically intertwined (GA 75: 86).

What the conversational pedagogy of this text emphasizes in a new and profound way is the essentiality of interpretation for teaching and learning. Of course, the importance of interpretation has extensive precedent in Heidegger's corpus. His abiding interest in hermeneutics extends at least as far back as *Being and Time* and will shortly reemerge in his final conversational text of the 1950s. Between these points in his corpus, it is readily apparent that reading and interpreting Hölderlin's poetry formed the heart of Heidegger's lecture courses on the poet, as well as many essays on Hölderlin's—and other poets including Hebel's, Trakl's, and Rilke's—poems. Heidegger resists buttressing the established industry of disciplinary criticism, which he argues in 1942 is established on metaphysical ground (GA 53: 17–24/16–21). Bambach emphasizes that "what transpires in the dialogue is less something that might be called 'interpretation' than it is a way of entering into the resonance of the word as it sounds in the very dwelling of the Ister. Here the poetic word comes to sound as an appropriating event."[63] Heidegger's interpretation of Hölderlin's poetizing is attempting to learn how to hear its resonating. Such a task demands a decidedly non-representational and non-metaphysical practice of poetic interpretation.

This form of interpretation is what the conversational partners in the "Western Conversation" teach themselves by following the traces of poetizing in Hölderlin's poems. The "Evening Conversation" concluded with the characters outlining a pedagogy of waiting, which meant learning how to teach the unnecessary. To attempt this, the Younger Man urged them to "think of what poetically condenses [*das Dichtende*]" (GA 77: 240/CPC 157). In the renewed setting of the "Western Conversation," these characters do just that, where such a pedagogy is concretely enacted. This attempt does not figure interpretation on the basis of metaphysical representation such that poetry-as-object is deciphered by a subject equipped with a rubric for "the elucidation [*Erläutern*] of stray verses and words" (GA 75: 66). The conversational partners believe they will never "fittingly" understand key words in the poem if they try "to represent and define the word as uniformly representational" (GA 75: 111). Rather, their interpretations strive to unfold the poetic by "sing[ing] with" the "toning" of Hölderlin's poetizing (GA 75: 111). The conversational partners are learning to dwell in this familiar-yet-strange sense of the poetic language of Hölderlin's river song, insisting that it is both "good" (GA 75: 71) to recite Hölderlin's hymn and "good" (GA 75: 110) to non-metaphysically interpret his poetizing.

In the first pages, the conversational partners impart that their hope in their conversation is to encounter how Hölderlin's poetic word "resonates [*schwinge*]"[64] (GA 75: 59) and to learn how to bring their "talk [*Rede*] . . . [into that which] resonates in counter-resonance [*Gegenschwung*] to the saying [*Sagen*] of the singer" (GA 75: 59). Any notion of metaphysically informed interpretation coming to bear is already undermined. Hölderlin's words do not hold still in space and time such that they are representable, but are already involved in movement. Their task is not to arrest this movement to represent its meaning, but to learn how to move in tandem with this poetizing. The Younger Man is worried he may not know for sure when such counter-resonance has been attained (GA 75: 59), but the Older Man is more concerned that "our conversation [*Gespräch*] gets into a resonating [*Schwingen*], that every clarity [*Deutlichkeit*] threatens to over-resonate [*überschwingen*]" (GA 75: 60). The Younger Man responds, "that is why we would surely like only slowly to interpret [*deuten*] what is heard [*das Gehörte*]" (GA 75: 60). They must not allow the metaphysical rubric of representational clarity to overdetermine their interpretation as counter-resonating with what they hear of Hölderlin's poetizing. Otherwise, they will swing past Hölderlin's poetic words. Only after they learn to let themselves resonate in response, the Older Man tells the Younger Man, "conversation is only hearing [*Gespräch ist nur Gehör*]" (GA 75: 190). To speak together of this poetic word, they must first hear it. Interpretation's fundamental posture must be such listening because what emerges in this event is "the freedom of the arrival of an always-other [*Immer-an-deren*]" (GA 75: 65).

The river itself offers an example of how the conversational partners might prepare for the arrival of such alterity.[65] Disabused entirely of the desire for an authoritative teacher to show them the way, the Older Man and the Younger Man follow the river as a "sign"[66] such that they are able, in "following the riverbank path, always only to interpret the river, without naming it [*nennen*] and without thereby having the right to know [*recht zu wissen*] it" (GA 75: 62). This allows the alterity of the river to remain unassailed. The river itself offers an example of such a released letting. The Older Man remarks, "have you not already noticed how sometimes its flow arrives in a rush and then is irresistibly drawn to a quiet patch of bank, where the rock steeply protrudes out of the dark waters, but simultaneously takes itself back into a secluded cove, as it should, whose mild rounding maintains the calmed river in poverty [*im Arm*] so that there in its own depth that which opens itself gladly at such rocky places rests?" (GA 75: 61). The river's flow is not uniform and consistent, but dynamic and self-involved. It first rushes forth, resonating with haste, but then resolves into a calm silence offered by the banks of the river and its rocky coves.[67] As the river resonates and counter-resonates with itself, so the conversational partners must learn not to represents its course, but rather to come into a non-metaphysical counter-resonance with the river's song, including even learning to offer a welcome refuge of silence for such otherness.

Particular to their attempt to interpret the Ister-song is the relation to what the conversational partners call its "grounding tone [*Grundton*]" (GA 75: 68). The characters discuss the grounding tone of various Hölderlinian poems, which means, as the Older Man says, that the poetic "word sounds [*klingt*] to us only out of the sound [*Klang*] of the grounding tone [*Grundton*] of the poem, which is a song" (GA 75: 68). The association of Hölderlin's poetizing with music and what is musical is one of the defining features of this text and one that I explore more fully below. At this point, it is important to note how the Ister-song's grounding tone is exceptional in being so strongly imbued into the first word of the poem that the Older Man notes how, "out of even only the written word and verse, we could never take away the fitting tone [*füglichen Ton*] from 'Now' [»*Jetzt*«]" (GA 75: 68). They need not even speak this written word aloud to find themselves gripped by its grounding tone. Even though the singing of this tone is radically sensual, in their attempt to interpret it, the conversational partners reliably veer away toward other poems. This dynamic illustrates again the enigma of nearness and farness, drawing attention to the Hölderlinian logic of the foreign colony as a necessary stage in a journey to learn how to properly inhabit the ownmost of the homeland.[68] Though the characters acknowledge how "awkward [*unbeholfen*]" (GA 75: 93) some of their interpretive renderings are, they thereby illustrate how counter-resonating does not follow pre-determined standards.

Heidegger's characters here also launch and sustain a critique of representational, metaphysical thinking. Where the "Triadic Conversation" was largely concerned with defining this critique for those resistant to it with only a few pages devoted to collaborative poetizing, in the "Western Conversation" the situation is reversed. The few pages devoted to an explicit critique of representational metaphysics only briefly detour away from the poem (GA 75: 78). The Older Man says that whatever resonates "never lets itself . . . be conceptualized [*be-greifen*], that is, through the grasping [*Griffe*] of mere representation [*Vorstellens*] to take hold of what is always a willful [*willentliches*] representational setting-before-us [*Vor-uns-gestellen*]" (GA 75: 77). The Younger Man earlier notes just such a mistake, where the characters briefly fell into metaphysical, representational thinking *about* thinking and poetizing rather than interpreting Hölderlin's song from out of its resonating (GA 75: 70). Instead of treating "thinking as equivalent to conceptualizing [*das Denken dem Begreifen gleichsetzen*]" (GA 75: 77), they stress that they must decline how conceptualizing claims to "render the clarity of the word; that it is valid to transform the meanings of words into conceptualizations everywhere and thus to render language as unambiguous [*eindeutige*] understanding" (GA 75: 78). They believe they have two choices when faced with the challenge to think of language without concepts: to understand this as a "lack [*ein Mangel*]" or as an instance of releasement or "let[ting] go [*ablassen*] of the assault that takes hold through the grasp [*Griff*] of representation (GA 75: 77).

Language need not be limited to expressing only one meaning. Such a view arises from a representational view of language. As Hölderlin's hymn illustrates, ambiguity is native to poetic language. The fantasy of absolute clarity that would banish all ambiguity to the realm of mere error is generated by metaphysics. Throughout the "Western Conversation," the conversational partners strive to amplify the ambiguity of language. The Older Man tells the Younger Man that a sensitivity to this "poetizing ambiguity is only granted to us when we beforehand hear the word and the saying never as a merely representational statement, but rather experience what essentially occurs in poems in the saying of poetizing" (GA 75: 184). Though their interpretations do construe the meaning of Hölderlin's poems in particular ways, they build out these interpretations through identifying something question-worthy and then working to elucidate it *without* eradicating its essential ambiguity. A conversation—*Gespräch*—also unfolds in this way. In remaining open to the event of language, the conversational partners each interpret and respond differently. In exploring the many meanings that could be drawn from any particular event, the varying responses that unfold in conversation need not be reduced to a single "correct" view, but rather must be allowed to resonate as multifaceted at the risk of erasing the alterity of those with whom one remains in conversation.

Their temporal unfolding is also important for both conversation and poetic interpretation. The Younger Man explains, "only within metaphysics is there the physical [*das Physische*] and the sensual [*Das Sinnliche*] in contrast to the not-physical [*Nicht-Physischen*] and the not-sensual [*Nicht-Sinnlichen*]. Metaphysics is even the prevailing [*Walten*] of this difference" (GA 75: 166). Such a distinction between the sensible and the suprasensible cannot be directly opposed. The Older Man replies to the Younger Man, "I presage after our frequent conversations about metaphysics, that we could not throw this off like a mantle [*wir diese nicht abwerfen können wie einen Mantel*]. We still don't have the fitting relation [*den gemäßen Bezug*] to it at all" (GA 75: 166). The way the conversational partners attempt to come into a fitting, non-oppositional[69] relation to metaphysics is by returning the meaning of time to it. Metaphysics is bound up with and emergent from a certain history, which originates with the Greeks and today is expressed through the representations of science and technology.[70] Heidegger holds that interrogating this distinction may reveal that the typical view of the world based in metaphysics is contingent and ungrounded. These characters must learn to contend with this abyssal[71] sense of ungroundedness, which Heidegger through Hölderlin variously calls "homelessness" or "uncanniness."[72]

Heidegger's characters explore this ungrounding through temporalizing metaphysics. The Younger Man suggests they should endeavor to "think everything sensual [*alles Sinnliche*] as the sensing [*das Sinnende*] and this as the be-spiriting [*Be-geisternde*]" (GA 75: 143). Shifting these terms into the present progressive participle emphasizes what they share in common, which is the way they unfold temporally and participate in the history metaphysics has traced. The ambiguity of poetizing serves to interrupt and resist the metaphysical work of fixing thinking in ostensibly supra-temporalized concepts, to seek instead what the conversational partners call "conceptless [*begriffloses*] thinking" (GA 75: 77). Rather than posit discrete concepts, the verses of the Ister-song "are in no way the signage [*Abschilderung*] of a landscape in the representational material of language [*im Darstellungsmaterial der Sprache*]" (GA 75: 185). Instead, in remarking upon the "beautiful dwelling [*schön Wohnende*]" (GA 75: 185) of the Ister, the verses themselves build a way of inhabiting the temporality opened by its poetizing. This possibility is due to "how wide [*wie weit*] it is around each poetizing word of poets" (GA 75: 189)—wide enough, for instance, to unfold the essential connection between the Ister and "*Der Ister*," showing how Hölderlin's riversong *is* the river, in a non-representational, non-metaphysical sense. The poetic word the conversational partners spend so long exploring is the meaning of the first word of "*Der Ister*"—"Now"—in relation to the word that later describes the desire to build on the river bank—"Here." As poetizing words, they are not demarcating a representational metaphysics of time and space. Rather, in the place they build together, the Younger Man notes that "the expanse [*Weite*] [of the 'Here'] and the abiding-while [*Weile*] [of the 'Now'] greet each other" (GA 75: 74). This expanse is nothing objectively present, but rather only "may abide [*verweilen darf*], so long as it listens to the poem of the poet" (GA 75: 190), that is as long as their interpreting remains in conversation with the poet's poetizing—to attend to the expanse and the abiding-while of that which they think and never to abstract concepts out of what is fundamentally a way of (beautifully) dwelling.

Such interpreting is less a discrete task than a way of learning to think otherwise. For this reason, there is no straightforward way to determine when it is finished. The "Western Conversation" performs this point. The conversation itself is not finished (as Heidegger indicates in a closing note), but instead "breaks off" (GA 75: 194) like the Ister-song. Such a performance echoes the response that the conversational partners have learned to the metaphysical thinking that threatens to overtake their counter-resonating: to attend to what is unfinished in such thinking, namely to an elaboration of its relation to the native habitat of such thought.[73] Their goal with representational, metaphysical thinking is not to finish its purported task—somehow demarcating its ground and inner logic—but rather to break off from it, to recognize how—as a way of thinking that denies its own origins—it is nevertheless "complete" in its fragmentary articulation of itself.

The unfinished quality of the Ister-song is also "precisely completed in this breaking off [*Abbrechen*]" (GA 75: 194), as the Younger Man notes, but not as something that maintains itself as separated from its native expanse, but rather as a poetizing that first animates the possibility of historical time.

Conversational and Musical Interpretation

Many dimensions of the interpretation Heidegger's characters unfold in the "Western Conversation" are found in his other writings on poetry, art, and language. What is distinct about the interpretation here is twofold: first, the conversational style in which it unfolds and second, its emphasis on musicality.

The conversational genre of the "Western Conversation" is the least dramatically significant in Heidegger's conversational corpus. The dramatic significance of the dynamic between the characters recedes before the resonating of Hölderlin's poetizing. Yet the conversational setting of coming into counter-resonance with poetizing subtly underscores the historical importance of collaboratively welcoming such an event. As each of Heidegger's preceding conversations have shown, the various paths they walk have been made possible with and on account of others. In the wake of defeat, Heidegger does not abandon the poet of the Germans, but rather turns to Hölderlin for reassurance and a path forward.[74] This is not meant for Heidegger alone, but for the entire Western, German community. What Heidegger is calling for by enacting such interpreting conversationally is an essentially historical and collaborative response to the event of the Second World War. At times, such conversation makes the mistake of ceding to the dominance of metaphysical ideology. But these mistakes are themselves gifts[75] and invitations to renew releasement toward learning non-representational, non-metaphysical thinking.

In the postwar landscape, Heidegger has become even more convinced that organizing such a pedagogy around Hölderlin's poetizing is vital. What these conversational partners have—unlike any preceding character in the *Country Path Conversations*—is the influence of the grounding tone of Hölderlin's poetizing to guide them. The distinction between cultivating a sensitivity to the resonating of this grounding tone and the "solidity of the letter" (GA 75: 181) of the written poems opens a space that allows the conversational partners to notice this distinction[76] when one spurns the other to hear such resonating differently. In one sense, these conversational partners are conversing with one another. But in another way, their conversation fundamentally remains in "twofold conversation [*Zweigespräch*] . . . with the singing of the singer" (GA 75: 158). The Older Man and the Younger Man are not conversing with Hölderlin as a distinct (pedagogical) figure, but with his singing. The conversation of the "Western Conversation" is fundamentally doubled.

The second distinct aspect of Heidegger's exploration of Hölderlin's poetizing in the text is its emphasis on music and musicality.[77] Where the form of the conversation as a historical and collaborative event evokes the pedagogical techniques of remembering and the import of otherness, the significance of the musical dimensions of Hölderlin's poetizing draws out the importance of sensitivity to affect, reversals, and silence, all of which I elaborate below. Heidegger's turn to musical language permeates the "Western Conversation" and is foreshadowed in the "Evening Conversation" when the Younger Man remarked, "we are like a string instrument [*Saiteninstrument*] of the most ancient provenance, in whose sound [*Klang*] the primordial play of the world resounds [*weiderklingt*]" (GA 77: 227/CPC 148). In the first pages of the "Western Conversation," this string instrument is the "lyre" (GA 75: 60)[78] whose resonance demonstrates how the Ister river serves as a sign for Hölderlin's "*Der Ister*" and vice versa (GA 75: 62). Heidegger's turn to music reaches beyond the depictions of poetry as written verses he offers earlier.[79] Exploring the distinctive *musicality* of Hölderlin's Western poetizing also provides the point from which Heidegger will launch his engagement with photographs, theater, and film of the Eastern world.[80]

The connection Heidegger draws between poetizing and music[81] is amplified in the years following the text's composition. In the 1957 Freiburg Lectures, Heidegger writes, "thinking is in its essence saying. Poetizing is singing. Every singing is a saying, but not every saying a singing" (GA 79: 71/161). Likewise, in "The Essence of Language," delivered in 1957/58, Heidegger writes, "the song is sung, not after it has come to be, but rather: in the singing the song begins to be a song. The song's poet is the singer. Poetry is song. Hölderlin, following the example of the ancients, likes to call poetry 'song'" (GA 12: 171/OWL 77). For Heidegger, song cannot be represented as a metaphysical object. Song can only be song in the event of singing.[82] Further in the same essay, Heidegger writes, "song is not the opposite of a discourse, but rather the most intimate kinship with it; for song, too, is language" (GA 12: 172/OWL 78). It is *language* that poetizing singing and conversation share; its *event* allows both to proceed. This insight is at the heart of Heidegger's "Western Conversation."

For Heidegger, music cannot be surrendered to aesthetics,[83] a metaphysical methodology of representationally studying a particular art form. When considering how to think of beauty in relation to the poem, the Younger Man cautions them against "misplac[ing] the beautiful [*Schöne*] in the αἴσθησις and think[ing] the beautiful aesthetically [*aesthetisch*]," to which the Older Man adds, "you can also say: 'metaphysically'" (GA 75: 175). Relying on aesthetic analysis would be a mistake. However, the conversational partners also acknowledge that the tendency toward "aesthetic exegesis [*Auslegung*]" (GA 75: 176) of the beautiful was helpful because resisting it prompted them to deepen their interpretation of dwelling. Veering toward, and then away from, this mistake further allows them to distinguish a problematic sense of "the aesthetic of viewing and enjoyment [*der Aesthetik des Betrachtens und des Genusses*]" from "the art of poetic saying [*der Kunst des dichterischen Sagens*]" (GA 75: 177). In accepting what the mistake of metaphysical representation drew their attention toward, they are nevertheless able to return to Hölderlin's poetic saying. The pedagogy of mistakes Heidegger began in the "Tower Conversation" finds its felicitous resolution in poetizing.

The "Western Conversation" does not limit its celebration of poetic saying to Hölderlin's poems. In orchestrating this encore of his readings of Hölderlin, Heidegger emphasizes the form of an essential response that listening to such saying-as-musical-singing must take: conversation. This philosophically announces both what is distinct about the "Western Conversation" in Heidegger's work concerning poetizing and in his conversational oeuvre. This conversation is oriented by the characters learning how to counter-resonate [*Gegenschwung*] with the resonating [*Schwung*] of Hölderlin's poetizing. They are learning interpretation, which, as the Older Man says, "consists then in hearing the grounding tone of the resounding-forth [*den Grunton des Anklangs*] and tuning [*stimmen*] all saying to this grounding tone so that it would become a singing [*damit es ein Singen werde*]" (GA 75: 69). Only in carefully allowing the resonating of the grounding tone to become "freer" (GA 75: 60)—through their "interpreting as setting to music [*Deuten als einem Vertonen*]" (GA 75: 69)—is Hölderlin's saying first able to become a singing:[84] "Interpretation is the more originary [*ursprüngliche*] setting to music, through which the poem becomes freed [*wird befreyt*] in its grounding tone" (GA 75: 70). Poetizing's music is essentially collaborative since interpretation itself is in no way derivative of Hölderlin's singing, but rather interpretation is revealed as essentially a "sing[ing] with" (GA 75: 111) Hölderlin's poetizing. This produces not a simple reduplication of the poem, but a *harmonizing* with it. As the Younger Man puts it, "the *resounding*-forth [An-*klang*] turns toward itself to us [*kehrt sich uns zu*] and turns *with* us back to itself into the harmony [*Einklang*], out of which it occurs [*sich ereignet*]" (GA 75: 60).

Pedagogical Topographies of (Musical) Interpretation

In the "Western Conversation," the five pedagogical techniques that recur across Heidegger's corpus of conversational texts are unfolded as elements of non-representational poetizing language, not metaphysical technologies. Poetizing language itself performs these pedagogical techniques. It invites the characters to take part in learning what it has to say, which includes its pregnant silences. This provides the occasion for Heidegger's pedagogy to unfold as inherently poetic and non-metaphysical—inhabiting and animating a locale where humans can dwell in the ambiguity of being, without reducing its meaning to what is legible for representational thinking. In what follows, I show how the "Western Conversation" enacts each technique: reversal, sensitivity to affect, remembrance, openness to others, and silence.

Reversal: Resonating and Counter-Resonating

The importance of reversals in the "Western Conversation" cannot be overstated. At moments, the characters suddenly change the course of their interpretive exchange. These are not guided by the conversational partners so much as enacted by poetizing language itself. For instance, at one point while interpreting several words from the poem the Younger Man says, "it just seemed like the essence of the trial [*Prüfung*] and what is destinal [*Geschicklichen*] was clear to us, as if it was accordingly decided and knowable what is fitting [*Schickliche*]. Suddenly it veils itself all again. I wonder why?" (GA 75: 138). The Younger Man notes a reversal has taken place in their efforts to interpret certain key terms of the Ister-song. Their poetic elucidations had been clear, but suddenly became veiled and obscure. The Older Man responds, "because we too hastily grasp everything and only want to understand, because we always again forget that . . . a long time is needed until what is true occurs [*sich ereignet*]; meanwhile much may happen, which always still is as if it would not concern us, because it does not draw near to us and cannot draw near" (GA 75: 139). This hasty grasping after understanding indicates a resurgence of metaphysical thinking, which can never participate in the enigma of nearness and farness. Whenever representational, metaphysical thinking is activated, that which is poetized reverses course and recedes.

Such instances of representational metaphysics intervening in the conversational partners' efforts in the "Western Conversation" are few and far between. When they do happen, there is an almost seamless reversing between metaphysical and non-metaphysical thinking. This exhibits a non-oppositional relation that allows for the mistake of grasping after understanding something that cannot draw near to the human to instead become the occasion for healing and enacting non-metaphysical thinking anew. This is precisely what occurs when non-metaphysical thinking withdraws at this textual moment. The Younger Man marks that it happened, the Older Man notes why it happened, and the two together move through this pendulum swing and return to interpreting Hölderlin within half of a page. This is a far cry from the reversals the Scientist experienced as violent and fearsome in the "Triadic Conversation." These conversational partners allow this swinging movement *between* metaphysical and non-metaphysical thinking to unfold, almost as if it were as natural as the coming and going of the tide.

Though this particular mistake is rare in the "Western Conversation," such reversing movement recurs in different ways. The most obvious site of reversal is the Ister itself. As was evident in the earlier lecture courses,[85] Heidegger understands the river to flow backward, as does Hölderlin. The Older Man notes, "the waters of this river always again flow back [*zurückfleißen*] to the source [*der Quelle zu*]" (GA 75: 64). In flowing backward toward its origin, the river only creates a locale by charting a course through Europe. In demarcating the East from the West and making the land arable for human habitation, the river also occasions the historical relation between Greece and Germany whereby Eastern, Greek thinking acts as a properly historical origin for Western, German thinking. This historical origin is both that from which it sprang *and* that which remains outstanding in its future. In this way, Hölderlin offers a historical, poetic geography as the essence of the riversong.[86]

Just as the river's flow enacts a reversal—flowing out and forth but also back to its source—so too does the poetizing song of the river resonate as an intensification of this very sense of reversal. These are not separate occurrences. As Heidegger insists, "*Der Ister*" *is* the river. Hölderlin's song does not represent the river through metaphor or any other representative symbolic function of language. It poetizes the river's essence (GA 53: 17–23/16–21) and reveals a non-metaphysical relation of selfsameness between the river and the riversong. The "Western Conversation" shows that the conversational partners' interpretive "sing[ing] with" (GA 75: 111) also resonates with the riversong's poetizing of the river's essence, intensifying it even more without seeking a "clarity [*Deutlichkeit*] [that] threatens to over-resonate [*überschwingen*]" (GA 75: 60). The riversong's poetizing and the characters' interpretive singing with this poetizing enable the river's essence to swing back and forth across the Upper Danube Valley, itself enacting a reversal.

In the opening line of the "Western Conversation," the Younger Man describes Hölderlin's saying as the word that "resonates [*schwinge*] in the gleaming valley over the hesitating river between the waitful forests, in the evening of a gracious day in the approaching summer" (GA 75: 59). This resonating of poetizing saying swings out from and returns back to its origin, always moving by reversing its movement, which is only intensified by emphasizing its locality and temporality. Ziarek offers the following depiction of the meaning of this resonating momentum—as he calls it—of poetic language: "This momentum—the way of language into language's appearance as words or signs—is always and already underway *as* language . . . This experience with language is occasioned not simply out of interest in poetry, let alone literary criticism or interpretation, but for the sake of thinking. What matters in the experience with language undergone through encounters with poetry is the opening onto the possibility of a different, nonmetaphysical language *of* and *in* thinking."[87] The momentum this non-metaphysical thinking of language and of being is attuned to is the proliferation of reversals that constitute the resonating of poetizing. These reversals are what allow language to release itself through acknowledging "how wide [*wie weit*] it is around each poetizing word of poets [*um jedes dichtende Wort des Dichters*]" (GA 75: 189), wide enough to unfold a non-metaphysical geography and history of the valley where it resonates already in the first lines of the "Western Conversation."

Affect: Non-Metaphysical Love

In the *Country Path Conversations*, the conversational partners touched upon the relevance of affects such as fear, anxiety, wonder, the uncanny, and pain, but also the feeling of being healed whenever calm releasement prevailed in their conversations. In the "Western Conversation," affects proliferate. The Scientist's major accomplishment in the "Triadic Conversation" consisted in transitioning from fear to anxiety and then (only in the final pages) into a trusting, collaborative poetizing with his conversational partners. In this text, anxiety resolves into trust in the very first pages (GA 75: 59–60). From the posture of "inexplicable trust [*unerklärlichen Vertrauen*]" (GA 75: 60) and guided by the river itself, the Older Man and the Younger Man find their way "into a resonating [*gelangt in ein Schwingen*]" (GA 75: 60) with the Ister-song. Where the characters in the "Tower Conversation" grappled with the distinction between wonder and the strange, in the "Western Conversation," wonder is not even mentioned here. Instead, the "strange" appears repeatedly (GA 75: 74, 86, 103, 184, and 189) and attends to the non-metaphysical sense of Hölderlin's poetizing in place of the "fright" (GA 75: 86) that had attended the withdrawal of metaphysical thinking for the Scientist. Allowing the strange to emerge through letting go of fear is, as in the "Tower Conversation," here again described as "good [*gut*]" (GA 75: 88).

The "Western Conversation" does more than echo the relation unfolding between non-representational, non-metaphysical thinking and feeling found in previous conversations. It introduces a new set of affects anchored by love, liking, and mania. Heidegger rarely discusses these affective states,[88] but such a constellation is also found in Plato's *Phaedrus*.[89] The importance of love is established in the text's opening pages. The conversational partners associate what they call "erstwhile love [*einstige Liebe*]" with a released, historical[90] sense of the river's essence. Responding to the Younger Man's evocation of this term, the Older Man says, "erstwhile love, which can release itself to let in [*sich gelassen einlassen kann*] what has been formerly and comes in the future" (GA 75: 64). This erstwhile love is the river's very temporal element that, as the Younger Man continues, "blows through our hearts [*Herz*] and blows away all willing [*Wollen*] in releasement [*Gelassenheit*] toward the favor [*Huld*] that all essence frees [*be-freyt*]" (GA 75: 64). This released, erstwhile love is further associated with mania, which defines love as such: "In this mania [*Irre*] we seem to belong . . . Would you like to dare [*wagen*] to name a measured [*maßvolle*] and calculated [*bemessene*] love as love?" (GA 75: 67). The mania of what must be a measureless and non-calculative love is essential for turning away from representational, metaphysical thinking. Such a turn sometimes requires "thanking" (GA 75: 67) and at other times "anger" (GA 75: 123) to sustain.

Such love capacitates releasement into "the expanse [*Weite*] of heart space [*des Herzraumes*]" (GA 75: 139). Poetically playing on etymological relations, in a few lines of the Ister-song the characters note the resonances between "capacity [*Vermögen*]," "to like [*mögen*]" and "to love [*lieben*]" (GA 75: 87). They determine that the meaning of "to like" [*mögen*] is probably double: both capacity [*Vermögen*] as "ability" and in the sense of "gladly have," or "to love" [*lieben*] (GA 75: 87). This secures the significance of such affects for capacitating the interpretation of Hölderlin's poetizing.[91] Feeling is not secondary to thinking or willing but is equally needful.[92] In love, the characters learn to open themselves up and reach out to what is *not* (in a metaphysical sense), but rather *is* only always already still *coming* as erstwhile and historical. As the Younger Man remarks, "we first love that, for which we reach [*gelangen*] and what we would like to gain [*Erlangen*]. Without the liking of love, we are capable of [*vermörgen*] nothing" (GA 75: 89). What love enables is their reaching toward a non-representational, non-metaphysical inhabitation of the resonating of Hölderlin's singing.

Remembrance: The Destiny of the (German) People

The importance of remembrance permeates the "Western Conversation."[93] Topics that arise early in the "Western Conversation" are initially left behind, but later reprised. This illustrates the importance of the historical sense of time the conversational partners are learning to inhabit, where what "has been" remains yet outstanding in their future.[94] For example, death appears early, as an instance of the inceptual (GA 75: 59–60). The importance of death is then recalled many pages later, when the conversational partners endeavor to interpret the closing stanza of the poem "Tears" (GA 75: 130). Likewise, love is found in the earliest pages of the conversation (GA 75: 64 and 67), only to be set aside until they need to continue reflecting on the meaning of love in the context of interpreting several of Hölderlin's lines (GA 75: 87, 88, 89, 90, and 110–35).

The characters also take moments to retrace their steps, attempting to recapitulate their own conversational journey at points, as did the conversational partners in the "Triadic Conversation."[95] In settling whether they have adequately determined the essence of "what is fitting [*Schiklichen*]" (GA 75: 95), the Younger Man offers a brief recapitulation, summarizing their conversation on the topic up to that point. However, in distinction from the Scientist's and the Scholar's attempts to summarize their discussion with *precision*, the Younger Man immediately also recognizes that attempting this kind of remembering, namely one that replicates exactly where they had just been, may be itself "an impossible plan [*Vorhaben*]" (GA 75: 95). It is not possible to simply extract the definition of what is fitting out of its contextual locale, "because the destining [*Schicken*] and that which is fittingly destined [*Geschickte*] and what is fitting [*Schickliche*] essentially occur [*wesen*] and therefore are only to be thought from out of this" (GA 75:

95). This remembering must remain within its proper place, which means it can never take the form of an extracted summary.

Such remembrance arises, in the "Western Conversation," as a call to listen to the singing of Hölderlin's poetizing. The word "remember [andenken]" is most reliably uttered[96] when the conversational partners introduce Hölderlin's poetry.[97] They also frequently recall particular lines or figures from the poems by calling on each another to *remember* the " 'fitting hands' of the singer" (GA 75: 162) or the "eagle"[98] (GA 75: 89 and 161). As the conversational partners first come to terms with interpreting Hölderlin's poetizing in this way, the Older Man asks, "are we walking along on the bank of the river toward its source in the evening light because the river-song of the poet has brought us here or do we only recall the Ister-Song because we have somehow reached the valley of the river?" (GA 75: 63). The Younger Man replies that neither is causal in the sense of realizing a metaphysical effect. Rather, it is the "selfsame" of the "singing of the river" and their being "here on its bank," which occasions the "letting [*Lassen*] as an allowing [*Zu-lassen*] that something matters [*daß etwas angeht*]" (GA 75: 63–64) with which their interpretation counter-resonates. It is not the (meta)physical location that incites them to recall Hölderlin's poems, nor are those poems recalled as artifacts of the past affixed in their memories. Rather, poetic remembrance unfolds in opening the possibility of thinking of space and time otherwise, as the first stanza of the Ister-Song does with its senses of "Here" and "Now" that occasion its selfsameness with the river.

For Heidegger's conversational partners, Hölderlin is a historical poet, one whose poetry is remembered *as* futural as it swings back and forth across the Upper Danube Valley and throughout the history of the people related to this place of dwelling. Who are these people, exactly? In his lectures, Heidegger called Hölderlin the poet of the Germans.[99] Heidegger's disavowal of nationalistic conceptions of what it means to be a people at the conclusion of the "Evening Conversation" may suggest that Heidegger has reconsidered this earlier pronouncement. As Savage notes, the *Abendland*—or occident—takes the place in this text that had previously been fulfilled by Germany in Heidegger's Hölderlin interpretations.[100] Indeed, the word "German" hardly appears in the "Western Conversation," except when interpreting a line from Hölderlin's "The Journey" (GA 75: 191). However, the absence of a particular term does not mean that its significance has faded. Bambach argues instead that the "Western Conversation" is an underground postwar protest, which aims at supporting "a Hölderlinian vision of German nationalism that presents the George Circle's suppressed dream of a secret Germany to fit the new postwar realities of an emasculated German *Volk* forced to accept the new victor's justice imposed by the occupying Allied powers."[101] Even though Heidegger here writes about the destiny of the West, Bambach contends that Heidegger is still essentially concerned with *German* destiny,[102] particularly whether the Germans are "chosen [*auserwählt*]" (GA 75: 98) to survive the "trial [*Prüfung*]" (GA 75: 135–37) facing them, in order to participate in the "great destiny of our land [*große Geschick unseres Landes*]" (GA 75: 105). For the conversational partners, "Hölderlin remembers the great destiny [*an das große Geschick denkt*]" (GA 75: 109). If they succeed in withstanding the poverty facing them, they too will become those (Germans) who can remember Hölderlin's futural, destinal poetizing.

Openness to the (Poetic) Other

Though it is (still) the Germans who are capable of this remembering in this text, it remains to be decided what it means to be "German" for Heidegger. Through learning how to counter-resonate with Hölderlin's poetizing, the conversational partners sense that they must learn to remember who they could (or even should) be as distinctly *other* than what they actually metaphysically are. As becomes apparent, part of what it means to become non-metaphysically German is to embark on a journey into the foreign of what is strange and other.

In the *Country Path Conversations*, one (or more) of the characters learning to enact proper openness to others served as centrally dramatically important. But from the outset of the "Western Conversation," the conversational partners are already remarkably open with and attuned to one another. They are not trying to learn releasement toward one another. The otherness with which they are trying to properly relate is the resonating of Hölderlin's riversong. The conversational partners understand they cannot interpret this poetizing directly as a metaphysical object: "[It is] almost like we should be prevented [*abgehalten*] from interpreting the river song immediately [*unmittelbar*]" (GA 75: 64). What arrives in interpretation is not a "correct" assessment of the poet's meaning. Rather, "interpreting is only replying [*Entgegnung*]" (GA 75: 65) as "a repeated-sign [*Wieder-Zeichen*], a repeated bringing back [*ein Wiederzurückbringen*] of what the sign gives away as a gift [*verschenkt*]" (GA 75: 65). What arrives is not the identical poem, but instead "more abiding remains the freedom of the arrival of an always-other [*Immer-an-deren*]" (GA 75: 65).

It is this always-other(ness) of poetizing with which non-representational, non-metaphysical interpretation harmonizes. The "repetition [*Wieder-holen*]" (GA 75: 65) of the alterity of what is poetized *as* other is why the conversational partners insist that "harmony [*Einklang*] never lets itself and what also resounds of it [*was ihm erklingt*] be conceptualized [*be-greifen*], that is to take hold of what is always a willful representational setting-before-us [*Vor-uns-gestellen*] through the grasping [*Griffe*] of mere representation [*Vorstellens*]" (GA 75: 76–77). For representational metaphysics, "a thinking that escapes the terms of conceptualizing seems to be a thoughtless thinking [*ein gedankenloses Denken*], whose inner impossibility lies out in the open" (GA 75: 77). It is impossible if non-representational, non-metaphysical thinking is understood as a "a lack [*ein Mangel*], an incapacity" (GA 75: 77). While this may be "correct," it is not true. Instead, it is a released "letting go . . . [which] springs from a capability, namely a capacity that would draw near to the non-conceptualizing in a different way [*anders nahe*] than by seizing the conceptualization [*Ansichreißen im Begriff*]" (GA 75: 77). Drawing nearer to what is inherently and radically other[103] is the different way this poetic interpretation seeks to capacitate. As the Younger Man later insists, this "difference must appear differently and announce itself to us . . . [through a] wholly different claim [*Anspruch*], which begins to resound [*erklingt*] in the singing of the poet [*im Gesang des Dichters*]" (GA 75: 81). Even difference can come to be thought differently, when it draws nearer in the alterity of poetizing.

Poetic difference is the way opened—the river's way [*Stromweg*], no longer the country path's way [*Feldweg*],—through which the otherwise-than-metaphysical draws near. This is described and performatively illustrated in the "Western Conversation." When the conversational partners begin to interpret "*Der Ister*" in earnest—exploring the meaning of the first line: "Now come, fire!"—the Older Man finds that "meanwhile a different [*anderer*] verse flashed out to me . . . , which I still now can only hear in a sounding-together [*Zusammenklang*] with the first" (GA 75: 73)—the final line in the first stanza: "Here, however, we want to build." They cannot immediately approach the riversong,[104] but rather the poetizing performs its own alterity by sending its interpreters away, not only from a particular line in "*Der Ister*" to another verse, but even eventually away from this particular poem entirely, to a multitude of other Hölderlinian poems, which are mutually needful of one another to properly resonate. This is further elucidated by the conversational partner's reflections on how Hölderlin's words "have a different weight [*ein anderes Gewicht*], because no matter how soft they sound [*so sanft sie auch klingen*], they nevertheless resound [*erklingen*] out of the abyssal grounding tone [*aus dem abgründigen Grundton*]" (GA 75: 96). This weight echoes the "abyssal sensual essence" (GA 75: 105) of poetizing, which capacitates non-representational, non-metaphysical thinking.

The essential otherness of poetizing unfolds in at least two ways in the "Western Conversation." On the one hand, the "other" of Hölderlin's poetizing is different. Not only is it different from representational, metaphysical thinking, but it is also self-different. The sensuousness of poetizing cannot be objectified because it is essentially related to its proper locale, which is other to it, and opens up the "proper realm [*Eigentum*]" (GA 75: 189) in which it can dwell. This shows that, on the other hand, this alterity is inherently related to plurality. For poetizing to *be* what it is, it is also what is *other* to it. This means that it itself is a plurality and is so by means of which a (plural) people is founded non-nationalistically. This community—enabled by a self-othering poetizing—finds its own proper realm because it has first sojourned in what is foreign to it. This is a sustained theme in Heidegger's readings of Hölderlin, yet it is not clear Heidegger ever truly comes to terms with it.[105] In the "Western Conversation," the characters concur that Western destiny can only be named "in difference to an other" (GA 75: 141), namely the East. For Hölderlin, the "'Eastern' [»*Morgenländische*«]" (GA 75: 141) is Greece. As I will show, Heidegger broadens his travels, considering East Asian thinking as a future potential foreign site in his final conversation.

Silence: Poetic Punctuation

Silence may be the most philosophically significant pedagogical technique Heidegger elaborates in the "Western Conversation." Beginning with its small but potent role in the "Triadic Conversation," silence gains in importance over the course of Heidegger's conversations, here reaching its epitome. In the locale cleared by the resonating of poetizing language, Heidegger shows the ambiguity of the poetic word is only possible because it guards a silence about its meaning. Hölderlin's poetic words bring with them their own width (GA 75: 189), gesturing toward the silence through which their resonating is first enabled, and inviting an even more receptive listening out of which conversation may be kindled (GA 75: 190).

The conversational partners remark upon specific instances in which silence is significant in Hölderlin's poems. In responding to some lines from "Bread and Wine," the Older Man notes how "being brought to rest

[*Beruhen*] . . . only prevails freely, when it is silent [*still*] on the earth" (GA 75: 126). For Hölderlin, it is necessary that a certain silence holds sway for the bridal festival between the demi-gods and the mortals. When the conversational partners later return to the poem "But When the Heavenly . . ." silence resounds again. The Younger Man remarks how "in this silence [*In dieser Stille*] the festive [*Festliche*] unfolds and calls all into blooming," which means that "fate is balanced [*ausgeglichen das Schicksal*]" (GA 75: 156). In the elegy "Homecoming," they remark how the "highest god . . . dwells alone in silence [*in der Stille*]" (GA 75: 181). Silence is poetized repeatedly in Hölderlin's poems.

But silence is more than a poetic theme under investigation. It is the very *medium* of poetizing itself insofar as it does not state its meaning unambiguously. As the Older Man says, "poetizing ambiguity [*dichtende Vieldeutigkeit*] is only granted to us [*gewährt sich uns*] when beforehand we hear the word and the saying never as a merely representational statement, but rather experience [*erfahren*] what essentially occurs of poems in the saying of poetizing" (GA 75: 184). To hear poetizing ambiguity as non-representational and non-metaphysical is to attend not only to *what* it says, but also to it as *capable* of saying what the Younger Man calls "a silent word [*ein verschweigendes Wort*]" (GA 75: 109). Silent words poetize through alethic concealing. Those who would learn to sing with the resonating of such poetizing are first let into non-representational, non-metaphysical thinking through listening as much to what is *not*, that is to the "abyssal essence of the sensuality of the word and of language [*das abgründige Wesen der Sinnlichkeit des Wortes und der Sprache*]" (GA 75: 105).

Beyond learning to listen to—and thus entering into conversation with—what metaphysically does not exist by attending to the ambiguity of poetic words, the conversational partners also show how language points to its sensuality through the spaces *between* words. At one point, Heidegger inserts a full break between two lines the Older Man speaks in response to the Younger Man's development of a sense of "relation [*Verhältnis*]" (GA 75: 61) that is non-metaphysical:

> OLDER MAN: Then the human essence would be nearer to the relation that holds and maintains everything, nearer to it than anything that otherwise still may "be."
>
> But take heed, we are already again talking in the resonating of an objectless, non-representational saying and would rather like to interpret what is heard. (GA 75: 61)

The silence of this line break is itself ambiguous and multifaceted. It opens a moment for the Older Man to listen to what he has just said, to enter into a kind of conversation with himself, and recognize the possibility that he has made a mistake in not properly heeding Hölderlin's poetizing. This allows him to call them both back toward such listening. This is not the only line break in the "Western Conversation." Later, the Younger Man also allows himself a moment to keep silent between quoting several lines from the first stanza of "*Der Ister.*" This performs a point they notice about the riversong itself. In its first stanza, it "so sharply names the 'Now' and the 'Here' but nevertheless still remains silent [*verschweigt*] about the Ister and only speaks of distant rivers, of the '*Indus*' and the '*Alpheus.*'" (GA 75: 74). *Der Ister* remains silent about the Ister.

The riversong guards its own essence in silence. These silences—both explicit in Hölderlin's poetizing and embedded between the characters' lines—newly amplify the musicality of the riversong, which can only build a rhythmic sense of time through the silences between its tonings. Nowhere is this more apparent than in the reading the characters give of the beginning of the second stanza of Hölderlin's "*Der Ister*" that emphasizes the silence garnered by its punctuation. Before the Younger Man speaks these lines again, he remarks, "we would do well to hear the verses anew, in which we pay attention to the tone and the pauses of sound, noted through the punctuation mark," specifically the work of a "semicolon" (GA 75: 178). The poetic work of punctuation is eminently more than grammatical. It functions as musical notation, accentuating harmony or dissonance, and above all draws the ear toward the spaces *between* words—to the ambiguity of rhythmic silence—as it unfolds within the lines of a poem and between those who would engage in conversation with one another.

Learning to Poetize the (East and) West

The "Western Conversation" unfolds the apogee of Heidegger's poetic pedagogy. In this text, two characters bereft of any particular teaching figure nevertheless manage to teach themselves to think beyond representational metaphysics through counter-resonating in conversational response to Hölderlin's resonating poetizing. A Heideggerian dynamic of teaching and learning would not be possible without a sense of language as ambiguous and multifaceted, which the poetic embodies. The pedagogical techniques that have appeared in Heidegger's conversations are finally elaborated as ways in which a non-representational, non-metaphysical thinking reveals itself in poetizing language.

And yet the "Western Conversation" is the dream that follows the reality of the "Evening Conversation." The possibility of this pedagogy is both yet-to-come and not-yet-arrived. Their conversation is preparatory for the climb they may make together next time, up to the "narrow peak of the highest cliff . . . [that will show] the open of the river's way, which you only enter if you have recognized *the* way in [*wenn du* den *Weg erkannt hast*] and know it from indwelling [*Innestehen*]" (GA 75: 60). Much still remains to learn once Heidegger returns to reality. Yet, in another way, the "Western Conversation" contests facile distinctions between dream and reality. Perhaps the "Evening Conversation" is a fantasy in which prisoners of war can engage in philosophical conversations and the "Western Conversation" portrays Heidegger's own reality of escape into scholarly work, which sharply contrasts with the realities of many others who did—or did not—survive the war. The Shoah was mobilized through propaganda that harnessed certain interpretations of Hölderlin's poetry to cultivate a fascistic German identity.[106]

In ways Heidegger both does and does not seem to realize, attempting to enact this poetic pedagogy ought to entail acute care to discern where and when it is appropriate. It should attend to harms that may result from avenues foreclosed along the way. In other words, the proper *limits* of this poetic pedagogy must be ascertained. In the "Western Conversation," Heidegger broached the relation of the West to the East (GA 75: 141). For Heidegger's Hölderlin, an exploration of this relation is constricted by a specific historical connection between the Greeks and the Germans. However, for the colonial and imperial history of the Western project of globalization, this has meant something quite different. The idea that colonies are "daughters of the motherland" (GA 75: 147) has many disturbing implications vis-à-vis the oppression organized by colonialism, racism, patriarchy, misogyny, and capitalism. Yet for Heidegger, the destinal sending Hölderlin poetizes in "*Der Ister*" is one that travels from the East to the West and therefore essentially involves them both. There are not two destinies at stake, but one. It is to the East that Heidegger turns next, or rather the conception of the East that he summons.

5

"From a Conversation of Language"
Endangering Pedagogy

Heidegger's final conversational text[1] concerns danger.[2] It is not about metaphysical danger. That is, it does not stage an exchange in which subjects discuss danger as an object. The danger it is concerned with cannot be objectified because it is always already at play, influencing what could even come forth to appear as dangerous in the first place. Heidegger is concerned with a danger that has already endangered those who would speak of it and continues to endanger them as conversation unfolds. In his first conversation, the "greatest danger" was "for a human to ever be called wise" (GA 77: 84/CPC 53). In his final conversation, danger threatens in a new way. Heidegger here engages with Eastern—specifically Japanese—thinking, culture, and language. Though this is not the only instance in his conversations where Heidegger draws from the Eastern world,[3] it does represent his most sustained encounter with this particular form of alterity in his conversational oeuvre. Its very openness to this alterity endangers the conversation from the outset. Until this point, the otherness Heidegger's pedagogy engaged emerged from the Western philosophical tradition and has therefore shared a philosophically idiomatic origin in representational metaphysics. Such a shared origin can no longer be presumed, even in the face of what these characters call the threatening of "complete Europeanization of the earth and of man" (GA 12: 98/OWL 15).

Much is at stake in this text. It offers a rich account of the oft debated turn from Heidegger's early interests in phenomenology[4] and hermeneutics to his later thinking of ontology and language. The title of this text—"*Aus einem Gespräch von der Sprache: Zwischen einiem Japaner und einem Fragenden*"[5]—indicates a distinct emphasis on Heidegger's thinking of language. Hertz has translated the title: "A Dialogue on Language between a Japanese and an Inquirer."[6] Parkes disputes this rendering, suggesting instead the title ought to be translated "From a Conversation on Language: Between a Japanese and an Inquirer":

> The assonance between the words *Gespräch* and *Sprache* intimates a close connection between the conversation and its concern. More important is that the conversation is not *über* but "*von der Sprache*": the *von* is ambiguous and suggests that the conversation is as much (or more) *from* or by language as it is about it. The interlocutors strive to avoid speaking *about* language, trying rather to let the conversation be led by and issue from out of the essential being of language itself (*vom Wesen der Sprache her*).[7]

Davis has translated the title simply as "A Conversation on Language between a Japanese and an Inquirer,"[8] though he states he would be comfortable using dialogue or conversation, "both because 'conversation' does not literally translate *Gespräch*[9] and because I am not convinced that 'dialogue' necessarily implies a problematic sense of intersubjectivity."[10]

For a text in which the question of translation is centrally at issue, I find this manifold of renderings apt. I translate the title "From a Conversation of Language between a Japanese and a Questioner."[11] I construe the prepositions as "from" and "of," respectively, to indicate that the task at hand is not to converse *about* language, as Parkes also stresses, but rather to let the conversation that language is engaged in with itself[12] draw near of its own accord. I continue to use "conversation" to translate *Gespräch*[13] because of Heidegger's own differentiation between *Dialog* and *Gespräch* (GA 77: 56–57/CPC 36–37) and the anxiety he expressed over being compared to Plato in his letters.[14] For Heidegger, *Dialog* is inextricably tied up with the Western philosophical tradition. Finally, though "Inquirer" is a fine translation of "*einer Fragender*," I choose to render this term "Questioner" to signal the connection between this character's name and the strange relation between questions and answers discussed in the "Triadic Conversation" (GA 77: 22–23/CPC 14–15). There is no definitive answer as to whether the danger of conversation between a Westerner and an Easterner can ever been resolved. As I will show, it is the *lack* of such an answer that allows the Questioner to continue unfolding his questioning along pedagogical lines.

On East-West Conversation

Many avenues may lead to "Conversation of Language." Those interested in cross-cultural dialogue or comparative philosophy have found Heidegger's engagement with East Asian themes ripe for consideration. There are generally three positions scholars have taken regarding Heidegger and intercultural exchange. Following Vetsch,[15] some have suggested Heidegger's work is paradigmatic of successful East-West exchange. In contrast, Ma[16] has argued Heidegger's work on East Asia advances the cultural appropriation of Western hegemony.[17] Davis[18] has attempted to forge a middle way, highlighting Heidegger's awareness of his lack of competence with Asian texts and tendencies toward Eurocentrism while noting how his ideas find resonances with elements of Eastern thought and certain Eastern thinkers. Heidegger was influenced by the Eastern tradition in certain instances,[19] but the extent to which this influence prompted a genuine attempt at cross-cultural philosophizing is still contested.[20] For instance, of "Conversation of Language," Ma writes, "in the latter half of this text, it *looks* as if East and West have entered into a 'deep-level' dialogue in the same mode as what he delineates as authentic *Gespräch*,"[21] but she concludes this appearance is deceiving. Against commentators such as Mehta,[22] Vetsch, Prins,[23] and May, Ma argues Heidegger fails to stage a genuine interchange between these two philosophical and cultural contexts.

In other contexts, Heidegger develops what could be understood as highly creative readings of philosophy and poetry over the course of his career.[24] That this proclivity for taking interpretive license—motivated though it was by the demands of non-representational, non-metaphysical thinking—extends to philosophically salient ideas and terms found outside the Western philosophical tradition (or the more restricted domain of German cultural history) can easily be construed as remarkably brazen, if not wildly irresponsible. While topics of East Asian origin are at play in "Conversation of Language," many more themes drawn from the German culture, the Western philosophical tradition, and a stylized version of Heidegger's own personal history permeate this text, down to the very language of its composition. The Japanese and East Asian references that do appear range from slightly misconstrued to patently distorted.

Comparative studies of the status of Eastern thought for Heidegger and the import of Heidegger for Eastern thinkers represent crucial and important scholarly efforts.[25] The importance of the particularity of the Eastern alterity at stake in this text cannot be overstated. However, my own reading does not seek to make a direct contribution to this body of scholarship. Rather, I approach "Conversation of Language" by way of Heidegger's preceding conversations, with a concern to elaborate the pedagogy at work in these texts. Heidegger may aspire to cross-cultural exchange, but a pedagogy of such exchange must be at work. Each conversational partner must teach their own world and learn the other's world for the sake of such an endeavor. I read "Conversation of Language" as an instance of conversation that is pedagogical in essence and relies on the pedagogical techniques at play in his other conversations, especially openness to the alterity of the other. The importance of properly relating to otherness comes into even sharper focus. "Conversation of Language" functions, I argue, as a coda to Heidegger's conversational oeuvre, one that urges a heightened awareness not only to the limits of representational, metaphysical thinking, but also to the proper limits of the poetic, conversational pedagogy Heidegger himself has been cultivating. This final installment suggests revisions of each preceding conversational text and, in certain instances, demonstrates Heidegger's failure to enact his own pedagogy.

Where the "Triadic Conversation" originated in strident disagreement and resolved into collaborative poetizing, "Conversation of Language" unfolds for conversational partners who are already speaking out of an accord with one another. In this text, their apparent *agreement* becomes potentially problematic, underscoring the importance of listening beyond this accord. The "Tower Conversation" exemplified a pedagogy of making mistakes. While here Heidegger emphasizes how dangerous cross-cultural conversation can be, he himself makes several mistakes in attempting to relate to the East, likely inadvertently demonstrating how in need of continually learning his own lesson he still is. The third "Evening Conversation" depicted how students-become-teachers learn to teach themselves in a confined and impoverished state. The "Conversation of Language" explores how even professional teachers must strive to remain students of one another, and to continue to acknowledge when they have reached the outer limits of their pedagogical fluency. Finally, the "Western Conversation" recast the "Evening Conversation," not in a prisoner of war camp in a foreign land, but in the heart of the German homeland—the Upper Danube Valley—and unfolded the possibility of a poetizing that attends to the silence that the conversation embodied in Hölderlin's poetry enables. "Conversation of Language" revisits this question of the homeland and reconsiders whether non-representational, non-metaphysical thinking is only possible for or from within the Western tradition.

"Conversation of Language" is the outlier in Heidegger's conversational oeuvre—an afterthought to the apogee of poetic pedagogy celebrated in the "Western Conversation." But it is one that nevertheless demonstrates the necessary risk the historically and culturally specific poetic pedagogy of the "Western Conversation" runs when it meets radical alterity, specifically the alterity of the East. As I will show, the Eurocentric[26] mistakes Heidegger makes in this text provide the occasion to flesh out the implications of his pedagogy much more fully than Heidegger ever did explicitly.

In this conversation, two professional teachers spend time reflecting together. These characters both teach their students many of the same texts from the German tradition. They are pedagogically related to one another by an absent, third figure who was a student to one character (the Questioner) and teacher to the other (the Japanese). They also teach and learn from one another at many points. Thus, pedagogy is vital in this text. On the one hand, "Conversation of Language" could be taken as a radical triumph of the poetic, conversational pedagogy Heidegger has been honing across his conversational corpus. But this would be too hasty. I instead argue for reading "Conversation of Language" as a text in which Heidegger—intentionally or not—enhances the danger of poetic, conversational pedagogy. The danger lies not only in the apparent distance between the Western and Eastern worlds. It is particularly enhanced when *agreement* between the two characters has been (apparently) reached. Representational, metaphysical thinking erases its own alterity, purporting to be self-identical and universal. The thinking supported by conversational, poetic pedagogy instead attends to that which is *excessive* in its self-difference as self-sameness. Sustaining such thinking even when a conversation seems successful proves even more difficult and is thereby dangerous in the extreme.

Conversational Context

(Three) Professional Teachers Meet

The characters of "Conversation of Language" differ from Heidegger's previous characters. They are locatable within distinct intellectual, social, and political milieus. Both are scholars and teachers at a university, but they come from different cultural backgrounds, speak different native languages, and are citizens of different countries. They are both fictional characters who nevertheless resemble real, historical people. Their intellectual genealogies became entangled because of a pedagogical relationship each character shares with a third, absent figure: "Kuki." Kuki has died, but his thinking efforts continue to permeate the conversation that takes place between his former teacher, "a Questioner [*einer Fragender*]," and his former student, "a Japanese [*einer Japaner*]."

Kuki is not merely a fictional character in "Conversation of Language." The Baron Kuki Shūzō (1888–1941) was a Japanese philosopher in his own right. He was the first scholar anywhere in the world to publish a book on Heidegger's work in 1933: *Haidegga no tetsugaku* or *The Philosophy of Heidegger*.[27] He introduced many other Japanese philosophers to Heidegger.[28] Baron Kuki spent almost eight years in Europe studying with Rickert, Husserl, Heidegger, and Bergson.[29] He met Sartre during his academic tour and was perhaps the first to introduce Sartre to Heidegger's work.[30] As a philosopher, Kuki worked on topics including time, repetition, contingency, art, and the Japanese notion of *iki*.

The fictionalized character Kuki is the functional inverse of the Guest in the "Tower Conversation" who gifted the Tower Warden a picture. The Teacher encountered this picture in the Tower Warden's room, prompting their subsequent conversation. The gift also foreshadowed and prepared the way for the encounter with its source—the Guest—by the text's end.[31] In contrast, Kuki's physical proximity long predates their conversation. He is the origin of the possibility of their meeting, and in a certain sense initiates their conversation since *he* is the topic of the first pages of the text. In a sense, Kuki's "gift" consists in passing along what the Questioner taught him across geographic, historical, linguistic, and cultural distance. Even after his physical death—on which both conversational partners dwell at length—Kuki's philosophical relevance endures.

The opening of their conversation is anchored in their memory of the man they call Count[32] Shuzo Kuki, who died "too early" (GA 12: 81/ OWL 1). They both recall him for the influential philosophical conversations they shared over the years. The Japanese speaks of a transcript of a lecture course the Questioner gave in 1921 titled "Expression and Appearance,"[33] which led to many discussions between the Japanese and his teacher Kuki concerning "the terms 'hermeneutics' and 'hermeneutic' . . . [that] Kuki did not succeed in explaining . . . [but] stressed constantly that the term was to indicate a new direction of phenomenology" (GA 12: 90/OWL 9). The Questioner spends much of their subsequent conversation clarifying the meaning of these terms for this student of his student. In so doing, he acknowledges how their conversation "has grown out of our memory of Count Kuki" (GA 12: 97/OWL 15), which binds them in pedagogical relation. He recollects that his conversations with Kuki "were not formal, scholarly discussions . . . The conversations of which I am thinking came about at my house, like a spontaneous game . . . [and] tried to *say* the essential nature of *East-asian* art and poetry" (GA 12: 84–85/OWL 4, tm.). Both the Questioner's and the Japanese's pedagogical relationships with Kuki were invigorating and frustrating. Kuki did not have complete, satisfactory explanations for his student, the Japanese. And as a student himself, Kuki only made unsuccessful attempts to bring his own culture to bear on informal conversations with his teacher, the Questioner. In these ways, Kuki's memory sets the stage for "Conversation of Language."

It is tempting to interpret the Japanese and the Questioner as stylized versions of the historical people who have these relations to the historical Kuki, namely Tezuka Tomio and Heidegger himself. "Conversation of Language" is the only Heideggerian conversation in which the characters bear such striking resemblances to real people. Yet Heidegger's articles caution against simple identification. In Heidegger's preceding conversations, characters were defined by professions, functions, or age relative to one another. He also always used definite articles. In this text, where such enticing resemblances to biography emerge, Heidegger instead uses indefinite articles to refer to his characters. The Japanese is "a Japanese" (not "the Japanese") and the Questioner is "a Questioner" (not "the Questioner"). Though I refer to these characters using definite articles in this chapter, this is only for want of grammatical ease. It is still the types or standpoints of his characters[34] that are philosophically relevant, not their personality or, in this case, their historical reality.

The Japanese character is a professor of German literature who is from and resides in Japan. He is traveling through Europe and stops to meet with the Questioner during his sojourn. He is an avid reader of Heidegger's work and a scholar of other major German figures. The Questioner mentions that the Japanese has "translated into Japanese a few of Kleist's plays, and some of my lectures on Hölderlin" (GA 12: 89/OWL 8). This again raises the question of the relation between the Japanese and Tezuka Tomio, who was a professor of German literature at Tokyo University and a translator of Heidegger in addition to Nietzsche, Goethe, Hesse, George, and Rilke. Heidegger appends a misleading statement as a note to the text, claiming that the conversation "originated in 1953/54, on the occasion of a visit by Professor Tezuka of the Imperial University, Tokyo" (GA 12: 259/OWL 199). In March 1954, Tezuka did visit Heidegger in Freiburg. However, from Tezuka's own account of his conversation with Heidegger,[35] it is clear that "Conversation of Language" is not a reconstruction of their actual conversation. The characters in the text share a significant connection with Kuki, but Tezuka did not know Kuki.[36] Further, Heidegger had been considering how his thinking may relate to the East long before this meeting, not least of all by way of the Hölderlin interpretations the Japanese seems to know intimately.[37] Davis suggests the Japanese should be constructed as a character based on "his conversations with numerous other Japanese scholars and philosophers,"[38] many of whom he both learned from and taught, suggesting a distinct pedagogical fluidity and reciprocity. At any rate, Tezuka's 1954 visit to Freiburg was only one of many inspirations for the "Conversation of Language."

The Japanese character fulfills many functions in this text. He was a student of Kuki and, by intellectual ancestry, thereby of the Questioner. But he is also a teacher in his own right, both professionally at his posting in Japan and of the Questioner during their conversation. He is a member of the scholarly German Studies community and clearly a reader and translator of the Questioner's (and, by implication, of Heidegger's) texts. In a certain way, he can also be read as Heidegger's mouthpiece. When compared with Tezuka's account of his actual conversation with Heidegger, it is clear that Heidegger fashioned a character amenable to his purposes, not one who presents the themes Tezuka had actually asked about.[39] Jean-Luc Nancy goes so far as to call the Japanese "the Western other."[40] Yet Heidegger chooses to write his character as a member of *Japanese* culture and as a speaker of the *Japanese* language.

The Japanese initially comports himself as one who is grieving and remembering his teacher Kuki. He savors the opportunity to share this with someone else who knew and experienced him as similarly (pedagogically) significant. This sharing of their loss with one another recalls the healing unfolded in the "Evening Conversation," which could only be found in welcoming the other into what had been presumed to be a solitary experience. Though the purpose of the "Conversation of Language" is not expressly pedagogical at the outset, it becomes so as they discuss the resonances of their shared relation to Kuki. This involves the Questioner's—but not the Japanese's—personal intellectual history, which he recounts in detail to teach the Japanese what Kuki had been unable to explain satisfactorily to him. In response, the Japanese becomes reticent and almost *too* accommodating to the Questioner's subsequent inquires of the Japanese about the Eastern world.[41]

Even though the Questioner does ask questions about *Japanese* thinking, art, and culture, the majority of the conversation unfolds with the Japanese asking the Questioner about the nature of *European* metaphysical thought, metaphysically informed aesthetics, and technical aspects of the Questioner's teachings and works. The characters explicitly determine to switch roles at a crucial point, allowing the Japanese to answer (and not only ask) questions, but this is largely the exception, not the rule of their interaction. By the conversation's midpoint, interest in Japanese culture is all but abandoned so that the Questioner can elaborate his hermeneutic sense of language. It may have been more accurate for Heidegger to name these characters "a German" and "a Questioner," especially given that the language and geographical location of their conversation are both German and the trajectory of the Western metaphysical tradition is the conversation's most central concern. Regardless, the Japanese's language and culture is inscribed into his name, and he is cast in the role of learning from the Questioner more often than he teaches the Questioner about non-Western thinking.

The Questioner character is also a professor whose proficiencies span German philosophy and literature. He teaches professionally and taught Kuki years earlier. But he is also a student of the various figures he names as influences. He appears to occupy a student role with the Japanese at certain points as well. The Questioner is obviously a stylized version of Heidegger himself. In the conversation, he claims to be the author of several of Heidegger's works, including *Being and Time* (GA 12: 91/OWL 9), "What is Metaphysics?" (GA 12: 103/OWL 19), and "Letter on Humanism" (GA 12: 105/OWL 21). Heidegger here describes his own works as the Questioners', but in "Triadic Conversation," he also mentioned a "contemporary book" (GA 77: 24/CPC 15) that addressed the truth of being. There, he did not go so far as to name the book or openly attribute authorship to one of the characters. By the time he composes "Conversation of Language" and fashions the character of the Questioner, Heidegger overtly claims ownership of his work and collapses the distance between his thinking and personal context. This conversation is more closely related to Heidegger's own world. He is no longer impelled to place his conversations in imaginary settings—distanced from any personal or political context—as he did in the 1940s. Though any simple identification between the Questioner and Heidegger is implausible, at the very least the Questioner is someone strongly influenced by Heideggerian thinking and shares at least some aspects of Heidegger's personal and professional history.

The Questioner's demeanor departs from his name. He certainly *asks* questions, but he spends more time *answering* questions posed to him by the Japanese about his life and work. He elucidates his own thinking more than he endeavors to learn about Japanese thinking, echoing the culminating of the "Triadic Conversation," in which the conversational partners all follow the Guide's attempts to think non-metaphysically. Yet in that text, the Guide was clear that not every answer is an answer to a question (GA 77: 22/CPC 14). To engage in authentic questioning—to invite a "counter word" to one's word—the "Tower Conversation" demonstrated that one must learn to resist wondering and instead to allow something to rest as strange (GA 77: 163–65/CPC 105–6). In the "Conversation of Language," is the Questioner engaged in *this* sort of questioning? Or has he become mired in producing mere answers?

In the extensive autobiographical intellectual retrospective Heidegger places in the Questioner's mouth, what is included is as telling as what is absent—particularly his political involvement with National Socialism. In the "Evening Conversation" and the "Western Conversation," Heidegger evidently finds Hölderlin's poetic history worth speaking of in light of the devastation facing Germany. However, "Conversation of Language" does not manage to escape (if this was Heidegger's intention) Germany's political history. The Questioner clearly enjoys the privilege of being German without acknowledging how or why that privilege has been recuperated and maintained.[42] As a character, it is so manifestly evident that the Questioner is German—in the political, national sense and in the sense depicted by Hölderlin—that Heidegger never mentions it. This Eurocentric bias is clear in the way the German character is never called upon to name his own identity as such, but the Japanese character is characterized solely by his. This informs the Questioner's pedagogical comportment as well. Though he states repeatedly he is not interested in simply procuring useful information from the Japanese, in many respects this is exactly what he does. The danger of cross-cultural exchange is eminently amplified.

Sheltered, by the Western Tradition

The setting of "Conversation of Language" is unique. While the other conversations took place outside while the conversational partners were (or recently were) walking through nature, "Conversation of Language" takes place inside, while the characters are stationary. They are presumably in Germany, likely in the Questioner's home or office. They mention the Japanese will be traveling to Florence in the coming days[43] and look at a number of books that seem to be readily at hand. At one point, the Questioner pulls out his copy of Franz Brentano's dissertation (GA 12: 88/OWL 7). The Questioner also reads a passage aloud from the general introduction to Schleiermacher's lecture "Hermeneutics and Criticism" (GA 12: 92/OWL 10). The Japanese states, "it is obvious that . . . you are at home in theology [*in der Theologie . . . beheimatet*]" (GA 12: 91/OWL 10). The Questioner responds that his theological background was crucial for his future path of thinking. The Japanese replies, "the two [the theology background and the eventual path of thinking] call to each other, and reflection makes its home [*einheimisch wird*] within that calling" (GA 12: 92/OWL 10). The theme of housing and home continues throughout their conversation. The Questioner tells the Japanese, "some time ago I called language, clumsily enough, the house of being [*das Haus des Seins*]. If the human being by virtue of his or her language [*Sprache*] dwells within the claim [*Anspruch*] of being, then we Europeans presumably dwell in an entirely different house than the Eastasian [*der ostasiatische Mensch*]" (GA 12: 85/OWL 5, tm.). There may be two houses in question here, but the question itself is unbalanced. For the Questioner, it can be posed both for him in particular and as a member of a "we." In contrast, the Japanese's house is implicitly assigned to the generic Eastasian person and remains abstract. After all, they are conversing together from within the Questioner's house. The sense of the foreign engendered by the Japanese's presence enables this (German) homecoming.[44]

Within the Questioner's house, the characters are not physically moving. They nevertheless cover an incredible amount of temporal and historical ground. Remembrance—of what remains outstanding in what has been—and history constitute the terrain over which their conversation roams. Though they remain sedentary, there are still many references to thinking as the walking of a path.[45] Perhaps their greater temporal scale explains why Heidegger does not bother mentioning whether the conversation takes place during the day or at night. On the one hand, being indoors and having protection from the natural elements means that these diurnal natural cycles are not as immediately significant. On the other, the sweeping global and historical scope of their conversation calls for a discussion measured by epochs and lifetimes, not hours or seasons. The Questioner seems particularly comfortable and settled in his home. He considers concrete personal histories in a more retrospective mode. The historical grounding of "Conversation of Language" is accomplished through the concrete temporality of specific peoples' lives. Perhaps this appreciation of memory has invited Heidegger toward a renewed sense of concreteness—and the relation sustained between the concrete and the philosophical—under the guise of the personal.

PEDAGOGICAL TECHNIQUES

Despite its remove from the preceding conversations, the same five pedagogical techniques Heidegger unfolded in those texts are found in "Conversation of Language": openness to others, sensitivity to affect, reversals, remembrance, and silence. However, in this text, these techniques are not as easily located as practiced by one of the characters. Rather, the conversation—especially the language of the conversation—enacts these techniques of itself.[46] The conversational partners respond to—rather than initiate—this pedagogy in its unfolding. There is a sense that the characters still have some capacity to guide the conversation, but the issues at play—namely culture, language, history, and alterity—are significantly larger than they are. Most distinctive about how these techniques are illustrated is the danger in which the pedagogy of the conversation unfolds. In addition to being an explicit and repeated topic, I argue this danger is implicitly performed throughout this conversation as well.

Danger is indicated through what Lin Ma has called the "asymmetry"[47] of the conversation. In addition to the asymmetries in how Heidegger fashions his characters noted above, for Ma, "Heidegger's discussion of the danger of language only bears upon the transit of Japanese notions into European languages. He has never entertained the danger involved in the reverse direction, that is, European notions may be distorted when entering into the Japanese language."[48] The Questioner seems unconcerned when the Japanese describes moving seamlessly between German and Japanese in his translation efforts. As Ma astutely points out, the danger Heidegger elaborates seems firmly grounded in a Western sense of language. The representational thinking Heidegger's pedagogy seeks to redress may be grounded in the beginnings of the Western metaphysical tradition of philosophizing. But that he does not even entertain the concern that the Eastern tradition may also have generated obstacles for learning non-representational, non-metaphysical thinking betrays orientalism and significant Eurocentric bias. Regarding this bias, Davis argues, "despite some undeniable moments and persistent elements of Eurocentrism in Heidegger's thought, the proper pathway of his step back, or at least the pathway it would be most proper for us to follow, leads to a place which allows us to step outward into a genuine dialogue with other traditions of thought."[49] Though Heidegger's stringent criticism of the Western philosophical tradition as a whole may contribute to clearing away colonialism, racism, sexism, and other forms of discrimination, his efforts in this particular text do not accomplish such a feat. They remain persistently asymmetrical, replicating and enhancing the danger of which he writes.

Danger also appears in the mistakes that abound. In particular, Heidegger misconstrues a number of the Eastasian themes. There are two possible interpretations of these mistakes. On the one hand, the errors in presenting elements of the Eastern world may be intentional mistakes, and Heidegger is well aware of falling prey to the very danger he repeatedly warns against—illustrating, performing, and underscoring his argument. On the other hand, Heidegger may have been entirely oblivious to committing these mistakes in the course of his project of enabling cross-cultural exchange. In this case, these mistakes perform—with even *more* urgency—the pervasiveness and seriousness of the danger Heidegger warns against in "Conversation of Language."

Whether he realizes it or not, Heidegger has persuasively demonstrated the very danger of which he speaks. As the structural inverse of the "Triadic Conversation," "Conversation of Language" explores how conversational partners who begin conversing in agreement must nevertheless remain vigilant to the danger of (mis)translation, particularly in the context of significant cultural, historical, and linguistic difference. Perhaps the ways in which Heidegger repeatedly (mis)uses Japanese culture demonstrate how drawing near to that which is far—the guiding enigma of Heidegger's conversations—demands the difficult and continual task of recognizing the other through a recognition of our own proper limits.

In this text Heidegger writes, the human being is "he who walks the boundary of the boundless" (GA 12: 129/OWL 41). In the early fifties, this will assume a new valence in the wake of his emergent re-thinking of technology. No longer will technological thinking be characterized by objectification imposed by a subject. Instead, it will be characterized by circulative replacement. In the "Triadic Conversation," Heidegger claimed that the essence of scientific and technological thinking consisted in the mathematical, but after the Bremen lectures, Mitchell clarifies that the circulative replacement of the standing reserve reveals it as "*essentially essenceless.*"[50] Technology becomes the means by which everything is available and always already replaceable—boundless, in a negative sense. It is no longer anything definite or objectified, but rather circulates ceaselessly. The human being must learn to respond to this essenceless boundlessness. Whereas the poetic pedagogy of the preceding conversations could contend with the objectification and subjectification of representational, metaphysical thinking by inaugurating its own singing with the poetic resonation of non-metaphysical thinking, perhaps Heidegger now realizes coming to agreement itself—even an agreement born out of poetizing accord—nevertheless harbors danger for those who would engage in such conversation.

Endangering Pedagogy

(Not) At Home

Intentionally or not, Heidegger's "Conversation of Language" performs the dangers of poetic pedagogy. This conversation seems to unfold at a standstill since the conversational partners are at the Questioner's home. But this is not the standstill of the "Evening Conversation." The Japanese has traveled long and far to a foreign place to enable this exchange, but this has fallen out of the text's frame. The conversational text does elaborate a far-reaching historical and cultural terrain across which the conversational partners roam. In a way, the act of physically walking across such terrain would be much too demanding. Their legs are insufficient. They must instead employ thinking to travel across both the non-metaphysical space of the East/West divide and non-metaphysical time of the world historical, but also the personal and biographical. To elucidate this journey's danger, I follow Ma's suggested six-part division of "Conversation of Language."[51]

As I read the text, I note the repeated appearances of the five pedagogical techniques that emerge in each of Heidegger's conversational texts. Each performs significant functions. However in his final conversation, they do not always perform the function Heidegger seems to intend or that to which his poetic pedagogy would seem to aspire. At points, they enable the conversational partners to move toward non-representational, non-metaphysical thinking, but at others, they seem to malfunction. These malfunctions—intentional or not—illustrate the danger that Heidegger's poetic pedagogy incites when it calls upon sensitivity to affect, reversals, remembrance, and silence in order to perform an openness to the alterity of an other with which Heidegger never quite contends.

Prelude: *Iki* and Danger

"Conversation of Language" opens with a remembrance of the pedagogical relations of each character to Kuki—as a student for the Questioner and as a teacher for the Japanese—and their differing connections to his burial site. The Japanese speaks first, mentioning that Kuki gave "lectures" and wrote a "book"[52] significant for the Japanese's learning (GA 12: 81/OWL 2). He mentions his frequent visits to Kuki's grave: "Yes, I know the temple garden in Kyoto. Many of my friends often join me to visit the tomb there. The garden was established toward the end of the twelfth century by the priest Honen, on the eastern hill of what was then the Imperial city of Kyoto, as a place for reflection and deep meditation" (GA 12: 81/OWL 1). His relationship to his teacher's tomb extends beyond a mere personal and social connection. The Japanese knows the history of the garden and the religious significance of the place. He is also familiar with the epitaph that a famous Japanese philosopher (who was also Kuki's teacher) worked on for over a year to perfect for Kuki's grave (GA 12: 81/OWL 1). Kuki died "too early"[53] (GA 12: 81/OWL 1) and thereby reversed the traditional pedagogical relation, forcing the teacher to secure the memory of the student. This reversal is the first indication that the pedagogy unfolding in this text is hardly predicated on a traditional student-teacher relationship.

The Questioner also has a connection to Kuki's burial place, but not one grounded in history or culture. He mentions that he is "happy to have photographs [*Aufnahmen*] of Kuki's grave and of the grove in which it lies" (GA 12: 81/OWL 1). It seems the Questioner has not physically visited the garden, nor does he have access beyond these images supplemented by the second-hand account of the place the Japanese provides. The German term translated as "photographs"—*Aufnahmen*—carries additional connotations of a recording, even a video recording in the form of a tape. The lens of a (Western) camera intruding upon Japanese culture will become an explicit issue. Even at this early point, it is notable that a technological mode of registering this burial site is the Questioner's only access to Japanese culture. In the "Tower Conversation," the picture that so unsettled the Teacher provided the occasion to learn releasement toward the strange. But these photographs are not described as anxiety provoking, nor is there any mystery about what they depict. There is instead a sense that these photographs grant the Questioner limited access to a world that is nevertheless foreign to him.[54] For the Questioner, the photographs do not allow him an authentic experience of the temple garden, but they nevertheless support a meaningful relation to Kuki's memory. Implied by the force of memory that compels their conversation is a sense that a human life can impact the world and others well beyond death.[55]

On the first page, the Japanese introduces *Iki,* recalling that this was what "all [Kuki's] reflection was devoted" (GA 12: 82/OWL 1) to understanding. As with the grave site, the term *iki* is not equally accessible to both characters. The Questioner is acquainted with Kuki's interest, but shares, "in my conversations with Kuki, I never had more than a distant inkling [*aus der Ferne ahnen*] of what that word says" (GA 12: 82/OWL 2, tm.). The Questioner again signals the farness of the Japanese world for him. *Iki* plays a central role in this text. It originates from their shared history with Kuki and his work.[56] From here, the characters discuss the potential to elaborate *iki* with the help of European aesthetic philosophy. The Questioner cautions against this and recalls how he similarly cautioned Kuki in their past conversations: "The name 'aesthetics' and what it names grow out of European thinking, out of philosophy. Consequently, aesthetic considerations must remain foreign [*fremd*] to East-asian thinking" (GA 12: 82/OWL 2, tm.).

This spurns the emergence of another central theme: danger. When the Japanese explains that Kuki had come to Europe to learn the conceptual system of aesthetics to "grasp [*um . . . zu fassen*] what is of concern to us as art and poetry" (GA 12: 82/OWL 2), the Questioner hesitates.[57] He worries it is dangerous "for Eastasians to chase after the European conceptual systems" (GA 12: 83/OWL 3). At first the Questioner seems to think that such an encounter is not possible because of the radical differences between Eastern and Western traditions. Yet he intimates "a far greater danger [*Gefahr*] threatens" (GA 12: 84/OWL 3) than a mere failure of exchange, one that remains "hidden in language itself, not in *what* we discussed, nor in the *way in which* we tried to do so" (GA 12: 85/OWL 4). The Japanese seems to sense what was at stake in those earlier conversations, though he himself was not present. As he puts it, the Questioner's and Kuki's conversations were dangerous because "the language of the conversation constantly destroyed [*zerstörte*] the possibility of saying what the conversation was about" (GA 12: 85/OWL 5, tm.). Though Kuki was fluent in the European languages, the Questioner recalls, "it was *I* to whom the spirit of the Japanese language [*der japanische Sprachgeist*] remained closed—as it is to this day" (GA 12: 85/OWL 4).

The Questioner and Kuki were attempting to discuss East Asian art and poetry in Germany against the backdrop of European philosophy. This conceptual system may appear to provide convenient parallel explanations, but this is misleading. The danger threatens that the conversational partners may "let [them]selves be led astray by the wealth of concepts which the spirit of the European languages has in store, and will look down upon what claims our existence, as on something that is vague and amorphous" (GA 12: 84/OWL 3). Or, even worse, they may only come to accept as valid that which can be articulated according to the rubric of representational metaphysics. Such reliance, the characters agree, would have devastating consequences for the Eastern world.

The danger of the very language of conversation is further evoked by a familiar Heideggerian phrase. When the Japanese comes to terms with the danger of the language of a conversation in German that nevertheless "tried to *say* the essence [*Wesentliche*] of *East-asian* art and poetry" (GA 12: 85/OWL 4, tm.), the Questioner responds, "some time ago I called language, clumsily enough, the house of being. If the human being by virtue of his or her language dwells within the claim of being, then we Europeans presumably dwell in an entirely different house than the Eastasian" (GA 12: 85/OWL 5, tm.) In addition to the pronominal asymmetry already noted, the characters determine that the pronouncement of radical alterity may render "a conversation from house to house . . . nearly impossible [*beinahe unmöglich*]" (GA 12: 85/OWL 5, tm.). Though the Questioner insists the Japanese world is closed to him, he has invited both the Japanese and Kuki into his home, where he keeps photographs of Kuki's grave. He already finds himself exposed to this world even if it does not thereby open itself to him. Likewise, the Japanese has traveled to Europe to meet with the Questioner, speaks German, and knows much about the Western tradition. Against all odds, these two find themselves engaging in this "nearly impossible" conversation, launched by the pedagogical techniques of remembrance and reversal, and headed straight toward the danger.

(The Questioner's) Intellectual Autobiography

The mention of Heidegger's famous phrase signals the centrality of language for this conversation. It also initiates the Questioner remembering and recounting his own intellectual autobiography. This account rehearses episodes selectively drawn from Heidegger's own life. The Japanese demonstrates significant familiarity with the Questioner's trajectory—which is not reciprocated—by filling out this retrospective, supplying facts, and asking questions as the Questioner reminisces about his life. This autobiography centers Heidegger's intellectual influences and academic achievements without any mention of his personal or political life—a highly stylized and fictionalized retrospective, indeed.

The Japanese begins retracing the Questioner's intellectual history by insisting that Kuki and the Questioner's conversations must have been fruitful despite their danger. Upon Kuki's return to Japan, the Japanese remembers that he and his fellow students "pressed him in our effort to understand more clearly the reason that had prompted him at that time to go to Germany to study with you. Your book *Being and Time* had then not yet been published. But after the First World War several Japanese professors, among them our revered Professor Tanabe, went to Husserl, in Freiburg, to study phenomenology with him. That is how my compatriots came to know you in person" (GA 12: 86/OWL 5). At the Japanese's prompting, the Questioner reminisces about a lecture course he gave in 1921 titled "Expression and Appearance"[58] and his dissertation "Duns Scotus' Doctrine of Categories and Theory of Meaning." The Questioner agrees with the Japanese's assessment that both his dissertation and his 1921 lecture course "circled around the problem of language and of being" (GA 12: 87/OWL 6, tm.) even as he remained "silent [*geschwiegen*] for twelve years" (GA 12: 87/OWL 6) about this relation between his dissertation and *Being and Time*.[59] He waited twenty years after his doctoral dissertation to again broach the topic of language in his teaching and another ten years after that before he felt he could properly articulate his concern with language, claiming "the fitting word [*das gemäße Wort*] is still lacking even today" (GA 12: 89/OWL 8). He nevertheless assures the Japanese that his silence in no way indicates that the dual question of language and being vanished, but rather that this silence is essential to it. The characters will take up this suggestion again, later performing how silence supports learning such thinking, which I discuss below. But in Heidegger's earlier conversations, the importance of silence as a pedagogical technique has already become apparent. During all these years, we might surmise that Heidegger was engaged in a conversation with himself structured by a self-pedagogy that informs all that comes after.[60]

The Questioner turns to a figure he and the Japanese share to illustrate the meaningfulness of charting his course in this way. For the Questioner, a line from Hölderlin's "*Der Rhine*"—". . . For as you began, so you will remain" (GA 12: 88/OWL 7)—encapsulates the connections he elaborates between his very early influences in Brentano, Scotus, Husserl, Dilthey, and Schleiermacher, and helps explain how it may seem he abandoned the strict confines of hermeneutic phenomenology "in order to abandon my own path of thinking to the nameless [*um meinem Denkweg im Namenlosen zu lassen*]" (GA 12: 114/OWL 29). In turning to hermeneutics and phenomenology, the Questioner says he tried to "attempt first of all to define the essence of interpretation on hermeneutic grounds" (GA 12: 93/OWL 11, tm.) and thereby to "think the essence [*Wesen*] of phenomenology more originarily [*ursprünglicher*]" (GA 12: 91/OWL 9, tm.). Yet his thinking of language and being could not follow the predetermined paths these methodologies set out. He set out on his own, understanding this early starting point as "merely a sojourn [*Aufenthalt*] along a way [*in einem Unterwegs*] . . . the lasting element in thinking is the way" (GA 12: 94/OWL 12, tm.). In remembering his own history of thinking, the Questioner concurrently clarifies his way of thinking. The Questioner situates his task as a futural thinking of the origin of language and being. His history is his way, and the reverse also holds, namely that his way is essentially historical.

But as he elaborates the path of the historicality of his thinking, there is no mention of danger. The question of whether the Questioner's account is somehow closed to the Japanese never arises. The Questioner preemptively justifies setting aside any such danger since in his judgment the Japanese has "a keener ear [*helleres Ohr*] for the questions that I addressed to your compatriots [*Landsleute*] almost thirty-five years ago" (GA 12: 89/OWL 8).[61] The Japanese is not invited to present a corresponding account of his own personal, intellectual journey. This shows what Ma calls the asymmetry of "Conversation of Language." Despite his critique of representational thinking, the Japanese character functions for Heidegger as a representative of the Japanese world, whose role is to receive the Questioner's narrative, not as a proper thinker.

The issue of danger explicitly arises when the Questioner begins wondering whether his way of thinking of language "is *also* adequate for the essence of the Eastasian language" (GA 12: 89/OWL 8, tm.). The characters here agree upon a guiding principle for their conversation. The Japanese says, "we Japanese [*Uns Japaner*] do not think it strange if a conversation leaves undefined [*im Unbestimmten läßt*] what is really intended, or even restores it back to the keeping of the undefinable," to which the Questioner responds, "that is part, I believe, of every conversation that has turned out well between thinkers" (GA 12: 95/OWL 13, tm.). They agree on the importance of guarding the (pedagogical) silence at the heart of their cross-cultural conversation. However, the asymmetry indicated by the difference in the pronouns used in coming to this agreement—the Japanese offers agreement as a "we" where the Questioner agrees as an "I"—is passed over as ostensibly unremarkable. The danger of cultural appropriation—shown where the Japanese character speaks as a member of a cultural group when the Questioner speaks as an individual—does not seem to even register as dangerous.

The Eastern World

A significant portion of "Conversation of Language" is dedicated to elaborating the Questioner's intellectual autobiography, but there is no corresponding account from the Japanese. Instead, in its third section, the conversation returns to the question of danger as the two characters converse about several topics and themes related to the Japanese tradition. Despite the ostensive openness to the alterity of the East that Heidegger may be attempting by considering the Japanese's culture and a concurrent turning away from Western themes for a time, it is critical to note that the Japanese continues to speak in the first-person plural "we," as a group representative. Heidegger also places general depictions of Japanese thinking and culture into the Japanese's mouth that range from slightly misconstrued to blatantly incorrect. They remain without the extensive citations the Questioner provided when giving an account of his relation to and place within the German, Western tradition. A generous reading of this disparity may suggest that Heidegger is practicing a form of epistemic humility in dramatizing the relative newness of his access to the Eastern world. However, it is possible to demarcate and respect cultural difference while nevertheless striving for accuracy.

Iki

The conversational partners already mentioned the Japanese term *iki* when remembering Kuki. *Iki* assumes vital importance throughout the text. The Japanese brings *iki* up again in lamenting that his own conversations with Kuki failed to turn out so well because of "our thirst [*Wissenwollen*] for handy information [*handliche Auskünfte*]" (GA 12: 95/OWL 13) that he and his fellow students had when Kuki returned from Europe. In particular, they hoped that European aesthetics might help clarify the essence of Japanese art and poetry. The Questioner reiterates that he barely understood the word when he discussed it with Kuki. Though the Questioner recalls that Kuki seemed to find his efforts in originary hermeneutics helpful for his own thinking, because "the language of the conversation was European" (GA 12: 96/OWL 13, tm.), for the Questioner the danger of mistranslation (or worse) remained. Despite this, the Questioner shares Kuki's depiction of *iki* as "sensuous radiance through whose lively delight here breaks the radiance of something suprasensuous" (GA 12: 96/OWL 14). As the conversational partners are quick to note, this references the sensuous/suprasensuous distinction promulgated by Western representational metaphysics and thus already obscures *iki*. A number of different descriptions and interpretations of *iki* emerge across the conversation, all of which serve Heidegger in elucidating non-representational, non-metaphysical thinking by dramatizing the inadequacy of Western philosophy.

That Heidegger's use of *iki* is delimited by his own project and not by its Japanese context is further shown by how the meaning of the term itself[62] and the historical Kuki's work on it are distorted. As commentators have shown, Heidegger's depiction of *iki*, including Baron Kuki's interest, constitutes a radical misconstrual. For instance, May notes that Heidegger's portrayal of *iki* "has nothing whatever to do with *iki*."[63] Davis concurs, complaining that the text "frustrates us with its arbitrary metaphysical misinterpretations of Kuki's hermeneutical phenomenology of the Japanese word *iki*."[64] Ma writes that its "complete meaning is beyond that of such words as raffiné, elegant and coquettish. *Iki* is not an abstract concept, but a distinctive ethnic consciousness the penetrates the minutest areas of the life of the Japanese people."[65] Parkes suggests one way to interpret this striking divergence between Heidegger's evolving portrayal of *iki* and Kuki's scholarly work on *iki* runs as follows: "If *iki* was not a topic of his conversation with Tezuka, since no German translation of Kuki's work was available, Heidegger would have had to cast his mind back quite some way in order to remember what Kuki had said about it—which no doubt explains why the explication of *iki* in the 'Conversation' bears so little relation to Kuki's own presentation of the idea."[66] Indeed, the historical Kuki's work on "the aesthetic sensibility of a merchant class that was developed in the pleasure quarters in the Edo period of Japan"[67] appears nowhere in "Conversation of Language" even though his "hermeneutics of ethnic being"[68] was particularly influenced by his studies with Heidegger about how language enacts the formation of a people in relation to culture and history.[69] Not only does Heidegger misrepresent the historical Kuki's interest in *iki*, but he also offers a highly creative interpretation of the term in this conversational text.

Iro (Shiki)/Kū

To redress the seeming infection of Eastern thinking with Western metaphysics in the depiction of *iki*, the Japanese suggests a non-metaphysical alternative. He volunteers that "our [Japanese] thinking . . . does know something similar to the metaphysical distinction; but even so, the distinction itself and what it distinguishes cannot be comprehended with Western metaphysical concepts. We say *Iro*, that is, color, and say *Ku*, that is, emptiness, the open, the sky. We say: without *Iro no Ku*" (GA 12: 97/OWL 14). Though this distinction seems metaphysical, the Japanese insists *Iro* "means essentially [*wesentlich*] more than whatever is perceptible by the senses" and *Ku* "means essentially more than that which is merely suprasensuous" (GA 12: 97/OWL 14–15). Nevertheless, the Questioner remains concerned. He mentions twice that he fears "the authentic essence of Eastasian art is obscured and shunted into an unfitting [*ungemäßen*] realm" (GA 12: 97/OWL 14, tm.).

This mention of fear is telling of a pedagogically significant moment. In the "Triadic Conversation," Heidegger's Guide helped the Scientist resolve his fear into the more proper comportment of anxiety. Here, the Questioner does not accomplish such a transition. Alongside his fear, the Questioner also notes he has "the expectation [*Erwartung*] within me that our conversation . . . could turn out well" (GA 12: 97/OWL 15). This prompts him to "now see *still* more clearly the danger that the language of our conversation might constantly destroy the possibility of saying that of which we are speaking [*was wir besprechen*]" (GA 12: 98/OWL 15, tm.). To expect such radical difference will be so neatly resolved is to engage in a technological thinking that seeks to make everything (and everyone) available for use. In the "Evening Conversation," it was clear that such an expectation is a distorted, metaphysical deviation from a proper waiting that is "otherwise than all awaiting and expecting [*Erwarten*], which are basically unable to wait" (GA 77: 227/CPC 148). In "Conversation of Language," these affects—fear and expectation—indicate pedagogical need for a poetic, conversational thinking enabled in the "Western Conversation."[70] The Questioner and the Japanese discuss how "reason" was "idolize[d]" in the Western tradition (GA 12: 98–99/OWL 15). In modernity's wake, affect seems able to do important work, to hint at other ways of thinking. These experiences of fear and expectation also provide the Questioner with the opportunity to continue practicing learning, as the teacher in the "Tower Conversation" did. The Questioner needs to continue to wait because of this amplification of danger. Here again, affect is detecting a particular threat generated by representational metaphysics. Yet this fear remains oriented by such thinking, not by any fear that he is actively representing the Japanese metaphysically by treating him as a spokesperson for a group of people.

Beyond the philosophical causes for concern Heidegger provides, scholars[71] have shown that the distinction Heidegger is attempting to unfold as signaling possibilities for thinking beyond Western metaphysics is incorrectly formulated. Ma writes,

> Heidegger invokes the famous Buddhist formula "*shiki* is *kū, kū* is *shiki*" ("form is emptiness; emptiness is form") . . . In his text, the twin words *shiki* and *kū* appear as *iro* and *kū* (IDL 14/120). In the context of the Buddhist ideas of *shiki* and *kū*, which cannot be clearly differentiated, the first character should read *shiki*, not *iro*. Heidegger might have misread *shiki* as *iro* from his notes, or he was later given another reading. Further, Heidegger made an obvious mistake in explaining *iro* (form) as meaning "colour" (DL 14/120); in fact, "colour" can only be said to be one aspect of the meaning of "form."[72]

The Questioner's concern about danger is well founded. This mistake works toward confirming the conversational partner's expressed worry. In discussing the Japanese world through a European lens, significant and unnoticed distortions are thereby generated. This exemplifies what the Questioner names "a process which I would like to call the complete Europeanization of the earth and of human beings" (GA 12: 98/OWL 15, tm.). Heidegger's characters are unwittingly performing this very process, demonstrating just how dangerous their undertaking is through this failure. There is no point in the conversation where this mistake is addressed as such.

Rashomon

Next, the characters turn to Kurusawa's film *Rashomon*.[73] The conversational partners refer to *Rashomon* as an example of how Europeanization—or Americanization, as is later suggested (GA 12: 101/OWL 17)—has infiltrated the Japanese world. The Questioner shares his experience screening the film: "I believed that I was experiencing the enchantment of the Japanese world, the enchantment that carries us away into the mysterious [*Geheimnisvolle*]" (GA 12: 99/OWL 16). The Questioner admits he exoticized the Eastern world at the same moment he believed it was rendered available to him through the film. The Japanese responds that the Japanese world is not unfolded, but rather "captured and imprisoned . . . in the objectivity of photography [*Gegenständliche der Photographie*], and is in fact especially positioned [*gestellt*] for photography" (GA 12: 100/OWL 17, tm.). The technology of film dictates what is represented, not the Japanese world the Questioner believed he was experiencing. This invites a reconsideration of the photograph of Kuki's grave discussed at the conversation's outset. The Questioner's experience of the tomb—including the cultural and relational world in which the tomb is situated—is also framed in advance. The Japanese's experience unmediated by technology is entirely different.

Attempting to follow the Japanese's criticism of the false realism the camera lens attributes to the Japanese world, the Questioner replies, "if I have listened rightly, you would say that the Eastasian world, and the technical-aesthetic product of the film industry, are incompatible" (GA 12: 100/OWL 17), which the Japanese affirms. But no matter how closely the Questioner listens, the conversational partners can never be sure their agreement is based in a shared understanding. The danger of distortion and mistranslation is concentrated and intensified even when it seems accord is reached. This is clear from Heidegger's portrayal of the film. He cautions against a romanticization of *Rashomon*, but simultaneously continues to perpetuate a selective interpretation fit for his purposes. In elaborating his criticism, the Japanese recounts a scene in the film of a hand in intense repose. This is supposed to help describe how the meaning of this gesture cannot be captured by the realism produced through Western technology, including film. He dwells on a specific example of a "hand resting on another person, in which there is concentrated a contact that remains infinitely remote from any touch, something that may not even be called gesture any longer in the sense in which I understand your usage" (GA 12: 99/OWL 16). However, as Ma notes, there is no such scene:

> Watching the film *Rashōmon* by oneself, one cannot find a scene in which a hand is given a focus of such kind, except the two hands of the murdered man sticking out of the shrubs when the woodcutter found the corpse . . . [which are a] pair of stiff hands of a dead man. As a matter of fact, the film *Rashōmon* is set in a milieu in which the world is thrown out of joint: the decrepit *Rashōmon* gate, the suspense of a Hitchcockian style before the corpse is discovered, the violence, the betrayal, the robbery, and the inscrutability of everything . . . From

this perspective, instead of treating it as an embodiment of the "enchantment" of traditional Japanese taste, it would be more apposite to describe this film as an allegory of the rootlessness of Japanese reality after the Second World War.[74]

Heidegger's reference to this film is misplaced and seems to result from the danger the conversational partners discuss, but never realize is concretized in their exchange.

No-Play

The mention of the importance of gesture (over and above realism) prompts the Japanese to draw a contrast between the film and the *No*-play of Japanese theatre. This continues their discussion of gesture as an alternative to the European (or American) camera's error of objectifying the Japanese world. The Questioner admits that he never attended such a play but has read "a book about the *No-play* . . . Benl's Academy treatise" (GA 12: 101/OWL 17).[75] Stressing that he has only read *about* such theatre reemphasizes his representationally and metaphysically informed access to this experience. He can only understand something *about* that which has been objectified through a study, he cannot unfold an experience *of* the play because it is bound up in the Japanese world that remains closed to him. The Japanese insists, "you would need to attend such plays. But even that remains hard as long as you are unable to live within the Japanese existence" (GA 12: 101/OWL 18). He nevertheless proceeds to assist the Questioner with an account (and small demonstration) of the importance of gesture for *No* play, showing how an actor's gestures allow a mountain landscape to appear.

The Japanese both tells and shows the Questioner that the emptiness of the stage is inhabited by the gestures of the actors: "For instance, if a mountain landscape, is to appear, the actor slowly raises his open hand and holds it quietly above his eyes at eyebrow level" (GA 12: 102/OWL 18). Heidegger inserts a rare parenthetic stage direction, writing "(The Japanese raises and holds his hand in the described way)" (GA 12: 102/OWL 18, tm.). The Questioner responds, "a [*ein*] European" (GA 12: 102/OWL 18)—not "we Europeans"—would not be content with such a simple gesture. The Questioner turns to the Heideggerian notion of "nothingness" as an analog for the fertility of this "emptiness" (GA 12: 103/OWL 19) of the Japanese stage, rather than listening further to the Japanese or quoting from the treatise just referenced. This ostensive tour through a foreign way of thinking concludes with a return to a discussion of the Questioner's (Heidegger's) own work, decentering the Japanese world for a distinctly Heideggerian description of the "the gathering of a bearing . . . which bears itself toward us" (GA 12: 102/OWL 18–19).

Language (Is the House of Being)

The fourth part of "Conversation of Language" resumes articulating Heidegger's (Western) orientation. This brief foray into the Japanese world yields the Questioner purchase on his own philosophical concerns, reversing course to return from the East to the West. They turn to language and naming as explored by the Questioner's phrase the "house of being" in his "Letter on Humanism" (GA 12: 105/OWL 21, tm.). The question of danger is reactivated in relation to the plurality of languages, translation, and East-West exchange.

This section begins with the Japanese sharing a worry that has plagued many of Heidegger's characters in his conversational texts: "I must consider that our conversation has strayed far from its pathway [*weit von seinem Weg*]" (GA 12: 106/OWL 21, tm.). In response, the Questioner assumes the familiar[76] role of pedagogically aiding the Japanese to remember the course of their conversation thus far. Together, the two conversational partners recall that they first discussed Kuki's aesthetic interpretation of *iki*, then considered the danger of bringing Western metaphysical aesthetics to bear upon the Eastasian world, and finally noted how the source of this danger is not particular to East-West exchange, but rather inheres in the concealed essence of language itself. This recapitulation of their conversation reveals that they have "stayed on the pathway [*Weg*] of the conversation" after all (GA 12: 106/OWL 22, tm.).

But the "way" of their conversation does not consist in anything metaphysically objectifiable. Though the Questioner prompts them to consider how they learned to do this by respecting the (pedagogical) silence at the heart of their conversation, together the conversational partners reflect upon the importance of leaving the essence of language unnamed:

Questioner: [. . .] we, without quite knowing it, were obedient to what alone, according to your words, allows a conversation to succeed.

Japanese: It is that undefined defining [*unbestimmte Bestimmende*] something . . .

QUESTIONER: . . . which we let remain untouched despite its coaxing voice [*Stimme*].

JAPANESE: At the risk that this voice [*Stimme*], in our case, is silence itself.

QUESTIONER: What are you thinking of now?

JAPANESE: Of the same that you think, of the essence of language.

QUESTIONER: That is what is defining [*Bestimmende*] our conversation. But even so we must not touch it.

JAPANESE: Surely not, if by touching you mean grasping it in the sense of your European conceptualizations. (GA 12: 106–7/ OWL 22, tm.)

This exchange unfolds a sense of conversation that accords with the supplement from the "Triadic Conversation": "Where else could the unspoken be purely kept, heeded, other than in true conversation" (GA 77: 159/CPC 104). The conversation's voice of silence must not be touched,[77] or rather it must not be represented metaphysically. Heidegger's guiding aspiration is disclosed just after this exchange, placed in the Japanese's mouth: that his phrase describing language as the "house of being" "touches upon the essence of language without doing it injury" (GA 12: 107/OWL 22, tm.). Such poetic, non-injurious touching is only possible through leaving its essence undefined and engaging in conversation with an other to whom one is open, which in turn accords with the conversation that language itself is.[78] Whether Heidegger achieves this aspiration—particularly in relation to his crafting of the Japanese character—remains in question. Nevertheless, the pedagogical techniques of silence and openness are here acknowledged as conversational practices in which both characters take part.

This accord enables an affective intensification of the conversation. It provides the Questioner the occasion to "take courage [*Mut*]" (GA 12: 107/OWL 22), as he puts it, and to ask something he has long resisted asking. Though he registers they are "going toward the danger" (GA 12: 108/OWL 23, tm.), the Questioner still ventures to ask, "what does the Japanese world understand by language? Asked still more cautiously: Do you have in your language a word for what we name [*nennen*] language? If not, how do you experience what is called language by us?" (GA 12: 108/OWL

23, tm.). The danger they are walking straight toward is not the danger of translating between languages. Rather, this danger is that the European, Western metaphysical concept of language may overwrite, distort, or otherwise obscure whatever answer the Japanese might provide. The Questioner does not harbor the converse worry that the Eastern experience of language distorts the European concept of language or he would not have asked his final question, which assumes his conversational partner already grasps what he means by "language."

The Japanese is a professional translator of German to Japanese. He mentions translating the Questioner's lecture on Hölderlin's elegy "Homecoming" and Kleist's *Penthesilea* and the *Amphitryon*. The Japanese tells the Questioner, "while I was translating, I often felt as though I were wandering back and forth between two different essences of language [*verschiedenen Sprachwesen*]" (GA 12: 109/OWL 24, tm.). For Ma, this shows Heidegger's interest in intercultural exchange is asymmetrical[79] insofar as German, with its inextricable grounding in metaphysical, representational, and technological thinking, will inevitably distort that with which it comes into contact. Ma notes that the converse—that Japanese would likewise distort German concepts—does not arise as significant: "What he is talking about is not the danger of any language when used to explain a notion embedded in another language, but specifically *the* danger inherent in European languages. Furthermore, the existence of this danger is independent of the actual use of European language(s), either in intercultural context or not."[80] The two essences of language the Japanese references do not carry equivalent ontological weight.

It might be argued that this asymmetry can be positively construed. The Eastern world is depicted as free from the corrosive effects of the representational metaphysics plaguing the West! However, this presumption reveals a deeper failure on Heidegger's part to heed the danger. The Questioner seems to forget he is assuming the Japanese already understands the Western concept of language and, further, that Western metaphysics is graspable for non-Westerners even though the reverse does not hold. Heidegger may be working to counter what he understands as the metaphysical drive toward planetary domination. However, this same line of thinking Heidegger is here exemplifying has also justified colonial expansion and ideologies of cultural and racial superiority. That Heidegger's understanding of endangerment runs only one way—from West to East—already calls into question whether he recognizes this alterity.

The Japanese responds to the Questioner's query in a remarkable way. After telling the Questioner that "no one has ever addressed this question to me" (GA 12: 108/OWL 23, tm.), the Japanese asks for a few moments to consider his reply. At this point, Heidegger inserts another stage direction: "*(The Japanese closes his eyes, lowers his head, and sinks into a long reflection. The Questioner waits until his guest resumes the conversation)*" (GA 12: 108/ OWL 23, tm.). This interlude marks the relation between this text and Heidegger's preceding conversations in several ways. First, the importance of silence is both discussed and performed during these moments. Since the "Evening Conversation," Heidegger has inserted sporadic paragraph breaks into his characters' contributions, indicating short bursts of silence punctuating their speech. Though waiting was especially emphasized in "Evening Conversation," it is not until approximately halfway through "Conversation of Language" that Heidegger provides an overt performance of such waiting. This further shows how now it is the conversation taken as a whole—not the characters—that unfolds the pedagogy of a poetic thinking, in which silence plays a significant role. Finally, in this brief note, it is telling that Heidegger refers to the Japanese as "his guest [*sein Gast*]." The "Tower Conversation" portrayed the Tower Warden and the Teacher walking out toward the Guest, despite the Teacher's distress associated with him as the origin of the unsettling picture. In "Conversation of Language," we may finally find Heidegger's teaching character ready to meet his guest, calmly and eagerly welcoming him into his home to discuss the picture in question (here of Kuki's grave). Though danger abounds, it seems Heidegger feels more equipped to stage a conversation that welcomes a guest now than he did in the second of the *Country Path Conversations*.

Upon breaking his performed silence, the Japanese reports that there is a Japanese word for the essence of language, but he does not share what it is. He instead withholds the word—much like the Scholar in the "Triadic Conversation" with the Heraclitus fragment—to ensure the Questioner is first prepared to receive it. The Japanese does disclose, however, that "from a great distance [*aus der Ferne*] I sense a kinship [*Verwandtschaft*] between our word that is now before my mind, and your phrase [the 'house of being']" (GA 12: 108/OWL 24). In the "Tower Conversation," the Teacher used the word acquaintanceship—*Kundschaft*—to describe the relation between the Guest and the picture. Here, a Guest proclaims an even closer relationship of *Verwandtschaft*—a familial relation—between his word for language and the interest in hermeneutics that first led the Questioner to his phrase.

Perhaps this too suggests that Heidegger now finds himself more adept at letting the strange be strange—drawing nearer to its farness—and thereby finding the possibility of an even more intimate relation to language and being. Or it evinces an overreach that shows Heidegger has yet more to learn than he realizes.

In what follows, the characters suggest the "hint [*Wink*]" (GA 12: 109/OWL 24) is related to this essence of language. The Japanese is afraid hinting may be conceptualized as a "guiding concept [*Leitbegriff*] into which we then bundle up everything" (GA 12: 109/OWL 24–25). As in the "Triadic Conversation," fear indicates a reliance on representational, metaphysical thinking that should be released into anxiety. The Questioner helps the Japanese release his fear through pointing out the inevitability of representational metaphysics. Even if they never succeed in guarding themselves entirely from such thinking, the Questioner suggests they will have done well enough if they manage to "build a bypath [*Seitenpfad*] toward those ways" (GA 12: 111/OWL 26) even as their thinking may be overtaken by representational metaphysics. The suggestion that these mistakes may even be *necessary* to build this bypath still resounds in this conversation from its first suggestion in "Tower Conversation." Silence is one way to attempt this. The Japanese suggests that "hold[ing] back [a] word" (GA 12: 111/OWL 26), or "hesitat[ing]" (GA 12: 113/OWL 28) would allow the word to unfold as a hint. The Questioner further describes hints: "They are enigmatic. They beckon to us. They beckon *away*. They beckon us *toward* that from which they unexpectedly bear themselves toward us" (GA 12: 111/OWL 26). To think the movement that these hints incite, the conversational partners begin to speak of the wide sphere in which these hints may "have the possibility of swinging [*weit auszuschwingen*] widely" (GA 12: 113/OWL 27). Only in such a "region" (GA 77: 114/CPC 73), as the characters from the *Country Path Conversations* would call it, can they begin to think beyond representational metaphysics: "I do not mean the being of beings represented metaphysically, but the essence of being, more precisely the two-fold of being and beings" (GA 12: 112/OWL 26, tm.).

(Conversational) Hermeneutics

In the fifth section of "Conversation of Language," Heidegger offers a dense philosophical elaboration of the role hermeneutics continues to play in his later thinking of language. Though the partners had just recently toured the Eastasian world in their conversation, Heidegger's Questioner appeals to the Greeks for this endeavor. It begins with a purported reversal of their pedagogical dynamic in which the Japanese takes up the role of questioner and the Questioner is called upon to provide responses. The Questioner suggests, "in order that your reflection may swing freely [*ausschwinge*], almost without your prompting, let us exchange roles [*Rollen vertauschen*], and let me be the one who would undertake to provide the answers [*das Antworten übernehme*], specifically the answer to your question about hermeneutics" (GA 12: 113–14/OWL 28, tm.). But this ostensive reversal of roles proves to mean little. In most cases, the Questioner has *already* been giving answers, especially about his personal intellectual history and his early thinking, which he employs to make sense of the Japanese's depictions of the Eastern world. This betrays his penchant for answering (rather than asking) questions, which has been sustained across the conversation. Yet it may also show that what it means to question, for Heidegger, is to be enmeshed in history. Perhaps radical difference can only be encountered from an already situated locale in the world. Though Heidegger may be illustrating this point in "Conversation of Language," it is not clear he is aware of doing so.

Endeavoring to seriously address what he means by hermeneutics, the Questioner resolves to not simply "t[ell] [hi]stories [*Geschichten*]" (GA 12: 114/OWL, 28, tm.), but to "show how I came to employ the word" (GA 12: 114/OWL 28). He unfolds an etymology, following the word back to its Greek source and "the name of the god Hermes by a playful thinking that is more compelling than the rigor of science" (GA 12: 115/OWL 29). Prior to the solidification of its meaning as interpretation, the Questioner claims hermeneutics has meant "the bearing of message [*Botschaft*] and tidings [*Kunde*]" (GA 12: 115/OWL 29). The Questioner clarifies that his phenomenological project from *Being and Time* was essentially hermeneutic in this sense, insofar as his attempt to think the being of beings as "the two-fold [*Zweifalt*] of the two in virtue of their simple oneness [*Einfalt*]" that required the human, who is only human in "corresponding to the call of the two-fold" (GA 12: 116/OWL 30), that is in receiving this message. Hermeneutics—and the sense of language hermeneutics supports—is pivotal because it is language that enables the ontological relation of the human and being. As the Questioner further describes, language is essentially historical—involved in a conversation with past thinkers and those yet to come (GA 12: 117/OWL 30–31). Of course, there is a danger interpretation could degenerate into an attempt to extract a merely correct definition.[81]

This danger, the Questioner says, can be "stave[d] off as long as we ourselves make an effort to think in conversation" (GA 12: 117/OWL 31). Not only is hermeneutics essentially ontological, it is also inherently conversational.

The Japanese and the Questioner struggle to understand what it could mean to think the relation that language supports beyond metaphysics. They attempt to forgo defining each word technologically by excavating its meaning and making it available, but rather aim to give "each word . . . its full—most often hidden—weight" (GA 12: 117/OWL 31).[82] When they allow language to emerge in its poetic essence, the reliance on a metaphysical rubric that determines beings or being as subjects or objects in advance is no longer needed. Instead, it becomes clear that the human herself is essentially "needed [*gebracht*]" (GA 12: 119/OWL 32) by being. Because the relation is not one that spans objective distance but rather elaborates an intimate belonging, this means that "relation to the two-fold . . . is not an object of mental representation, but is the sway of usage [*das Walten des Brauches*]" (GA 12: 119/OWL 33). That which allows language to properly sway and to reveal itself as concealed is—as the "Western Conversation" insisted—the poetic. Heidegger's characters elaborate that this also means they must strive to think together with (and thereby remain open to) others, that conversation itself enables such an inhabitation of language. The Japanese tells the Questioner, "when I can follow you in conversation, I succeed. Left *alone*, I am helpless" (GA 12: 120/OWL 33, tm.). What it is to be in conversation is to never be left alone, but to remain walking a path that many before and many after will also take. It is to belong to a community—a condition enabled by poetizing. This poetizing sense of conversation is what the conversational partners conclude is most properly enabled by—and essentially *is*—language. Language is most essentially itself in conversation and in poetizing.

The conversational partners insist that the sense of language they have just unfolded stands in stark contrast to a metaphysical representation of language in which it is predicated on expression of a correspondence between that which is inward—the soul—and that which is exterior—the object. On the one hand, the Questioner is critical of phenomenology for seemingly always referring "life and lived experience back to the 'I' [*ein Ich*]" (GA 12: 122/OWL 35). Returning again to his 1920 lecture course "Expression and Appearance," the conversational partners wrestle with whether the Questioner had there already moved beyond a metaphysical sense of phenomenology. At first, the Japanese thinks the Questioner had activated this non-metaphysical view of language precisely by following the path of hermeneutics in his engagement with phenomenology. The Questioner, however, suggests this would be a "mistake" (GA 12: 121/OWL 34) and that he had not yet seen what was at stake in the thinking he began as "youthful capers" (GA 12: 121/OWL 35). He suggests that his work was still caught in metaphysical thinking, indicated in the subject-object relation:

> JAPANESE: [. . .] By giving your lecture the title, you did commit yourself to the subject-object relation.
>
> QUESTIONER: In a certain respect, your objection is justified, if only because much had to remain unclear in that lecture. (GA 12: 123/OWL 36, tm.)

But on this point, the Questioner also equivocates. Though metaphysics may have permeated his earlier thinking to a greater extent, he does not believe he was fully swept up by it then either. The Questioner suggests that he may have made a mistake in his youth, but a productive, creative mistake that allowed him to begin to make the leap from representational, metaphysical thinking, even as he was finding a springboard of sorts in such thinking itself. As the "Triadic Conversation" emphasized, the relation between metaphysical and non-metaphysical thinking cannot be simply oppositional. The "Tower Conversation" elaborates that mistakes are not missteps, but rather occasions to continue to learn non-metaphysical thinking. The youth of the "Younger Man" in both "Evening Conversation" and "Western Conversation" attest to how helpful abandoning caution can be. The Questioner in "Conversation of Language" emphasizes that "nobody can in just one single leap [*Sprung*] take distance from the predominant circle of ideas [*aus dem herrschenden Vorstellungskreis*]" (GA 12: 123/OWL 36). He claims he is not trying to escape the velocity of history, but rather "to bring together what is concealed [*verbirgt*] within the old [*im Alten*]" (GA 12: 124/OWL 36). For this, he needs not only youthful daring, but also an older (even ancient) sense of the origin of history.

In this respect, the Questioner understands himself as working with the history of representational metaphysics, unfolding how it has misunderstood its own meaning. Even in his earliest thinking attempts, he clarifies he was in this sense already moving beyond metaphysics even in turning back to Kant's thinking of appearance through his "object [*Gegenstand*] of our representation" (GA 12: 124/OWL 37), which the Japanese further elaborates as that which stands "in opposition [*Gegenstehen*] to us" (GA 12: 125/OWL 37). Unlike Kant, the Questioner is not interested in the object of appearance, but rather in the originary "appearing of the appearance [*Erscheinen der Erscheinung*]" (GA 12: 125/OWL 37), echoing his concern not with hermeneutics as (representational, metaphysical) interpretation, but as the (non-representational, non-metaphysical) interpretation that underlies such methodology. To elaborate this origin of the phenomenon of appearance, the Questioner turns to the Greeks, specifically the Greek experience of the presence of present beings without forcing them into "opposing objectness," and instead as an experience of the "radiance [*Scheinen*]" of "unconcealment [*Entbergung*]" (GA 12: 125/OWL 38).

There are several important aspects of this turn toward the Greeks. Most significantly, the Questioner has just been met with the Eastern world. Rather than continuing to question and think with the Japanese, he chooses to remain firmly within the historical boundaries of the Western tradition. But this choice is nuanced. The Questioner insists that the word "Appearance" in the title of his lecture course both does and does not take on the Greek meaning. It does insofar as "for me the name 'appearance' does not name objects as objects" (GA 12: 125/OWL 38), but it also does not because merely contrasting the Greek and Kantian experiences of appearance is not enough. Even if it were possible to obvert the Kantian view of metaphysical objectivity, the Questioner emphasizes we would "still in no way be thinking of appearance in the Greek sense" (GA 12: 125, OWL 38, tm.) because our thinking is still overdetermined by representational subjectivity as well, thanks to "the manner of Descartes: in terms of the 'I' as the subject" (GA 12: 125/OWL 38). The West is caught up in a history of representational, metaphysical thinking that must be thought otherwise-than-oppositionally.

The Questioner is not trying to replicate or simply "return to Greek and even pre-Socratic thinking" (GA 12: 126/OWL 38). Yet he does hold that "our thinking today is charged with the task to think what the Greeks have thought in an even more Greek manner [*noch griechischer*]" (GA 12: 127/OWL 39). The Questioner notes this claim will be open to all sorts of "new misinterpretation" (GA 12: 126/OWL 39). Throughout this section, the Japanese—attempting to follow the responses offered by the Questioner to his questions—has been misinterpreting and misunderstanding much. Yet these misinterpretations provide precisely those occasions by which the two continue to walk the path of their conversation together.[83] Neither character expresses embarrassment or frustration in getting it wrong. They hardly even remark upon these mistakes, instead effortlessly weaving them into the fabric of their conversational exchange.

The Questioner then describes the essence of alethic appearance: appearance as "the emergence into openness [*ins Lichte*] in the sense of unconcealedness [*Unverborgenheit*]" (GA 12: 127/OWL 39). This way of seeing may be "Greek," but what this way of seeing sees is "never again, Greek" (GA 12: 127/OWL 39). The Questioner does not aim to replicate the Greek experience of the world, but rather to "catch sight of appearance as the essence of presence in its essential origin" (GA 12: 127/OWL 40, tm.). At this elaboration of *aletheia*, the Japanese expresses his own hope that in thinking in both this Greek and no-longer-Greek way, they will "abandon the region of the subject-object relation when thinking is let into the experience just mentioned" (GA 12: 127–28/ OWL 40, tm.). The Questioner replies, "hardly. But you are touching on something essential" (GA 12: 128/ OWL 40). What remains to be seen is whether the Japanese is touching upon this insight without injuring it. Nothing so simple as leaving behind or exchanging one way of thinking for another is at stake. Rather, they must assume a pedagogical stance toward representational metaphysics itself, to learn to think of it non-representationally and non-metaphysically. This can only be undertaken, as "Conversation of Language" repeatedly suggests, hermeneutically, by way of the poetizing interpretation that the "Western Conversation" showed counter-resonates with poetizing's own resonating. The Questioner tells the Japanese, "in the source of appearance, something comes toward the human being that holds the two-fold of presence and present beings" (GA 12: 128/OWL 40, tm.). What comes toward the human is the message of the hermeneutical relation they spoke of earlier. Listening to the message is what the Questioner calls "*being* human [*Mensch*-sein]" (GA 12: 128/OWL 40).

At this point, the Japanese mentions that he senses "a "deeply concealed kinship [*Verwandtschaft*] with our thinking, precisely because your way of thinking [*Denkweg*] and its language are so wholly other" (GA 12: 129/OWL 41). This suggestion of a relatedness to Japanese thinking deeply "agitates [*erregt mich*]" (GA 12: 129/OWL 41) the Questioner. He admits that he can only handle his agitation "because we remain in conversation" (GA 12: 129/OWL 41, tm.) and can raise the question of the "place [*Ort*]" (GA 12: 129/OWL 41, tm.) of this kinship while again failing to register the pronominal asymmetry. Nevertheless, this intensification of the importance of conversation evokes the most condensed illustration of the task in which they are engaged in the "Conversation of Language" and perhaps in the conversational corpus as a whole:

JAPANESE: [The belonging together of hermeneutics and language carries us] toward a transformation of thinking—a transformation which, however, is not like a course correction [*Kursänderung*] is set up, and even less as the consequence [*Folge*] of an accumulation of the results of philosophical research.

QUESTIONER: The transformation happens as a walking [*Wanderung*] . . .

JAPANESE: . . . in which one place [*Ort*] is abandoned [*verlassen*] in favor of another . . .

QUESTIONER: . . . which requires an emplacing discussion [*Erörterung*].

JAPANESE: The one place is metaphysics.

QUESTIONER: And the other? We leave [*lassen*] it without a name [*Namen*]. (GA 12: 130/OWL 42, tm.)

To leave this other place without a name—and further to leave unanswered the question of the place that would make possible drawing these two sites into discussion—leaves much unsaid. Yet this silence is not mute. Rather, in its silence, it is (pedagogically) evocative. It guards against the possibility of thinking these two sites in opposition. If one is not named, it cannot oppose metaphysics because it is not an "it." Further, the conversation itself allows the characters together to speak *of* but not *about* the (cross-cultural) possibility of non-metaphysical thinking.

The conversational partners' decision to leave the site in silence does not mean they cease speaking. Rather, the conversation turns back to Kuki's interest in *iki* and how it related to his interest in metaphysics and the Questioner's critiques thereof. The Questioner suggests that Kuki's interest in European aesthetics was perhaps not for the purpose of interpreting *iki* according to its rubrics, but rather to determine the relevant difference between Eastern and Western thinking of the aesthetic. Up to this point, the Japanese has been unwilling to venture his own translation of *iki*. The Questioner clarifies "the essence of the aesthetic" (GA 12: 131/OWL 43, tm.) is mired in a metaphysical view of the artist "as a subject who remains related to the work as his object" (GA 12: 132/OWL 43). Together, the characters acknowledge this metaphysical "framework is so treacherous [*verfänglich*]" in that it is "all-embracing [*umgreifend*]" but encircles it in such a way that it can "never make its own [*aneignen*]" (GA 12: 132/OWL 43) what it claims to represent.

With this, the Japanese becomes willing to hazard a translation of *iki*—or rather two attempts between which a priority is never determined. This undecidability staves off the interpretation that the Japanese's translations seek to correctly represent the word. First, he describes *iki* as "the gracious" (GA 12: 132/OWL 43). As suggestive as this translation is, it rather quickly conjures Schiller, Kant, and Hegel, and thereby activates the history of Western metaphysical thinking, which stands at the ready to make the translation representable. Despite this, the Japanese announces his intention to "attempt to detach [*herauszunehmen*] *iki*" (GA 12: 133/OWL 44) from this way of thinking. In elaborating what he means by "the gracious" beyond the Western tradition, the Japanese offers a second, more poetic translation: "*Iki* is the breath of the stillness of luminous delight" (GA 12: 133/OWL 44). This translation fares better in offering a bypath around metaphysical thinking, at least at first blush. Metaphysical thinking can never be entirely avoided. It is the site that first enables non-metaphysical thinking to emerge. But in choosing a phrase that works as a "hint that beckons on, and beckons to and fro" (GA 12: 133/OWL 44), the Japanese's translation holds it at bay just long enough for the site beyond metaphysics to be glimpsed.

The (Same?) Conversation

In the final section of "Conversation of Language," the characters are still grappling with the danger of their conversation, specifically with the relation of their two languages, cultures, and histories to a hermeneutic and phenomenological sense of language beyond metaphysics. Are there multiple houses of being? Or do the two characters occupy different rooms (so to speak) within the same house of being? At the closing of their conversation, this question remains salient.

The Questioner earlier asked after the Japanese word for language, which the Japanese elected to withhold. They return to this word in the wake of having learned to rescue their thinking from overdetermination by metaphysics, illustrated by the Japanese's poetic translations of *iki*. The Japanese finally reveals the word for language—*Koto ba*—after he shares that he was afraid that his translation would too easily be metaphysically rendered as "a mere pictograph [*Bilderschrift*]" (GA 12: 154/OWL 45). In other words, the Japanese's fear teaches caution because metaphysics threatens to turn his world into mere representational pictures, exemplified earlier with Kurosawa's film and the Questioner's photograph of Kuki's grave.[84] These representational images distort, but as products of technology they are not only or inherently negative. Though they first appear representationally, the potential remains to think beyond and through this distortion. Perhaps these pictures provide the occasion for poetic interpretation by critiquing metaphysics in order to bring it back within its proper limits.[85]

The Japanese discloses the word but does not venture its definition for some time. He first describes each word that makes it up: "*ba* means leaves [or] petals" (GA 12: 134/OWL 45) and *koto* requires an extensive contextualization by way of the graciousness[86] associated with *iki* and the non-metaphysical distinction between *iro*[87] and *ku*, with a detour through the Greek understanding of "what poetically condenses [*Dichtende*]" (GA 12: 135/OWL 46, tm.). Finally, the Japanese ventures stating what *koto ba* says: "the petals that stem from *koto*" as "the event [*Ereignis*] of the opening message of the grace that brings forth" (GA 12: 136/OWL 47, tm.). This word does not *define* language—it *poetizes* its essence.

In response to the sharing of this word he calls "wonderous"[88] and "inexhaustible" (GA 12: 136/OWL 47), the Questioner shares a word for language of his own that he finds "more fitting [*Gemäßeres*]" (GA 12: 137/OWL 47) because it works to evade metaphysics. Instead of "language," the Questioner prefers the word "saying [*die Sage*]" (GA 12: 137/OWL 47). This word means to "let appear [*erscheinen*] and let shine [*scheinenlassen*], but in the way [*Weise*] of hinting" (GA 12: 137/OWL 47). Yet even this poetic depiction of saying can only, the Questioner insists, be "the beginning of that path [*Weg*] which takes us back out of merely metaphysical representations" (GA 12: 137/OWL 48). This path must lead not to any question "*about* language [*über* die Sprache]" (GA 12: 139/OWL 49)[89] because "speaking *about* language turns language almost inevitably into an object," to which the Japanese replies, "and then its essence vanishes" (GA 12: 141/OWL 50, tm). They must learn to practice a poetic saying *of* language instead.

The conversational partners search for a way of speaking that builds a bypath through and beyond the metaphysical objectification of representational language. They decide that their task is "to guard the purity of the [mystery's] source" (GA 12: 140/OWL 50, tm.), not by simply abstaining from the "risk [*Wagnis*] of speaking about language" (GA 12: 141/OWL 50) but by striving to allow this speaking to retain its "movement [*Bewegung*]" (GA 12: 141/OWL 50). They have already illustrated this in providing elucidations of their respective words for language—*koto ba* and saying—that are mysterious and poetic on their own, and also by providing multiple depictions of these words, which shows that no single definition represents this meaning. In addition to these implicit illustrations, the conversational partners further discern a way of speaking that best supports this movement. As the Questioner puts it, "a speaking *of* [*von*] language could only be a conversation" (GA 12: 141/OWL 51), which accords with Heidegger's 1936 contention that language is conversational in essence.[90] Conversation has quietly anchored Heidegger's thinking of poetic language across multiple decades of his work.

In the final moments of their conversation, the characters reflect on conversation as a form of saying. Many of these reflections accord with remarks already found in "Triadic Conversation" that distinguish certain forms of talking from the sense of conversation at play here and insist that silence (more than talking) characterizes the corresponding saying of conversation. The Questioner also clarifies that what he was trying to think as "the hermeneutic circle" (GA 12: 142/OWL 51) in his early work was actually a listening that is simultaneously an (interpretive) saying. He no longer calls this the hermeneutic circle, but rather *conversation*. It is the saying of language itself—not human beings—that brings "about authentic conversation" (GA 12: 143/OWL 52, tm.). While the Questioner elects to leave the "question open" when the Japanese asks whether "in this sense, then, even Plato's *Dialogues*[91] would not be conversations?" (GA 12: 143/OWL 52), evidently Heidegger now understands this form of saying as fundamental to (and in no way derivative from) his thinking of language. The silences of conversation have the character of a "constant coming" as a "prologue [*Vorspiel*] to the authentic [*eigentlichen*] conversation *of* language" (GA 12: 144/OWL 52–53, tm.). Insofar as silence is the essence of poetizing, the silence of conversation is also inherently related to the poetic. Learning to listen to language in this way is the essence of the poetic pedagogy Heidegger stages in his conversational texts.

But it is not clear that Heidegger has enacted his own poetic pedagogy in this conversational text, particularly in relation to the Eastasian world he draws from in elaborating this sense of conversation. Though the Questioner and Japanese reference *iki*, ancient Japanese poetry, and return to *koto ba* in the concluding pages of the conversation, these Japanese themes act as foils to amplify the Questioner's attempt to bid "farewell" (GA 12: 146/OWL 54) to metaphysics. Ma argues that this conclusion is strikingly monological[92] despite its celebration of conversation. This could be understood in two ways. One the one hand, there are formal similarities between this conclusion and the conclusion of the "Triadic Conversation." The ending of "Conversation of Language" also contains many lines that begin and end in ellipses, and the characters seem to be participating in the same saying rather than offering distinct contributions. There seems to be deep agreement and collaborative poetizing here—engendered by language itself—that rejects that any "serviceable clarification of the essence of language" can be found in "information in the form of theorems and cue words" (GA 12: 145/OWL 54, tm.). But on the other hand, there is a sustained asymmetry between the two characters at this closing. In the final ten lines of each character, the Questioner makes nine statements and asks one (rhetorical) question, whereas the Japanese makes four statements and asks six (apparently genuine) questions. Though Heidegger may have articulated a prologue toward the Questioner's thinking of the essence of saying, this was not accomplished through remaining open to the alterity of his Eastern guest.

Dangerous Conclusions

I have shown that the pedagogical techniques Heidegger relies upon in his other conversational texts are also at play in this conversation. At various points, the conversational partners underscore the importance of silence, enact reversals, remember, and notice affect. Arguably, Heidegger intends for the "Conversation of Language" as a whole to demonstrate the fifth pedagogical technique—openness to the other. Heidegger likely composed this text to demonstrate both how open the Eastern philosophical world had been to him and that he reciprocated this gesture. But it is readily apparent that Heidegger did not achieve a meaningful cross-cultural philosophical conversation in this text, which rightly emphasizes how dangerous such an endeavor would be. Another interpretation therefore becomes possible. Perhaps Heidegger is revising what shape such openness can take, emphasizing how historical, linguistic, and cultural contexts cannot be technologically rendered as available, interchangeable resources and that history significantly delimits our capacity for radical openness to alterity. Heidegger's very performance of his own failure may argue not that we should forgo attempting to engage across and through difference, but that we should be ever more sensitive to the amplified possibilities for making mistakes that we may or may not ever become aware of making. This is a dangerous pedagogy, indeed.

In the Bremen lectures, Heidegger writes, "what is most dangerous in the danger consists in the danger concealing itself as the danger that it is" (GA 79: 54/52). Danger's self-concealment as such is both its most essential trait and that which makes it dangerous toward itself. The danger of a conversation that spans cultural, historical, and linguistic contexts is finally articulated not as anything as blatant as the European conceptual system threatening to overwrite Japanese meaning. Even more essentially, the danger consists in the threat that one might sense in otherness only what is familiar, despite every attempt to listen beyond one's biases and prejudices. Even in trying to reach out beyond oneself, it could be that one may only ever be able to sense as problematic what one is already equipped to recognize and address. The deeper danger is that nothing might be registered as dangerous at all.

This is the pedagogical force of Heidegger's "Conversation of Language." On my reading, Heidegger has demonstrated—knowingly or unknowingly—the danger of conversational, poetic pedagogy. As Heidegger's characters repeatedly emphasize, this danger is enhanced when apparent agreement has been reached. Even when it seems a Japanese word or concept is successfully translatable into a Western vernacular—even into Heidegger's non-metaphysical (but still Western) thinking—the characters feel agitation and unease, as well they should. Heidegger's mistakes in attempting to relate his thinking to the Eastern world shows how relevant ongoing engaging in his poetic, conversational pedagogy remains, especially for *him*. In this conversation between professional teachers, it is even more urgent for these characters to practice becoming ever more student-like to begin to learn the difficulty and danger of teaching itself. Despite his own well-formulated criticisms of representational metaphysics, Heidegger does not manage to think of the Japanese character as anyone more than a representative of a certain strata of Japanese culture as it has been objectified for him. That is, he does not learn to think of the *Japanese* non-representationally or non-metaphysically. The danger remains—as does the ongoing task of learning to listen ever more closely to the poetic silences of alterity.

Conclusion

Learning from/through/beyond Heidegger

In enacting a thinking beyond representational metaphysics, Heidegger's route takes him toward a sense of language that could enable such thinking. This is poetic language—language that allows poetizing to resound. In this book, I have argued that Heidegger's endeavor to evoke non-representational, non-metaphysical thinking—which both leaps beyond and returns to that which is originary of representational, metaphysical thinking—relies on what had yet to be acknowledged as the poetic pedagogy performed in conversation. Because the representational metaphysics of the Western philosophical tradition has ideologically dominated the history of thought, Heidegger's attempt to think otherwise must simultaneously unfold a way by which such radical thinking can be learned and taught. This way is not static or fixed. It cannot be captured as a set of step-by-step directions without risking reverting into representational, metaphysical thinking. This pedagogy instead emerges from its own locale in/as the event of its unfolding. It is a *way* in Heidegger's sense. We do not willfully travel such a road as isolated subjects moving through objective space; it is the way that moves us. This way is not simply a space for movement, it *itself* is "the movement (on the way) [*Bewegung*]" (GA 77: 118/CPC 76–77)—less a noun than a verb. Further, it moves *us* as a plurality, which means that such movement is collaborative—a distinguishing feature of conversation as such. This collaboration first affords the possibility of building a dwelling together as a non-metaphysical community. Because such pedagogy can only emerge from its unfolding, any attempt to produce such pedagogy from an authoritative teacher or teaching will necessarily fail. Poetic pedagogy can only take shape as non-metaphysical teaching when its posture of learning to listen to the saying of the alterity of language is radically intensified.

I have argued that Heidegger elaborates this poetic pedagogy in his five conversational texts. This is no accident of genre. For Heidegger, language is essential only as conversation. Because of the radicality of Heidegger's thinking relative to the tradition of Western philosophy, he must reformulate the basic meaning of many fundamental words harnessed by theory in his effort to dislodge them from their grounding in representational metaphysics. He must learn to *speak* otherwise so as to learn to *think* otherwise. As Aristotle first noted, simply speaking a language with others functions simultaneously as a teaching and learning of that language. In this sense, Heidegger's thinking has always already been a pedagogy.[1] This primarily ontological pedagogy is dramatically staged in his conversational texts, in which his characters teach and learn the meaning of thinking of being otherwise. My reading has drawn out the ways in which Heidegger's staging of the action, setting, and characters in these texts enable a unique vantage point from which to understand *how* Heidegger thinks as essential for enabling *what* he thinks and, further, how he endeavors to unfold this thinking for others. I have uncovered five pedagogical techniques—reversal, sensitivity to affect, remembrance, openness to otherness, and silence—supporting the elaboration of this poetic pedagogy. These are found in each of Heidegger's conversational texts and offer the basis from which to understand these texts as philosophically integrated (over and above sharing a common genre) as they perform learning and teaching non-representational, non-metaphysical thinking.

I have also shown that each conversational text mobilizes these pedagogical techniques uniquely. Each conversation articulates a particular element of Heidegger's poetic pedagogy, which together constitute it as a coherent whole. In the "Triadic Conversation," the characters learn the importance of non-oppositionality, particularly for teaching non-representational, non-metaphysical thinking to a resistant student. In the "Tower Conversation," the conversational partners learn that even a teacher making a mistake does not constitute a failure, but rather offers an invitation to sustain the posture of learning. The "Evening Conversation" illustrates the need for such pedagogy as a practice of building community because learning—even (or perhaps especially) in the absence of a distinct teacher—becomes teaching when such experiences are opened out toward others. In the "Western Conversation," the call for interpretation that issues from poetizing language—particularly Hölderlin's poetizing—is unveiled as what uniquely enables this pedagogy. Finally, the "Conversation of Language" demonstrates the danger of such poetic pedagogy exceeding its proper limits.

This developmental arc demonstrates the path Heidegger walked as he worked through the implications of what it means to teach and learn non-representational, non-metaphysical thinking. Though this development is clear, Heidegger has not offered a progressive account of pedagogy. Instead, he challenges the very notion of progress itself as able to claim pedagogical compatibility with non-representational, non-metaphysical thinking. The "Triadic Conversation" exhibits the most apparently "successful" conversation, in which the Scientist and the Scholar are persuaded to learn to think non-representationally and non-metaphysically. Each subsequent conversation unravels this ostensive accomplishment through decoupling pedagogy from any (authoritative) teaching figure until the final conversation becomes inextricably embroiled in its own dangerous undertaking. Yet this apparent journey from success to failure may instead speak of Heidegger's own sense of what has gone awry in the traditional student-teacher relationship and why it ought to be unraveled. Learning in a non-metaphysical sense offers no clearly discernible objective. When encountered alongside a metaphysical representation of "successful" education—as the assimilation and subsequent deployment of useful information—a pedagogy of non-metaphysical thinking appears as (at best) whimsy or (at worst) incompetence. The non-metaphysically representable outcome of Heidegger's pedagogy is not mastery, but rather a praxis of sustaining a posture of learning. In other words, the Heideggerian teacher has not "succeeded" when she has taught her students everything she knows. Instead, she must learn to enable her own irrelevance as an apparently authoritative teacher and to motivate an *unlearning* of the justification that would underwrite any possibility of authoritarianism in pedagogy. She must help her students learn that there is no essential difference between teacher and student. They are all collaboratively becoming a community of non-metaphysical thinkers through enacting poetic pedagogy.

Though this book unfolds the pedagogy underlying Heidegger's conversations in particular, several commentators have identified a pedagogy attending to Heidegger's thinking in other areas of his corpus. Focusing on *Being and Time*, Sacha Golob[2] explores how Heidegger's broken tool analysis can be harnessed for its pedagogical insights. Golob argues that the significance of the broken tool—reworked as a contemporary information tool—is to "activate and then disrupt"[3] its context, making visible the world in which the tool operates. He further claims this disruption "is not simply descriptive: it is not simply to highlight the world and the tool for further philosophical description. Instead, that process involves improving the tools we use."[4] While the initial moment of disruption of one's usual frame of reference is critical for learning and is often, as Golob underscores, up to the teacher to initiate, Heidegger's pedagogy extends far beyond any pragmatic use-value that would be aimed at improving our tools. In his later work, Heidegger's reconsideration of technology casts in doubt the very metric of "use." Michael Bonnett[5] also argues for an implicit philosophy of education in *Being and Time*. Bonnett finds a pedagogy suggested by Heidegger's existential analytic of Dasein and its emphasis on what he terms Dasein's "personal authenticity."[6] From his reading, Bonnett determines, "perhaps what emerges most powerfully is the importance of learners having the opportunity, encouragement, and support to decide how they will *value* what they learn, to decide how it should affect their outlook and their actions."[7] Opening space for learners to come into relation to what they are learning is undoubtedly important for Heidegger, but not as a site for evaluation. This issue of value is marked as distinctly metaphysical and the source of Nietzsche's error in the "Evening Conversation"—bypassed as significant for those who would truly learn.

Bonnett does not limit his analysis to *Being and Time*, however, and also highlights the distinction that later emerges between calculative and poetic thinking as significant for educational efforts. Moving beyond the instrumental view of education espoused by Golob, Bonnett finds poetic thinking a needed remedy in an inhuman landscape dominated by calculative thinking spurned on by a drive for technological advancement. For Bonnett, poetic thinking rests on the possibility of recognizing the "uniqueness of individual things"[8] and assuming a "*co-responsibility* . . . [in any] making and building"[9] responsive to this uniqueness. In the educational context, poetic modes of education involve what Bonnett calls a "triadic interplay between the teacher, learner, and what calls to be learned"[10] that involves particularly "a relationship that is radically non-instrumental,"[11] "requires a genuine *listening*,"[12] "openness to things,"[13] is "based on *trust* . . . [that acknowledges] such learning will require emotional support,"[14] and is necessarily related to the "different locations . . . [and] different times"[15] where learning may unfold. In following this sense of the poetic in Heidegger's later thinking, Bonnett articulates a striking constellation of elements and techniques also enacted in Heidegger's conversations. This guiding thread of the poetic in the later work offers more than the existential analytic of *Being and Time* for making sense of Heidegger's broader pedagogy. Bonnett concludes, "the teacher-pupil relationship is not to be conceived as a vehicle for the attainment of some set of prespecified standards in education—in effect as a management tool—but as a genuinely creative, because genuinely open, encounter in which the teacher attempts to sense both the quality of the learner's current engagement and to help him to hear for himself the call of what calls to be thought in this engagement."[16] The later Heidegger thinks the meaning of the poetic because he discerns that technology is no longer operating according to the tool-logic of *Being and Time*, but rather has become something entirely (post-)modern.[17]

The urgency of contending with the increasing domination of *Gestell* motivates many scholars who have sought educational insights from Heidegger. Indeed, the "Triadic Conversation" begins by staging a confrontation with scientific and technological thinking, though his mature understanding of this form of thought—first articulated in the *Bremen* lectures—is yet to come. Patrick Fitzsimons[18] explores how the relation between human beings and technology has also impacted education. Offering a close reading of the "Question Concerning Technology," Fitzsimons shows how Heidegger diagnoses a contemporary dissolution of the relation between *techne* and *poiesis*, which results from the elevation of Aristotle's *causa efficiens* above all others:[19] "When we take education primarily as a technology for national economic development, that "technology" is focused on some predetermined goal, itself already evaluated as of value. Education so configured does not suggest or ask about education's purpose. The process to the ends is purely to produce the predetermined ends, and the human is part of that structure."[20] When the human being becomes just another resource within the totalization of the standing reserve, the question of "value"—insofar as it remains at all legible as such—is taken entirely out of human hands, and instead becomes a function of calculative thinking. Any claim to humanistic[21] values can only serve to deflect inquiry into the essence of technology, which forecloses the possibility of dwelling[22] on the earth in equilibrium with it, a practice it seems education ought to support.

Iain Thomson[23] also argues that, for Heidegger, the meaning of education—especially higher education—is today determined by "enframing"[24] because the essence of truth varies according to the prevailing epoch of the history of being. For Thomson, the state of today's fractured multi-versity depicts, for Heidegger, an "ontohistorical dissolution of Plato's original conception of education."[25] Though Heidegger's project is deconstructive of the way Plato has been co-opted by the metaphysical tradition, Thomson argues that Heidegger finds a "long-obscured essence of education"[26] concealed in Plato's Allegory of the Cave. Heidegger's own return to the cave in "Plato's Doctrine of Truth" is in fact a recovery of what had been lost to metaphysics.

Thomson shows how Heidegger charts a course to "transcend enframing"[27] in four phases that align with Plato's allegory: first, students encounter the shadows as resources to be optimized; second, once students can see the fire, they experience negative freedom and realize that things aren't already showing themselves as themselves; third, daylight enables effective or positive freedom to dwell in the openness of being; and fourth, in their return to the cave, the students-become-teachers work to free other potential students.[28] Learning quite naturally becomes teaching as it reveals a shared subject matter in "whatever essentials address us at a given time."[29] For Thomson, Heidegger pedagogically transcends the current metaphysical epoch by seeking "to educate his students *against* their preexisting ontotheological education"[30] to awaken instead a true pedagogy: "Genuine education leads us back to ourselves, to the place we *are* (the *Da* of our *Sein*), teaches us 'to dwell' (*wohnen*) 'there,' and transforms us in the process . . . The goal of this educational odyssey is simple but literally *revolutionary*: to bring us full circle back to ourselves, first by turning us away from the world in which we are most immediately immersed, then by turning us back to this world in a more reflexive way."[31] In my view, an examination of the post-1942 pedagogy underlying his conversational texts reveals that Heidegger developed an even more complex sense of teaching and learning. Without a doubt, seeds of Heidegger's thinking on this topic are discernible as early as *Being and Time*.[32] His impending mature engagement with technology and the poetic certainly attenuated the dramatic staging he grants to his pedagogy in the conversations. However, only a close reading of the performance of pedagogy—alongside the explicit interspersed discussions of teaching and learning in these texts—discloses these nuances.

Heidegger's poetic pedagogy performed in the conversations is not concerned with honing instrumental or humanistic values for education. His call for revolutionary or radical resistance to the domination of representational, metaphysical thinking runs much deeper. The enactment of such a pedagogy would engender a dwelling that forgoes technological use, but Heidegger depicts this dwelling in a particularly concrete, textured way in the drama of the conversations. In the face of a technology that would, among other things, reduce education to a model of information transmission, a break first must be made with such metaphysical overdetermination. Thomson's reading of Heidegger's reading of Plato's allegory of the cave shows this. Despite Thomson's suggestion, however, that it is an "us" that first turns "away from the world in which we are most immediately immersed," Heidegger's "Triadic Conversation" shows that it is the atomized, isolated subject of representational metaphysics that first turns away, not only from the world, but also from one's own metaphysical subjectivity, which the Scientist, Scholar, and Guide enact in learning to leave their distinct personalities behind. Only such poetic pedagogy can constitute the plural, collective "we" needed for such revolutionary transformation, which can no longer be one of educating students "*against*" anything at all. Heidegger's Guide has cautioned that such a polemic is doomed to replicate the metaphysics it would attack. Non-oppositional pedagogy does not seek for superficial liberation, but the profound realization that we are already "between" metaphysical and non-metaphysical thinking. Once anyone who lays claim to the role of teacher realizes that they are perhaps even more vulnerable to mistakes than any student, a community of learners can only then realize their role is not to break each other's chains or lead one another anywhere. Instead, they must listen to the silence of what they are still not hearing in what already addresses them. Where Thomson renders Heidegger's reading of Plato's Cave Allegory as a story in which students become teachers, I read Heidegger's conversations as performing the (d)evolution of teaching into an intensified stance of learning.

A strange sort of ontological egalitarianism marks the collaborative non-metaphysical pedagogy of these texts. While these scholars of Heidegger's pedagogy have made invaluable contributions toward uncovering this educational dimension of Heidegger's ontology, they nevertheless presuppose the teacher-student relation as inviolable. On my reading, this is precisely a dangerous trope and hierarchical vestige of representational, metaphysical thinking that Heidegger unravels to instead enact non-representational, non-metaphysical pedagogy anew. The development Heidegger performs across his conversational corpus stages this very dissolution. While various figurations of the teacher appear throughout these texts, the meaning of this name is so transformed that the distinction between teacher and student no longer holds. Perhaps Heidegger realizes it was the *teacher* chained in Plato's cave instead, rescued by the student who invites her out for a nighttime stroll.

The reading I've just provided of Heidegger's pedagogy as collaborative, pluralist, open to alterity, and in a certain sense egalitarian is entirely at odds with the form of education Heidegger himself actually enacted in his classrooms and—during his rectorship—in the university as a whole. As Heidegger worked to marry his philosophy with the politics of Nazi Germany, his education theory and praxis took its cue from a pointed authoritarianism. Thomas Peterson[33] takes Heidegger to task on precisely this point. Pursuing a reading of his pedagogy inferred from Heidegger's "framing and presentation of intellectual issues,"[34] Peterson argues Heidegger is "seemingly hostile to progress in the sciences and the related field of epistemology."[35] For Peterson, Heidegger's willful "pedagogy of not-knowing"[36] means

> Heidegger's students are placed in the position of being told that the assembled order of gathered scientific thought is delusional, in so far as it is leading civilization down the path to its destruction. To regain one's humanity one must return to the wisdom of the ancient Greeks by making oneself open. While the teacher apprises his students of the difficulty of this task, he provides no mediating disciplines such as the economic, ethical, or political sciences, by which to articulate and thus better achieve it. What seems most egregiously lacking—again in the pedagogical context of his lectures—is the practical and ethical stratum.[37]

Peterson argues that "Heidegger revealed an educational method incapable of integrating concrete experience with abstraction, facts with values,"[38] but at the same time, this cypher of humanistic or scientific values installed Heidegger as a fascist dictator of "an extreme logology,"[39] the very obscurity of which necessitated authoritarianism.

Peterson points toward a paradox at the heart of Heidegger's work that anyone who engages with it must contend. On the one hand, Heidegger offers a critical reading of the representational and metaphysical domination engendered by those "mediating disciplines" such as science, economics, ethics, or politics that offer practical modes of valuation. For Heidegger, pronouncements of "ethics" may themselves be found to be profoundly unethical[40] and should be regarded with ontological caution. Yet, on the other hand, Heidegger's own actualization of his pedagogy falls prey to this very critique. When he maneuvered into a position of political and academic administrative power, he leveraged it in the service of the very "conformism"[41] that characterized Nazi ideology. Though the technological thinking Heidegger argues is driving the scientific disciplines has led to current and ongoing mass extinction events in the form of climate change, Heidegger's actions taken as a member of the Nazi party wholeheartedly reinforced the domination of representational, metaphysical thinking.

Perhaps the pedagogy Heidegger develops in his conversations suggests a meager sort of recognition and response to his own momentous failure, which attempts anew to think non-polemically, non-willfully, and to embrace mistakes as gifts that allow danger to presence amid the formation of any community. Without a doubt, Heidegger failed to concretely embody the conversational, poetic pedagogy I have shown that he performs in his pedagogical texts. This failure is absolute and should never be excused or defended. As Peterson rightly warns, his very invocation of the poetic and of silence harbors the danger that Heidegger did not understand any of this as *his* failure, but instead that the Nazi's particular historical movement to reinscribe the Germans as the leaders of Western civilization failed in achieving its aspirations, which nevertheless remain perhaps in the form of a doctrine of a secret Germany.

The ethnonationalist ambiguity of Heidegger's work cannot be excised. Just as it is undeniable that Heidegger put his philosophy to work for the antisemitism of National Socialist Germany, it is also possible to generate interpretations of his thinking that exceed and diverge from the purposes he intended. The work of reclaiming tainted conceptual resources presents a set of unique and demanding opportunities, routinely taken up by critical theorists including feminist, anti-racist, and post- and de-colonial theorists, among many others. The master's tools will never dismantle the master's house, as Audre Lorde emphasizes, but in any effort to enact radical, revolutionary change, Heidegger's own attempt to enact a radical, revolutionary ontology might be born in mind. All too easily, radical movements can be co-opted by empire and travel as fodder for extreme, reactionary conservatism while such ideologies may also re-deploy revolutionary organizing practices in order to stunt them.

While Heidegger's actual pedagogical practices stand firmly in support of the German conservative revolution, the pedagogy he performs in his conversational texts implies an aspiration to non-representational, non-metaphysical thinking pregnant with *other* possibilities, beyond those that were actualized. In the disjunctive interstices between his own deployment of metaphysical educational theory and praxis and his conversational performance of non-metaphysical pedagogy, possibilities for learning to think otherwise remain to be taken up. We need not follow Heidegger even as we explore the pedagogical way he opens. Those committed to a very different vision of philosophical and political community may nevertheless find insights in this poetic pedagogy that contribute to collaborations that engender more just, inclusive, and equitable futures. In his conversations at least, Heidegger refrains from offering any step-by-step instructions that would reinstate him as an authoritative teacher. Instead, he undermines the representational, metaphysical terms that would maintain any distinction between teacher and student.

I argue this becoming-obsolescent of the traditional student-teacher relationship is performed across Heidegger's five conversational texts. Such a (d)evolution of the traditional pedagogical relationship may, upon interpretation, nevertheless yield the following sketch:

1. The teacher and student first assume a non-oppositional stance toward what they are to learn and toward one another. They build trust with one another and are willing to teach and learn by experimenting with a variety of ways to approach one another, practicing patience while they wait for learning to take place.

2. The teacher and student then discover how important and fertile mistakes are for learning, including the teacher's mistakes, which demonstrate that learning is never-ending. Learning is a way of being, never a completed or completable process. Despite being frustrating and distressing at times, learning is ultimately rewarding in that it provides opportunities to collaborate with others.

3. The original distinction between teaching and learning begins to fade away. Those endeavoring to learn—including both student and teacher—cannot be said to have learned something if one or the other is not able to share in that insight. Obviously, a teacher has not successfully taught if only she—but not the student—understands what she teaches. Likewise, a student has only truly learned when she can articulate what she has learned back to her teacher, effectively learning to teach her teacher what she has learned. Learning is collaborative and builds a sense of community.

4. The pedagogical community members come to see that even what they have shared in their collaborative learning practice is not self-sufficient. Rather, it further calls for interpretation. In exploring how the meaning of what they learn can be determined in a multiplicity of ways, the learners are further divested of any idea that learning is a completable process and assured that learning instead raises more questions than it answers.

5. Finally, in pursuing an exploration of the complexities of interpretation, learners must remain on guard for misapprehensions. Even though they are engaging in learning together, they must be alert to the danger that apparent agreement may conceal misunderstanding that remains unnoticed. There is no

way to guarantee this will not happen. However, remaining in sustained conversation may encourage such uninterrogated misunderstandings to emerge in due course.

Such a generalized view of the pedagogy developed across the conversational texts—divorced as it is from Heidegger's philosophical commitments—is illuminating even as it may also be misleading. Again, Heidegger is not developing a progressive account of pedagogy. He performs poetic pedagogy to enable non-representational, non-metaphysical thinking. Any attempt to extract a methodology of teaching and learning from Heidegger's conversational texts without also endeavoring to allow for such thinking may engender catastrophe. But perhaps this very failure too provides the occasion for further reflection on what it means to teach and learn.

These further reflections could take many forms. Heidegger's pedagogy may be brought into fruitful relation with other philosophies of pedagogy. Comparing his pedagogy with that of Ralph Waldo Emerson and Friedrich Nietzsche, but also Paulo Freire, bell hooks, Eve Sedgwick, Enrique Dussel, and Nel Noddings, among others,[42] could illuminate the stakes of Heidegger's particular commitment to pedagogy while also highlighting the impact of the privileges of Heidegger's particular social and political situatedness on his philosophizing. Drawing out his pedagogy may also offer a new avenue by which to assess and criticize Heidegger's failure to learn from his own pedagogy in his support for National Socialism. In the context of his political life, Heidegger set himself up as an authoritative teacher. The developmental arc of his pedagogy across the conversational texts may suggest an implicit self-critique, or at the very least a criticism that should be launched in response to the political uses to which he sought to put his philosophical work.

In many pedagogical contexts today, representational, metaphysical thinking dominates and remains largely unchallenged in so doing. In educational institutions across the globe at all levels, there is increasing emphasis on assessments grounded in "measurable" learning outcomes. The "value" of philosophical reflection—or inquiry practiced under the umbrella of the humanities more broadly—can hardly be articulated convincingly, except in terms borrowed from scientific methodology. In making legible the pedagogy latent in Heidegger's conversations—which constitute one of the many "ways, not works" he traveled in his attempts to leap beyond metaphysical thinking—I hope to have opened up new vistas from which to consider the lasting significance of Heidegger's philosophy, including its limitations and dangerous pitfalls. The pedagogy I have described need not lead *us* to ethnonationalist politics, misogyny, or anti-Semitism, though Heidegger as its progenitor supported the maintenance of these forms of discrimination and, ultimately, genocide. In so doing, he clearly and repeatedly failed to live up to the aspirations of his own philosophy. Perhaps certain elements of Heidegger's poetic pedagogy can be reoriented in renewed and ameliorative political registers. Though Heidegger did not realize or actualize it, his poetic pedagogy aspires to strive toward collaborative conversation with others in increasingly profound and meaningful ways. What his readers may learn from his thinking *and* his failure to embody this thinking will hopefully inspire more just and inclusive philosophical and pedagogical futures from, through, and beyond formal educational environments, in conversations we motivate with others, as well as in those we hold with ourselves.

Notes

Introduction

1. See Daniela Vallega-Neu, *Heidegger's Poietic Writings: From "Contributions to Philosophy" to "The Event"* (Bloomington: Indiana University Press, 2018).

2. That Heidegger composed in such a wide variety of genres presents significant interpretive challenges for readers of his work. Though Heidegger's works could be rather straightforwardly located on a spectrum ranging from public to personal writings, this sliding scale of publicity does not necessarily shed light on which texts more or less authoritatively present Heidegger's "authentic" view of any particular topic, philosophical or otherwise. For an illuminating recent discussion of these interpretive challenges, see Adam Knowles's chapter "Heidegger's Politics of Silence," in *Heidegger's Fascist Affinities* (Stanford: Stanford University Press, 2019). Knowles claims that Heidegger's reliance on silence fulfills a vital ontological function in his thinking of language that is politically inexcusable and further illustrates the attendant privileges of his own socially and politically constructed identity that Heidegger never acknowledges.

3. Demonstrating the plausibility of this claim as it would apply to each of the genres Heidegger employs across his corpus falls outside the scope of this monograph. However, I hope my dedicated reading of Heidegger's conversations contributes to supporting future scholarly efforts.

4. I agree with Holger Zaborowski's claim in "Origin, Freedom, and Gelassenheit: On Heidegger's Second 'Country Path Conversation,' " trans. Gregory Canning, in *Phenomenological Perspectives on Plurality*, ed. Gert-Jan van der Heiden (Leiden, Netherlands: Brill, 2015) that "the significance of conversation in Heidegger (and this means: the conversational character of his entire way of thinking) has been considered insufficiently by the scholarship to date" (140). This book endeavors to respond directly to this lack.

5. See the chapters "After the War, the Void," "Coming to Terms with the Political Past" and "Towards a Rehabilitation of Heidegger" in Hugo Ott, *Martin Heidegger: A Political Life*, trans. Allan Blunden (London: HarperCollins, 1993) and

the chapters "Heidegger Faces the Denazification Committee: Barred from University Teaching" and "Heidegger's Other Public" in Rüdiger Safranski, *Martin Heidegger: Between Good and Evil*, trans. Ewald Osers (Cambridge, MA: Harvard University Press, 1999) for pertinent overviews of Heidegger's biography in this decade and its relation to the historical events of the period.

6. During this time, Heidegger frequently travels by bicycle between the Upper Danube Valley and Meßkirch to check on his manuscripts. After the bombing of Meßkirch on February 22, Heidegger located a cave in the Upper Danube Valley where his manuscripts are stored alongside many of Hölderlin's manuscripts. See his letter to Elfride on April 15, 1945, in Martin Heidegger, *Letters to His Wife, 1915–1970*, ed. Gertrud Heidegger, trans. R. D. V. Glasgow (Malden, MA: Polity Press, 2010), 189–90.

7. Heidegger, *Letters to His Wife*, 184.

8. See Dieter Speck, "Vorlesungen im Phantomsemester: Die Freiburger Philosophische Fakultät in Beuron zwischen Flucht und Fiktion," in *Mittelalterliches Mönchtum in der Moderne? Die Neugründung der Benediktinerabtei Beuron 1863 und deren kulturelle Ausstrahlung im 19. und 20. Jahrhundert*, ed. Karl-Heinz Braun, Hugo Ott, and Wilfried Schöntag (Stuttgart: Kohlhammer, 2015), 169–89.

9. As Ian Moore notes in *Eckhart, Heidegger, and the Imperative of Releasement* (Albany: State University of New York Press, 2019), there is evidence that Heidegger may have even taught the first of the *Country Path Conversations* because of the existence of a "typescript summarizing the trajectory of the dialogue in four sections dated April 18, April 30, May 22, and May 29" (124) as well as "a later, unpublished recollection by Hermine Lossman (who was one of the students there) proves that Heidegger was at least talking about themes that appear in his text" (125).

10. Moore writes, "in a letter to his brother from June 28, 1945, Heidegger thanks him for sending a transcript of the dialogue. He also mentions that he is ruminating on ten (!) interrelated evening dialogues, and that the first serves as a sort of introduction to the others and contains all of the themes that will be developed in them" (*Eckhart, Heidegger, and the Imperative of Releasement*, 267, fn. 8).

11. For an analysis of Heidegger's breakdown in relation to his own philosophy of health and healing as well as that of Gebsattel's, see Andrew Mitchell, "Heidegger's Breakdown: Health and Healing Under the Care of Dr. V.E. von Gebsattel," *Research in Phenomenology* 46 (2016): 70–97.

12. See his letter to Elfride on November 18, 1948 (*Letters to His Wife*, 205).

13. See Reinhard May, "Tezuka Tomio 'An Hour with Heidegger,'" in *Heidegger's Hidden Sources: East Asian Influences on His Work*, trans. Graham Parkes (New York: Routledge, 1996), 59–64.

14. I have chosen to translate *Gespräch* as "conversation" whenever possible to preserve Heidegger's philosophical distinction between *Gespräch* and *Dialog*. While Hyland and Gonzalez use "dialogue" as a more conventional and accessible translation of *Gespräch*, as do the translators of the Hölderlin lecture courses, I prefer to preserve

the difference Heidegger demarcates with his use of the word that most literally means a collection or gathering (*Ge-*) of language (*Sprache*). Davis is also sensitive to the historical distance Heidegger is taking from Plato in drawing this distinction in his foreword to the *Country Path Conversations* (viii–ix), though he is not convinced that " 'dialogue' necessarily implies a problematic sense of intersubjectivity" ("Heidegger's Orientations: The Step Back on the Way to Dialogue with the East," 165, fn. 52). However, translating *Gespräch* as "conversation" is not entirely satisfactory. German also has the term *Konversation*, which would be mostly obviously and easily translated as "conversation." In the 1951/2 lecture course, Heidegger distinguishes between *Konversation* and *Gespräch*, writing that "Conversation [*Konversation*] consists in slithering along the edges of the subject matter, precisely without getting involved in the unspoken" (GA 8: 182/WCT 178), where *Gespräch* involves inhabiting the "realm and abode about which they are speaking" (GA 8: 182/WCT 178). Ma, for instance, argues "dialogue" as a translation is more appropriate precisely because it signals a relation to Plato (Ma, *Heidegger on East-West Dialogue*, 189–92). Though I would most prefer to leave *Gespräch* untranslated, I follow Davis in rendering *Gespräch* as "conversation" whenever possible because English offers no ready term beyond dialogue or conversation. I have done this to allay Heidegger's own fear of being directly compared with Plato and to indicate his resistance to his depiction of Platonic metaphysics.

15. However, scholars such as Drew Hyland (1995 and 2015), Francisco Gonzalez (2009 and 2015), and myself (2018 and 2020) have argued that the relationship between Heidegger and Plato is more nuanced than it may appear.

16. In particular, see *Plato's Sophist*, *The Essence of Truth: On Plato's Cave Allegory and Theaetetus*, and the *Nietzsche* lecture courses.

17. Though, this culmination is presented in a transformed and abridged way. For a nuanced and rigorous account of the development of Heidegger's earlier readings of Plato, see especially Francisco Gonzalez, "Heidegger's Transformation of Plato into Platonism," in *Plato and Heidegger: A Question of Dialogue* (University Park, PA: The Pennsylvania State University Press, 2009): 107–72.

18. *Letters to His Wife*, 187.

19. *Letters to His Wife*, 187.

20. *Letters to His Wife*, 187.

21. "Saying" is one of Heidegger's favored terms for "language." See GA 12: 137/OWL 47 and GA 80.2: 1190/140.

22. This raises the issue as to whether Heidegger may distinguish between a Plato who is also engaged in a *Gespräch* and a Platonism that has enshrined a *Dialog* of metaphysics into doctrine. At the closure of his final conversational text, Heidegger leaves this question entirely open. Given Heidegger's characterization of the distinction between *Dialoge* and *Gespräche*, it is not necessarily obvious that Plato's Socrates is interested in pursuing "dialogues." On this point, see my article "The Resistant Interlocutor: Plato, Heidegger, and the End of Dialogue," in *Epoché:*

A Journal for the History of Philosophy 23 (2018): 165–90. In the concluding pages of Heidegger's last conversational text of 1953/54, the "Japanese" interlocutor asks, "in this sense, then, even Plato's *Dialoges* would not be *Gespräche*?," to which the "Inquirer" responds, "I would like to leave that question open" (GA 12: 143/OWL 52, tm.). Heidegger pens these lines after writing in the 1951/52 lecture course that "a dialogue of Plato is inexhaustible—not only for posterity and the changing forms of comprehension to which posterity gives rise; it is inexhaustible of itself, by its nature. And this is forever the mark of all creativeness" (GA 8: 76/WCT 72). Heidegger's relationship to Plato is far from settled. Further, letters he wrote to Elfride indicate that he had planned, but never executed, a project devoted entirely to Plato, which may have upended his earlier readings.

23. Martin Heidegger, *Country Path Conversations*, trans. Bret W. Davis (Bloomington: Indiana University Press, 2010).

24. See Bret Davis, *Heidegger and the Will* (Evanston: Northwestern University Press, 2007) and also "Returning the World to Nature: Heidegger's Turn from a Transcendental-Horizonal Projection of World to an Indwelling Releasement to the Open-Region," *Continental Philosophy Review* 47 (2014): 373–97, and "Will and *Gelassenheit*," in *Martin Heidegger: Key Concepts*, ed. Bret W. Davis (New York: Routledge, 2014), among other works that engage the question of the will in relation to Heidegger's conversational texts.

25. See also William Richardson's chapter "Towards an Analysis of Release" in *Heidegger: Through Phenomenology to Thought* (New York: Fordham University Press, 2003).

26. Drew Hyland, "Heidegger's (Dramatic?) Dialogues," *Research in Phenomenology* 45 (2015): 341–57. Hyland was also the director of the 2013 Collegium Phaenomenologicum "Heidegger: Gelassenheit, Ethical Life, Ereignis, 1933–1946," which launched my interest in Heidegger's conversations. This project is indebted to that event and especially to the three rich and thought-provoking lecture courses given by Bret Davis, Dennis Schmidt, and Daniela Vallega-Neu, as well as the individual lectures by Andrew Mitchell, Silvia Benso, and Robert Bernasconi.

27. Drew Hyland, "Heidegger's Plato," in *Questioning Platonism: Continental Interpretations of Plato* (Albany: State University of New York Press, 2004), especially 68–83.

28. Andrew Mitchell, *The Fourfold: Reading the Late Heidegger* (Evanston: Northwestern University Press, 2015).

29. Silvia Benso, "When Heidegger's Tower Dweller Takes a Walk: On Thinkers, Poets, and Mysterious Guests," Collegium Phaenomenologicum Individual Lecture, Città di Castello (Italy), July 9, 2013.

30. Charles Bambach, "Heidegger in Dialogue with Hölderlin: 'The Western Conversation,'" in *Of an Alien Homecoming: Reading Heidegger's Hölderlin* (Albany: State University of New York Press, 2022).

31. Robert Bernasconi, "Being is Evil: Boehme's Strife and Schelling's Rage in Heidegger's 'Letter on Humanism,'" *Gatherings: The Heidegger Circle Annual* 7 (2017): 164–81.

32. Bret Davis, "Heidegger's Orientations: The Step Back on the Way to Dialogue with the East," *Heidegger-Jahrbuch 7: Heidegger und das ostasiatische Denken* (2013): 153–80, and "Heidegger on the Way from Onto-Historical Ethnocentrism to East-West Dialogue," *Gatherings: The Heidegger Circle Annual* 6 (2016): 130–56, including his works already cited.

33. Lin Ma, *Heidegger on East-West Dialogue: Anticipating the Event* (New York: Routledge, 2008).

34. Ian Moore, *Eckhart, Heidegger, and the Imperative of Releasement*, cited above.

35. Eric Nelson, "Heidegger's Daoist Turn," *Research in Phenomenology* 49 (2019): 362–84.

36. Robert Savage, *Hölderlin after the Catastrophe: Heidegger—Adorno—Brecht* (Rochester: Camden House, 2008).

37. Francisco Gonzalez, *Plato and Heidegger: A Question of Dialogue*, cited above.

38. Holger Zaborowski, "Origin, Freedom, and *Gelassenheit*: On Heidegger's Second 'Country Path Conversation,'" cited above.

39. Tobias Keiling, "Letting Things Be for Themselves: *Gelassenheit* as Enabling Thinking," in *Heidegger on Technology*, ed. Aaron James Wendland, Christopher Merwin, and Christos Hadjioannou (New York: Routledge, 2019).

40. Shane Ewegen, "The Thing and I: Thinking Things in Heidegger's *Country Path Conversations*," *Gatherings: The Heidegger Circle Annual* 6 (2016): 114–29.

41. Katherine Davies, "The Resistant Interlocutor: Plato, Heidegger, and the End of Dialogue," cited above, "Heidegger's Reading(s) of the *Phaedrus*," *Studia Phaenomenologica* XX (2020): 191–21, and "Heidegger's Conversational Pedagogy," *Research and Phenomenology* 52 (2022): 399–424.

42. Heidegger does use this term to refer to the philosophical science by this name, but this is only one of many meanings it bears in his thinking. See James Bahoh's compilation of ten different definitions that the term "metaphysics" bears in Heidegger's philosophy in *Heidegger's Ontology of Events* (Edinburgh: Edinburgh University Press, 2021), 61. Mark Wrathall also offers an incisive overview of the meanings of this term for Heidegger, condensing them to four distinct senses. See "Metaphysics (Metaphysik)," in *The Cambridge Heidegger Lexicon*, ed. Mark Wrathall (Cambridge: Cambridge University Press, 2021), 482–90.

43. For an overview of the role of "nothing" in Heidegger's work, see Iain Thomson, "Nothing (Nichts)," in *The Cambridge Heidegger Lexicon*, ed. Mark Wrathall (Cambridge: Cambridge University Press, 2021), 520–28.

44. See Gregory Fried, "Introduction to Metaphysics," in *The Bloomsbury Companion to Heidegger*, ed. François Raffoul and Eric Nelson (London: Bloomsbury, 2016), 207–13.

45. For an overview of this aspect of Heidegger's thinking, see Mark Wrathall, "History of Being (Geschichtes des Seins)," in *The Cambridge Heidegger Lexicon*, ed. Mark Wrathall (Cambridge: Cambridge University Press, 2021), 385–96, and Peter Warnek, "The History of Being," in *Martin Heidegger: Key Concepts*, ed. Bret Davis (New York: Routledge, 2010), 155–67.

46. As Wrathall shows in "History of Being (Geschichtes des Seins)," Heidegger later offers finer grained delineations between and within these various epochs (390–91).

47. In this book, I am examining Heidegger's formulation of "representational metaphysics" in the conversational texts. Typically, I include both terms to indicate this. On the occasions where I may write of "representation" or "metaphysics" without referring to the other term, I still have this philosophical coupling distinctive of Heidegger's sense of modernity in mind.

48. This is arguably the mistake Heidegger makes in the 1930s with his investment in the will, decision, and the politics of National Socialism. His turn toward releasement and letting be in the 1940s marks a different comportment. See Bret Davis, *Heidegger and the Will*.

49. Several scholarly studies have been made of Heidegger's pedagogy, but none has examined Heidegger's conversational texts for this purpose. Many of these studies have focused on Heidegger's reading of Plato's Allegory of the Cave or the implications of his thinking of technology for educational praxis. In his monograph *Heidegger's Philosophic Pedagogy* (New York: Continuum, 2010), Michael Ehrmantraut sets out to demonstrate a pedagogical concern that permeates Heidegger's early thinking, developing significantly into what he calls a "new pedagogy" after *Being and Time*. Ehrmantraut is interested in language, comportment, and the pedagogical implications of the genre differences between Heidegger's treatise and his lecture courses, which are interests that I also share. However, Ehrmantraut limits his study to comparing *Being and Time* with the lecture courses from 1927–34 and argues that Heidegger's philosophy as a whole has a pedagogical aim. I instead elaborate Heidegger's particular pedagogy. I also take seriously Heidegger's contention that the essence of language is conversational and therefore examine the pedagogy Heidegger's characters perform in the conversations from this later period. An important collection edited by Michael Peters, titled *Heidegger, Education, and Modernity* (Lanham, MD, Rowman & Littlefield, 2002), presents significant contributions on Heidegger and education by Cooper, Thomson, Fitzsimons, Bonnet, and others, but none of these essays examines the pedagogy enacted in the conversations. Peters also edited a special issue of the journal *Educational Philosophy and Theory* 41 (2009) that collects phenomenological work by educational theorists and practitioners. Iain Thomson, *Heidegger on Ontotheology: Technology and the Politics of Education* (New York: Cambridge University Press, 2005) and Anna Kouppanou, *Technologies of Being in Martin Heidegger: Nearness, Metaphor and the Question of Education in Digital Times* (New York: Routledge, 2018) each concurrently approaches the question of

education alongside Heidegger's considerations of technology, albeit from different vantage points. Additional contributions to the topic of Heidegger and pedagogy include Babette Babich, "On Heidegger on Education and Questioning" (2017); Thomas Peterson, "Notes on Heidegger's Authoritarian Pedagogy" (2005); Dawn Riley, "Heidegger Teaching: An Analysis and Interpretation of Pedagogy" (2011); Doron Yosef-Hassidim, "Rethinking Education: Heidegger's Philosophy in the Service of Education" (2014); Mark Sinclair, "Heidegger, Von Humboldt and the Idea of the University" (2013); Jonathan Neufeld, "The (In)vocation of Learning: Heidegger's Education in Thinking" (2012); David Lewin, "Heidegger East and West: Philosophy as Educative Contemplation" (2015); Sacha Golob, "A Heideggerian Pedagogy of Disruption" (2021); and Iain Thomson, "Heidegger on Ontological Education, or: How We Become What We Are" (2001); and "Heidegger's Perfectionist Philosophy of Education" (2004). Finally, much has also been published under the guise of applied Heideggerian pedagogical research: Paul Standish, "Heidegger and the Technology of Further Education" (2007); Lynda Stone, "From Technologization to Totalization in Education Research: U.S. Graduate Training, Methodology, and Critique" (2006); Nancy Diekelmann, "Learning-as-Testing: A Heideggerian Hermeneutical Analysis of the Lived Experiences of Students and Teachers in Nursing" (1992); Robert Shaw, "Heidegger and E-Learning: Overthrowing the Traditions of Pedagogy" (2014) and "Toward a Heideggerian Pedagogy" (2004); Paul Gibbs, "A Heideggerian Phenomenology Approach to Higher Education as Workplace: A Consideration of Academic Professionalism" (2010); and Haim Gordon, *Dwelling Poetically: Educational Challenges in Heidegger's Thinking of Poetry* (2000).

50. See Heidegger's analysis of language rendered as information in the age of technology (GA 80.2: 1188/139).

51. Evident from his efforts to further distance his depiction from the metaphysical presuppositions of subjectivity and objectivity that he will later assign to dialogue in 1944.

52. A version of which he later published as *The Question Concerning the Thing* (GA 41).

53. In this respect, Heidegger and Paulo Friere agree. Friere calls this the "banking concept of education" (*Pedagogy of the Oppressed*, 72) and argues that pedagogy must be rethought to achieve social and political liberation for oppressed peoples. These two thinkers of pedagogy both reject this model, though their reasons for doing so diverge considerably.

54. Heidegger reiterates this point a decade later at the outset of his 1962 lecture "Traditional and Technological Language" (GA 80.2: 1174/129).

55. whom he later renames "the Teacher," as I note in chapter 1.

56. Hyland, "Heidegger's (Dramatic?) Dialogues," 343.

57. Hyland, "Heidegger's (Dramatic?) Dialogues," 344.

58. In the *Research in Phenomenology* article cited above, in *Questioning Platonism*, and in *Finitude and Transcendence in the Platonic Dialogues*.

59. Davis, "Translators' Foreword," in *Country Path Conversations*, viii.
60. Davies, "Heidegger's Reading(s) of the *Phaedrus*," 195–96.
61. Zaborowski, "Origin, Freedom, and *Gelassenheit*," 141.
62. Zaborowski, 140. See further Zaborowski's section "In-Between Thinking," 137–42, and compare with Sean Kirkland, "Thinking the Between with Heidegger and Plato," *Research in Phenomenology* 37 (2007): 95–111.
63. See Plato's meditation on writing at the end of *Phaedrus*. See further Hyland, "Heidegger's (Dramatic?) Dialogues," and Davies, "Heidegger's Reading(s) of the *Phaedrus*."
64. In "The Assayer," Galileo writes: "Philosophy is written in this great book which is continually open before our eyes—I mean the universe—but before we can understand it, we need to learn the language and recognize the characters in which it is written. It is written in the language of mathematics" (*Selected Writings*, 115).
65. For an elaboration of this account, see especially Heidegger's essay "Age of the World Picture" (GA 5: 75–96/207–23).
66. See Andrew Mitchell's "Translator's Foreword" for an explanation of his decision to translate *Gestell* as "positionality" rather than "enframing"; Heidegger insists that this term does not mean anything like a framing or frame-work (Mitchell, *Bremen and Freiburg Lectures*, xi).
67. Mitchell, *The Fourfold*, 24.
68. For an illuminating account of the philosophical stakes of this emphasis on representation, see Mitchell, "Machination as Representational Objectification," in *The Fourfold*, 26–32.
69. See Mitchell, "Positionality as Circulative Replacement," in *The Fourfold*, 49–63.
70. Mitchell clarifies what is at stake in this reconsideration: "Under the aegis of positionality all that exists is transformed into standing reserve (*Bestand*), and this is something quite far from the modern philosophical conception of objectivity proffered by machination . . . The technological challenge to the thing is thus no simple opposition of representational objectivity, on the one hand, and the relationality of the thing on the other. Instead it is a tension between two departures from objectivity, that of the thing and that of the standing reserve. As a result, there is a strange alliance between the thing and the standing reserve in their distance taking from modern objectivity as encapsulated self-identical presence" (*The Fourfold*, 25).
71. Four out of five of Heidegger's conversations precede this breakthrough. As I will show, the fifth, 1953/54 conversation that follows it elaborates some of the dangers of the pedagogy that leads up to this transition.
72. Zaborowski agrees: "It is, therefore, not enough to go alone on the country path between the fields. It depends on a modification of the relation to the country path so that one is moved by it and its course or can listen to its assertion. Movement is then no longer the action of an autonomous subject, but rather something that occurs to the one who goes on the country path. Such movement

on the country path (as will become clearer) assumes an other thinking" ("Origin, Freedom, and *Gelassenheit*," 139).

73. I use the term "poetic" as an adjectival form of "poetizing," not "poetry." The subtitle of this book does not refer to the instances in which poetry is recited or referred to in Heidegger's conversations. Rather, "poetic pedagogy" describes a pedagogy that is essentially engaged with poetizing.

74. Krzysztof Ziarek, *Inflected Language: Toward a Hermeneutics of Nearness: Heidegger, Levinas, Stevens, Celan* (Albany: State University of New York Press, 1994), 24–25.

75. John Lysaker "Language and Poetry," in *Martin Heidegger: Key Concepts* (New York: Routledge, 2010), 205.

76. Here (and whenever Heidegger writes of Hölderlin's poetry) the German *Dichten* is used (see GA 7: 203) to indicate these poems participate in the essential poetizing of *Dichtung* rather than merely imitating the linguistic form of *Poesie*.

77. As Heidegger writes in "The Origin of the Work of Art," "Building and plastic creations . . . always happen already, and happen only, in the Open of saying and naming. It is the Open that pervades and guides them. But for this very reason they remain their own ways and modes in which truth orders itself into work. They are an ever special poetizing within the clearing of what is . . . Art, as the setting-into-work of truth, is poetry" (GA 5: 62/PLT 72).

78. See particularly *Being and Time* (GA 2: 214–19/206–10), *On the Essence of Truth* (GA 9: 177–202/136–54), and *Plato's Doctrine of Truth* (GA 9: 203–38/155–82) for an elaboration of Heidegger's critique of the derivative status of such theories of truth.

79. Heidegger does not use the word "affect." Instead, he is known for his rich thinking of attunement or mood. See Katherine Withy, "Mood (Stimmung)" in *The Cambridge Heidegger Lexicon*, ed. Mark Wrathall (Cambridge: Cambridge University Press, 2021), 500–3. My account does not directly intervene in Heidegger's thinking of *Stimmung*. I am interrogating these texts for their performative dimensions, not only for their philosophical content. This means I am studying the embodied or staged performance of Heidegger's thinking. To mark this distinction, I have elected to use the term "affect" to describe the fear, anxiety, distress, love, etc. of these specific characters in these conversational, dramatic performances. These performative affects certainly relate to what Heidegger means by attunement, but an elaboration thereof falls outside the scope of this project.

80. Martin Heidegger, "Αγχιβασίη: Ein Gespräch selbstdritt auf einem Feldweg zwischen einem Forscher, einem Gelehrten und einem Weisen," in *Feldweg-Gespräche*, ed. Ingrid Schüßler, *Gesamtausgabe* 77 (Frankfurt: Vittorio Klostermann, 1995). Published in translation as "Αγχιβασίη: A Triadic Conversation on a Country Path between a Scientist, a Scholar, and a Guide," in *Country Path Conversations*, trans. Bret W. Davis (Bloomington: Indiana University Press, 2010), 77. Hereafter "Triadic Conversation."

81. Martin Heidegger, Der Lehrer trifft den Türmer an der Tür zum Turmaufgang," in Martin Heidegger, *Feldweg-Gespräche*, ed. Ingrid Schüßler, *Gesamtausgabe* 77 (Frankfurt: Vittorio Klostermann, 1995). Published in translation as "The Teacher Meets the Tower Warden at the Door to the Tower Stairway," in *Country Path Conversations*, trans. Bret Davis (Bloomington; Indiana University Press, 2010). Hereafter "Tower Conversation."

82. Martin Heidegger, "Abendgespräch in einem Kriegsgefangenenlager in Rußland zwischen einem Jüngeren und einem Ältern," in Martin Heidegger, *Feldweg-Gespräche*, ed. Ingrid Schüßler, *Gesamtausgabe* 77 (Frankfurt: Vittorio Klostermann, 1995). Published in translation as "Evening Conversation: In a Prisoner of War Camp in Russia, between a Younger and an Older Man," in *Country Path Conversations*, trans. Bret Davis (Bloomington; Indiana University Press, 2010). Hereafter "Evening Conversation."

83. Martin Heidegger, "Das abendländische Gespräch," in *Zu Hölderlin-Griechenlandreisen*, ed. Curd Ochwadt, *Gesamtausgabe* 75 (Frankfurt am Main: Vittorio Klostermann, 2000). Hereafter the "Western Conversation." This volume remains untranslated. All translations into English are my own provisional renderings.

84. Martin Heidegger, "Aus einem Gespräch von der Sprache," in *Unterwegs zur Sprache*, ed. Friedrich-Wilhelm von Hermann, *Gesamtausgabe* 12 (Frankfurt: Vittorio Klostermann, 1985). Published in translation as "A Dialogue on Language between a Japanese and an Inquirer," in *On the Way to Language*, trans. Peter D. Hertz (New York: HarperCollins Publishers, 1971), tm. The German title of this text is *"Aus einem Gespräch von der Sprache."* Though Hertz chose "Dialogue" to render the title, the German is *Gespräch*. Hereafter "Conversation of Language."

Chapter 1

1. Martin Heidegger, "Αγχιβασίη: A Triadic Conversation on a Country Path between a Scientist, a Scholar, and a Guide," in *Country Path Conversations*, trans. Bret W. Davis (Bloomington: Indiana University Press, 2010). Hereafter "Triadic Conversation."

2. Heidegger intended for this first text to introduce the themes of the ten interrelated conversations he planned to write. See Moore, *Eckhart, Heidegger, and the Imperative of Releasement*, 267, fn. 8.

3. Bret Davis (2007, 2010, 2014, and 2014) explores the shape and importance of *Gelassenheit* as it is first elaborated in the "Triadic Conversation." Ian Moore (2019) depicts Heidegger's indebtedness to Eckhart for his thinking of *Gelassenheit*. Tobias Keiling (2019) draws from Heidegger's depiction of *Gelassenheit* in this text to illuminate his thinking of technology. Shane Ewegen (2016) explores the development of Heidegger's thinking of the thing. Drew Hyland (2015) emphasizes the

significance of the character's lack of personal names, the setting of the conversation on a country path, and the importance of the role of night. Andrew Mitchell (2015) shows how precursors to the Fourfold may be found in the *Country Path Conversations*. I (2018) have explored how this text sets Heidegger in conversation with Plato, drawing from the work of many of these scholars as well as Sean Kirkland (2007) and Francisco Gonzalez (2009).

4. With this provocation I do mean to raise the question of whether Heidegger's performative staging may inadvertently disclose a sense of an ethics that undergirds his philosophy. This is not, however, a question I am able to respond to here.

5. As I discuss below, in the selection of the "Triadic Conversation" that Heidegger published in 1959 in *Gelassenheit*, Heidegger renamed "*Der Weise*" "*Der Lehrer*" or "the Teacher"—a modification that brings this first of the *Country Path Conversations* into thematic uniformity with the others, which explicitly discuss teaching or contain the figure of the teacher.

6. Both Keiling ("Letting Things Be for Themselves," 100) and Moore (*Eckhart, Heidegger, and the Imperative of Releasement*, 128, fn. 13) argue that it would be more apt to translate "*Der Forscher*" as "the Researcher" and "*Der Weise*" as "the Sage" or "the Wise One." While I agree these English translations may follow neatly from the German, Davis's translational choices take their cue from the text itself and the philosophical relevance of Heidegger's depictions of these characters. As Moore notes, there is a passage within the text (GA 77: 84–85/CPC 54) where the Guide explicitly rejects the interpretation of his role as one of expressing wisdom. Further, the Scientist engages in one form of research (pertaining to the sciences) while the Scholar engages in another type of research (pertaining to the humanities). To align the Scientist with research without signaling a parallel association for the Scholar would be to overdetermine his role.

7. Hyland, "Heidegger's (Dramatic?) Dialogues," 341–57 and 345–46.

8. Francisco J. Gonzalez, *Plato and Heidegger: A Question of Dialogue* (University Park: The Pennsylvania State University Press, 2009), 277.

9. This is a striking difference between Heidegger's conversations and the Platonic dialogues. Hyland comments that the personal specificity of interlocutors "forms part of the dramatic existential concreteness of Plato's dialogues . . . Each character is a specific individual with a specific personality, whose personality usually plays a significant part in the events of the dialogue" ("Heidegger's (Dramatic?) Dialogues," 345).

10. In differentiating between the who-ness and the what-ness of these characters, I echo Hannah Arendt's distinction (*The Human Condition*, 179).

11. Hyland argues that even though Heidegger's conversations are not dramatic in the sense of a Platonic dialogue, Heidegger missed something in his own reading of Plato that draws the work of these two philosophers into proximity. He writes,

The dialogue form enabled Plato to allow to emerge in his writing more than could be articulated as the propositional content of the sentences he wrote. That is, in the drama of the dialogues, in the interactions of the characters, in the place and time of each dialogue, in the contrast or symmetry between word and deed, even in the occasional silences of this or that character (including Socrates!), Plato could allow to show forth something like what Heidegger himself has called "the unsaid;" he could allow what is hidden from explicit articulation to show forth, but to show forth as *hidden* . . . Even though in his earlier work on Plato, Heidegger remains unfortunately oblivious to this dramatic and therefore poetic aspect of Plato's dialogues . . . , I want to entertain the hypothesis . . . that the possibilities of exceeding the propositional content of sentences uttered, of allowing the unsaid and that which withdraws to emerge as such, which the Platonic dialogues exhibit, is just what Heidegger now comes to appreciate and is why he turns to the dialogue form. (Hyland, 343–44)

I agree that the conversations offer a corrective to his earlier readings of Plato and may even provide the occasion for a subtle acknowledgement of the "poetic" aspect of Plato's writings. See further Katherine Davies, "Heidegger's Reading(s) of the *Phaedrus*" (2020), and chapter 4 of the present volume. Yet there is even more philosophically relevant dramatic staging informing the "Triadic Conversation" than has yet been acknowledged, as this current chapter shows.

12. The metaphysical and epistemological analogy of the light radiating from the sun forms the crux of Plato's analogy of the sun (and Heidegger's reading of this analogy in "Plato's Doctrine of Truth"), drawing attention to the grounding of the Scientist's philosophical orientation in this form of metaphysics on the first page.

13. See Hyland (346) and Davis's "Translators' Foreword" (xi–xii).

14. In his foray into the conversation, the Scholar describes the Kantian account of cognition, thereby aligning himself with this metaphysician. Kant is repeatedly mentioned, and the insights the characters develop concerning both the value of Kant's thinking and its limits seem to reflect the Scholar's own realizations about his historiographical epistemology.

15. For the seeds of this insight, I thank Mathieu Debic.

16. Among the many things to be learned from Heidegger's "Rectorship Address: The Self-Assertion of the German University," it is clear that, on his view, a proper questioning will "shatter the encapsulation of the various fields of knowledge into separate disciplines" and that "the teachers of the university must really advance to the outermost dangerous position of uncertainty concerning the world" (GA 16: 111–12/112).

17. It is worth noting Heidegger was deeply influenced both by Husserl, who endeavored to develop phenomenology as a science of consciousness with the motto

"back to the things themselves," and by Dilthey, who worked as an intellectual historian to show how the human sciences are essentially historical and therefore require interpretation. See Richard Polt's *Heidegger: An Introduction* (12–16) for a brief yet vigorous overview. Though I do not pursue such an interpretation here, one may find that Heidegger's invention of these two characters recalls his own influences in Husserl and Dilthey and contains a subtle critique of their metaphysical presuppositions, which Heidegger's inheritance of their work seeks to remediate.

18. I argue that this point holds regardless of whether these are simple authorial misattributions on Heidegger's part, which is plausible given his incredible compositional speed. If Heidegger himself misremembers which character first articulated a given idea or question, this further shows that the Scientist and the Scholar fulfill similar functions, likely as research practitioners of (albeit distinct forms of) metaphysical thinking.

19. In explaining his decision to translate *der Weise* as he does, Davis cites the following passage as highlighting a multifaceted sense of this word, which extends beyond the typical rendering of the term as the "wise man" or the "sage" (Davis "Translators' Foreword," xi, fn. 14).

20. For an extended study of the crucial and novel role of *Gelassenheit* in Heidegger's thinking, see Bret Davis's monograph *Heidegger and the Will* and Ian Moore's *Eckhart, Heidegger, and the Imperative of Releasement*.

21. See the introduction for an overview of his remarks about the teacher's pedagogical role.

22. At two points, Heidegger substitutes "Truth" and "World" where he originally referred to the "Open Region," which Davis indicates in notes to his translation. Moore (134) has also shown that Heidegger works to better elaborate what he means by "*Gelassenheit*" by changing "activity" to "doing" in the Scholar's mouth (GA 77: 108 and *Gelassenheit*, 35) and that the Guide strengthens his claim that *Gelassenheit* may come to pass without necessarily being first released from transcendental-horizonal thinking (GA 77: 121 and *Gelassenheit*, 51).

23. This resonates with how they engage with many other interlocutors from the history of philosophy during their walk, whom even the Guide agrees were great and originary thinkers despite their capitulation to metaphysics.

24. See "Primordial Movedness of Fundamental Attunement: Having-Been and Past," in *Hölderlin's Hymns "Germania" and "The Rhine"* (GA 39: 107–9/98–99).

25. This is a reference to a line from Hölderlin's hymn "*Der Ister*." See especially part one of Heidegger's lecture course *Hölderlin's Hymn "The Ister"* (GA 53).

26. Heraclitus's fragment is found in both the opening and closing lines of the "Triadic Conversation" and in moments between (though without yet being named), acting as a guiding thread that can only be properly disclosed after much preparation.

27. Heidegger will later compose a short text titled "*Der Feldweg*," translated by O'Meara and Sheehan as "The Pathway." Davis translates the same term as

"Country Path" in his rendering of the title of the "Triadic Conversation." Sheehan indicates "*Der Feldweg*" may have been written between 1947 and 1948, but the editors of GA 13 date its composition to 1949. In either case, "*Der Feldweg*" was composed after the "Triadic Conversation," and many of the descriptions of this path recollected from his childhood in this later text also fit with features of the path in the "Triadic Conversation" (GA 13: 87–90/69–72).

28. The characters decide to forgo explicitly discussing politics. Yet, as Hyland points out, Heidegger gives both a time and date to the "Triadic Conversation." In the spring of 1945 outside Freiburg, it would have been impossible to take the idyllic walk Heidegger describes. What are we to make of this feat of the imagination? According to Hyland, "the setting of the country path conversation indicates clearly enough, no one is more attuned to the problematic of such a releasement than Heidegger himself, for he places the conditions of that problematic in the very setting in which he stages his country path conversation" (Hyland, 351).

29. See Plato's *Republic*, VII, 514a–517a.

30. Though it is dated both 1931/32 and 1940, Francisco Gonzalez argues that Heidegger only claims that his "*Gedankengang* extends back to the lecture courses of the early 1930s, and the essay was only *zusammengestellt* in 1940" (Gonzalez, 147, fn. 31).

31. What Heidegger forgets is that Plato acknowledges the role of the night and the light of the stars and moon at a crucial point in the Allegory of the Cave, when the learner has just left the cave. This is a moment where Plato is remarkably gentle with the learner, allowing him to get accustomed to seeing in darkness first. Heidegger does not remark upon this passage in "Plato's Doctrine of Truth." Perhaps his silence invites a reading of the "Triadic Conversation" as inspired by this episode in Plato's Allegory.

32. Hyland goes so far as to argue that the night itself is "a concrete, sensuous, and *simple* image of that which regions, of *Ereignis*, and of its happening. Night is that sensible, one could even say visible, image of that revealing/concealing that is the regioning of that which regions, the *ereignet* of *Ereignis*. Night is the simple that Heidegger has learned to say" (Hyland, 356). Though Heidegger might object to a characterization that he is simply responding to Plato's image of the sunlight with his own image of the night, he is undoubtedly highlighting a contrast.

33. Hyland, 353.

34. Heidegger still agrees nearly a decade later. In the 1951/52 lecture course, he writes, "it would be both tactless and tasteless to take a stand against science upon the very rostrum that serves scientific education . . . Any kind of polemics fails from the outset to assume the attitude of thinking. The opponent's role is not the thinking role. Thinking is thinking only when it pursues whatever speaks *for* a subject" (GA 8: 16/WCT 13). This depiction of polemics apparently contrasts with his work from the 1930s, which seems to exalt willfulness, resolute decisiveness, and even violence. However, Gregory Fried offers an astute and provocative study

of the role of *polemos* or *Auseinandersetzung* in Heidegger's thinking that accounts for the so-called turn in Heidegger's thinking in *Heidegger's Polemos: From Being to Politics* (New Haven: Yale University Press, 2000) and *Toward a Polemical Ethics: Between Heidegger and Plato* (Lanham, MD: Rowman & Littlefield, 2021), which argue that *polemos* cannot be reduced to a facile ontology of opposition.

35. The night is gendered as a "seamstress" of the stars who stitches them together "without seam or hem or yarn" in their final collaborative poetizing (GA 77: 156–57/CPC 102). No explanation for this feminization of the night is provided, nor for the gender traditionalism that is reinforced in identifying her with homemaking practices. In this instance, however, the Guide does further qualify that the night is a seamstress "for the child in the human" (GA 77: 156/CPC 102), recalling perhaps the Nietzschean child who learns to say "yes" from the "Three Metamorphoses" in *Thus Spoke Zarathustra*, but also suggesting a further maternal dimension of the night's femininity that remains yet unexplored. For further analysis of Heidegger's invocation of the feminine, see Shane Ewegen, "Gestures of the Feminine in Heidegger's 'Die Sprache,'" *The Journal of Speculative Philosophy* 30 (2016): 486–98 and a forthcoming edited collection titled *Heidegger, Dasein, and Gender: Thinking the Unthought* in Rowman & Littlefield's New Heidegger Research series.

36. Mitchell, *The Fourfold*, 24.

37. Though *Gestell* has been translated as "enframing," Andrew Mitchell shows that translating the term as "positionality" better resists any temptation to interpret Heidegger's consideration of *Gestell* as "some kind of framework of scaffolding" that is "thrown over" but remains separate from the world such that it would "leave our existence ultimately untouched . . . an idea that Heidegger excoriates" (Mitchell, 50–51).

38. As I noted in the introduction, Heidegger uses the plural term *Beständen* in the "Tower Conversation" (GA 77: 198) but does not use it with the precise meaning he will grant it in 1949. The *Country Path Conversations* may articulate the last gasp of the dominance of representational, metaphysical thinking on Heidegger's own understanding of technology.

39. Though the meaning this depiction develops—that technology is not a category of objects but rather a way of knowing—is sustained. See especially "The Question Concerning Technology" (GA 7: 13–44/QCT in BW 311–41).

40. See Mitchell's introduction "The Fourfold: On the Relationality of Things" and chapter "The Technological Challenge to Things" in *The Fourfold: Reading the Late Heidegger* for a cogent account of how Heidegger's thinking of the thing and technology crescendos in his later work.

41. Heidegger's inaugural 1929 lecture to the faculty of Freiburg University, "What Is Metaphysics?," suggested as much. Though he insists that the history of Western metaphysics interprets beings while forgetting being, he closes by writing that "the truth of metaphysics . . . stands in closest proximity to the constantly lurking possibility of deepest error" (GA 9: 18/BW 109–10).

42. See for example GA 77: 10, 17, and 25–26/CPC 6, 11, and 16.

43. See for example GA 77: 40, 46–47, 58, 63, and 92–93/CPC, 26, 30, 37, 40, and 59.

44. See for example GA 77: 105, 116, 129–30, and 137/CPC 67–68, 76, 84, and 89.

45. I am not the first commentator to note the importance of this structure in Heidegger's thinking. Jean-François Mattéi has shown the replete usage (approximately 220 cases) of ten different forms of the chiasmus across the work available to Mattéi in French in 1983. See "The Heideggerian Chiasmus or the *Setting Apart* of Philosophy," in *Heidegger: From Metaphysics to Thought*, ed. Dominique Janicaud and Jean-François Mattéi, trans. Michael Gendre (Albany: State University of New York Press, 1995). The majority of the forms of chiasmus Mattéi identifies take place at the level of the sentence or passage. My reading of the "Triadic Conversation" shows that this text writ large exemplifies this structure.

46. "Collaborative poetizing" is a term I coined to describe Heidegger's unique staging of poetizing through conversation in this text. See Katherine Davies, "The Resistant Interlocutor: Plato, Heidegger, and the End of Dialogue" (2018).

47. In the opening pages, winter, autumn, and summer are mentioned (GA 77: 4/CPC 2). Spring is conspicuously absent. This omission looks forward to the completion of the philosophical and seasonal cycle with the springtime "Western Conversation." See chapter 4.

48. This metaphysical form of mathematics can in no way be equated with the (non- or pre-metaphysical) Greek sense of τὰ μαθήματα that he describes as meaning "the *learnable* and hence, simultaneously, the teachable" (GA 41: 69–70/47), which I discussed in the introduction. That the Scientist is so uncritically invested in mathematics (figured as the calculable) shows both that he is suffering from the domination of metaphysics and that he wants to learn what nature is and thereby is teachable. In other words, that which shows the Scientist is in need of learning is also that which allows the Guide the opening he needs to teach.

49. Keiling, drawing from Golob, depicts what I am calling representational, metaphysical thinking as follows: "specific subjective forms of the representation of an object mediate and in this way determine how the object appears as meaningful to a subject. The semantics of setting and positioning expresses how this medium is brought to bear on what it is to represent: it is a *set* form of representing objects in thought, prior to any particular object that is to be represented; it is *positioned* in such a way as to capture what it should represent; their representation is *imposed* upon objects" (Keiling, 101). I am arguing that there is a division of labor in how Heidegger presents representational, metaphysical thinking in the dramatic staging of this text—the Scientist is hyper-invested in the objectivity demanded by representational, metaphysical thinking where the Scholar embodies the subjectivity Keiling mentions as also crucial for this form of thinking.

50. Davis, *Country Path Conversations*, 9, fn. 6.

51. In this sense, the Guide may be offering a critique of science rather than a criticism or straightforward disavowal of it. For an analysis of the nuances of Heidegger's thinking of science in his work more broadly, see Trish Glazebrook, *Heidegger's Philosophy of Science* (New York: Fordham University Press, 2000).

52. These include how to distinguish between annihilation and destruction, the essence of the human, whether every answer responds to a question, whether thinking itself is an object, the enigma of nearness and farness thought on its own terms without reference to an object (which the Guide finds beautiful, the Scientist finds oppressive, and the Scholar finds freeing), the distinction (or lack thereof) between methodological and historiological study, the distinction between the identical and the selfsame, and what it means to adorn a matter, among other topics.

53. For instance, the Guide surmises a distinction between the identical (which affords no possibility of relation) and the selfsame (which is thoroughly relational because grounded in difference), but then keeps silent as the Scientist and Scholar work out for themselves what this means (GA 77: 38–42/CPC 25–27).

54. This is presumably because of the distinction between fear and anxiety vis-à-vis the presumption of objectivity. In *Being and Time*, Heidegger distinguishes between fear and anxiety in relation to being-toward-death. Only anxiety as that affect that does not prematurely fashion death into an object-to-be-feared can attenuate an authentic being-toward-death. The claim that fear is always directed at some object whereas anxiety is necessarily object-less is also found in Freud's essay "Beyond the Pleasure Principle."

55. The "strange" and the stranger are centrally important in the second of the *Country Path Conversations*. The "strange" will mark a non-metaphysical comportment toward alterity in distinction from a metaphysics of "wonder" that would seek to solve otherness as a problem in need of definitive resolution. See chapter 2.

56. For an expanded and comparative account of this exchange with the fear driving Callicles in Plato's *Gorgias*, see Katherine Davies, "The Resistant Interlocutor: Plato, Heidegger, and the End of Dialogue" (2018).

57. The soul also appears in Heidegger's 1932 seminar on Plato's *Phaedrus*. See Katherine Davies, "Heidegger's Reading(s) of the *Phaedrus*" (2020), and Francisco Gonzalez's "'I Have to Live in Eros': Heidegger's 1932 Seminar on Plato's *Phaedrus*" (2015).

58. This excerpt was titled *"Zur Erörterung der Gelassenehit: Aus einem Feldweggespräch über das Denken,"* translated as "Conversation on a Country Path about Thinking" by John M. Anderson and E. Hans Freund, thereby omitting the reference to releasement.

59. The "Memorial Address" was delivered ten years *after* Heidegger first articulated *Gelassenheit* in the "Triadic Conversation." However, Heidegger placed it first—before the earlier conversational excerpt—in the published volume. Moore notes, "although the thoughts of the dialogue provide the philosophical foundation for the memorial address, the address serves as an excellent entry point into the

themes of the dialogue. It is presumably for this reason that Heidegger placed the memorial address first in his volume" (126).

60. Translated and published as *Discourse on Thinking*, trans. John M. Anderson and E. Hans Freund (New York: Harper and Row, 1996).

61. See principally *Heidegger and the Will*, among Davis's other scholarly works.

62. See Davis's comment on the appearance of Eckhart in the "Triadic Conversation" in his "Translators' Foreword" to the *Country Path Conversations* (xii–xiii). Additionally, see Moore's monograph *Eckhart, Heidegger, and the Imperative of Releasement* for an extensive analysis of these thinkers and of Heidegger's selective appropriation of Eckhart's thinking.

63. Davis, "Will and Gelassenheit," in *Martin Heidegger: Key Concepts* (New York: Routledge, 2014), 168.

64. Davis, 168–69.

65. Moore, 135.

66. In agreeing to transition away from cognition as the guiding thread of their conversation, the Scientist is already beginning to learn releasement in that he lets (*lassen*) this topic go. However, he is only exchanging one representational framework (science) for another (the soul) and thereby not yet practicing releasement as a gathering of a letting (*ge-lassen*) that in turn gathers him. This can only happen after night falls, an event predicated on a turning (of the earth in relation to the heavens) that they can prepare for but can in no way will to bring about.

67. In no way is this the becoming homely of dwelling that the later Heidegger—drawing from Hölderlin—will articulate. On this topic, see Charles Bambach, *Of an Alien Homecoming: Reading Heidegger's Hölderlin* (Albany: State University of New York Press, 2022).

68. with the Guide even affirming his appropriation at one point. See GA 77: 51, 56, 59, 60, 66, and 79/CPC 33, 36, 38, 42, and 50.

69. Even when pressed, the Guide declines to assert definitively that plants or jugs don't think (GA 77: 67–68/CPC 43).

70. Heidegger's Guide muses further, "I would like to say that the essence of an authentic conversation is determined from out of the essence of language. Perhaps, however, it is the other way around" (GA 77: 57/CPC 36), suggesting language is conversational in essence. See the introduction for an account of this sustained strand of Heidegger's thinking of language, first notable as early as 1936.

71. The distinction Heidegger draws between *Dialog* and *Gespräch* is relevant to his worry that his texts may be compared to Plato's works. See the introduction.

72. Keiling suggests this may implicitly recall Husserl as well ("Letting Things Be for Themselves," 101).

73. On this topic see also Keiling (100–9) and Moore (130–31).

74. The inclusion of "love" in this list deserves underscoring. Though it passes without remark here, in Heidegger's fourth conversational text, "*Das abendländische Gespräch*," love will become an important point of philosophical reflection.

75. He is also, as Davis's footnote astutely points out, "critically reflecting on the manner in which transcendental-horizonal thinking and the metaphysics of production have responded to [the question of how something lets itself show itself as the being that it is]" (CPC 55). This reiterates the Guide's earlier point that technological thinking—that which would manipulate and produce for gain—is the essence of the mathematical projection of nature, which scientific thinking relies on to first understand nature.

76. Davis argues that Heidegger's criticism must also "be understood in part as a self-critique of Heidegger's own Kantian-inspired thinking of transcendence in the late 1920s as well as the voluntarism of his thinking in the first half of the 1930s" ("Returning the World to Nature," 378). Though Heidegger does not explicitly emphasize that any teacher also makes mistakes as she learns until the "Tower Conversation" (see chapter 2), Davis's argument that Heidegger's turn is also crucially a turn away from his earlier thinking supports the reading that the teacher is already becoming student in the "Triadic Conversation." However, Heidegger does not allow the Guide to acknowledge his own historical adherence to this view, perhaps indicating that Heidegger himself still has more to learn about the importance of making and acknowledging his own mistakes.

77. Though I do not elaborate extensively on the importance of the open-region, see Davis (377–78), Moore (132), and Keiling (107–9) for excellent work on the topic. The open-region may be understood as playing the role typically accorded to being in Heidegger's thinking. See especially the scholarly consensus Moore traces (132, fn. 15).

78. For an illuminating analysis of the impact of Kant's thinking of anthropology on racism in the Western philosophical canon, see Peter Park, *Africa, Asia, and the History of Philosophy: Racism in the Formation of the Philosophical Canon, 1780–1830* (Albany: State University of New York Press, 2013).

79. Keiling describes this as a "*reduction ad absurdum*" that shows "the idea that there is no final horizon amounts to a rejection of the idea that there is a single meaning of Being that makes meaningful experience possible," which further may even be understood as "a comment on Heidegger's own philosophical project" (Keiling, 106).

80. For an illuminating reading of the importance of things in Heidegger's *Country Path Conversations*, including the jug, see Shane Ewegen, "The Thing and I: Thinking Things in Heidegger's *Country Path Conversations*," *Gatherings: The Heidegger Circle Annual* 6 (2016): 114–29.

81. Though not explicitly designated as such, this initial exposition of the jug aligns with Aristotle's four causes. In "The Question Concerning Technology," Heidegger refers to the four causes to ascertain the connection between causality and instrumentality inhering in representational thinking. This alerts readers of the "Triadic Conversation" to the return to the technological and scientific thinking afoot in this conversational development.

82. This becomes the teaching character's own task in the second of the *Country Path Conversations*. See chapter 2.

83. This is an allusion to Hölderlin's poetizing of the festival. See further Mathias Warnes, "Heidegger on Hölderlin's Festival: The Wedding Dance as the Inceptual Event," *Epoché* 18 (2014): 503–24; Charles Bambach, "The Time of the Festival and the Graeco-German Beginning," in *Of an Alien Homecoming*, 136–53; and Andrew Mitchell, "The While of the Festival (Hölderlin)," in *The Fourfold*, 280–86.

84. Davis, "Returning the World to Nature," 377.

85. Though Heidegger lays groundwork in the "Triadic Conversation," it is not until the "Western Conversation" where the importance of poetic saying—and learning to resonate with poetic saying through interpretation—is fully elaborated. See chapter 4.

86. See especially Heidegger's characterization of the metaphysical interpretation of art and why Hölderlin's poetizing is not symbolic or metaphorical in the *Ister* lecture course (GA 53: 17–24/16–21). This is further expounded in the "Western Conversation." See chapter 4.

87. As Zaborowski has compellingly shown in "Origin, Freedom, and *Gelassenheit*," the question of the between (field) is precisely what remains at issue in the next installment of the *Country Path Conversations*. I turn to a more detailed assessment of this question in chapter 2.

88. The poem is left without attribution. The Scholar says he read these lines at a friend's house and that this friend had apparently copied them down from somewhere. Of course, Heidegger himself wrote poetry. Three years later he would compose the poems from *Aus der Erfahrung des Denkens*, translated as "The Thinker as Poet" in *Poetry, Language, Thought*. Though this poem is not found there, the styles are commensurate.

89. In his work of the 1940s and beyond, Heidegger has been deeply engaged in unfolding this possibility in the wake of his own interpretive encounter with Hölderlin. The importance of this poet will come to the fore in the "Western Conversation," which I discuss in chapter 4.

90. For an erudite account of Heidegger's critique of the correspondence theory of truth (or truth as *adaequatio*) and his alternative senses of truth, see James Bahoh, *Heidegger's Ontology of Events* (Edinburgh: Edinburgh University Press, 2020), especially chapters 3 and 4.

91. As Davis points out in his footnote (CPC 101, fn. 60).

92. See the introduction for my analysis of Heidegger's abiding interest in conversation and early assertion that the essence of language itself is conversational.

93. There are mentions of Leibniz, Kant, and the intimation of Heidegger himself as the thinkers whose major contribution consists in the introduction of a "single word" that leaves much unthought and thus much more to be thought within it. Heidegger seems to suggest his own single word is "aletheia" (GA 77: 99/CPC 64).

94. This way is unique in Heidegger's corpus. See Davies, "The Resistant Interlocutor: Plato, Heidegger, and the End of Dialogue," *Epoché* 23 (2018): 165–90.

95. Hyland, 347.

96. Hyland, 354.

97. Though I agree with Keiling in principle that the released thinking Heidegger is here developing "eschews a mediational form of representationalism but is not committed to a specific understanding of Being" (97), the rhetorical genre of this conversational text does not allow us to ignore who is (and who isn't) in the (politically) privileged position of remaining philosophically uncommitted in this way.

98. Hyland, 349–50.

99. On the political and philosophical ramifications of "silence" in Heidegger, see Adam Knowles, *Heidegger's Fascist Affinities: A Politics of Silence*.

Chapter 2

1. Martin Heidegger, "The Teacher Meets the Tower Warden at the Door to the Tower Stairway," in *Country Path Conversations*, trans. Bret W. Davis (Bloomington: Indiana University Press, 2010). Hereafter "Tower Conversation."

2. In the 1940s and 1950s, the notion of the "mistake" comes to the fore at various points in Heidegger's conversational texts. In the 1930s, however, Heidegger was briefly occupied with elucidating a particular ontological dimension of being he named "errancy." See Richard Capobianco, "Errancy (Irre)," in *The Cambridge Heidegger Lexicon*, ed. Mark Wrathall (Cambridge: Cambridge University Press, 2021), 289–90. An argument could be developed that this notion of mistake continues a certain strain of his earlier thinking. However, in the context of this project, I use "mistake" to refer to the performative dynamic that elucidates Heidegger's pedagogy, not to describe an ontological feature of being Heidegger had earlier called "errancy."

3. See Holger Zaborowski, "Origin, Freedom, and *Gelassenheit*: On Heidegger's Second 'Country Path Conversation,' " trans. Gregory Canning, in *Phenomenological Perspectives on Plurality*, ed. Gert-Jan van der Heiden (Leiden, Netherlands: Brill, 2015).

4. This will be pursued non-subjectively in the "Evening Conversation. See chapter 3.

5. It is even clearer in this text that Heidegger is preparing to think the Fourfold several years later, focusing on the relationality things mark between earth and sky.

6. Silvia Benso, "When Heidegger's Tower Dweller Takes a Walk: On Thinkers, Poets, and Mysterious Guests in Heidegger's Second Country Path Conversation (GA 77)" (unpublished text of lecture, Collegium Phaenomenologicum, Città di Castello Italy, July 9, 2013), 23.

7. Heidegger, "The Origin of the Work of Art," in *Poetry, Language, Thought* (New York: HarperCollins, 1971), 70.

8. Benso, 16. At this time, Heidegger had also recently abandoned a project to renovate a tower in which he planned to work. This suggests Heidegger may aspirationally self-identify with the Tower Warden in this text rather than with the Teacher.

9. Benso takes her insight into the poetic essence of both the picture and the tower even further, identifying the Tower Warden as Hölderlin: "my interpretative surmise and contention is that the second of the country path conversations provides us not only with the staging of a 'dialogue between poets and thinkers' but more specifically with the enactment of a historically impossible dialogue precisely with the poet Heidegger reveres the most, the poet's poet—Hölderlin, or at least a Hölderlin-like figure indeed interpreted through the lens of Heidegger's predilection for such a poet: a Heideggerianized Hölderlin, to be sure, but still Hölderlin" (8). I agree there are clear indications toward the poetic and even the specific poetizing of Hölderlin in the "Tower Conversation." But when this text is read as the second installment of a series of five conversational texts, it seems to me that Heidegger does not launch a full-scale dialogue with Hölderlin until the "Western Conversation," which is the subject of chapter 4. It is also worth noting that Heidegger had been considering the philosophical meaning of the tower and towering in Sophocles' *Antigone* in both his lecture courses *Introduction to Metaphysics* and *Hölderlin's Hymn "The Ister."*

10. A fourth character is indirectly mentioned several times when the Teacher and Tower Warden reference previous conversations they held with a "neighbor" (GA 77: 171 and 176/CPC 111 and 115). No further details about this figure are disclosed, but a "neighborhood" (GA 75: 93) is mentioned in the "Western Conversation."

11. The plausibility of this claim rests both on the resonances of topics discussed in the "Triadic Conversation" that seem to come through in the Teacher's thinking in this text and on Heidegger's own assertion that his conversations are "interrelated" (Moore, 267), presumably philosophically and dramatically.

12. thereby deemphasizing the supposed importance of the "look" (GA 77: 86–87/CPC 55) described in the "Triadic Conversation" that dominates Western metaphysics and sets the standard for truth as correct representation.

13. See Davis, "Translators' Foreword," xvii–xix.

14. Benso, 8.

15. This is not the first time a philosopher formulated this claim about pedagogy. In the *Physics*, Aristotle argued that one can only become a good teacher if one is not innately talented regarding the content or skill to be learned, but rather first struggled to discern and grasp the cause. Only someone experienced in this struggle can teach a student.

16. Benso, 27–28.

17. Zaborowski, 150–55.
18. Zaborowski, 154–55.
19. Heidegger is here interpreting these lines from Hölderlin: ". . . Since we have been a conversation / And able to hear from one another . . ." (GA 4: 39/56). See the introduction.
20. Zaborowski, 152.
21. See Mark Wrathall, "History of Being (Geschichte des Seins)," in *The Cambridge Heidegger Lexicon*, ed. Mark Wrathall (Cambridge: Cambridge University Press, 2021), 385–96.
22. If the Teacher is the same character as the Guide in the "Triadic Conversation" (as Heidegger's later edit may suggest), then this shows that the Guide was listening to the Scientist and the Scholar quite closely and ultimately learning about their perspectives.
23. or "too early" (GA 77: 198/CPC 129), as the Teacher will worry in the case of the approaching Guest near the end of their conversation.
24. The Teacher seems to revert to representational, metaphysical thinking most easily when negative or challenging affects prevail.
25. See Heidegger's essays "Plato's Doctrine of Truth" and "The End of Philosophy and the Task of Thinking" for an elaboration of this charge.
26. See chapter 1.
27. The conversational partners in this text are only prepared to endure this natural landscape for a short time and in a blunted way. In the "Western Conversation," however, the characters undertake a walk through a forest, guided only by (Hölderlin's) "*Der Ister*." This supports my developmental reading of Heidegger's conversations, which demonstrates that in each text Heidegger is equipping his characters to make ever bolder and more meaningful forays into non-representational, non-metaphysical thinking.
28. Zaborowski emphasizes the importance of *Gelassenheit* for the futural thinking of the origin practiced in the "Tower Conversation," offering an exceptional reading of the centrality of *Gelassenheit* for the thinking of "provenance" (155–57).
29. The question of the "who" arises explicitly in the third (and final) of the *Country Path Conversations*.
30. Though Nietzsche is later invoked as exemplifying a metaphysical philosophy of art because he falls into the trap of anti-metaphysical rather than non-metaphysical thinking, the task of this conversation is to illustrate how the mistake of metaphysical representation provides the occasion for this very turning-back. The conversational partners acknowledge that "Nietzsche moves on a borderline" even though "the idea of value led his thinking . . . to fall back into metaphysics" (GA 77: 187/CPC 122). His earlier thinking shows that Nietzsche too had inklings of what it means to think the human in its locale rather than as a metaphysical subject, specifically in "looking away from ourselves in order to find ourselves" (GA 77: 172/CPC 112). In "Schopenhauer as Educator," Nietzsche issues a call influenced

heavily by his own reading of Emerson that resonates with Heidegger on this point:

> Let the youthful soul look back on its life with the question: what have you truly loved up to now, what has drawn your soul aloft, what has mastered it and at the same time blessed it? Set up these revered objects before you and perhaps their nature and their sequence will give you a law, the fundamental law of your own true self. Compare these objects one with another, see how one completes, expands, surpasses, transfigures another, how they constitute a stepladder upon which you have clambered up to yourself as you are now; for your true nature lies, not concealed deep within you, but immeasurably high above you, or at least above that which you usually take yourself to be. (129)

31. Though there may be further ethical implications to this claim, Heidegger does not draw them. Heidegger's use of the term "good" is restricted to describing the comportment of *Gelassenheit* in the *Country Path Conversations*, which only implicitly includes our relations to other human beings, animals, the environment, etc. Such implications could perhaps be grounded in the performative dimensions of these texts.

32. perhaps in the sense of "being-towards-death" or even approaching the later sense of the "mortals" Heidegger uses to rethink his earlier conception of death. See my essay "Antigone's (Poetic, Queer) Death: Heidegger, Butler, and Mortality," in *Heidegger, Dasein, and Gender: Thinking the Unthought* and Andrew Mitchell, "Mortals, Being-in-Death," in *The Fourfold* (211–13) for a brief overview of the differences between these two distinct Heideggerian philosophies of death.

33. See GA 39: 107–8/98–99.

34. The philosophical importance of swinging or resonating is underscored in the fourth "Western Conversation." It there becomes clear that swinging is the essence of poetizing language.

35. This is another allusion to Hölderlin's poetizing of the festival, which lends support to Benso's suggestion that the Tower Warden is Hölderlin personified. See further Mathias Warnes, "Heidegger on Hölderlin's Festival: The Wedding Dance as the Inceptual Event," *Epoché* 18 (2014): 503–24; Charles Bambach, "The Time of the Festival and the Graeco-German Beginning," in *Of an Alien Homecoming*, 136–53; and Andrew Mitchell, "The While of the Festival (Hölderlin)," in *The Fourfold*, 280–86.

36. Heidegger uses two different terms translated in context as "mistake" or "to be mistaken": *sich täuschen* and *sich verschätzen*. I am not identifying a particular term Heidegger uses by grounding my reading of this text in this notion of the "mistake." Rather, I am elucidating a pedagogical dynamic that performatively undergirds the text.

37. Heidegger's characters call out Nietzsche specifically as falling prey to this error in his thinking of art as the countermovement against metaphysics (GA 77: 187–88/CPC 122).

Chapter 3

1. Martin Heidegger, "Evening Conversation: In a Prisoner of War Camp in Russia, between a Younger and an Older Man," in *Country Path Conversations*, trans. Bret W. Davis (Bloomington: Indiana University Press, 2010). Hereafter "Evening Conversation."

2. It later came to light that both of Heidegger's sons were in POW camps—Jörg in Czechoslovakia and Hermann in Russia—during the spring of 1945. Hermann Heidegger later published a memoir about his time as a prisoner.

3. In 1935, Heidegger developed a claim that Russia and America are, metaphysically speaking, the same (GA 40: 40–41/40). This may raise further questions about the stakes of this nationalistic location.

4. Andrew Mitchell, "Heidegger's Breakdown: Health and Healing under the Care of Dr. V. E. von Gebsattel," *Research and Phenomenology* 46 (2016): 70–97, 78.

5. This term will take on central importance in the "Western Conversation." There it becomes clear that while the forest is the place where such resonating may occur, it is poetizing language that swings out across this capaciousness. See chapter 4.

6. Mitchell, "Heidegger's Breakdown," 79.

7. See chapter 1 for discussion of the enigma of nearness and farness.

8. Mitchell, "Heidegger's Breakdown," 77–78.

9. Again, see Knowles, *Heidegger's Fascist Affinities*.

10. particularly regarding the trap of Nietzsche's anti-metaphysics.

11. Heidegger repeatedly urges a letting of polemical thinking pass by so that it can be learned from the Guide how to not "go forth 'against' anything at all" (GA 77: 51/CPC 33).

12. Arendt, Levinas, and Husserl, for instance, did not experience the privilege Heidegger did to refrain from considering the implications of the failures of ethics and politics. Their lived experiences precluded understanding ethics and politics as derivative, which simultaneously highlights the ethical and political status of Heidegger's focus on ontology.

13. There is an extensive body of literature on this topic. Some recent examples published since the *Black Notebooks* include the exchange between Emmanuel Faye and Gregory Fried; see Gregory Fried, "A Letter to Emmanuel Faye," in *Confronting Heidegger*, ed. Gregory Fried (Landham, MD: Rowman & Littlefield, 2020), 1–52; Donatella Di Cesare, *Heidegger and the Jews: The Black Notebooks*, trans. Murtha Baca (Medford, MA: Polity, 2018); Peter Trawny, *Heidegger and the Myth of a Jewish World Conspiracy*, trans. Andrew Mitchell (Chicago: University of Chicago Press,

2015); and the collection *Heidegger's Black Notebooks: Responses to Anti-Semitism*, ed. Andrew Mitchell and Peter Trawny (New York: Columbia University Press, 2017).

14. Robert Bernasconi shows that the concept of non-moral evil in the "Evening Conversation" is indebted to Schelling in "Being is Evil: Boehme's Strife and Schelling's Rage in Heidegger's 'Letter on Humanism,'" *Gatherings: The Heidegger Circle Annual* 7 (2017): 164–81. Though Bernasconi is interested in elucidating four sentences on evil from the "Letter on Humanism," he engages with the description of evil Heidegger launches in the "Evening Conversation." He writes, "to understand what was meant by both the 'malice of rage' and 'the insurgency' we must go back behind both 'Letter on Humanism' and 'Evening Conversation' to Heidegger's 1936 lectures on Schelling's *Philosophical Investigations into the Essence of Human Freedom*. Heidegger read Schelling's essay as an essay on evil and it is, like these two other texts by Heidegger, about evil as, in Schelling's own words, 'a universal activity,' 'an unmistakable general principle,' and not a discussion of how evil becomes actual in individuals" (169).

15. See the "Triadic Conversation"—particularly GA 77: 35–48/CPC 22–31—for an exposition of Heidegger's distinction between the "selfsame" and the "identical."

16. Again, for a rigorous account of the importance of the will in Heidegger's thought, see Bret Davis, *Heidegger and the Will* (Evanston: Northwestern University Press, 2007).

17. The Younger Man in the "Tower Conversation" diagnoses Nietzsche's thinking of morality, which in attempting to think "beyond good and evil" only succeeds as an "extreme affirmation of morality" (GA 77: 209–10/CPC 135).

18. Bernasconi, "Being Is Evil," 167.

19. Bernasconi, 166–67.

20. and do not even try to describe, unlike the Teacher in the "Tower Conversation."

21. Here, the conversational partners echo Heidegger's remarks concerning the relation between being and nothing in "What Is Metaphysics?"

22. Several years later in the essay "Language," Heidegger seemingly recalls this theme and further reflects on the question of intimacy and being as pain. See further Ian Moore, *Dialogue on the Threshold: Heidegger and Trakl* (Albany: State University of New York Press, 2022).

23. Heidegger centers his fourth "Western Conversation" on the importance of poetic *Schwung*, which can be variously translated as swing, oscillation, or resonation. See chapter 4.

24. Calvin Warren shows how Heidegger's "What Is Metaphysics?" illustrates the logic of anti-Black racism as structurally embedded within humanistic principles. See *Ontological Terror: Blackness, Nihilism, and Emancipation* (Durham: Duke University Press, 2018).

25. This will gain in philosophical importance in chapter 4, where characters of the same names will attempt to hear and interpret Hölderlin's poetry.

26. but not the last time. See chapters 4 and 5.

27. This lends support to Mitchell's claim that for Heidegger, "'the mortals' is always plural, even when, on the rare occasion, Heidegger uses it in the singular" (*The Fourfold*, 212).

28. This is the proper comportment toward poetizing, which will become even more evident in the "Western Conversation." See chapter 4.

29. Though I am not able to elaborate on this issue in depth here, it is important to note (as Arendt was first to do) that Heidegger's later philosophy of death develops significantly from his earlier view of Dasein's being-toward-death in *Being and Time*. For an overview of this evolution, see Iain Thompson, "Death and Demise in *Being and Time*"; Linnell Secomb, "Philosophical Deaths and Feminine Finitude"; Andrew Mitchell, "Mortals, Being-in-Death," in *The Fourfold: Reading the Late Heidegger*; and my essay "Antigone's (Poetic, Queer) Death: Heidegger, Butler, and Mortality."

30. Heidegger composed and delivered "Poverty" within one month of writing the "Evening Conversation."

31. "Poverty," 8.

32. "Poverty," 6.

33. "Poverty," 9, tm.

34. As with the poem in "Triadic Conversation," this seems to be of Heidegger's own composition.

35. For further elaboration of the connection between poetizing and conversation in Heidegger's earlier work, see the introduction.

36. This raises the question of the relation between poetizing and thinking. For a considered study of this relation in Heidegger's broader work, see Keith Hoeller, "Is Heidegger Really a Poet?," *Philosophical Topics* 12 (1981): 121–38. Also, see chapter 4 for a reply to this question as Heidegger addresses it in the "Western Conversation."

37. However, his next two conversational texts will suggest reasons for this retention.

38. See the introduction for a discussion of the evolution of Heidegger's view as to whether learning or teaching is more difficult. The way in which he shifts his view is arguably informed by the depiction of pedagogy he offers here.

39. On March 2, 1945, Heidegger wrote to Elfride that he "recently found the short conversation between two Chinese thinkers that I'm copying out for you" (*Letters to His Wife*, 187). Perhaps it was this very conversation.

40. This is Heidegger's preferred term for non-representational, non-metaphysical language. See chapter 5.

41. Published in translation as "Dialogue on Language." See chapter 5.

Chapter 4

1. Martin Heidegger, "Das abendländische Gespräch," in *Zu Hölderlin-Griechenlandreisen*, ed. Curd Ochwalt, *Gesamtausgabe* 75 (Frankfurt am Main: Vittorio Klostermann, 2000). "*Das abendländische Gespräch*" has not been translated into English. All provisional translations are my own, unless otherwise indicated. Hereafter the "Western Conversation."

2. See the introduction for further discussion of Heidegger's relevant biography.

3. Robert Savage, *Hölderlin after the Catastrophe: Heidegger—Adorno—Brecht* (Rochester, Camden House, 2008), 66.

4. Charles Bambach, *Of an Alien Homecoming: Reading Heidegger's Hölderlin* (Albany: State University of New York Press, 2022), 263.

5. Katherine Davies, "Heidegger's Reading(s) of the Phaedrus," *Studia Phaenomenologica* 20 (2020): 191–221. In this article, I agree with and extend Savage's reading that Plato's *Phaedrus* is philosophically relevant in Heidegger's text.

6. which the characters in the "Evening Conversation" first raised. See chapter 3.

7. Charles Bambach's 2022 monograph—*Of an Alien Homecoming*—represents the most significant and cumulative scholarly endeavor to elucidate the meaning of this relationship.

8. In his discussion of Heidegger's conversations, Francisco Gonzalez focuses on the first three texts in *Country Path Conversations* and the final conversation with the Japanese, neglecting "*Das abendländische Gespräch*" entirely. Bret Davis also omits consideration of this conversation in "Heidegger on the Way from Onto-Historical Ethnocentrism to East-West Dialogue." Likewise, in his article "Heidegger's (Dramatic?) Dialogues," Drew Hyland passes over this dialogical text. Perhaps these omissions are because the "Western Conversation" is not yet available in English translation or is due to its significant length and relative difficulty.

9. The collaborative poetizing in "Triadic Conversation" undoubtedly provides a preview of this poetic thinking, but it does so in a limited way. Where the "Triadic Conversation" ends with poetizing, the "Western Conversation" is permeated by it from the outset.

10. Savage, *Hölderlin after the Catastrophe*, 78.

11. See Hugo Ott's chapters "After the War, the Void," "Coming to Terms with the Political Past," and "Towards a Rehabilitation of Heidegger," in *Martin Heidegger: A Political Life*, trans. Allan Blunden (London: HarperCollins, 1993) and Rüdiger Safranski's chapters "Heidegger Faces the Denazification Committee: Barred from University Teaching" and "Heidegger's Other Public," in *Martin Heidegger: Between Good and Evil*, trans. Ewald Osers (Cambridge, MA: Harvard University Press, 1999) for pertinent overviews of Heidegger's biography in this decade and its relation to the historical events of the period.

12. Andrew Mitchell, "Heidegger's Breakdown: Health and Healing Under the Care of Dr. V.E. von Gebsattel," *Research in Phenomenology* 46 (2016): 70–97.

13. Savage, *Hölderlin after the Catastrophe*, 54–55.

14. Heidegger emphasizes that the conversations between these two men unfold in the plural. This buttresses further the interpretation that these conversational partners are friends, a moniker that is explicitly invoked (GA 75: 158).

15. including a poor woman who is especially in need of milk (GA 75: 93).

16. For instance, *Gelassenheit* appears within the first five pages of the conversation (GA 75: 64) without even a hint of confusion for either conversational partner. The enigma of nearness and farness, previously endlessly debated in the "Triadic Conversation," is also mentioned (GA 75: 103) without engendering any trouble or resistance.

17. See Krzysztof Ziarek, "Refiguring Otherness: A Heideggerian Bypass of Ethics?," in *Inflected Language: Toward a Hermeneutics of Nearness: Heidegger, Levinas, Stevens, Celan* (Albany: State University of New York Press, 1994).

18. See Katherine Davies, "Heidegger's Conversational Pedagogy," *Research in Phenomenology* 52 (2022): 399–424, specifically, 412–17.

19. This limited the "Evening Conversation" characters' success while confined in the camp.

20. Ziarek, *Inflected Language*, 26–27.

21. As Heidegger makes clear in the 1934/35 lecture course, there are two pasts: the (merely) past [*die Vergangenheit*] and the having-been [*die Gewesenheit*]. The past is "unalterably closed off, unable to be brought back" (GA 39: 108/98). *Gewesenheit* "is that which still presences, which we ourselves in a certain way are, insofar as, bringing it before us, preserving it and carrying it forward, or even pushing it away or wanting to forget it" (GA 39: 108/99). The has-been is futural and thereby historical.

22. As I argued was the primary element of his pedagogy of non-metaphysical thinking that Heidegger developed in the second "Tower Conversation."

23. Recall that Heidegger's Guide in the "Triadic Conversation" tells his conversational partners, "I don't want to go forth 'against' anything at all. Whoever engages in opposition loses what is essential, regardless of whether he is victorious or defeated" (GA 77: 51/CPC 33).

24. This 1940 essay is an abridged version of a more sensitive and careful reading of the Allegory of the Cave in the earlier 1931/32 lecture course. See Francisco Gonzalez's tracking of the differences between these texts (*Plato and Heidegger*, 107–61).

25. See especially his 1951/52 lecture course *What is Called Thinking?* in which Heidegger writes positively,

> A dialogue of Plato—the *Phaedrus*, for example, the conversation on Beauty—can be interpreted in totally different spheres and respects, according to totally different implications and problematics. This multiplicity of possible interpretations does not discredit the strictness of the thought content. For all true thought remains open to more

than one interpretation [. . .] multiplicity of meanings is the element in which all thought must move in order to be strict thought. (GA 8: 75/WCT 71)

and

A dialogue of Plato is inexhaustible—not only for posterity and the changing forms of comprehension to which posterity gives rise; it is inexhaustible of itself, by its nature. And this is forever the mark of all creativeness—which, of course, comes only to those who are capable of reverence. (GA 8: 76/WCT 72)

The *Phaedrus* seems to have especially captured Heidegger's attention. In the *Black Notebooks* from the 1930s, Heidegger includes it on an essential philosophical reading list:

From now on the only possible preparation for philosophy is to master the small extent of what's essential to her heritage: the saying of Anaximander, the sayings of Heraclitus, the "doctrine" of Parmenides, Plato's *Phaedrus*, Aristotle's *Metaphysics* VII–IX; Descartes' *Meditations*, Leibniz' "Monadology," Kant's "Critique" (the threefold); Hegel's *Phenomenology of Spirit*, Schelling's treatise on liberty, Nietzsche's "fragments" for his "major work" [his *Will to Power*]. To keep each of these present in conversation, in its uniqueness, without falling into historical scholarship and clever reckoning [comparing/contrasting with others, and with flatland exigencies]. Such mastery can only spring from an original questioning emergent out of the exigency of being[-as-event] itself, and first of all necessitated from the loss-of-being of the things [otherwise] determined to be: As a consequence, there'll be the complete dissolution of the form philosophy has hitherto assumed. (GA 94: 492–93/BN 492–93)

If Heidegger is engaging in an original questioning of Plato's *Phaedrus* in the "Western Conversation," he has perhaps realized his own prescription to keep this text "present in conversation [*Gespräch*]" in a quite literal way.

26. It is the Older Man who tells the Younger Man that perhaps he is enthralled with Hölderlin's Ister hymn in part because "the simple house of your father" (GA 75: 59) stands nearby. In the footnote appended to this line, Heidegger discloses that his family owned the shepherd's farm in the area and his grandfather was born in the sheep's stall. Though this makes no direct impact on the text of the "Western Conversation," this would suggest that the Younger Man occupies the genealogical position of Heidegger's father.

27. In the "Tower Conversation," genealogy is not yet at play but rather only *Kundschaft* or acquaintanceship, which seems to be what was finally achieved in the conclusion to Heidegger's "Triadic Conversation." This arc—from colleagues to acquaintances to friends and now to family—suggests Heidegger is building toward articulating his ancestry (and concurrently the ancestry of the West) as the pinnacle of the possibilities relationality affords for (historical) thinking.

28. Bambach, *Of an Alien Homecoming*, 268. For Bambach, there are "four intersecting themes" of the "Western Conversation": "the *arche* of Heidegger's biographical-familial origin; the *arche* of the Ister as river; the *arche* of the Occident as the origin of German dwelling, and the *arche* of language as poetry" (268).

29. Bambach, 273.

30. Bambach, 268.

31. See the introduction for biographical and historical detail about this time in Heidegger's (and Germany's) life.

32. On this point, Bambach and Savage agree. Bambach writes, "what we find in 'The Western Conversation' is a Hölderlinian vision of German nationalism that presents the George Circle's suppressed dream of a secret Germany to fit the new postwar realities of an emasculated German *Volk* forced to accept the new victor's justice imposed by the occupying Allied powers" (308). Savage concurs that the "Western Conversation" is "recognizably a *postwar* reading, despite . . . [Heidegger's] best efforts to ignore the German catastrophe or to downplay its significance" (72).

33. Again, see Mitchell, "Heidegger's Breakdown."

34. Bambach, xxiii.

35. As I have argued in the preceding chapters, all of Heidegger's conversations are attempting to launch a pedagogy of learning to think beyond representational metaphysics. The first of the *Country Path Conversations* interrogates the importance of the night, the second does the same for art, and the third finds the possibility of a renewed relation to the natural world as significant for healing from political wounding.

36. Savage, 56.

37. See Bambach (267), Savage (58–67), and Davies, "Heidegger's Reading(s) of the *Phaedrus*" (207–16).

38. Davies, 210.

39. Bambach, 271.

40. In the "Triadic Conversation," Heidegger writes of the enigma of nearness and farness (GA 77: 29–31/CPC 18–19), in which to draw near to some*thing*, one must first draw even further away from it. This logic is enacted in the "Tower Conversation" as the conversational partners walk away from the tower to come to understand the relationality it enacts between the upward and the downward. It is also echoed and developed further in "The Point of Reference" in the *Bremen* lectures (GA 79: 3–4/3–4).

41. Heidegger first develops his notion of the selfsame [*das Selbe*] as the alternative to positing identity as the identical [*das Gleiche*] in the "Triadic Conversation" (GA 77: 35–40/CPC 22–26). He sustains this logic in the "Western Conversation" (GA 75: 63, 64, 76, 98, 104, 124, 133, 158, 176, and 193).

42. when compared, for instance to the "Triadic Conversation," in which the Heraclitus reference is made in the opening line, but only explicitly engaged in the final pages of that conversation.

43. Just before the text's end, the conversational partners remark upon how "*Der Ister*" is unfinished and stands as completed in such a breaking off. As both Savage and Bambach note, several pages later the "Western Conversation" also breaks off without any discernible ending, resonating with the poem even at its closure.

44. This would stage the inverse of the "Tower Conversation," in which the conversational partners continued speaking after the text of the written conversation ended.

45. The conversational partners in the "Tower Conversation" were also unprepared to climb upward (in that case back into the tower room) and instead covered geographical ground to come to a non-metaphysical way of thinking of the tower before presumably later climbing up to take in what was also not simply a "mere view" offered by the picture. It was in part the possibility for taking in a view from a height that the devastated metaphysical geography of what Heidegger called the "desert" (GA 77: 211/CPC 136) or the "ocean" (GA 77: 212/CPC 137) in the "Evening Conversation" foreclosed.

46. Bambach writes, "Hölderlin offers a poetic geography and a poetic history for thinking through the turning at the limit, border, and boundary between East and West, Orient and Occident" (271).

47. See further part three of *Hölderlin's Hymn "The Ister"* (GA 53).

48. Bambach, 306.

49. See Hölderlin's "Böhlendorff Letter," trans. Dennis Schmidt, in *On Germans and Other Greeks: Tragedy and Ethical Life* (Bloomington: Indiana University Press, 2001).

50. See chapter 1 for my analysis of the pedagogical function of this chiastic structure in the "Triadic Conversation."

51. On the distinction between waiting and awaiting, see the "Triadic Conversation" (GA 77: 115–16/CPC 75) and the "Evening Conversation" (GA 77: 227/CPC 148).

52. Bambach writes, "the conversations 'vom' Abendland—that is, 'from,' 'out of,' 'in terms of' the West, recognizing all the while that 'the West' is nothing objectively present but, rather, exists as what is coming, what is still to come, and what will be decided upon depending on how 'we' respond to the poetic word of Hölderlin" (305).

53. Bambach, 284.

54. Savage, 74.

55. See Bambach, 298–312.

56. On this point, see Bret Davis's article "Heidegger on the Way from Onto-Historical Ethnocentrism to East-West Dialogue," *Gatherings* 6 (2016): 130–56. Davis contends that Eastern themes run throughout the *Country Path Conversations*, which offers evidence for continuity rather than discontinuity between the first three conversations and the final conversation (138–39). I suggest that including a consideration of the "Western Conversation" offers a Hölderlinian perspective on the relevance of the East that ought to be taken into account to make the case for the "arc" that Davis argues spans the four conversational texts he considers.

57. This authorial decision—to pursue an engagement with the East differently—shows Heidegger may have found a Hölderlinian rendering of the East/West relationship—or at least his understanding of Hölderlin's geo-poetic cartography—lacking in some way. For an overview of Hölderlin's logic of the relation between the foreign and what is one's own, see Charles Bambach, *Thinking the Poetic Measure of Justice* (Albany: State University of New York Press, 2013), 46–56. In *Of an Alien Homecoming* (2022), Bambach argues the "Western Conversation" shows that Heidegger does not adequately come to grips with what he calls the ethopoetic insight: "Heidegger never properly acknowledges the full otherness of the foreign. Rather, for him, the foreign presents a way station on the path of spirit's journey to self-recognition" (300).

58. Though German soldiers were issued a wartime, Insel edition of Hölderlin to be carried in their backpacks, the prisoners in the "Evening Conversation" did not seem to have had recourse to these verses at this time.

59. In "Poverty," Heidegger writes, "genuinely being poor is in itself be-ing rich" (8). Seen in this light, Hölderlin's absence as a character may be rendered as a kind of poverty, distinctive to the postwar historical moment in which Heidegger finds himself.

60. For example, Heidegger inserts a parenthetical note, referring readers on page 146 back to page 136 to make sense of a comment about how the togetherness of the heavenly ones and the earthly sons is granted.

61. This implicit dramatic interpretive dynamic may continue illustrating how laudable the achievements of the confined characters in the "Evening Conversation" truly are.

62. Including *"Der Ister,"* approximately twenty-seven of Hölderlin's poems appear in the "Western Conversation": "Germania" (GA 75: 75), "Mnemosyne" (GA 75: 75), "The German Song" (GA 75: 82), "The Journey" (GA 75: 84), "At the Source of the Danube" (GA 75: 88), "Winter" (GA 75: 90), "The Rhine" (GA 75: 92), "Timidness" (GA 75: 96–97), "The Poet's Courage" (GA 75: 97), "Bread and Wine" (GA 75: 99), "The Only One" (GA 75: 99), "The Walk in the Country" (GA 75: 109), "The Archipelago" (GA 75: 110–11), "As on a Holiday" (GA 75: 112), "Tears" (GA 75: 114), "Sappho's Swan Song" (GA 75: 115), "Love" (GA 75: 119–20), "Exhortation" (GA 75: 120), "But When the Heavenly" (GA 75: 124–25),

"The Poet's Vocation" (GA 75: 141), "The Titans" (GA 75: 143), "Homecoming" (GA 75: 145), "To the Virgin Mary" (GA 75: 147), "Patmos" (GA 75: 179), "The Ages of Life" (GA 75: 179), and "What Is God?" (GA 75: 189–90). In addition, the conversational partners mention Hölderlin's *Nightsongs* as a collection (GA 75: 96), drafts of his theoretical essays (GA 75: 142), and (implicitly) the Böhlendorff letter (GA 75: 151).

63. Bambach, 274.

64. The term *Schwung* has many possible meanings and translations, including resonation, but also oscillation, swinging or swaying, and even force. Heidegger plays upon this multivalent word throughout the conversation.

65. in a more skillful way than the Teacher in the "Tower Conversation," who was unable to properly welcome the arriving Guest.

66. This sense of "sign" stands in stark contrast to what Heidegger in the 1942 lecture course called a "symbol" or a "metaphor" (GA 53: 17–23/16–21).

67. mimicking, in a certain sense, the pedagogical dynamic of making mistakes in the "Tower Conversation," in which a character would hasten to make a philosophical assertion and only later slow down to reconsider the meaning of the danger of such haste.

68. Regarding Heidegger's sense of the importance of the homeland, see Bambach, 268 and 307.

69. See chapter 1 for my analysis of the importance of learning a non-oppositional relation to metaphysics. This, I argue, enables the first step toward the poetic pedagogy celebrated here.

70. as Heidegger variously asserts, in Plato's thought.

71. The conversational partners describe language as having an "abyssal sensual essence" (GA 75: 105) See further Katherine Davies, "Heidegger's Conversational Pedagogy," *Research in Phenomenology* 52 (2022): 399–424, 415–16.

72. Particularly in his 1935 reading of the choral ode from *Antigone* and his 1942 reading of the character Antigone herself. See my "Antigone's (Poetic, Queer) Death: Heidegger, Butler, and Mortality."

73. In the "Triadic Conversation," it was clear science couldn't study its own foundations by way of scientific methodology, and historiology was similarly bereft of its disciplinary resources when attempting to analyze itself. The limitations of these iterations of representational, metaphysical thinking demonstrated their lack of any articulated relation to its origin.

74. As Bambach writes, "for Heidegger, the essential question still remained: would the Germans be able to draw upon a historical faith in their singular role in Occidental history and come to terms with their appointed task as saviors of the Western tradition? For Heidegger, the answer to this question could come only from Hölderlin and his poetic bequest to the German *Volk*. Yes, the language and political form of this message would need to change, given the dominance of Allied

bureaucracy over central Europe. But Heidegger's underlying faith in the Hölderlinian task of the Germans to provide an alternative path to Anglo-American/Soviet machination never faltered" (293). Bambach also insists—and I wholeheartedly agree—that we must read Heidegger's adherence to a notion of a "secret Germany" critically and as distinctly dangerous (277 and 309).

75. as Heidegger demonstrated in the "Tower Conversation." See chapter 2.

76. recalling a similar discussion of the limitations of the written word in Plato's *Phaedrus*.

77. As Bambach notes, "this *Gespräch* takes place as the musical, rhythmic play of language" (266).

78. The lyre may also be a veiled reference to Plato. In the *Phaedo*, Socrates finds himself compelled by a dream to begin composing lyrics and verses in addition to philosophizing. One of the arguments offered to support the immortality of the soul he posits uses a lyre as an example.

79. in the "Triadic Conversation" (GA 77: 145/CPC 94) and the "Evening Conversation" (GA 77: 232/CPC 151). It also extends his consideration of the role of the various arts in non-metaphysical thinking beyond the (non-) appearance of visual art in the "Tower Conversation" (GA 77: 167/CPC 108).

80. in his fifth and final conversation. See chapter 5.

81. For an illuminating account of the connections Heidegger draws between the end of metaphysics, poetizing, music, and interpretation beyond the "Western Conversation," see John Lysaker, "Heidegger's Absolute Music, or What Are Poets for When the End of Metaphysics is at Hand?," *Research in Phenomenology* 30 (2000): 180–210.

82. Echoing the sense the characters discuss in the "Triadic Conversation," that movement can only be "movement (on a way) [*Bewegung*]" (GA 77: 118/CPC 77).

83. In both "The Origin of the Work of Art" and the "Age of the World Picture," Heidegger has already denounced aesthetics as a metaphysical, reductive, and distinctly modern methodology that obscures the essence of the artwork.

84. The Older Man is careful to insist that Hölderlin's poem is already resonating, even before it would be non-metaphysically interpreted: "The interpreting sets to music, that is it pays attention to the grounding tone in the resounding-forth and lets the word abide in its tone. Setting-to-music *[Ver-tonen]* I mean here in this sense: to let purely into the grounding tone" (GA 75: 69).

85. See especially "The river as the locality of journeying and the journeying of locality" in *Hölderlin's Hymn 'The Ister'* (GA 53: 40–62/33–50).

86. On this point, see Bambach, 271.

87. Krzysztof Ziarek, "The Poietic Momentum of Thought," *Philosophers and Their Poets: Reflections on the Poetic Turn in Philosophy since Kant*, edited by Charles Bambach and Theodore George (Albany: State University of New York Press, 2019), 185–86.

88. A marked exception is found in Heidegger's *Nietzsche* lectures, which contain a detailed consideration of love, arguably extending his consideration of fundamental attunements. See Ricky DeSantis, "Love's Resistance: Heidegger and the Problem of First Philosophy," *Journal of the British Society for Phenomenology* 53 (2022): 61–74.

89. which further intimates a subterranean dialogue with Plato. See my article "Heidegger's Reading(s) of the *Phaedrus*," 210–13.

90. The conversational partners emphasize the historical character of erstwhile love by contrasting it to "eternal love" (GA 65: 54), which aspires to a metaphysical atemporality.

91. The connection between *mögen* and *Vermögen* permeates Heidegger's later thinking, even beyond the context of interpreting Hölderlin's poetry. See Mitchell, *The Fourfold*, 223–31.

92. Heidegger developed this point in the "Triadic Conversation." See chapter 1.

93. recalling instances of remembering in the *Country Path Conversations*.

94. See again, GA 39: 107–9/98–99.

95. The "Triadic Conversation" is the only conversational text of such impressive length, comprising 159 pages. Such a lengthy exchange benefits from these summaries at various points. By contrast, the "Western Conversation" is only 137 pages.

96. often in the form of a grammatical imperative.

97. For instance, the characters say to one another, "I remember the song 'Germania' . . ." (GA 75: 85), "Remember the inception of the Ister-song . . ." (GA 75: 112), "And remember the hymn 'As when on a Holiday . . . ,' . . ." (GA 75: 112), "You remember now the inception of the last section of the elegy 'The Autumn Festival' ['Stuttgart'] . . ." (GA 75: 136), "You remember the only recently become known verse: . . ." (GA 75: 140), "Remember the word of 'Fate' . . ." (GA 75: 186), "You remember now probably the late poem: 'What Is God?' . . ." (GA 75: 189), and "Again you remember the word in 'Bread and Wine' . . ." (GA 75: 191).

98. On the significance of the eagle as the emissary from the Greeks to the Germans for Hölderlin, see Bambach, 275–76.

99. See "The Metaphysical Locale of Hölderlin's Poetizing, GA 39: 288–94/261–67.

100. Savage offers a reason for this significant shift: " 'Das abendländische Gespräch' thus legitimates Heidegger's turning to Eastern (especially Taoist) thought at just this time in a common world-destiny: if the voyage away from the Orient drives the spirit from the heavenly fire of Being—a supposition supported by the word *Abendland*, with its associations of twilight and decline—then the reappropriation of the flame, which is the prerequisite for the free use of the occidental ownmost, enails a movement toward the Orient or *Morgenland* that mirrors and undoes Plato's achievement. Whereas Plato, the great transitional figure in an age of transition, occidentalized the Orient, the task confronting post-metaphysical

thinking is an Orientalization of the Occident" (64–65). Such a reading accounts for the turn to Eastern thinking in Heidegger's fifth and final conversational text.

101. Bambach, 308.

102. Bambach, 310.

103. For an incisive account of the role drawing into nearness to otherness plays in Heidegger's hermeneutics writ large, see Krzysztof Ziarek, *Inflected Language: Toward a Hermeneutics of Nearness: Heidegger, Levinas, Stevens, Celan* (Albany: State University of New York Press, 1994). Though Ziarek's study was published before GA 75 was available, the "Western Conversation" attests to Ziarek's prescient analysis.

104. Especially the poetic historical geography Hölderlin is laying out with his singing of the "Here" and "Now" in the first stanza, rather than metaphysical representations of space and time.

105. For Bambach, Heidegger never understands Hölderlin's ethics: "Heidegger never properly acknowledges the full otherness of the foreign. Rather, for him, the foreign presents a way station on the path of spirit's journey to self-recognition" (300). This echoes Arendt's reading of Heidegger as continuing the legacy of German Idealism.

106. Savage argues that even "if Heidegger's turn to Hölderlin represents a turn away from Nazism, it nonetheless remains open to readings that find, in its continuing fixation upon the national as well as in its lofty indifference toward the politics of the day, an effective distraction from an ever-worsening political reality" (45).

Chapter 5

1. Though this is the final conversation in the chronological series of texts Heidegger wrote between 1944 and 1954, it was the first conversation to be published in its entirety in 1959 (an excerpt from the "Triadic Conversation" appeared in the *Gelassenheit* volume, also in 1959). Hertz's English translation appeared in 1971. This text has received substantially more scholarly attention by the Anglophone Heidegger Studies community than the earlier conversations, which were published in German in 1995 (GA 77) and 2000 (GA 75). Davis's English translation of GA 77 appeared in 2010. No English translation of the "Western Conversation" is currently available.

2. Danger becomes significant in Heidegger's work between "*Das abendländische Gespräch*" and this final conversational text, principally in his lecture "The Danger" presented twice in Bremen in 1949. See GA 79: 46–67/44–63. In this lecture, Heidegger contends with a sense of technology that is no longer a process of objectification but instead exemplifies circulative replacement. See Mitchell, "Positionality as Circulative Replacement," in *The Fourfold*, 49–63.

3. The "Evening Conversation" ends with a quotation (which Heidegger fails to properly cite) to a short dialogue in chapter 26 of the *Zhuangzi*. See chapter 3.

This quoted dialogue may have helped inspire the project of composing conversations for Heidegger. On March 2, 1944, Heidegger wrote to Elfride about a "short conversation between two Chinese thinkers" (*Letters to His Wife*, 187), and less than two weeks later he wrote to her again about his experience composing the *Country Path Conversations*. See the introduction. As Bret Davis argues, Eastern themes inform all three *Country Path Conversations*. See Davis, "Heidegger on the Way," 138–39.

4. For an illuminating interrogation of the relation between phenomenology and *Gelassenheit* across Heidegger's corpus, see Will McNeill, *The Fate of Phenomenology: Heidegger's Legacy* (Lanham, MD: Rowman & Littlefield, 2020).

5. Martin Heidegger, "Aus einem Gespräch von der Sprache: Zwischen einem Japaner und einem Fragenden," in *Unterwegs zur Sprache*, ed. Friedrich-Wilhelm von Herrmann, *Gesamtausgabe*, vol. 12 (Frankfurt: Vittorio Klostermann, 1959).

6. Martin Heidegger, "A Dialogue on Language between a Japanese and an Inquirer," in *On the Way to Language*, trans. Peter D. Hertz (New York: HarperCollins Publishers, 1971).

7. Graham Parkes, "Afterwords—Language," in *Heidegger and Asian Thought*, ed. Graham Parkes (Honolulu: University of Hawai'i Press, 1987), 213.

8. Bret Davis, "Heidegger's Orientations: The Step Back on the Way to Dialogue with the East," in *Heidegger-Jahrbuch 7: Heidegger und das ostasiatische Denken*, ed. Alfred Denker, Holger Zaborowski, Georg Stenger, Ryôsuke Ohashi, and Shunsuke Kadowaki (2013), 157.

9. For my own view of this issue, see the introduction.

10. Davis, "Heidegger's Orientations," 165, fn. 52.

11. Hereafter "Conversation of Language."

12. That is, the task of conversation is to allow the conversational essence of language—which Heidegger first elaborated in the 1936 essay "Hölderlin and the Essence of Poetry" (GA 4: 38–39/EHP 56)—to emerge. See the introduction.

13. See the introduction for my rationale.

14. Heidegger, *Letters to His Wife*, 187.

15. Florian Vetsch, *Heideggers Anfang der interkulturellen Auseinandersetzung* (Würzburg: Königshausen and Neumann, 1992).

16. Lin Ma, *Heidegger on East-West Dialogue: Anticipating the Event* (New York: Routledge, 2008).

17. which may be understood along the lines of Said's critique of Eurocentrism.

18. See Davis, "Heidegger's Orientations," 154, fn. 3.

19. See Reinhard May, *Heidegger's Hidden Sources: East-Asian Influences on His Work* (London: Routledge, 1996) and Graham Parkes's "Translator's Preface" thereof and complementary essay "Rising Sun over Black Forest: Heidegger's Japanese Connections," in May (1996), vii–xv and 79–117.

20. See, for instance, Lin Ma and Jaap van Brakel, "Heidegger's Comportment toward East-West Dialogue," *Philosophy East and West* 56 (2006): 519–66.

21. Ma, *Heidegger on East-West Dialogue*, 210–11.

22. Jarava Lal Mehta, "Heidegger and the Comparison of Indian and Western Philosophy," *Philosophy East and West* 20 (1970): 303–18.

23. A. W. Prins, " 'Im Westen nur Neues.' Martin Heidegger und die interkulturelle Auseinandersetzung," in *Das Multiversum der Kulturen. Beitrage zu einer Vorlesung im Fach 'Interkulturelle Philosophie an der Erasmus Universität Rotterdam*, ed. H. Kimmerle (Amsterdam: Rodopi, 1996).

24. Heidegger's educational training equips him to understand the scope of just how creative his interpretations in these domains are (and need to be, to accomplish his philosophical intervention).

25. In addition to the scholarship already mentioned, see Graham Parkes, ed., *Heidegger and Asian Thought* (Honolulu: University of Hawai'i Press, 1987); Yasuo Yuasa, "The Encounter of Modern Japanese Philosophy with Heidegger," in Parkes (1987): 155–74; Joan Stambaugh, "Heidegger, Taoism, and the Question of Metaphysics," in Parkes (1987): 79–92; Robert Mugerauer, *Heidegger's Language and Thinking* (Atlantic Highlands, NJ: Humanities Press International, 1988); Jean-Luc Nancy, "Sharing Voices," in *Transforming the Hermeneutic Context: From Nietzsche to Nancy* (Albany: State University of New York Press, 1990); Robert Bernasconi, "On Heidegger's Other Sins of Omission: His Exclusion of Asian Thought from the Origins of Occidental Metaphysics and His Denial of the Possibility of Christian Philosophy," *American Catholic Philosophical Quarterly* 69 (1995): 333–50; Bradley Douglas Park, "Differing Ways, Dao and Weg: Comparative, Metaphysical, and Methodological Considerations in Heidegger's 'Aus einem Gespräch von der Sprache' " *Continental Philosophy Review* 37 (2004): 309–39; Bret W. Davis, "Heidegger and Asian Philosophy," in François Raffoul and Eric S. Nelson, eds., *Bloomsbury Companion to Heidegger* (London: Bloomsbury Press, 2013), 459–71; David Lewin, "Heidegger East and West: Philosophy as Educative Contemplation," *Journal of Philosophy of Education* 49 (2015): 221–39; Eric S. Nelson, *Chinese and Buddhist Philosophy in Early Twentieth-Century German Thought* (London: Bloomsbury, 2017); Bret Davis, "East-West Dialogue After Heidegger," in *After Heidegger?*, ed. Gregory Fried and Richard Polt (Lanham, MD: Rowman & Littlefield, 2018); Eric S. Nelson, "Heidegger's Daoist Turn," *Research in Phenomenology* 49 (2019): 362–84; and Bret Davis, "Heidegger and Daoism: A Dialogue on the Useless Way of Unnecessary Being," in *Daoist Encounters with Phenomenology*, ed. David Chai (London: Bloomsbury, 2020), 161–96.

26. Of Heidegger's ethnocentric biases, Davis writes, "despite some undeniable moments and persistent elements of Eurocentrism in Heidegger's thought, the proper pathway of his step back . . . leads to a place which allows us to step outward into a genuine dialogue with other traditions of thought" ("Heidegger's Orientation," 173). This may be a possibility for Heideggerian thinking. However, I contend such a dialogue is not realized by Heidegger in this text.

27. See Davis, "Heidegger's Orientations," 167 fn. 55 and Ma, *Heidegger on East-West Dialogue*, 10.

28. Including Tsjimura Kōichi, a prominent philosopher of the Kyoto school who later studied with Heidegger from 1956 to 1958 (Ma, *Heidegger on East-West Dialogue*, 14).

29. For a thorough and entertaining account of the historical Baron Kuki, see Hans Ulrich Gumbrecht, "Martin Heidegger and His Japanese Interlocutors: About a Limit of Western Metaphysics," *Diacritics* 30 (2000): 83–101.

30. See Ma, *Heidegger on East-West Dialogue*, 12 and Stephen Light, *Shuzo Kuki and Jean-Paul Sartre: Influence and Counter-influence in the Early History of Existential Phenomenology* (Carbondale: Southern Illinois University Press, 1987).

31. See chapter 2.

32. He is inappropriately referred to as "Count" rather than "Baron" Kuki in "Conversation of Language." See Ma, *Heidegger on East-West Dialogue*, 12.

33. Presumably referring to the lecture course that Heidegger delivered in summer semester 1920, titled "*Phänomenologie der Anschaung und des Ausdrucks*," published as GA 59.

34. On this point, see Hyland, "Heidegger's (Dramatic?) Dialogues," 346.

35. See Reinhard May, "Tezuka Tomio, 'An Hour with Heidegger,'" in *Heidegger's Hidden Sources: East Asian Influences on His Work*, trans. Graham Parkes (New York: Routledge, 1996), 59–64. This account was published as an afterword to Tezuka's own Japanese translation of "Conversation of Language."

36. See Reinhard May, "The 'Conversation,'" in *Heidegger's Hidden Sources*, 15–16.

37. In "Heidegger on the Way," Davis shows how Heidegger's readings of Hölderlin prepare for his encounter with Eastern thought (139–42) and that the *Country Path Conversations* already contain Eastern themes (137–39), which Davis argues are already preparing Heidegger to move beyond the confines of the Western tradition before he composed "Conversation of Language."

38. Davis, "Heidegger on the Way," 137. Davis also lists many of these scholars: 161, fn. 39.

39. Including especially the question of the import of Christianity for European civilization.

40. Nancy, "Sharing Voices," 226.

41. This dynamic—where the Questioner speaks on his own behalf about the personal details of his life, but the Japanese must speak only as a representative of various groups—is one example of what Ma will diagnose as perniciously asymmetrical in "Conversation of Language." I elaborate on this dynamic below.

42. Nor is there any reflection on the political context of why this German Questioner worked with Japanese students so closely.

43. The Questioner says, "tomorrow you will leave again, to go to Florence" (GA 12: 126/OWL 39), indicating that the Japanese has been there before and is leaving yet again.

44. For an elaboration of this sense of homecoming that seems to subordinate the foreign to one's own in Heidegger's work, see Charles Bambach, *Of an Alien Homecoming: Reading Heidegger's "Hölderlin"* (Albany: State University of New York Press, 2022).

45. See GA 12: 87, 88, 91, 105, 106, 114, 137/OWL, 6, 7, 10, 21, 22, 29, and 48.

46. As in the "Western Conversation." See chapter 4.

47. Ma, *Heidegger on East-West Dialogue*, 168.

48. Ma, 172.

49. Davis, "Heidegger's Orientations," 173. For an elaboration of his argument considering ethnocentrism, see also Davis's urging that Heidegger's emphasis on the unspoken and silence may be "the 'single source' (*die einzige Quelle*) of Eastern as well as Western languages and thought" ("Heidegger on the Way," 147).

50. Mitchell, *The Fourfold*, 59.

51. Ma, *Heidegger on East-West Dialogue*, 168.

52. Likely *Reflections on Japanese Taste: The Structure of Iki* or perhaps *The Philosophy of Heidegger*, both written by the historical Baron Kuki Shūzō.

53. There may be resonances with this invocation of the unliving Kuki all the way back to *Being and Time*, in which Heidegger offers an analysis of corpses as objects that nevertheless are never reducible to their mere objecthood, instead preserving their history even after death.

54. Perhaps foreshadowing the comportment Heidegger will come to suggest is possible toward technology in the 1955 "Memorial Address": "We can use technical objects [*technischen Gegenstände*], and yet with proper use also keep ourselves so free [*freihalten*] of them, that we may let go [*loslassen*] of them at anytime . . . We let technical objects enter into our daily world [*tägliche Welt*], and at the same time leave them outside [*draußen*]" (*Gelassenheit*: 24–25/54, tm.).

55. This supports Mitchell's contention that Heidegger's thinking of death evolves beyond this earlier, existential account of being-toward-death and is now anchored by a sense of plurality signaled by his term "the mortals" in *The Fourfold*. On this point see Mitchell, "Mortals, Being-in-Death," in *The Fourfold*, 211–58 and my "Antigone's (Poetic, Queer) Death: Heidegger, Butler, and Mortality," in *Heidegger, Dasein, and Gender: Thinking the Unthought*.

56. Ma notes, the term *iki* "refers to the aesthetic sensibility of a merchant class that was developed in the pleasure quarters in the Edo period of Japan" (Ma, *Heidegger on East-West Dialogue*, 169). She also references Hisumatsu, who describes *iki* as "an aesthetic complex—connotatively, as combining outward coquetry with inner boredom; denotatively, as embracing such contrasting qualities as refinement and coarseness, or showiness and restraint" (Hisamatsu, *The Vocabulary of Japanese Literary Aesthetics*, 64). Ma goes on to show how the historical Kuki's theorizing of this term bears little to no resemblance to the way Heidegger depicts it in "Conversation of

Language." Davis concurs, writing that this text "frustrates us with its arbitrary metaphysical misinterpretations of Kuki's hermeneutical phenomenology of the Japanese word *iki*" ("Heidegger's Orientations," 179). The historical Kuki's work does engage Heidegger's work on the "relation between a language and a people" (Ma, *Heidegger on East-West Dialogue*, 169), but this is not discussed in "Conversation of Language."

57. It does not seem too farfetched, given Heidegger's interest in "hesitation" as the proper comportment of the human being to her essence in the "Western Conversation" (see chapter 4) to read this moment as a performance of and reference to this previously developed analysis and therefore as no mere instance of dramatic flair.

58. Again, presumably referring to the 1920 lecture course.

59. About the publication of *Being and Time*, the Questioner remarks that when he broke his silence, he did not do so in a way that remained attenuated to the need of that silence: "The fundamental flaw of the book *Being and Time* is perhaps that I ventured forth too far too early" (GA 12: 89/OWL 7). It would follow that Heidegger may have subsequently endeavored to learn how to keep silent in a pedagogical sense, so as not to repeat this particular mistake.

60. This pedagogy is what Heidegger is disclosing in his conversational texts.

61. This is perhaps partially because the Japanese has translated some of the Questioner's lectures.

62. Again, Hisamatsu describes *iki* as "an aesthetic complex—connotatively, as combining outward coquetry with inner boredom; denotatively, as embracing such contrasting qualities as refinement and coarseness, or showiness and restraint" (*The Vocabulary of Japanese Literary Aesthetics*, 64).

63. May, "The 'Conversation,' " in *Heidegger's Hidden Sources*, 19.

64. Davis, "Heidegger's Orientations," 179.

65. Ma, *Heidegger on East-West Dialogue*, 169.

66. Parkes, "Rising Sun over Black Forest," in May, *Heidegger's Hidden Sources*, 96.

67. Ma, 169.

68. Kuki Shūzū, *Reflections on Japanese Taste. The Structure of Iki*, trans. J. Clark (Sydney: Power Publications, 1997), 118.

69. "Language is nothing but the self-manifestation of the past and present mode of being of a people, and the self-unfolding of a specific culture endowed with history . . . The relations between the two indicate organic compositional relations where the whole prescribes the part" (Kuki, 28).

70. If the poetic pedagogy developed therein can find traction or purchase beyond the Western, German context. This is the question at the heart of this text.

71. May concurs with Ma on this point: "Since it is highly unlikely that Tezuka would have pronounced it *iro* in his explanation to Heidegger (though he may have mentioned it as an alternative reading in other contexts), one must suppose that Heidegger misread his notes on the discussion and/or that he was later given

a reading of the character by another Japanese who was unaware of the Buddhist context" (May, 66, fn. q.).

72. Ma, 182.

73. This film made an August 26, 1950, debut in Japan and had an August 4, 1952, release date in West Germany.

74. Ma, 186–87.

75. Above, I drew a contrast between the replete references to the Western tradition the Questioner relies on to explore and elaborate his own intellectual trajectory and Heidegger's portrayal of the Eastern world. This reference to Oscar Benl is a notable exception. However, Heidegger will soon turn to his own philosophical work to make sense of this theatrical form. Further, the use Heidegger makes of Benl's work extends far beyond this isolated mention of it. Heidegger uses this single source extensively throughout this text without citing it. As May shows, Heidegger seems to draw on it to define what he means by mystery, as a source for a Japanese poem by a supposedly unknown poet he later places in the Japanese's mouth, and for the idea of grace he (inappropriately) uses to describe *iki* ("The 'Conversation,'" in *Heidegger's Hidden Sources*, 17–19). Rather than using many sources (as he did to elaborate his own autobiography), Heidegger instead uses this single source in a myriad of semi-disguised ways to speak on behalf of the Eastern world.

76. familiar to readers of Heidegger's earlier conversations, that is.

77. At the outset of "Language," Heidegger writes, "to talk about language is presumably even worse than to write about silence. We do not wish to assault language" (GA 12: 10/PLT 188).

78. See "Hölderlin and the Essence of Poetry" as discussed in the introduction.

79. c.f. Ma 172–77.

80. Ma, 172.

81. This was also a pervasive worry in the "Western Conversation," but one that the resonating of poetizing addressed. See chapter 4.

82. In the "Western Conversation," the conversational partners spoke of the poetic word having a width too: "how wide [*wie weit*] it is around each poetizing word of poets (GA 75: 189).

83. as mistakes had done for the Teacher and Tower Warden in the "Tower Conversation." See chapter 2.

84. The picture [*Bild*] in the "Tower Conversation" may also speak to this point.

85. Such an interpretation would foreshadow Heidegger's "Memorial Address."

86. For an extended discussion of the role grace plays in Heidegger's later work, see Andrew Mitchell, "The Exposure of Grace: Dimensionality in Late Heidegger," *Research in Phenomenology* 40 (2010): 309–30.

87. This should read "*shiki*," but Heidegger misrepresents it. See above.

88. perhaps indicating that he has learned how to let the wonderous be in all its strangeness, the outstanding task remaining from the "Tower Conversation."

89. The Questioner shares that he made this remark in a lecture called "Language." At the point of composition, it was unpublished, but later collected into GA 12 and published alongside "Conversation of Language."

90. See "Hölderlin and the Essence of Poetry" and my discussion of the relevance of this essay for Heidegger's project of composing conversations in the introduction.

91. The letter to his wife and his own insistence on the distinction between *Dialog* and *Gespräch* in the "Triadic Conversation" show that Heidegger was eager to distance himself from Plato at the outset of his sojourn in the conversational genre. But at its conclusion, he seems to signal an openness to reconsidering the nearness of Plato's thinking to his own.

92. Ma, 168.

Conclusion

1. This is Michael Ehrmantraut's contention in *Heidegger's Philosophic Pedagogy*, though he limits his claim to the period of 1928 to 1935. I argue that this later articulation of his pedagogy via the conversational texts is much richer and more mature than the implications in *Being and Time* and other earlier work.

2. Sacha Golob, "A Heideggerian Pedagogy of Disruption," *Educational Philosophy and Theory* 54 (2022): 194–203.

3. Golob, "A Heideggerian Pedagogy of Disruption," 198.

4. Golob, 198.

5. Michael Bonnett, "Education as a Form of the Poetic: A Heideggerian Approach to Learning and the Teacher-Pupil Relationship," in *Heidegger, Education, and Modernity* (Lanham, MD: Rowman & Littlefield, 2002), 229–43.

6. Bonnett, "Education as a Form of the Poetic," 230. Bonnett here sets aside the thorny issue of whether Dasein constitutes a person capable of authenticity as a matter of the personal. I would argue Dasein is not a person, but regardless of this interpretive issue of the text of *Being and Time*, it becomes exceedingly clear in the *Country Path Conversations* that personhood is precisely what must be left behind, as Drew Hyland puts it, to undertake educational transformation.

7. Bonnett, 232.

8. Bonnett, 234.

9. Bonnett, 236.

10. Bonnett, 238.

11. Bonnett, 239.

12. Bonnett, 239.

13. Bonnett, 239.

14. Bonnett, 240.

15. Bonnett, 241.

16. Bonnett, 240.

17. Again, see Andrew Mitchell, *The Fourfold: Reading the Late Heidegger* (Evanston: Northwestern University Press, 2015).

18. Patrick Fitzsimons, "Enframing Education," in *Heidegger Education, and Modernity* (Lanham, MD: Rowman & Littlefield, 2002), 171–90.

19. Fitzsimons, "Enframing Education," 177.

20. Fitzsimons, 184.

21. Fitzsimons, 185.

22. Fitzsimons, 187.

23. A prolific and well-respected commentator on this topic. For the purposes of these remarks, I focus on his book chapter: Iain Thomson, "Heidegger on Ontological Education, or How We Become What We Are," in *Heidegger Education, and Modernity* (Lanham, MD: Rowman & Littlefield, 2002), 123–50. However, for a richer and more detailed presentation of many of the themes demonstrated in this chapter, see Iain Thomson, *Heidegger on Ontotheology: Technology and the Politics of Education* (New York: Cambridge University Press, 2005).

24. Iain Thomson, "Heidegger on Ontological Education, or How We Become What We Are," 129. Thomson uses this term to translate *Gestell*, which earlier in this manuscript I've referred to as "positionality," following Mitchell's translation.

25. Thomson, 133.

26. Thomson, 125.

27. Thomson, 137.

28. Thomson, 137–39.

29. Thomson, 139.

30. Thomson, 137.

31. Thomson, 135.

32. This includes the account offered by Michael Ehrmantraut in *Heidegger's Philosophic Pedagogy* (New York: Continnuum, 2010), 16–17.

33. Thomas Peterson, "Notes on Heidegger's Authoritarian Pedagogy," *Educational Philosophy and Theory* 37 (2005): 599–623.

34. Peterson, "Notes on Heidegger's Authoritarian Pedagogy," 600.

35. Peterson, 600.

36. Peterson, 606.

37. Peterson, 611–12.

38. Peterson, 620.

39. Peterson, 615.

40. For an example, see Adolf Eichmann's invocation of Kant's Categorical Imperative to defend his actions as a Nazi bureaucrat as described by Hannah Arendt in *Eichmann in Jerusalem* (New York: Penguin Books, 2006).

41. Peterson, 610.

42. I hope to explore such comparative projects in the future, or to inspire my readers to do so, if or when the critical pedagogical tools harbored within Heidegger's thinking could help illuminate efforts to reimagine what it means to learn.

Bibliography

Works by Martin Heidegger

HEIDEGGER GESAMTAUSGABE

Heidegger, Martin. *Gesamtausgabe.* 102 vols. Projected. Frankfurt Am Main: Vittorio Klostermann, 1975.

GA 2. *Sein und Zeit* (1927). Edited by Friedrich Wilhelm von Herrmann, 1977. / *Being and Time.* Translated by Joan Stambaugh. Revised and with a foreword by Dennis J. Schmidt. Albany: State University of New York Press, 2010.

GA 4. *Erläuterungen zu Hölderlins Dichtung* (1936–68). Edited by Friedrich-Wilhelm von Herrmann, 1981, 2012 (rev. ed.). / *Elucidations of Hölderlin's Poetry.* Translated by Keith Hoeller. Amherst, NY: Humanity Books, 2000.

GA 5. *Holzwege* (1935–46). Edited by Friedrich-Wilhelm von Hermann, 1977. / *Off the Beaten Track.* Translated by Julian Young and Kenneth Haynes. Cambridge: Cambridge University Press, 2002.

GA 6.1. *Nietzsche I.* Edited by Brigitte Schillbach. 1996. / *Nietzsche: Volumes One and Two.* Translated by David Farrell Krell. New York: HarperCollins, 1991.

GA 6.2. *Nietzsche II* (1939–46). Edited by Brigitte Schillbach, 1997. / *Nietzsche: Volumes Three and Four.* Translated by Joan Stambaugh, David Farrell Krell, and Frank A. Capuzzi. New York: HarperCollins, 1991.

GA 7. *Vorträge und Aufsätze* (1936–53). Edited by Friedrich-Wilhelm von Herrmann, 2000. / ". . . Poetically Man Dwells . . ." In *Poetry, Language, Thought,* 209–27, translated by Albert Hofstadter. New York: Harper & Row, Publishers, 1971. "The Question Concerning Technology." In *Basic Writings,* edited by David Farrell Krell, 307–42. New York: HarperCollins, 1993.

GA 8. *Was heißt Denken?* (1951–52). Edited by Paola-Ludovika Coriando, 2002. / *What Is Called Thinking?* Translated by J. Glenn Gray. New York: Harper & Row, 1968.

GA 9. *Wegmarken* (1919–61). Edited by Friedrich-Wilhelm von Herrmann, 1976, 1996 (rev. ed.). / *Pathmarks.* Edited by William McNeill. Cambridge: Cambridge University Press, 1998.

GA 12. *Unterwegs zur Sprache* (1950–59). Edited by Friedrich-Wilhelm von Herrmann, 1985. / *On the Way to Language*. Translated by Peter D. Hertz and Joan Stambaugh. New York: Harper & Row, 1971.

GA 13. *Aus der Erfahrung des Denkens* (1910–76). Edited by Hermann Heidegger, 1983, 2002 (rev. ed.). / "The Pathway." In *Heidegger: The Man and the Thinker*, edited by Thomas Sheehan, 69–72. Chicago: Precedent, 1981.

GA 14. *Zur Sache des Denkens* (1927–68). Edited by Friedrich-Wilhelm von Herrmann, 2007. / *On Time and Being*. Translated by Joan Stambaugh. New York: Harper & Row, 1972.

GA 16. *Reden und andere Zeugnisse eines Lebensweges* (1910–76). Edited by Hermann Heidegger, 2000. / "Rectorship Address: The Self-Assertion of the German University." In *The Heidegger Reader*, edited by Günter Figal. Bloomington: Indiana University Press, 2009.

GA 19. *Platon: Sophistes* (1924–25). Edited by Ingeborg Schüßler, 1992. / *Plato's "Sophist."* Translated by Richard Rojcewicz and André Schuwer. Bloomington: Indiana University Press, 1997.

GA 34. *Vom Wesen der Wahrheit. Zu Platons Höhlengleichnis und Theätet* (1931–32). Edited by Hermann Mörchen, 1988, 1997 (rev. ed.). / *The Essence of Truth: On Plato's Cave Allegory and "Theaetetus."* Translated by Ted Sadler. London: Continuum, 2002.

GA 40. *Einführung in die Metaphysik* (1935). Edited by Petra Jaeger, 1983. / *Introduction to Metaphysics*. Translated by Gregory Fried and Richard Polt. 2nd ed. New Haven: Yale University Press, 2014.

GA 41. *Die Frage nach dem Ding. Zu Kants Lehre von den transzendentalen Grundsätzen* (1935–36). Edited by Petra Jaeger, 1984. Also published by Niemeyer (1962). / *The Question Concerning the Thing: On Kant's Doctrine of the Transcendental Principles*. Translated by James Reid and Benjamin Crowe. London: Rowman & Littlefield International, 2018.

GA 50. *Nietzsches Metaphysik; Einleitung in die Philosophie—Denken und Dichten* (1941–42, 1944–45). Edited by Petra Jaeger, 1990, 2007 (2nd rev. ed.). / *Introduction to Philosophy—Thinking and Poetizing*. Translated by Phillip Jacques Braunstein. Bloomington: Indiana University Press, 2011.

GA 53. *Hölderlins Hymne "Der Ister"* (1942). Edited by Walter Biemel, 1984. / *Hölderlin's Hymn "The Ister."* Translated by William McNeill and Julia Davis. Bloomington: Indiana University Press, 1996.

GA 59. *Phänomenologie der Anschauung und des Ausdrucks: Theorie der philosophischen Begriffsbildung*. Edited by Claudius Strube. 1993 / *Phenomenology of Intuition and Expression: Theory of Philosophical Concept Formation*. Translated by Tracy Colony. New York: Continuum, 2010.

GA 77. *Feldweg-Gespräche* (1944–45). Edited by Ingrid Schüßler, 1995, 2007 (2nd rev. ed.). / *Country Path Conversations*. Translated by Bret Davis. Bloomington: Indiana University Press, 2010.

GA 75. *Zu Hölderlin—Griechenlandreisen* (1939–70). Edited by Curd Ochwadt, 2000. / "The Western Conversation," provisional self-translation.
GA 79. *Bremer und Freiburger Vorträge* (1949, 1957). Edited by Petra Jaeger, 1994. / *Bremen and Freiburg Lectures: Insight Into That Which Is and Basic Principles of Thinking*. Translated by Andrew Mitchell. Bloomington: Indiana University Press, 2012.
GA 80.2 *Vorträge. Teil 2: 1932–1967*. Edited by Günther Neumann, 2020. / "Traditional Language and Technological Language" (1962). Translated by Wanda Torres Gregory. *Journal of Philosophical Research* 23 (1998): 129–45.
GA 94. *Überlegungen II–VI* (Schwarze Hefte 1931–38). Edited by Peter Trawny, 2014. / *Ponderings II–VI: Black Notebooks 1931–1938*. Translated by Richard Rojcewicz. Indiana University Press, 2016.

OTHER EDITIONS OF HEIDEGGER

"Die Armut." *Heidegger Studies* 10 (1994): 5–11. Republished in GA 80.2: 1173–96. / "Poverty." Translated by Thomas Kalary and Frank Schalow. In *Heidegger, Translation, and the Task of Thinking: Essays in Honor of Parvis Emad*, edited by Frank Schalow, 3–10. Dordrecht: Springer, 2011.
Gelassenheit. Pfullingen: Neske, 1959. / *Discourse on Thinking*. Translated by John M. Anderson and E. Hans Freund. New York: Harper and Row, 1996.
Aus der Erfahrung des Denkens. Pfullingen: Neske, 1954. / "The Thinker as Poet." In *Poetry, Language, Thought*, translated by Albert Hofstadter. New York: Harper & Row Publishers, 1971.
"Mein liebes Seelchen!" Briefe Martin Heideggers an seine Frau Elfride 1915–1970. Edited by Gertrud Heidegger. Munich: Deutsche Verlags-Anstalt, 2005. / *Letters to His Wife 1915–1970*. Translated by R. D. V. Glasgow. Cambridge: Polity, 2008.
Überlieferte Sprache und Technische Sprache. Edited by Hermann Heidegger. Copyright 1989 by Erker-Verlag, Franz Larese, und Jürg Jannett, Gallusstrasse 32, CH-90000 St. Gallen. / "Traditional Language and Technological Language" (1962). Translated by Wanda Torres Gregory. *Journal of Philosophical Research* 23 (1998): 129–45.

HEIDEGGER IN ENGLISH TRANSLATION: ABBREVIATIONS

BT *Being and Time*. Translated by Joan Stambaugh. Revised and with a foreword by Dennis J. Schmidt. Albany: State University of New York Press, 2010.
BW *Basic Writings*. Edited by David Farrell Krell. New York: HarperCollins, 1993.
CPC *Country Path Conversations*. Translated by Bret W. Davis. Bloomington: Indiana University Press, 2010.
HR *The Heidegger Reader*. Edited by Günter Figal and translated by Jerome Veith. Bloomington: Indiana University Press, 2009.

N1 *Nietzsche, volume 1: The Will to Power as Art*. Edited and translated by Joan Stambaugh, David Farrell Krell, and Frank A. Capuzzi. San Francisco: Harper, 1991.
N2 *Nietzsche, volume 2: The Eternal Recurrence of the Same*. Edited and translated by Joan Stambaugh, David Farrell Krell, and Frank A. Capuzzi. San Francisco: Harper, 1991.
N3 *Nietzsche, volume 3: The Will to Power as Knowledge and Metaphysics*. Edited and translated by Joan Stambaugh, David Farrell Krell, and Frank A. Capuzzi. San Francisco: Harper, 1991.
N4 *Nietzsche, volume 4: Nihilism*. Edited and translated by Joan Stambaugh, David Farrell Krell, and Frank A. Capuzzi. San Francisco: Harper, 1991.
OWL *On the Way to Language*. Translated by Peter D. Hertz. New York: Harper & Row Publishers, 1971.
PLT *Poetry, Language, Thought*. Translated by Albert Hofstadter. New York: Harper & Row Publishers, 1971.
QCT "The Question Concerning Technology." In *Basic Writings*, edited by David Farrell Krell, 307–42. New York: HarperCollins, 1993.

Other Works

Arendt, Hannah. *Eichmann in Jerusalem: A Report on the Banality of Evil*. New York: Penguin Books, 2006.
Arendt, Hannah. *The Human Condition*. Chicago: University of Chicago Press, 1998.
Babich, Babette. "On Heidegger on Education and Questioning." In *Encyclopedia of Educational Philosophy and Theory*, edited by Michael A. Peters, 1–13. Singapore, 2017.
Bahoh, James. *Heidegger's Ontology of Events*. Edinburgh: Edinburgh University Press, 2020.
Bambach, Charles. *Of an Alien Homecoming: Reading Heidegger's Hölderlin*. Albany: State University of New York Press, 2022.
Bambach, Charles. *Thinking the Poetic Measure of Justice: Hölderlin—Heidegger—Celan*. Albany: State University of New York Press, 2013.
Benso, Silvia. "When Heidegger's Tower Dweller Takes a Walk: On Thinkers, Poets, and Mysterious Guests." Lecture, Collegium Phaenomenologicum, Città di Castello (Italy), July 9, 2013.
Bernasconi, Robert. "Being Is Evil: Boehme's Strife and Schelling's Rage in Heidegger's 'Letter on Humanism'." *Gatherings: The Heidegger Circle Annual* 7 (2017): 164–81.
Bernasconi, Robert. "On Heidegger's Other Sins of Omission: His Exclusion of Asian Thought from the Origins of Occidental Metaphysics and His Denial

of the Possibility of Christian Philosophy." *American Catholic Philosophical Quarterly* 69 (1995): 333–50.

Bonnett, Michael. "Education as a Form of the Poetic: A Heideggerian Approach to Learning and the Teacher-Pupil Relationship." In *Heidegger Education, and Modernity*, edited by Michael Peters, 229–43. Lanham, MD: Rowman & Littlefield, 2002.

Capobianco, Richard. "Errancy (Irre)." In *The Cambridge Heidegger Lexicon*, edited by Mark Wrathall, 289–90. Cambridge: Cambridge University Press, 2021.

Davies, Katherine. "Antigone's (Poetic, Queer) Death: Heidegger, Butler, and Mortality." In *Heidegger, Dasein, and Gender: Thinking the Unthought*, edited by Tricia Glazebrook and Susanne Claxton. Lanham, MD: Rowman & Littlefield, 2024.

Davies, Katherine. "Heidegger's Conversational Pedagogy." *Research in Phenomenology* 52 (2022): 399–424.

Davies, Katherine. "Heidegger's Reading(s) of the Phaedrus." *Studia Phaenomenologica* 20 (2020): 191–221.

Davies, Katherine. "The Resistant Interlocutor: Plato, Heidegger, and the End of Dialogue." *Epoché: A Journal for the History of Philosophy* 23 (2018): 165–90.

Davis, Bret. "East-West Dialogue after Heidegger." In *After Heidegger?*, edited by Gregory Fried and Richard Polt, 335–45. Lanham, MD: Rowman & Littlefield, 2018.

Davis, Bret. "Heidegger and Asian Philosophy." In *Bloomsbury Companion to Heidegger*, edited by François Raffoul and Eric S. Nelson, 459–71. London: Bloomsbury Press, 2013.

Davis, Bret. "Heidegger and Daoism: A Dialogue on the Useless Way of Unnecessary Being." In *Daoist Encounters with Phenomenology*, edited by David Chai, 161–96. London: Bloomsbury, 2020.

Davis, Bret. *Heidegger and the Will*. Evanston: Northwestern University Press, 2007.

Davis, Bret. "Heidegger on the Way from Onto-Historical Ethnocentrism to East-West Dialogue." *Gatherings: The Heidegger Circle Annual* 6 (2016): 130–56.

Davis, Bret. "Heidegger's Orientations: The Step Back on the Way to Dialogue with the East." In *Heidegger-Jahrbuch 7: Heidegger und das ostasiatische Denken*, edited by Alfred Denker, Holger Zaborowski, Georg Stenger, Ryôsuke Ohashi, and Shunsuke Kadowaki, 153–80. Freiburg im Breisgau: Alber Karl, 2013.

Davis, Bret. "Returning the World to Nature: Heidegger's Turn from a Transcendental-Horizonal Projection of World to an Indwelling Releasement to the Open-Region." *Continental Philosophy Review* 47 (2014): 373–97.

Davis, Bret. "Translators' Forward." In *Country Path Conversations*, translated by Bret W. Davis, vii–xxiv. Bloomington: Indiana University Press, 2010.

Davis, Bret. "Will and *Gelassenheit*." In *Martin Heidegger: Key Concepts*, edited by Bret W. Davis, 168–82. New York: Routledge, 2014.

DeSantis, Ricky. "Love's Resistance: Heidegger and the Problem of First Philosophy." *Journal of the British Society for Phenomenology* 53 (2022): 61–74.
Di Cesare, Donatella. *Heidegger and the Jews: The Black Notebooks*. Translated by Murtha Baca. Medford, MA: Polity, 2018.
Diekelmann, Nancy. "Learning-as-Testing: A Heideggerian Hermeneutical Analysis of the Lived Experiences of Students and Teachers in Nursing." *Advances in Nursing Science* 14 (1992): 72–83.
Ehrmantraut, Michael. *Heidegger's Philosophic Pedagogy*. New York: Continuum, 2010.
Ewegen, Shane. "Gestures of the Feminine in Heidegger's 'Die Sprache.'" *The Journal of Speculative Philosophy* 30 (2016): 486–98.
Ewegen, Shane. "The Thing and I: Thinking Things in Heidegger's Country Path Conversations." *Gatherings: The Heidegger Circle Annual* 6 (2016): 114–29.
Fitzsimons, Patrick. "*Enframing* Education." In *Heidegger Education, and Modernity*, edited by Michael Peters, 171–90. Lanham, MD: Rowman & Littlefield, 2002.
Freire, Paulo. *Pedagogy of the Oppressed*. Translated by Myra Bergman Ramos. New York: Bloomsbury, 2018.
Freud, Sigmund. "Beyond the Pleasure Principle." In *The Freud Reader*, edited by Peter Gay, 594–625. New York: Norton & Company, 1989.
Fried, Gregory. "A Letter to Emmanuel Faye." In *Confronting Heidegger*, edited by Gregory Fried, 1–52. Landham, MD: Rowman & Littlefield, 2020.
Fried, Gregory. *Heidegger's Polemos: From Being to Politics*. New Haven: Yale University Press, 2000.
Fried, Gregory. "Introduction to Metaphysics." In *The Bloomsbury Companion to Heidegger*, edited by François Raffoul and Eric Nelson, 207–13. London: Bloomsbury, 2016.
Fried, Gregory. *Toward a Polemical Ethics: Between Heidegger and Plato*. Lanham, MD: Rowman & Littlefield, 2021.
Galilei, Galileo. "The Assayer." In *Selected Writings*, translated by William R. Shea and Mark Davie, 115–21. Oxford: Oxford University Press, 2012.
Gibbs, Paul. "A Heideggerian Phenomenology Approach to Higher Education as Workplace: A Consideration of Academic Professionalism." *Studies in Philosophy and Education* 29 (2010): 275–85.
Glazebrook, Trish. *Heidegger's Philosophy of Science*. New York: Fordham University Press, 2000.
Golob, Sacha. "A Heideggerian Pedagogy of Disruption." *Educational Philosophy and Theory* 54 (2022): 194–203.
Gonzalez, Francisco. "'I Have to Live in Eros': Heidegger's 1932 Seminar on Plato's Phaedrus." *Epoché: A Journal for the History of Philosophy* 19 (2015): 217–40.
Gonzalez, Francisco. *Plato and Heidegger: A Question of Dialogue*. University Park: The Pennsylvania State University Press, 2009.
Gordon, Haim. *Dwelling Poetically: Educational Challenges in Heidegger's Thinking of Poetry*. Atlanta: Brill, 2000.

Heidegger, Hermann. *Heimkehr 47: Tagebuch-Auszüge aus der sowjetischen Gefangenschaft*. Steigra, Edition Antalios, 2007.
Hisamatsu, Shinichi. *The Vocabulary of Japanese Literary Aesthetics*. Tokyo: Centre for East Asian Cultural Studies, 1963.
Hoeller, Keith. "Is Heidegger Really a Poet?" *Philosophical Topics* 12 (1981): 121–38.
Hölderlin, Friedrich. "Letter to Böhlendorff." In *On Germans and Other Greeks: Tragedy and Ethical Life*, translated by Dennis Schmidt, 165–67. Bloomington: Indiana University Press, 2001.
Hyland, Drew. *Finitude and Transcendence in the Platonic Dialogues*. Albany: State University of New York Press, 1995.
Hyland, Drew. "Heidegger's (Dramatic?) Dialogues." *Research in Phenomenology* 45 (2015): 341–57.
Hyland, Drew. *"Questioning Platonism: Continental Interpretations of Plato*. Albany: State University of New York Press, 2004.
Keiling, Tobias. "Letting Things Be for Themselves: *Gelassenheit* as Enabling Thinking." In *Heidegger on Technology*, edited by Aaron James Wendland, Christopher Merwin, and Christos Hadjioannou, 96–114. New York: Routledge, 2019.
Kirkland, Sean. "Thinking the Between with Heidegger and Plato." *Research in Phenomenology* 37 (2007): 95–111.
Knowles, Adam. *Heidegger's Fascist Affinities: A Politics of Silence*. Stanford: Stanford University Press, 2019.
Kouppanou, Anna. *Technologies of Being in Martin Heidegger: Nearness, Metaphor and the Question of Education in Digital Times*. New York: Routledge, 2018.
Kuki, Shūzō. *Reflections on Japanese Taste: The Structure of Iki*. Translated by J. Clark. Sydney: Power Publications, 1997.
Lewin, David. "Heidegger East and West: Philosophy as Educative Contemplation." *Journal of Philosophy of Education* 49 (2015): 221–39.
Light, Stephen. *Shuzo Kuki and Jean-Paul Sartre: Influence and Counter-Influence in the Early History of Existential Phenomenology*. Carbondale: Southern Illinois University Press, 1987.
Lysaker, John. "Heidegger's Absolute Music, or What Are Poets for When the End of Metaphysics Is at Hand?" *Research in Phenomenology* 30 (2000): 180–210.
Lysaker, John. "Language and Poetry." In *Martin Heidegger: Key Concepts*, edited by Bret W. Davis, 195–207. New York: Routledge, 2014.
Ma, Lin, and Jaap van Brakel. "Heidegger's Comportment toward East-West Dialogue." *Philosophy East and West* 56 (2006): 519–66.
Ma, Lin. *Heidegger on East-West Dialogue: Anticipating the Event*. New York: Routledge, 2008.
May, Reinhard. *Heidegger's Hidden Sources: East-Asian Influences on his Work*. Translated by Graham Parkes. New York: Routledge, 1996.
May, Reinhard, ed. "Tezuka Tomio 'An Hour with Heidegger'." Translated by Graham Parkes. In *Heidegger's Hidden Sources: East Asian Influences on His Work*, by Reinhard May, 59–64. New York: Routledge, 1996.

McNeill, Will. *The Fate of Phenomenology: Heidegger's Legacy*. Lanham, MD: Rowman & Littlefield, 2020.

Mehta, Jarava Lal. "Heidegger and the Comparison of Indian and Western Philosophy." *Philosophy East & West* 20 (1970): 303–18.

Mitchell, Andrew. "The Exposure of Grace: Dimensionality in Late Heidegger." *Research in Phenomenology* 40 (2010): 309–30.

Mitchell, Andrew. *The Fourfold: Reading the Late Heidegger*. Evanston: Northwestern University Press, 2015.

Mitchell, Andrew. "Heidegger's Breakdown: Health and Healing under the Care of Dr. V.E. von Gebsattel." *Research and Phenomenology* 46 (2016): 70–97.

Mitchell, Andrew, and Peter Trawny, eds. *Heidegger's Black Notebooks: Responses to Anti-Semitism*. New York: Columbia University Press, 2017.

Moore, Ian. *Dialogue on the Threshold: Heidegger and Trakl*. Albany: State University of New York Press, 2022.

Moore, Ian. *Eckhart, Heidegger, and the Imperative of Releasement*. Albany: State University of New York Press, 2019.

Mugerauer, Robert. *Heidegger's Language and Thinking*. Atlantic Highlands, NJ: Humanities Press International, 1988.

Nancy, Jean-Luc. "Sharing Voices." In *Transforming the Hermeneutic Context: From Nietzsche to Nancy*, edited by Gayle L. Ormiston and Alan D. Schrift, 211–60. Albany: State University of New York Press, 1990.

Nelson, Eric. *Chinese and Buddhist Philosophy in Early Twentieth-Century German Thought*. London: Bloomsbury, 2017.

Nelson, Eric. "Heidegger's Daoist Turn." *Research in Phenomenology* 49 (2019): 362–84.

Neufeld, Jonathan. "The (In)vocation of Learning: Heidegger's Education in Thinking." *Studies in Philosophy and Education* 31 (2012): 61–76.

Nietzsche, Friedrich. *Thus Spoke Zarathustra*. Translated by Walter Kaufmann. New York: Penguin, 1978.

Nietzsche, Friedrich. "Schopenhauer as Educator." In *Untimely Meditations*, edited by Daniel Breazeale and translated by R. J. Hollingdale, 125–94. New York: Cambridge University Press, 1997.

Ott, Hugo. *Martin Heidegger: A Political Life*. Translated by Allan Blunden. London: HarperCollins, 1993.

Park, Bradley Douglas. "Differing Ways, *Dao* and *Weg*: Comparative, Metaphysical, and Methodological Considerations in Heidegger's 'Aus einem Gespräch von der Sprache'." *Continental Philosophy Review* 37 (2004): 309–39.

Park, Peter. *Africa, Asia, and the History of Philosophy: Racism in the Formation of the Philosophical Canon, 1780–1830*. Albany: State University of New York Press, 2013.

Parkes, Graham, ed. *Heidegger and Asian Thought*. Honolulu: University of Hawai'i Press, 1987.

Parkes, Graham. "Rising Sun over Black Forest: Heidegger's Japanese Connections." In *Heidegger's Hidden Sources: East-Asian Influences on his Work*, by Reinhard May, 79–117. London: Routledge, 1996.

Parkes, Graham. "Translator's Preface." In *Heidegger's Hidden Sources: East-Asian Influences on his Work*, by Reinhard May, vii–xv. London: Routledge, 1996.

Peters, Michael. "Editorial: Heidegger, Phenomenology, Education." *Educational Philosophy and Theory* 41 (2009): 1–6.

Peters, Michael, ed. *Heidegger, Education, and Modernity*. Lanham, MD: Rowman & Littlefield, 2002.

Peterson, Thomas. "Notes on Heidegger's Authoritarian Pedagogy." *Educational Philosophy and Theory* 37 (2005): 599–623.

Plato. "Republic." Translated by G. M. A. Grube and revised by C. D. C. Reeve. In *Plato: Complete Works*, edited by John Cooper, 971–1223. Indianapolis: Hackett, 1997.

Polt, Richard. *Heidegger: An Introduction*. Ithaca: Cornell University Press, 1999.

Prins, A. W. " 'Im Westen nur Neues.' Martin Heidegger und die interkulturelle Auseinandersetzung." In *Das Multiversum der Kulturen. Beiträge zu einer Vorlesung im Fach 'Interkulturelle Philosophie an der Erasmus Universität Rotterdam*, edited by H. Kimmerle, 77–101. Amsterdam: Brill Rodopi, 1996.

Riley, Dawn. "Heidegger Teaching: An Analysis and Interpretation of Pedagogy." *Educational Philosophy and Theory* 43 (2011): 797–815.

Richardson, William. *Heidegger: Through Phenomenology to Thought*. New York: Fordham University Press, 2003.

Safranski, Rüdiger. *Martin Heidegger: Between Good and Evil*. Translated by Ewald Osers. Cambridge, MA: Harvard University Press, 1999.

Said, Edward. *Orientalism*. New York: Random House, 1994.

Savage, Robert. *Hölderlin after the Catastrophe: Heidegger—Adorno—Brecht*. Rochester: Camden House, 2008.

Secomb, Linnell. "Philosophical Deaths and Feminine Finitude." *Mortality* 4 (1999): 111–25.

Shaw, Robert. "Heidegger and E-learning: Overthrowing the Traditions of Pedagogy." *E-Learning and Digital Media* 11 (2014): 123–34.

Shaw, Robert Keith. "Towards a Heideggerian Pedagogy." Paper presented at the 33rd Annual Conference of the Philosophy of Education Society of Australasia, Melbourne, Australia, 16–28 November 2004.

Sinclair, Mark. "Heidegger, Von Humboldt and the Idea of the University." *Intellectual History Review* 23 (2013): 499–515.

Speck, Dieter. "Vorlesungen im Phantomsemester: Die Freiburger Philosophische Fakultät in Beuron zwischen Flucht und Fiktion." In *Mittelalterliches Mönchtum in der Moderne? Die Neugründung der Benediktinerabtei Beuron 1863 und deren kulturelle Ausstrahlung im 19. und 20. Jahrhundert*, 169–89. Edited by

Karl-Heinz Braun, Hugo Ott, and Wilfried Schöntag. Stuttgart: Kohlhammer, 2015.
Stambaugh, Joan. "Heidegger, Taoism, and the Question of Metaphysics." In *Heidegger and Asian Thought*, edited by Graham Parkes, 79–92. Honolulu: University of Hawaiʻi Press, 1987.
Standish, Paul. "Heidegger and the Technology of Further Education." *Journal of Philosophy of Education* 31 (2007): 439–59.
Stone, Lynda. "From Technologization to Totalization in Education Research: U.S. Graduate Training, Methodology, and Critique." *Journal of Philosophy of Education* 40 (2006): 527–45.
Thomson, Iain. "Death and Demise in Being and Time." In *The Cambridge Companion to Heidegger's "Being and Time,"* edited by Mark A. Wrathall, 260–90. New York: Cambridge University Press, 2013.
Thomson, Iain. "Heidegger on Ontological Education, or: How We Become What We Are." *Inquiry* 44 (2001): 243–68.
Thomson, Iain. "Heidegger on Ontological Education, or How We Become What We Are." In *Heidegger Education, and Modernity*, edited by Michael Peters, 123–50. Lanham, MD: Rowman & Littlefield, 2002.
Thomson, Iain. *Heidegger on Ontotheology: Technology and the Politics of Education*. New York: Cambridge University Press, 2005.
Thomson, Iain. "Heidegger's Perfectionist Philosophy of Education in *Being and Time*." *Continental Philosophy Review* 34 (2004): 439–67.
Thomson, Iain. "Nothing (*Nichts*)." In *The Cambridge Heidegger Lexicon*, edited by Mark Wrathall, 520–28. Cambridge: Cambridge University Press, 2021.
Trawny, Peter. *Heidegger and the Myth of a Jewish World Conspiracy*. Translated by Andrew Mitchell. Chicago: University of Chicago Press, 2015.
Ulrich Gumbrecht, Hans. "Martin Heidegger and His Japanese Interlocutors: About a Limit of Western Metaphysics." *Diacritics* 30 (2000): 83–101.
Vallega-Neu, Daniela. *Heidegger's Poietic Writings: From "Contributions to Philosophy" to "The Event."* Bloomington: Indiana University Press, 2018.
Vetsch, Florian. *Heideggers Anfang der interkulturellen Auseinandersetzung*. Würzburg: Königshausen and Neumann, 1992.
Warnek, Peter. "The History of Being." In *Martin Heidegger: Key Concepts*, edited by Bret Davis, 155–67. New York: Routledge, 2010.
Warnes, Mathias. "Heidegger on Hölderlin's Festival: The Wedding Dance as the Inceptual Event." *Epoché: A Journal for the History of Philosophy* 18 (2014): 503–24.
Warren, Calvin. *Ontological Terror: Blackness, Nihilism, and Emancipation*. Durham: Duke University Press, 2018.
Wrathall, Mark. "History of Being (*Geschichte des Seins*)." In *The Cambridge Heidegger Lexicon*, edited by Mark Wrathall, 385–96. Cambridge: Cambridge University Press, 2021.

Wrathall, Mark. "Metaphysics (*Metaphysik*)." In *The Cambridge Heidegger Lexicon*, edited by Mark Wrathall, 482–90. Cambridge: Cambridge University Press, 2021.
Withy, Katherine. "Mood (*Stimmung*)." In *The Cambridge Heidegger Lexicon*, edited by Mark Wrathall, 500–3. Cambridge: Cambridge University Press, 2021.
Yosef-Hassidim, Doron. "Rethinking Education: Heidegger's Philosophy in the Service of Education." *Philosophy of Education* 70 (2014): 434–42.
Yuasa, Yasuo. "The Encounter of Modern Japanese Philosophy with Heidegger." In *Heidegger and Asian Thought*, edited by Graham Parkes, 155–74. Honolulu: University of Hawai'i Press, 1987.
Zaborowski, Holger. "Origin, Freedom, and *Gelassenheit*: On Heidegger's Second 'Country Path Conversation'." In *Phenomenological Perspectives on Plurality*, edited by Gert-Jan van der Heiden and translated by Gregory Canning, 135–57. Leiden, Netherlands: Koninklijke Brill, 2015.
Ziarek, Krzysztof. *Inflected Language: Toward a Hermeneutics of Nearness: Heidegger, Levinas, Stevens, Celan*. Albany: State University of New York Press, 1994.
Ziarek, Krzysztof. "The Poietic Momentum of Thought." In *Philosophers and Their Poets: Reflections on the Poetic Turn in Philosophy since Kant*, edited by Charles Bambach and Theodore George, 185–99. Albany: State University of New York Press, 2019.

Index

abandon, 20, 30, 146, 154, 177, 201; metaphysics, 33, 59, 80–81, 89, 115, 187, 203–204
abiding-while, 142, 153
abyss, 96, 152, 165–66, 256n71
accord: conversational, 23, 36, 97, 112, 172, 192, 194–95; disciplinary, 32, 204; with essence, 34, 38, 88, 170; with metaphysics, 40, 83, 102, 136, 185; poetic, 17, 182
achievement: calculative manipulation as, 25, 33, 37; humanistic ideal of, 114, 126; pedagogical, 36, 58; work and, 33, 37, 45. *See also* calculation; technology; work
aesthetics, 156, 177, 184, 188–89, 192, 194, 204, 257n83, 263n56, 264n62. *See also* art; camera; film; music; painting; photograph(y); picture; theatre; *Rashomon* (film); string instrument; value
age: of characters, 103, 122, 136–37, 175; historical, 8, 14, 60, 98, 116–17, 129, 141, 146, 229n50. *See also* ancient; elderly; epoch; history; modern(ity); youth
aletheia, 51, 62, 166, 203, 242n93. *See also* enigma; truth
Alpheus (river), 167. *See also* river

alterity: of conversational partners, 18, 152, 172, 180, 182; of the East, 169, 171, 173, 188, 196, 208; as non-metaphysical comportment, 239n55; of the poetized, 164–65; radical, 21, 173, 185, 208; of the river, 150; of students, 12, 217; of the (un)said, 13, 209, 211. *See also* plural(ity); river; saying; sensitivity; sing (with); speaking (together)
ambiguity: of being, 115–16, 129, 131, 140, 157; of ethnonationalist community, 103, 131, 219; of learning, 57–58, 129; metaphysical banishment of, 151; of night, 145; of poetizing, 134, 139, 151–53, 165–67. *See also* enigma; hint; mystery; night; movement; obscurity; oscillation; swing; unambiguous
America, 191, 193, 247n3, 257n74. *See also* nation (state)
ancestors, 140. *See also* genealogy; son(s)
ancient, 11, 14, 124, 155, 201, 207; Greek, 16, 45, 92, 104, 155, 218. *See also* Greek(s); history; modern(ity)
animal, 121, 246n31; rational, 50, 52, 107

annihilation, 50, 112, 239n52. *See also* desert; destruction; evil; wasteland

answer, 51, 53, 65, 72, 82, 170, 177–78, 196, 199, 239n52; as (counter) word, 60, 63. *See also* counter-word; word

antisemitism, 219. *See also* Holocaust; Jewish; National Socialism; Nazi; Shoah

anxiety, 34, 40, 73, 95, 140, 159, 170, 183, 190, 198, 231n79, 239n54. *See also* distress; fear; trust; unsettling; worry

appearance, 38, 83, 89, 116, 201–203, 257n79. *See also* outward look; view(s)

appropriate, 64, 98, 121, 148. *See also* cultural appropriation

Aristotle, 1, 26, 41, 212, 215, 241n81, 244n15, 252n25

art, 6, 71, 154, 156, 174, 253n35, 257n79; of conversation, 12, 18, 27–28, 41, 66; Japanese, 175, 177, 184–85, 188, 190; metaphysical interpretation of, 7, 242n86, 245n30, 247n37; poetic character of, 71, 138, 141, 156, 231n77. *See also* aesthetics; music; painting; picture; poem; theatre; work

articles: definite, 175; indefinite, 175. *See also* pronoun(s)

artificial, 76, 94, *See also* nature

Asia. *See* East Asia(n)

astonishment, 41, 64. *See also* wonder(ous)

attention, 37, 50, 53, 55, 74, 78, 82, 92, 121, 126, 156, 167, 257n84

authoritarianism, 65–67, 213, 217–18; of teacher, 19, 20, 39, 41, 80, 150, 211, 213, 219, 221. *See also* student-teacher relationship

autumn, 29, 32, 37, 137, 145, 238n47, 258n97. *See also* season

await, 124, 146, 190, 254n51. *See also* expectation; wait(ing)

beauty, 140, 141, 153, 156, 239n52, 251n25

beckon, 198, 205. *See also* enigma; hint; word

between-field, 70, 73, 81, 86, 98–99, 107–108, 115, 129, 242n87. *See also* critical point; cross over; transition; turn back

bidirectional, 80–81. *See also* movement; way

biography, 175; auto-, 185–86, 188, 265n75

Black Forest, 2, 144. *See also* forest

breakdown, 2, 3, 135, 224n11. *See also* sanatorium

brightness, 31–32, 48, 52, 66, 145. *See also* clarity; darkness; day; light; night; obscurity; sun; star(s)

bypath, 41, 85, 133, 198, 205–206. *See also* country path; way

calculation, 8, 16, 33, 37, 102, 160, 214–15, 238n48. *See also* achievement; manipulate; mastery; mathematics; meditation; science(s); technology

camera, 183, 192–93. *See also* aesthetics; film; photograph(y); picture

capaciousness, 105, 110, 247n5. *See also* expanse; swing

care, 103, 108

chiasm, 19, 35–36, 45, 52, 60, 65, 81, 238n45, 254n50. *See also* crossing

Chinese: thinkers, 249n39, 260n3; philosophy, 104, 130. *See also* East Asia(n)

circle: around, 186; as circular, 30, 50; en-, 205; full, 145, 216; hermeneutic, 207; of ideas, 201; of

vision, 49, 127; walking in a, 30. See also route; way
circulation 182; as replacement 15, 33, 181, 259n2. See also *Gestell*; positionality; replaceability; standing reserve(s); technology
city, 30, 140, 183. See also nature; *polis*
clarity, 8, 22, 48, 53, 56, 61, 137, 143, 145, 149, 151, 159, 188, 208. See also light; obscurity
cognition, 29, 32, 37, 39, 42–46, 62, 65, 234n14, 240n66. See also concept; feeling; reason(ing)
collaboration, 49, 70, 219; in conversation, 14, 17, 32, 47–48, 72, 88–89, 118, 132, 154–55, 211, 222; in interpretation, 120–21, 124, 154; in pedagogy, 1, 17, 20, 36, 99, 104, 131, 138, 213, 217; in poetizing, 19, 22, 32, 36, 63, 65–66, 78, 99, 132, 151, 156, 159, 172, 208, 220, 237n35, 238n46, 250n9; in sharing, 101, 103, 123; in thinking, 102, 130. See also healing; individual; plural(ity); speaking (together); student-teacher relationship; vulnerability
colonial(ism), 168, 181, 196, 219. See also foreign; home
colony, 151, 168. See also foreign; home; sojourn
commemoration, 35, 40, 65
community: come together in, 18, 20, 102; exclusion from, 103, 108, 127; formation of, 85, 122–23, 127, 212, 218–19; German, 13, 100, 127, 131–32, 154, 176; healing as, 106, 108, 116, 124, 127; historical, 29, 127, 142; members of, 137; non-metaphysical, 85, 104, 131, 134, 211, 213; pedagogy and, 19, 213, 217, 220; poetizing and, 108–109, 124, 143–44, 165, 200, 213. See also healing; history; human being; individual; plural(ity); politics
comparative: names, 104, 118; philosophy, 171; temporality, 82. See also East Asia(n); older definition (of the human); superlative; younger definition (of the human)
comportment: of language, 16; to nearness, 62; non-metaphysical, 91, 239n55; pedagogical, 178; proper, 12, 104, 190, 249n28, 264n57; of releasement, 12, 17, 95, 108, 228n48, 246n31; temporal, 117; of thinking, 17; of welcoming, 78. See also *Gelassenheit*; releasement; self-restrained comporter; temporal(ity); time; welcome
concept: systematic, 184–85; Western metaphysical, 26, 52, 96, 142, 151, 153, 162, 164, 168, 189–90, 195–96, 198, 209, 215, 219. See also cognition; grasp; rationality; truth; universal
confidence, 39, 72, 74, 83, 124. See also courage; trust; worry
correspondence, 17, 28, 31, 33, 62, 200, 242n90. See also truth
counter-resonance, 149–51, 153–54, 156, 162–63, 167, 203, See also resonation; song; tuning
counter-word, 60–61, 63. See also answer; word
country path, 12, 29–32, 41, 66, 77–78, 81, 85–87, 89, 95–96, 98, 107–108, 144, 164, 230–31n72, 233n3, 236n28. See also city; movement; *polis*; route; walk(ing); way
courage, 73, 75, 92, 99, 195. See also confidence; fear; magnanimity; trust
crisis, 92–93, 145
critical point, 81, 90, 92–94. See also between-field

cross-cultural exchange, 6, 171–72, 178, 181, 188, 204, 208. *See also* East Asia(n); intercultural (exchange); speaking (together)
cross over, 81, 87, 88. *See also* between-field; transition; turn back
crossing, 36, 48. *See also* chiasm; transition
cultural appropriation, 130, 171, 188. *See also* cross-cultural exchange; East Asia(n); intercultural (exchange)

Danube River, 3, 135, 142, 255n62. *See also* river; Upper Danube Valley
daring, 135–37, 201. *See also* youth
darkness, 31, 76, 88, 94, 106, 128, 145, 150, 236n31. *See also* clarity; day; light; night; obscurity; star(s); sun
day, 8, 27, 31–32, 36–37, 48–49, 76, 82–83, 106, 137, 144–46, 159, 179, 216, *See also* brightness; clarity; light; night; obscurity; sky; star(s); sun
death, 22, 101–102, 117, 121, 131, 161, 174; according to *Being and Time*, 239n54, 246n32, 249n29; beyond, 184, 263n53, 263n55. *See also* mortal(s); perish
decision, 30, 36, 48, 87, 104, 111, 119, 204, 228n48
defeat, 2, 4, 32, 42, 141, 146, 154, 251n23. *See also* postwar
Descartes, Rene, 1, 8, 202, 252n25
desert, 115, 254n45. *See also* annihilation; devastation; evil; expanse; ocean; wasteland
destiny, 82, 107, 109, 140, 142, 145–46, 161, 163, 165. *See also* history; sending
destruction, 4, 112, 239n52. *See also* annihilation; desert; postwar

detour, 2, 39, 42, 85, 87, 99, 124, 206. *See also* movement; route; way
devastation, 20, 22, 66, 108, 110, 112, 114–17, 119, 123–24, 126–27, 129, 131, 135, 178. *See also* annihilation; evil; wasteland
discipline, 7, 17, 24, 27, 32–34, 36–38, 41–42, 44–45, 47, 49, 51–52, 54–55, 57–58, 60, 65, 70, 148, 218, 234n16, 256n73. *See also* historiology; humanities; methodology; research(er); science(s)
dissolution, 215, 217, 252n25
dissonance, 112, 167. *See also* harmony; music
distress, 19, 70, 73, 76–77, 80, 82, 87, 99, 197, 220, 231n79. *See also* anxiety; fear; frustration; worry
divinity, 120. *See also* fourfold; gods; immortals; theology
domination: as feeling, 25–26; planetary, 196; of positionality, 215; of representational metaphysics, 9, 90, 102, 110–11, 216, 218, 238n48. *See also* manipulate; mastery; technology; universal
downward, 77, 85, 87, 253n40. *See also* stair(s); tower; upward
drink, 56–57. *See also* festival; jug; wine
dwelling, 71–72, 137, 141–42, 144, 148, 153, 156, 162, 211, 215–16, 240n67. *See also* human being; indwelling; locale

early, 95–96, 174, 183, 245n23, 264n59. *See also* late
earth: arable, 29; devastation of, 112, 114–15, 127; dwelling on, 215; engagement in, 72, 90; Europeanization of, 169, 191; festival and, 57, 70, 166; mother,

75; relations with, 240n66, 243n5, 255n60. *See also* festival; fields; fourfold; land(scape); nature; terrain
East Asia(n), 165, 171, 175, 179, 181, 184–85, 187, 190, 192, 194, 199, 207. *See also* alterity; Chinese; cross-cultural exchange; cultural appropriation; house; Japan; *Rashomon* (film); world
Eckhart, Meister, 6, 43, 323n3, 240n62. See also *Gelassenheit*
economy, 33, 129
elderly, 126. *See also* age; comparative; older definition (of the human)
emptiness, 45, 55, 57, 190–91, 193. *See also* jug; *ku*; nothing; wine
enigma: of *aletheia*, 5; of the Guest, 75; of hints, 198; of Hölderlin's poetizing, 148; of nearness and farness, 59, 72, 74, 80, 151, 157, 181, 239n52, 247n7, 251n16, 253n40. *See also* ambiguity; hint; infinite; mystery; surmise; truth
environment, 32, 246n31. *See also* world
epoch, 8–9, 14, 23, 55, 146, 179, 215–16, 228n46. *See also* age; history
errancy, 116, 129, 147, 243n2. *See also* truth
Eurocentrism, 171, 173, 178, 180, 261n26. *See also* colonial(ism); nation (state)
Europeanization, 169, 191. *See also* globe
evil, 6, 20, 101–102, 107–17, 129, 131, 248n14, 248n17. *See also* annihilation; devastation; good; insurgency; malice; moral(ity); rage; value; wasteland
expanse: of abandonment of life, 115; of the forest, 105, 110, 113–14; of

heart space, 160; as released, non-metaphysical space, 142, 153–54. *See also* capaciousness; desert; forest; measure; open; width
expectation, 190. *See also* await, wait(ing)
expropriation, 121. *See also* appropriate

faculties (of the soul), 44–47, 49. *See also* human being; soul
failure, 20, 47, 57, 84, 99, 113, 115, 121, 130, 172, 184, 191, 196, 208, 212–13, 218–19, 221–22. *See also* haste; student-teacher relationship
favor, 86, 119, 160, 204. *See also* grace
fear, 34, 39–44, 51, 73, 94, 101, 119–20, 122, 158–60, 190–91, 198, 206, 225n14, 231n79, 239n54, 239n54. *See also* anxiety; confidence; courage; distress; trust; worry
feeling, 25, 34, 41, 44, 57, 74, 87, 117, 142, 159–61. *See also* cognition; rationality; sensing; sensuous
festival, 57, 96, 98, 145, 166, 242n83, 246n35. *See also* drink; Hölderlin, Friedrich; jug; wine
fields, 4, 78, 81, 86, 142, 230n72. *See also* between-field; country path; earth; route
film, 155, 191–93, 206, 265n73. *See also* aesthetics; camera; hand; photograph(y); picture; *Rashomon* (film)
fire, 31, 164, 216
fitting, 45, 80, 83, 89, 92, 94, 149, 151–52, 157, 161–62, 186, 206. *See also* unfitting; measure; word
forbearance, 12, 18, 27–28, 41, 61. *See also* speaking (together)
foreign, 75, 103, 120, 122, 130, 144, 146–47, 151, 163, 165, 172, 179,

foreign *(continued)*
182–84, 193, 255n57, 259n105, 263n44. *See also* colonial(ism); colony; home; native; sojourn
forest, 4, 30, 36, 48, 105, 107, 109–10, 113–15, 142, 144, 159, 245n27, 247n5. *See also* Black Forest; expanse; land(scape); mountain; river; Russia; terrain; valley; swing; way
fourfold, 6, 15, 34, 57, 233n3, 243n5. *See also* divinity; earth; gods; immortals; mortal(s); sky
fragment, 1, 153; of Heraclitus, 30, 62–63, 85, 87, 91–92, 197, 235n26; of Nietzsche, 252n25. *See also* Heraclitus; Nietzsche, Friedrich; word
free: engagement (with metaphysics), 58, 65, 258n100; for/to, 85, 97, 98, 135; from, 43–44, 48, 87, 196, 263n54; poetic interpretation, 145, 150, 156, 160, 163, 166; thinking, 5, 114, 124, 199, 239. *See also* imprisonment; liberation; play
Freiburg (Germany), 2–4, 7, 22, 66, 135, 155, 175–76, 186, 224n8, 236n28, 237n41
friend, 72, 82, 117, 120, 128, 130, 134, 137, 183, 242n88, 251n14, 253n27. *See also* neighbor(hood)
frustration, 26, 39, 44, 175, 202, 220. *See also* distress
future, 3, 29, 76, 104, 106, 118, 127, 158, 160–61, 165, 179, 219, 222; futural, 29, 91, 129, 139, 162–63, 187, 245n28, 251n21. *See also* history; past; present; temporal(ity); time

game, 175
garden, 183–84

Gelassenheit, 6, 12, 20, 23, 28, 43–44, 48–49, 53, 58, 73, 87, 97, 108, 114, 125, 232n3, 235n20, 235n22, 239n59, 245n28, 246n31, 251n16, 260n4. *See also* comportment; Eckhart, Meister; non-willing; releasement; will(ing)
genealogy, 135, 140, 173, 252n26, 253n27. *See also* ancestors; kinship; son(s)
genocide, 101, 131–32, 222. *See also* Holocaust; Shoah
genre, 1, 2, 4, 8, 13, 16, 22, 154, 212, 223n2–3, 228n49, 243n97, 266n91
George, Stefan, 175; Circle, 162, 253n32
geography, 24, 29, 31, 38, 141–42, 144–45, 158–59, 174, 177, 254n45–46, 259n104. *See also* history; land(scape); terrain
Germany, 2–4, 13, 66, 99, 102, 112, 141, 146, 158, 162–63, 178, 185–86, 217, 219, 253n31–32, 257n74. *See also* history; nation (state)
Gestell, 15, 33, 215, 230n66, 237n37, 267n24. *See also* circulation; machination; positionality; replaceability; standing reserve(s); technology
gesture, 39, 118, 165, 192–93, 208. *See also* hand; theatre
gift, 75, 86–87, 163, 174; of a mistake, 80, 121, 154, 218; of non-metaphysical thinking, 9; of picture, 71, 80, 86, 174; of word, 86–87. *See also* picture; strange(r); thank(ing); welcome; word
globe, 168, 179, 221. *See also* Europeanization
gods, 75, 144, 166, 199. *See also* divinity; fourfold; immortals

Goethe, Johann Wolfgang von, 74, 175
good: and letting/releasement, 87, 160, 246n31; as metaphysical valuation, 116, 248n17; Plato's idea, 31; and poetic language, 149; as unsettling, 25. *See also* evil; *Gelassenheit*; moral(ity); Plato; value; unsettling
grace, 159, 205, 206, 265n75, 265n86. *See also* favor; *iki*; *koto* (*ba*)
grammar, 7, 9, 60, 79, 136–37, 167, 175, 258n96. *See also* line break; poem; punctuation; rhyme; stanza; verse(s)
grasp, 39, 55, 196; as mistake, 57, 73, 158; of moral superiority, 112, 114; of representational metaphysics, 9, 16, 65, 73, 151, 157, 164, 184, 195; of world picture, 71. *See also* cognition; concept; domination; moral(ity); picture; willing
grave (of Kuki), 183–85, 192, 197, 206. *See also* tomb (of Kuki)
Greek(s), 96, 104, 141, 152, 202–203, 206, 218; in historical relation with Germans, 144, 158, 168, 258n98; language/word(s), 11, 37, 49, 62, 120, 199, 238n48. *See also* ancient; Heraclitus; history; poet(s); word
ground(ing): in difference, 239n53; geographical, 30–31, 74, 254n45; hermeneutic, 187; historical, 7, 179, 180, 183; in language, 10, 16, 22, 124, 134; metaphysical, 7, 27, 31–32, 42, 73, 78, 90, 92, 98, 108, 119, 124, 127, 148, 153, 196, 212, 221, 234n12; in morality, 115; and provenance, 96; in releasement/ *Gelassenheit*, 19; tone, 150–51, 154, 156, 165, 257n84; ungrounding, 152; and will, 83. *See also* geography; hermeneutics; history; *Gelassenheit*; moral(ity); poem; provenance; tone; will(ing)
guard(ing), 13–14, 16–18, 28, 83, 121–22, 129, 145, 165, 167, 187, 198, 204, 206, 220. *See also* veil(ing)

hand: of the singer, 162, in a film scene, 192–93. *See also* gesture; film; theatre
harmony, 21, 30, 156–57, 164, 167. *See also* counter-resonance; dissonance; music; sing (with); song; resonation; tone; tuning
haste, 81, 83–84, 86–87, 99, 118–21, 129–30, 150, 157, 256n67. *See also* failure
healing, 20, 101–11, 113–19, 122–32, 142, 144–45, 158, 176, 224n11, 253n35. *See also* collaboration; community; devastation; evil; expanse; forest; speaking (together); swing
hear(ing), 10, 63, 75, 85, 98, 113, 125, 138–39, 149–50, 152, 154, 156, 164, 166–67, 215, 217 245n19, 249n25. *See also* listening
heart, 61; space, 160. *See also* love
Hebel, Johann Peter, 11, 148
Hegel, Georg Wilhelm Friedrich, 1, 26, 205, 252n25
Heidegger, Elfride, 2–3, 9, 13, 224n6, 224n12, 226n22, 249n39, 260n3
height, 64, 74, 144, 254n45. *See also* measure; tower; sensitivity; width
Heraclitus, 1, 26, 62–63, 85, 87, 90, 92, 197, 235n26, 252n25, 254n42. *See also* fragment; Greek(s); poet(s); word
hermeneutics, 148, 169, 174, 177, 187, 189, 197–207 passim, 259n103, 264n56; circle, 207. *See also* ontology; phenomenology

Hermes, 199. *See also* gods, hermeneutics; message
Hesse, Hermann Karl, 175
hint, 27, 39, 83, 190, 198, 205–206. *See also* ambiguity; beckon; enigma; mystery; surmise; unsurmised; word
historiography, 26, 234n14
historiology, 27, 33, 41, 45, 47, 52, 63, 73, 89, 91, 99, 104, 118–19, 121, 130, 145, 239n52, 256n73. *See also* methodology; research(er); university
history, 2, 76, 90, 128, 168, 171, 176–80, 183–84, 186–87, 189, 199, 201, 208, 263n53, 264n69; of being/beyng, 24, 80, 140, 215, 228n45–46; as discipline, 32; as futural, 91, 162; of metaphysics, 23, 65, 145, 152–53, 201–202, 205, 211, 237n41; of philosophy, 4, 7, 24, 26, 31, 235n23; as poetic, 141–42, 144, 159, 162, 178; of politics, 99, 100; of thinking, 91. *See also* ancient; destiny; future; geography; Germany; Greek(s); modern(ity); past; present; sending; temporal(ity); time
Hölderlin, Friedrich, 1–7, 10–11, 16, 20–21, 29, 35, 72, 74–75, 80, 104, 123, 132–68, 172, 175–76, 178, 186, 196, 212, 224n6, 224n14, 231n76, 235n25, 240n67, 242n83, 242n86, 242n89, 244n9, 245n19, 246n35, 249n25, 252n26, 255n56–59, 255n62, 257n84, 258n91, 258n98, 259n104–106. *See also* counter-resonation; festival; oscillation; poem; poet(s); resonation; river; saying; sing (with); song; swing
Holocaust, 102, 108, 110–12, 129–30. *See also* antisemitism; genocide; Nazi; National Socialism; Shoah

home, 3, 30, 44, 48, 57, 74, 141, 179, 182, 185, 197; homecoming, 166, 179, 196, 263n44; homeland, 128, 130, 146, 151, 172, 256n68; homelessness, 152; homeliness, 44; homely, 75, 240n67. *See also* colony; foreign; journey; native; sojourn; uncanny
horizon, 25, 50, 54–55, 241n79; horizonal essence (of the human), 50–52; horizonality, 49–50, 53; horizonal-transcendental thinking, 25, 49, 51–52, 54, 58, 235n22, 241n75. *See also* human being
house, 219, 242n88, 252n26; of being, 179, 185, 194–97 passim, 205; of Eastasians, 179, 185; of Europeans, 179, 185; of Questioner, 175, 179; of Scientist, 41, 44. *See also* home; office; room
human being, 5, 10, 29, 42, 49, 50, 52–54, 61, 94, 105–27 passim, 179, 181–82, 185, 191, 203, 207, 215, 246n31, 264n57. *See also* cognition; community; dwelling; faculties (of the soul); feeling; horizon; mortal(s); older definition (of the human); rationality; reason(ing); soul; subjectivity; younger definition (of the human)
humanities, 26, 42–44, 221, 233n6; humanist, 42, 44, 114, 116, 215–16, 218, 248n24; humanistic inquiry, 26–27, 34; humanity, 45, 114, 218. *See also* philosophical anthropology; research(er); science(s); university
Husserl, Edmund, 174, 186–87, 234–35n17, 240n72, 247n12. *See also* phenomenology

identical, 113, 116, 163, 173, 230n70, 239n52–53, 248n15, 254n41. *See also* relationality; selfsame

iki, 174, 184, 188–91, 194, 204–207, 263n56, 264n56, 264n62, 265n75. *See also* East Asia(n); grace
immortals, 120, 257n78. *See also* divinity; fourfold; gods; mortal(s)
impatience, 57, 126, 130. *See also* patience
imperative, 21, 113, 136–37, 258n96, 267n40
imprisonment, 102, 105, 127, 192. *See also* evil; free; liberation; prisoner(s)
impoverishment, 106, 124, 172. *See also* poor; poverty; rich
inceptual, 86–87, 94, 161. *See also* origin(ary); provenance
individual, 20, 24, 49, 70, 88, 108–109, 111, 124–25, 131, 188, 214, 233n9, 248n14. *See also* collaboration; community; imprisonment; singular; solitary
Indus (river), 167. *See also* river
industry, 148, 192
indwelling, 58, 60–61, 144, 168. *See also* dwelling
infinite: regress, 53, 96; remainder, 62; remoteness, 192. *See also* enigma
injury, 195, 203. *See also* pain; touch; wound
inside, 85, 178. *See also* outside; room; tower
insight, 7, 11, 26, 32, 36, 39, 43, 48, 54, 56–57, 61–63, 74, 90–91, 102, 115–18, 122, 124, 127–28, 131, 148, 155, 203, 213, 215, 219, 220, 234n14. *See also* enigma; hint; surmise; unsurmised
instrument (musical), 124–25, 155. *See also* lyre; music; string instrument; violin; tuning
insurgency, 113, 117, 129, 131, 248n14. *See also* evil; malice; rage; rebellious

intercultural (exchange), 171, 196. *See also* cross-cultural exchange; East Asia(n); speaking (together)
international, 125, 127. *See also* nation (state); politics
intimacy, 4, 115, 136, 155, 176, 198, 200, 248n22. *See also* love; sensual
iro, 190–91, 206, 246n71. *See also* East Asia(n); *ku*; *shiki*
Ister, 3, 7, 75, 133, 135, 140, 142–45, 148, 150, 153–68 passim, 235n25, 242n86, 244n9, 245n27, 252n26, 253n28, 254n43, 254n47, 255n62. *See also* Hölderlin, Friedrich; poem; river; song

Japan, 175–76, 186, 189, 263n56. *See also* East Asia(n); nation (state)
Jewish, 101, 108, 131–32. *See also* antisemitism
journey, 2, 19, 30–31, 72, 74, 138, 142–44, 151, 161–63, 182, 187, 213, 255n62, 257n85. *See also* colony; foreign; home; native; sojourn
jug, 49, 54–57, 70, 72, 240n69, 241n80–81. *See also* drink; emptiness; wine

Kant, Immanuel, 1, 8, 26, 32, 37, 49, 50, 52, 201–202, 205, 234n14, 241n76, 241n78, 242n93, 252n25, 267n40
kinship, 155, 197, 203. *See also* genealogy
Kleist, Heinrich von, 175, 196
koto (*ba*), 205–207. *See also* East Asia(n); grace; *iki*; *iro*; *ku*; pictograph; *shiki*
ku, 190–91, 206. *See also* East Asia(n); emptiness; *iro*; *koto* (*ba*); *shiki*
Kuki: Baron Kuki Shūzō (historical figure), 174–76, 189, 262n29–32

Kuki *(continued)*
  passim, 263n52, 263–64n56;
  Count (character), 174–77, 183–86,
  188–89, 192, 194, 197, 204, 206,
  262n32, 263n53. *See also* East
  Asia(n); grave (of Kuki); *iki*; Japan;
  student-teacher relationship; tomb
  (of Kuki)
Kyoto (Japan), 183, 262n28. *See also*
  Japan

land(scape), 29, 86, 103, 142, 144–46,
  153–54, 158, 163, 168, 172, 193,
  214, 245n27. *See also* earth; forest;
  geography; mountain; river; rock(y);
  sensitivity; terrain; valley
late, 82, 95, 106, 137. *See also* early
Leibniz, Gottfried Wilhelm, 26, 47,
  242n93, 252n25
Levinas, Emmanuel, 247n12
liberation, 20, 217, 229n53. *See also*
  free; imprisonment
life, 49, 115, 184, 200
light, 8, 19, 30–32, 36, 48–50, 52,
  64, 76, 106, 143, 145–46, 162,
  216, 234n12, 236n31–32. *See also*
  brightness; clarity; darkness; day;
  night; obscurity; Plato; star(s); sun
like, 160–61, 166. *See also* love
limit(s), 7, 9, 14, 16, 19, 21–22,
  34–39, 48, 49, 51, 58, 62, 65, 74,
  78–79, 96, 106, 115, 141, 168,
  172, 181, 206, 212
line break, 167. *See also* grammar;
  poem; punctuation; rhyme; stanza;
  verse(s)
listening, 75, 120, 139, 150, 156,
  165–67, 172, 193, 203, 207, 214,
  245n22. *See also* hear(ing); speaking
  (together)
literature, 4, 16, 175, 177

locale, 69, 73, 80–81, 88, 106–107,
  134, 140, 142–44, 157–59, 161,
  165, 199, 211, 245n30. *See also*
  dwelling; region(ing); space
logos, 120–21. *See also* word
love, 6, 49, 136, 140–41, 160–61,
  231n79, 240n74, 255n62, 258n88,
  258n90. *See also* heart; intimacy;
  like; mania
lyre, 155, 257n78. *See also* instrument
  (musical); music; Plato; string
  instrument; violin; tuning

machination, 15, 33, 230n70, 257n74.
  See also *Gestell*; objectivity; standing
  reserve(s); technology
magnanimity, 61, 145. *See also* courage
malice, 113, 116–17, 129, 131,
  248n14. *See also* evil; insurgency; rage
mania, 141, 160. *See also* love
manipulate, 25–26, 33, 38, 44, 96,
  102, 241n75. *See also* calculation;
  domination; nature; science(s);
  technology
manufacture, 54
mastery, 19, 105, 213, 252n25. *See
  also* domination; nature; science(s);
  technology; tool
mathematics, 8, 11, 14, 238n48. *See
  also* calculation; modern(ity); nature;
  science(s); technology
measure, 16, 45, 65, 77, 104, 116,
  118–19, 122, 160, 179. *See also*
  calculation; expanse; fitting; height;
  unfitting; weight; width; word
meditation, 28, 43, 53, 117, 129, 183.
  See also calculation; thank(ing)
message, 86, 87, 199, 203, 206. *See
  also* Hermes; hermeneutics
methodology, 25–27, 33, 41–42,
  45, 91, 145, 156, 187, 202, 221,

Index | 291

239n52, 256n73, 257n83. *See also* historiology; research(er); science(s); technology; university; view(s)

mobility, 30, 63, 98, 108. *See also* ambiguity; movement; walk(ing)

modern(ity), 8, 11, 14, 27, 31, 37–38, 44–46, 58, 63, 71, 90–91, 141, 190, 215, 228n47, 230n70, 257n83. *See also* age; ancient; epoch; history

moral(ity), 101, 112–17, 130, 248n14, 248n17. *See also* evil; good; value

morning, 104–105, 109, 117–18, 128, 144, 146. *See also* day

mortal(s), 92, 107, 119–21, 166, 246n32, 249n27, 263n55. *See also* death; fourfold; gods; human being; immortals

mountain, 144, 193. *See also* forest; land(scape); river; rock(y); terrain; valley

movement, 15, 29–30, 56–57, 62, 74, 77, 81, 98, 105, 107–108, 110, 149, 158–59, 198, 206–207, 211, 230n72, 257n82, 258n100. *See also* ambiguity; bidirectional; detour; mobility; oscillation; standstill; sway; swing; walk(ing); way

music, 141, 150, 154–56, 167, 257n77, 257n81, 257n84. *See also* aesthetics; dissonance; harmony; instrument (musical); lyre; sing (with); song; string instrument; violin; tone; tuning

mystery, 115, 136, 183, 191, 206–207, 265n75. *See also* ambiguity; enigma; hint

nation (state), 125, 127, 130; (ethno) national(ist), 113, 126–27, 132, 162, 165, 178, 219, 222, 247n3, 259n106; nationalism, 126, 129, 162, 253n32. *See also* America; Germany; Japan; Russia

National Socialism, 99, 101, 108, 111–12, 129, 178, 219, 221, 228n48. *See also* antisemitism; Holocaust; Nazi; Shoah

native, 8, 111, 145, 151, 153–54, 173. *See also* colony; home; foreign; land(scape); sojourn

nature, 25–26, 69, 75, 92, 105, 141–42, 178, 238n48, 241n75; human, 96; law of, 7; mathematical projection of, 8, 14, 16, 33, 37–40, 42, 44, 55, 60; metaphysical, 126. *See also* artificial; city; land(scape); manipulate; mastery; mathematics; technology; terrain; world

Nazi, 2–3, 99, 101–102, 108, 129, 131, 135, 217–19, 259n106, 267n40. *See also* antisemitism; Holocaust; National Socialism; Shoah

neighbor(hood), 6, 137, 244n10. *See also* friend

Nietzsche, Friedrich, 1, 2, 26, 104, 175, 214, 221, 237n35, 245n30, 247n37, 247n10, 248n17, 252n25, 258n88. *See also* fragment; value

night, 8, 19, 30–32, 36, 48–49, 51, 64–65, 70, 76–77, 82, 105, 130, 141, 145–46, 179, 217, 233n3, 236n31–32, 237n35, 240n66. *See also* darkness; day; light; obscurity; sky; star(s)

no-play, 193. *See also* theatre

non-willing, 28, 43–45, 48, 53–54, 58, 114, 218. *See also* comportment; *Gelassenheit*; releasement; will(ing)

nothing, 7, 12, 28, 53, 55, 115–16, 118, 193, 209, 227n43, 248n21. *See also* emptiness; thing objectivity, 19, 28, 36, 38–49 passim, 58, 147, 192, 202, 229n51, 230n70, 238n49, 239n54. *See also* identical; machination; relationality; subjectivity; standing reserve(s); thing

obscurity, 8, 9, 31, 53, 59, 95, 130, 157, 189, 190, 196, 215, 257n83. *See also* ambiguity; clarity; darkness; light; night; star(s)

occident, 139, 141, 146, 162, 253n28, 254n46, 256n74, 258–59n100. *See also* orient

ocean, 115, 254n45. *See also* desert; wasteland; water(s)

office, 4, 179. *See also* house

older definition (of the human), 118–22. *See also* age; elderly; human being, younger definition (of the human)

one: all-unifying, 120–21; oneness, 199. *See also* relationality; singular; thing; twofold; world

ontology, 7, 15, 33, 57, 87, 112–13, 126, 169, 196, 199–200, 212, 217–19, 243n2, 247n12. *See also* fourfold; hermeneutics; phenomenology

open: circle-of-vision, 49; region, 55, 54–61 passim, 235n22, 241n77. *See also* expanse; region(ing); view(s)

oscillation, 72, 74, 115, 248n23, 256n64. *See also* ambiguity; mobility; movement; string instrument; swing; tuning

orient, 141, 254n46, 258n100; orientalism, 180. *See also* occident

origin(ary), 7–8, 15–16, 22, 31, 34, 38, 50, 58, 63, 76, 80–81, 86, 95–96, 109, 113, 116, 122, 138–40, 143, 156, 158–59, 169, 171, 174, 187, 189, 197, 201–203, 211, 235n23, 245n28, 253n28, 256n73. *See also* inceptual; provenance

outside, 30, 66, 140, 143, 171, 178, 236n28, 263n54. *See also* inside; land(scape)

outward look, 49, 55. *See also* appearance; view(s)

pain, 104, 106–107, 117–18, 159, 248n22. *See also* injury; wound

painting, 71. *See also* aesthetics; picture

past, 9, 29, 32, 60, 76, 91, 104, 106, 110, 118, 127, 162, 184, 199, 251n21, 264n69. *See also* future; history; present; temporal(ity); time

patience, 41, 83, 220. *See also* impatience

people, 1, 100, 102, 105, 107, 110, 112, 123, 125–26, 128, 146, 165, 191, 229n53, 264n56, 264n69; elderly, 126; founding of a, 80, 127, 129; German, 100, 107, 162; historical, 106, 109, 162, 189; national, 113, 126–27; real, 173, 175. *See also* community; Germany; history; nation (state); plural(ity); politics; wait(ing)

performative, 9, 12, 17–18, 22–23, 35–36, 44–45, 62–63, 65, 117–18, 128, 153, 157, 164, 167, 180–82, 186, 191, 197, 208, 211–12, 216–19, 221, 228n49, 231n79, 233n4, 243n2, 246n31, 246n36, 264n57

perish, 115, 121. *See also* death; mortal(s)

personal(ity), 4, 7, 13, 24–25, 48, 65–66, 99–103, 112, 131, 135, 141, 171, 175–87 passim, 199, 214, 216; 223n2, 233n3, 233n9, 262n41, 266n6

phenomenology, 169, 174, 186–87, 189, 199–200, 205, 234n17, 260n4,

264n56. *See also* hermeneutics; Husserl, Edmund; ontology
philosophical anthropology, 71, 49, 52–53. *See also* humanities; research(er)
photograph(y), 155, 183, 185, 192, 206. *See also* aesthetics; camera; film; picture
physics, 25, 32, 37, 40–42, 55. *See also* science(s); technology; radiation; research(er)
pictograph, 205. See also *koto (ba)*
picture, 19, 70–77 passim, 80–87 passim, 95–99 passim, 174, 183, 197, 206, 244n9, 254n45, 265n84; world, 8, 71, 76, 94–95. *See also* aesthetics; camera; grasp; gift; film; painting; photograph(y); tower; world
Plato, 1, 5–6, 8, 13–14, 22, 24–26, 31, 33, 50, 52, 82, 134, 139–41, 160, 170, 207, 215–17, 225n14–17, 225–26n22, 228n49, 230n63, 233n3, 233n9, 233–34n11–12, 236n31–32, 240n71, 250n5, 251–52n25, 256n70, 257n76, 257n78, 258n89, 258n100, 266n91. *See also* ancient; faculties (of the soul); good; Greek(s); history; sensuous; soul; sun
play: Kleist's 175; *No-*, 193; primordial, 124, 155. *See also* free; theatre
plural(ity), 6, 18, 20, 79, 97, 102, 108–109, 111, 116, 123–24, 126, 137, 165, 188, 194, 211, 217, 237n38, 249n27, 251n14, 263n55. *See also* alterity; collaboration; community; people; singular
poem, 16, 19, 60–63, 125, 130, 133–35, 138, 143, 147–57 passim, 161–67, 231n76, 242n88, 249n34, 254n43, 255n62, 257n84, 258n97,

265n75. *See also* Hölderlin, Friedrich; grammar; ground(ing); line break; poet(s); punctuation; rhyme; saying; stanza; tuning; verse(s); word
poet(s), 20–21, 74, 80, 133, 140, 146, 148, 153–55, 162, 164, 242n89, 244n9, 265n75. *See also* Greek(s); harmony; Hölderlin, Friedrich; music; oscillation; poem; pre-Socratic (poets); resonation; saying; sing (with); song; swing; tone; tuning; word
polemic, 14, 36, 57, 111, 119, 129, 217–18, 236n34, 247n11. *See also* Nietzsche, Friedrich
polis, 30, 107, 141–42. *See also* city
politics, 30, 66, 101, 106–108, 111–12, 117, 124–27 passim, 132, 217–18, 222, 228n48, 236n28, 247n12, 259n106. *See also* community; nation (state); international; plural(ity)
poor, 123, 251n15, 255n59. *See also* impoverishment; poverty; rich
positionality, 15, 33, 230n66, 230n70, 237n37. *See also* circulation; *Gestell*; replaceability; standing reserve(s); technology
postwar, 2, 33, 101, 133, 135, 141, 154, 162–63, 253n32, 255n59. *See also* defeat; destruction; Germany
poverty, 3, 20, 123, 141, 150, 163, 255n59. *See also* impoverishment; poor; rich
present, 53, 104, 118, 152, 264n69. *See also* future; history; present; temporal(ity); time
pre-Socratic (poets), 104, 121, 202. *See also* Greek(s); Heraclitus; poet(s)
prisoner(s), 20, 103, 105–106, 108, 110, 131, 134–35, 145–46, 168,

prisoner(s) *(continued)*
172, 247n2, 255n58. *See also* free; imprisonment; liberation; wound

profession, 4, 21, 25–27, 72, 75, 103, 111, 172–73, 175–77, 196, 209. *See also* research(er)

professor, 2, 4, 21–22, 175, 177, 186. *See also* authoritarianism; student-teacher relationship; university

progress(ive), 6, 8, 25, 39, 51–52, 55, 79, 114, 126, 148, 152, 213, 217, 221

pronoun(s), 79, 85, 97, 108, 111, 118, 137, 188. *See also* articles

proposition(al), 9, 13, 60, 107, 124, 127, 234n11. *See also* rationality

provenance, 9, 61, 74, 83, 87, 94, 96–97, 115, 118, 124, 155, 245n28. *See also* inceptual; origin(ary)

punctuation, 167. *See also* grammar; line break; poem; rhyme; stanza; verse(s)

radiance, 189, 202, 234n12. *See also* shine

radiation, 25. *See also* physics; science(s); sun

rage, 113, 117, 131, 248n14. *See also* evil; insurgency; malice

Rashomon (film), 191–92. *See also* camera; East Asia(n); film; hand

rationality, 8, 119–20. *See also* cognition; concept; human being; proposition(al); reason(ing)

realism, 192–93. *See also* film

reason(ing), 47, 49, 50, 98, 102, 141, 186, 190. *See also* cognition; concept; feeling; grasp; rationality

rebellious, 46, 127. *See also* insurgency

region(ing), 43–44, 51, 54–61 passim, 198, 203, 235n22, 236n32, 241n77. *See also* locale; open

relationality, 17, 34, 53, 70, 72, 74, 80, 88, 91–99 passim, 106, 113, 116, 118, 121, 126, 134, 136, 139, 230n70, 243n5, 253n27, 253n40. *See also* feeling; fourfold; identical; one; selfsame; thing; twofold; world

releasement, 15, 17, 19, 23, 27–29, 43, 54, 56–58, 61, 90, 96, 109, 116, 151, 154, 159–60, 163, 183, 228n48, 236n28, 239n58, 240n66. *See also* comportment; *Gelassenheit*; non-willing; will(ing)

rephrase, 61, 63, 65. *See also* word

replaceability, 15, 181. *See also* circulation; *Gestell*; positionality; standing reserve(s); technology

research(er), 25–27, 32–34, 36–37, 42, 45, 47, 63, 204, 233n6, 235n18. *See also* humanities; methodology; philosophical anthropology; physics; profession; science(s); university

resistance, 24, 53, 78, 81, 86, 129, 216, 225n14, 251n16

resonation, 7, 134, 136, 141, 143, 147–67 passim, 203, 242n85, 246n34, 247n5, 254n43, 257n84, 265n81; counter-, 149–56 passim, 162–63, 167, 203; over-, 149, 159; poetic, 182, 248n23, 256n64. *See also* counter-resonance; harmony; Hölderlin, Friedrich; music; oscillation; poem; sing (with); singer; song; swing; tone; tuning

resounding(-forth), 63, 143, 156–57, 257n84. *See also* ground(ing); music; poem; sing (with); song; tone; tuning

revolution(ary), 15, 216–17, 219

rhetorical, 125, 148, 208, 243n9

rhyme, 125. *See also* grammar; line break; poem; punctuation; stanza; verse(s)

rich, 123, 147, 255n59. *See also* impoverishment; poor; poverty
Rilke, Rainer Maria, 1, 11, 148, 175
river, 72, 80, 135, 142–45, 147, 150, 155, 158–60, 168, 253n28; banks, 4, 138, 146, 150, 153; of Hölderlin's poetizing, 29, 143, 148; song, 136, 144, 146, 149–50, 153, 158–59, 162–64, 167; spirit, 137. *See also* alterity; Alpheus (river); Danube River; forest; Hölderlin, Friedrich; Indus (river); Ister; land(scape); poem; rock(y); song; spirit; terrain; water(s); valley; way
rock(y), 150. *See also* land(scape); mountain; river; terrain
room, 205; tower, 70, 71, 77, 80, 82, 84, 86, 87, 96–99, 145, 174, 254n45; class-, 1, 4, 22, 27, 217. *See also* house; picture; stair(s); tower; view(s)
route, 30, 39, 142, 211. *See also* circle; country path; detour; fields; walk(ing); way
rubric (of representational metaphysics), 8, 17, 40, 60, 88, 98, 102, 134, 149, 185, 200, 204. *See also* humanities; methodology; objectivity; science(s); technology; totality; research(er); subjectivity; universal
Russia, 105–106, 108, 110, 127, 247n2–3. *See also* forest; nation(state)

sanatorium, 135. *See also* breakdown
saying, 5–7, 14, 16–17, 24, 47, 60–63, 65–66, 87, 130, 134, 145, 149, 152, 155–56, 159, 166, 184, 190, 206–208, 211, 225n21, 231n77, 242n85, 252n25. *See also* harmony; Hölderlin, Friedrich; oscillation; poem; poet(s);

resonation; sing(with); singer; speaking (together); sway; swing; tone; tuning; unsaid; unspoken; voice
scene, 3, 66, 81–82, 86, 95, 192
science(s), 33, 41–44, 57, 199, 217–18, 233n6, 234–35n17, 236n34, 239n51, 240n66, 256n73; of metaphysics, 7, 227n42; of nature, 11, 27, 37, 63, 71, 90, 92; and technology, 8, 14, 16, 23–24, 37–40, 55, 71, 81, 90–91, 94–95, 152. *See also* calculation; manipulate; mastery; nature; humanities; phenomenology; research(er); technology; university
Schelling, Friedrich Wilhelm Joseph, 248n14, 252n25
Schleiermacher, Friedrich, 179, 187
Schiller, Friedrich, 205
season, 145, 179, 238n47. *See also* spring; summer; autumn; winter
security, 113. *See also* world
self-restraining comporter, 91. *See also* comportment; human being
selfsame, 81, 85, 88, 96, 98–99, 107, 113, 116, 120–22, 126, 128, 139, 143, 158, 162, 239n52–53, 248n15, 254n41. *See also* identical; relationality
sending, 8, 58, 80, 164, 168. *See also* destiny
sensing, 137, 152. *See also* feeling
sensitivity, 14, 18, 21, 31, 34, 39, 46, 47, 65, 70, 72, 74, 79, 83, 88, 90, 122, 138, 147, 152, 154–55, 157, 180, 182, 208, 212. *See also* alterity; harmony; land(scape) resonation; song; tower
sensual, 151–52, 165–66, 256n71. *See also* intimacy
sensuous, 165, 189, 236n32; supra, 189–90. *See also* feeling; Plato

shake (as act of will), 94. *See also* will(ing); swing

shiki, 191, 265n87. *See also* East Asia(n); emptiness; *iro*

shine, 31, 46, 57, 117, 206. *See also* radiance

Shoah, 112, 168. *See also* antisemitism; genocide; Holocaust; Nazi; National Socialism

sign, 20, 150, 155, 163, 256n66. *See also* river; symbol

sing (with), 134, 138, 147, 149, 156, 159, 166. *See also* alterity; counter-resonation; harmony; Hölderlin, Friedrich; poem; poet(s); resonation; song; singer; tone; tuning; voice; word

singer, 134, 139, 149, 155, 162. *See also* harmony; Hölderlin, Friedrich; poem; poet(s); saying; sing (with); song; tone; tuning; voice

singular, 15, 79, 82–83, 108, 111, 119, 249n27. *See also* individual; one; plural(ity); thing

sky, 57, 66, 70, 72, 90, 134, 190, 243n5. *See also* day; fourfold; gods; night; star(s); sun; wine

sobriety, 144

society, 116

Socrates, 22, 225n22, 234n11, 257n78. *See also* death; Plato

sojourn, 86, 91, 94, 107, 146, 165, 175, 187, 266n91. *See also* foreign; home; journey

soldier(s), 103, 105, 255n58

solitary, 1, 17, 176. *See also* individual

son(s), 2–3, 101, 135, 140, 247n2, 255n60. *See also* ancestors; genealogy

song, 136, 141, 144–45, 148–67 passim, 255–55, 258n97. *See also* counter-resonation; dissonance; harmony; Hölderlin, Friedrich; instrument (musical); music; poem; poet(s); resonation; river; saying; sing (with); tone; tuning; voice

soul, 42, 44–49 passim, 141, 200, 239n57, 240n66, 246n30, 257n78. *See also* faculties (of the soul); human being; Plato; spirit

space, 57, 91, 105, 110, 142, 149, 153–54, 160, 162, 166–67, 182, 211, 214, 259n104. *See also* locale; time

speaking (together), 12, 18, 27, 41, 60, 66, 94. *See also* alterity; collaboration; cross-cultural exchange; forbearance; intercultural (exchange); saying; sing (with)

spirit, 75, 137, 144, 148, 152, 184–85, 252n25, 255n57, 258n100, 259n105. *See also* river; soul

spring, 66, 140, 145, 164, 236n28, 238n47, 247n2. *See also* season

stair(s), 77, 85; -way, 19, 69, 70, 73, 76, 232n81, 243n1. *See also* downward; room; tower; upward

standing reserve(s), 15, 33, 135, 181, 215, 230n70. *See also* circulation; *Gestell*; objectivity; positionality; replaceability; technology

standstill, 105, 108, 182. *See also* movement; route; walk(ing); way

stanza, 134, 143, 148, 161–62, 164, 167, 259n104. *See also* grammar; line break; poem; punctuation; rhyme; verse(s)

star(s), 32, 64, 66, 106, 236n31, 237n35. *See also* brightness; clarity; light; night; obscurity; sky; sun

strange(r), 19, 25, 30–31, 41, 48, 69–70, 72, 80–90 passim, 95–98, 118, 149, 160, 163, 170, 178, 183, 187, 198, 217, 230n70, 239n55,

265n88, *See also* gift; journey; picture; welcome; wonder(ous)
string instrument, 124, 155. *See also* instrument (musical); lyre; music; tone; tuning; violin
student-teacher relationship, 183, 213, 217, 219. *See also* authoritarianism; collaboration; failure; professor; unlearning
subjectivity, 19, 27–28, 36, 42–47 passim, 52–54, 58, 105, 109, 127, 147, 202, 216, 229n51, 238n49. *See also* human being; objectivity
summer, 145, 159, 238n47. *See also* season
sun, 8, 31–32, 48, 57, 106, 144–46, 234n12, 236n32. *See also* brightness; clarity; darkness; light; night; obscurity; radiation; sky; star(s)
superlative, 82. *See also* comparative
surmise, 26, 28, 39, 51, 56, 62, 73, 75, 78, 83–84, 104, 107, 113–14, 117–18, 122–31 passim, 135–36, 186, 239n53, 244n9. *See also* enigma; hint; insight; unsurmised
sway, 105, 166, 200, 256n64. *See also* movement; oscillation; resonation; sing (with); song; swing; word
swing, 94, 99, 105, 110, 113, 115–17, 121, 128, 132, 150, 158–59, 162, 198–99, 246n34, 247n5, 248n23, 256n64. *See also* ambiguity; capaciousness; forest; healing; mobility; movement; oscillation; poem; poet(s); resonation; shake (as act of will); sing (with); song; tuning; word
symbol, 60, 143, 158, 242n86, 256n66. *See also* river; sign

techne, 14, 34, 38, 49, 50, 55, 215. *See also* technology

technology, 6, 14–15, 33–34, 38, 44, 47, 69, 181, 192, 206, 214–16, 228n49, 229n50, 232n3, 237n38–40, 259n2, 263n54; science and, 8, 14, 16, 23–24, 37–40, 55, 71, 81, 90–95 passim, 152; techne and, 38, 55. *See also* calculation; circulation; domination; *Gestell*; machination; manipulation; mastery; nature; positionality; replaceability; research(er); science(s); standing reserve(s); *techne*; tool; university
temporal(ity), 7, 8, 29, 31, 33, 37, 82, 91, 104–105, 108–109, 117–18, 135, 144–45, 152–53, 159–60, 179–80, 258n90. *See also* future; history; past; present; time
terrain, 76, 78, 144, 179, 182. *See also* country path; earth; fields; geography; land(scape); rock(y); way
Tezuka Tomio, 4, 175–76, 189, 264n71
thank(ing), 53, 62, 122, 130, 160. *See also* gift; meditation
theatre, 193. *See also* aesthetics; gesture; *no*-play; play
theology, 43, 120, 179. *See also* divinity
thing, 5, 15, 23, 34, 38–39, 53–58, 60, 70–72, 74, 77–78, 88, 90, 94–96, 214, 216, 230n70, 235n17, 237n40, 241n80, 243n5. *See also* fourfold; nothing; objectivity; one; relationality; tower; world
time, 29, 66, 91, 97, 117, 122, 128, 135, 137, 139–40, 144–46, 152, 157, 162, 167–68, 174, 214, 234n11, 236n28; epoch of, 6, 31; historical, 154, 161; metaphysical, 95, 104, 117, 126, 142, 149, 153, 259n104; non-metaphysical, 82, 91, 98, 142, 182; still concealed

time *(continued)*
  dimension of, 104, 109, 118, 126, 128. *See also* age; epoch; future; history; past; present; space; temporal(ity); wait(ing)
Tokyo (Japan), 175
tomb (of Kuki), 183, 192. *See also* grave (of Kuki)
tone, 36, 78, 102, 149–51, 154, 156, 165, 167, 257n84. *See also* harmony; ground(ing); music; resonation; saying; sing (with); singer; song; tuning; voice
tool, 10, 16, 35, 55, 213–15, 219, 267n42. *See also* manipulate; mastery; technology; work
totality, 7, 17, 215. *See also* universal
touch, 52, 74, 105, 192, 195, 203. *See also* injury; untouched
tower, 70–72, 74, 76–78, 80, 82, 84–88, 90, 95–99, 145, 244n8–9, 253n40, 254n45. *See also* downward; height; room; sensitive; stair(s); thing; upward
Trakl, Georg, 1, 11, 148
transition, 23–24, 33, 52–53, 59, 69, 79, 115, 145, 159, 190, 230n71, 240n66, 258n100. *See also* between-field; cross over; crossing; turn back
trauma, 111. *See also* breakdown; healing
trial, 157, 163. *See also* postwar
trust, 40–41, 47, 51, 72–75, 80, 87, 93, 99, 159–60, 214, 220. *See also* anxiety; confidence; failure; fear; unlearning; worry; vulnerability
truth, 9, 13, 17, 31, 50, 61–62, 71, 92, 94, 129, 143, 215, 231n77–78, 242n90, 244n12; of being, 115, 177; of metaphysics, 237n41. *See also aletheia*; concept; correspondence; domination; enigma; errancy; grasp; reason(ing); rubric (of representational metaphysics); saying; song; universal; wait(ing)
tuning, 156. *See also* string instrument
turn back, 7, 55, 72, 77–78, 81, 88, 90, 96, 99. *See also* between-field; cross over; origin(ary); transition
twofold, 11, 134, 139, 148, 154–55, 198–200, 203. *See also* one; relationality

unambiguous, 63, 151, 166. *See also* ambiguity; rubric (of representational metaphysics)
uncanny, 41, 152, 159. *See also* home
unfitting, 190. *See also* fitting; measure
universal, 7, 9, 14, 38, 42, 116, 173, 248n14. *See also* concept; domination; objectivity; rubric (of representational metaphysics); totality; truth
university, 2, 3, 13, 22, 27, 33, 103, 173, 175, 217, 234n16, 237n41. *See also* humanities; professor; research(er); science(s); technology
unlearning, 9, 26, 213. *See also* student-teacher relationship
unnecessary, 85, 117, 119, 126, 128–30, 149
unsaid, 13, 14, 18, 28, 204, 234n11. *See also* saying; unspoken; word
unsettling, 19, 20, 25, 83, 96, 109, 119, 183, 197. *See also* distress; good; worry
unspoken, 13, 17, 18, 31, 35, 121–22, 124, 195, 225n14, 263n49. *See also* saying; unsaid
unsurmised, 83–84. *See also* enigma; hint; surmise
untouched, 195, 237n37. *See also* touch
untranslated, 92, 225n14, 232n83

Upper Danube Valley, 2, 3, 135, 140–41, 159, 162, 172, 224n6. *See also* Hölderlin, Friedrich; mountain; river; valley

unveiled, 79, 212. *See also* guard; veil(ing)

upward, 77, 85, 87, 253n40, 254n45. *See also* downward; room; stair(s); tower

valley, 143, 147, 159, 162. *See also* forest; land(scape) mountain; river; terrain; Upper Danube Valley

value, 142, 214–16, 218, 221, 245n30. *See also* aesthetics; evil; good; moral(ity); Nietzsche, Friedrich

van Gogh, Vincent, 71. *See also* painting

veil(ing), 13, 35, 51, 110, 113–14, 136, 157. *See also* guard; unveiled

verse(s), 125, 134, 139, 149–50, 153, 155, 164, 167, 255n58, 257n78, 258n97. *See also* grammar; line break; poem; punctuation; rhyme; stanza

view(s), 14, 37–38, 45, 47, 50, 54, 88, 91–92, 144, 151–52, 156, 200, 202, 204, 254n45; bringing-into-, 34, 38; historiological, 41, 45; methodological, 41, 45; tower, 74, 77, 85, 95; world, 29, 36, 108, 129. *See also* appearance; circle; historiography; historiology; methodology; open; outward look; research(er); room; science(s); technology; tower; world

violin, 125. *See also* instrument (musical); lyre; music; string instrument; tuning

voice, 43–44, 66, 112, 195. *See also* saying; sing (with); singer; song

vulnerability, 72, 74–75, 80, 116, 126, 217. *See also* collaboration; trust

wait(ing), 5, 9, 17, 19–20, 46, 53–54, 56–58, 60, 64, 101–102, 106–108, 116–18, 121–31, 137, 145–46, 149, 159, 190, 197, 220, 254n51. *See also* await; expectation; people; time

walk(ing), 15, 18, 28–30, 35–37, 39, 48, 62–63, 66, 72, 76–78, 80–81, 85–86, 89, 95, 98, 105–108, 142–43, 145–46, 154, 162, 178–79, 181–82, 197, 200, 202, 204, 213, 236n28, 245n27, 253n40. *See also* country path; mobility; movement; route; standstill; way

wasteland, 115. *See also* annihilation; desert; devastation; ocean

water(s), 118, 150, 158. *See also* ocean; river

way: forest, 48; movement on the, 15, 29–30, 56, 59, 63, 206, 211, 257n82; path 142, 164, 194, 206; river, 142, 144, 150, 164, 168; thinking, 187, 203. *See also* country path; detour; forest; mobility; movement; river; route; standstill; terrain; walk(ing)

weight, 119, 164–65, 196, 200. *See also* measure

welcome, 51, 73–74, 78, 82, 95–96, 103, 150, 154, 176, 197, 256n65. *See also* gift; strange(r)

welfare, 114. *See also* workers

width, 128, 153, 159, 165, 198, 265n82. *See also* height; measure

will(ing), 6, 12, 28, 43–50, 53–54, 58, 61, 66, 82–83, 86–87, 94, 105, 112–14, 118, 125, 140, 151, 160–61, 164, 205, 211, 217, 226n24, 228n48, 236n34, 240n66, 248n16. *See also* faculties (of the soul);

will(ing) *(continued)*
  Gelassenheit; non-willing; releasement; shake (as act of will)
wine, 57. *See also* drink; festival; jug
wings, 141
winter, 145, 238n46. *See also* season
withhold, 91, 197, 205
wonder(ous), 57, 82–84, 86, 90, 96–97, 118–19, 157, 159, 160, 178, 187, 206, 239, 265n88. *See also* astonishment; picture; strange(r)
word: and counter-word, 60–61, 63, 178; as fitting, 83, 89, 186; as gift, 86–87; as Greek fragment, 37, 62–63; as hint, 198–99; as inexhaustible, 59, 206, 242n93; and language, 75, 111; for language, 10, 195, 197, 205–208; as poetic, 125, 148–50, 152–53, 157, 159, 164–66, 200, 254n52, 256n64, 257n84, 265n82; as silent, 166; as written, 150–51, 257n76. *See also* answer; community; counter-resonation; counter-word; fragment; gift; grammar; logos; poem; poet(s); rephrase; resonation; song; student-teacher relationship; written (texts); writing
work: and achievement, 33, 37, 45; of art, 71, 231n77, 257n83; place, 105, 109; of representing, 74; and rest, 47, 64; shop, 57. *See also* achievement
workers, 114. *See also* welfare
world, 10, 17, 21, 22, 30, 32, 53, 58, 72, 74, 82, 105, 107, 115–17, 124, 131, 141, 155, 172, 177, 183–84, 192, 199, 206, 213, 216, 234n16, 235n22, 237n37, 258n100, 263n54; of the East, 155, 169, 173, 181, 185, 188, 191–92, 194, 196, 199, 202, 207–209, 265n75; of the Greeks, 203; historical, 182; of Japan, 176, 184–85, 187, 191–95; of nature, 141, 143, 253n35; order, 46, 113, 129; picture, 8, 71, 76, 94–95; as secure, 116; view, 29, 36, 108, 152; War I, 186; War II, 2, 15, 99, 114, 154, 193; of the West, 139, 146, 173. *See also* East Asia(n); fourfold; Japan; Germany; Greek(s); history; nature; one; picture; postwar; relationality; security; thing; view(s)
worry, 30, 96, 112, 116, 120, 135, 191, 194, 196, 240n71, 245n23, 265n81. *See also* anxiety; confidence; distress; fear; trust; unsettling
wound, 104, 106–107, 110–12, 116, 118–19, 253n35. *See also* injury; pain; prisioner(s)
writing: (conversational genre of), 2, 4, 6, 8, 9, 13, 17, 22
written (texts), 3, 76–77, 95, 98, 141, 150–51, 154–55, 230n63–64, 254n44, 257n76. *See also* word; writing

younger definition (of the human), 119–21. *See also* age; human being; older definition (of the human); comparative
youth, 104, 114, 119, 122, 126, 136–37, 201, 246n30. *See also* age; comparative; daring; younger definition (of the human)

www.ingramcontent.com/pod-product-compliance
Lightning Source LLC
Chambersburg PA
CBHW020638230426
43665CB00008B/230